Praise for
To Speak the Truth in Love

"An astonishing story of one woman's moral leadership in collaboration with communities of her dedicated Sisters. The church and world are still in desperate need of such courageous speaking, born of deep faith and great kindness. Sparks fly out from this book to inspire a new generation."
—Elizabeth Johnson, CSJ
Distinguished Professor of Theology Emerita, Fordham University

"This deeply researched and well written biography of Sister Theresa Kane, RSM, not only brings historical thoroughness and interpretive acumen to the story of Kane's courageous and enormously effective leadership but also vividly exposes in Theresa's life and ministry the violent nature and operation of the moral evil—namely, clericalism—which Pope Francis has identified as the root cause of the current scandal in the Church."
—Sandra M. Schneiders
Professor Emerita of New Testament and Spirituality
Jesuit School of Theology

"This well-researched book shows why Sr. Theresa Kane's prophetic and courageous call to Pope John Paul II for women's ordination was only a part of her many efforts for reform in our patriarchal Church. She is a wise, deeply spiritual, and totally committed person who used her participative leadership of the Sisters of Mercy and the Leadership Conference of Women Religious to work for reform in the Church despite opposition and surprises."
—Charles E. Curran
Elizabeth Scurlock University Professor of Human Values
Southern Methodist University

"It's been a long time since I've felt so good reading a book. Chris Schenk's *To Speak the Truth in Love: a Biography of Theresa Kane* is a spirit lifter. Well-researched, simply-organized, cleanly-written, Kane's fearless, gospel-tethered character and crystal-clear integrity jump from each chapter. The book captures a special time in church history when confused and confounded men were first forced to deal seriously with educated women religious, who ended up praying circles around them. Further, the book speaks to the undeniable power of gospel love, especially when packaged in an intelligent and cunning character. With the publication of this fine biography, it becomes undeniable, were there ever a question, that Theresa Kane personifies the best of feminine church leadership. Make that church leadership."
—Tom Fox
former *NCR* Editor; current *NCR* CEO/President

"This is not one book, but two. The first tells a story of unquenchable commitment, personal faith, and the expenditure of irrepressible energy by religious orders of women to move religious life beyond its medieval European roots to become a dynamic presence in the modern world. The second story is about the commitment, faith, and irrepressible energy of Sr. Theresa Kane, RSM, a woman who not only embodies that change but is herself a major factor in making it happen. This well documented and historically precise work teaches us all the kind of courage it took to make that great transition in a church that ordered changes in religious life and then resisted them all the way."

—Sister Joan Chittister, OSB
former President, LCWR

"This very welcome book is about the life of Theresa Kane, RSM, as well as the lives of many other contemporary Catholic Women Religious in the U.S. after Vatican II. It offers a bold narrative of Kane's experiences and the major changes that catapulted so many nuns (as well as lay women) to discern new ministries in the world, new visions of religious life, alternate structures in women's forms of governance, and pastoral concerns. All of this required courage and leadership, as well as new ways of relating to the church. In this gripping story, Kane and her congregation manage to hold together mercy and justice, though struggles remain."

—Margaret A. Farley
Gilbert L. Stark Professor Emerita of Christian Ethics
Yale Divinity School

"Theresa Kane is a person remembered for the simple manner in which she engaged the ordinary experiences of her own story and, in doing so, embodied an age. Her life of faith and integrity reveals the wonder that, given the right moment and circumstances, ordinary persons hold the possibility of extraordinary human experience. All that is required is faithfulness to self, awareness of the moment, and courage in the face of opposition."

—Helen Marie Burns, RSM
former President LCWR (1988–91)
and Vice President, Sisters of Mercy 1984–91, 1999-2005

"Courageous, compassionate, and deeply human, this portrait of a leader is essential reading. A compelling narrative of an important chapter of the Catholic Church's history, *To Speak the Truth in Love* sheds new light on the longstanding tensions between the Vatican and U.S. women religious, and the price of prophetic perseverance. Sr. Theresa Kane and the collective witness of the Sisters of Mercy will embolden advocates to embrace the risks of pursuing justice."

—Kate McElwee
Executive Director, Women's Ordination Conference

To Speak the Truth in Love

December 2019
Dear Marjorie,

Many blessings and gratitude
for your friendship.

Love and Mercy
Theresa Kane, RSM

Sister Theresa Kane, RSM,
President of the Leadership Conference of
Women Religious, addresses the 1979 Assembly.

To Speak the Truth in Love

A Biography of Theresa Kane, RSM

Christine Schenk, CSJ

ORBIS BOOKS

Maryknoll, New York 10545

ORBIS BOOKS
Maryknoll, New York 10545

Fathers and Brothers
MARYKNOLL™

Founded in 1970, Orbis Books endeavors to publish works that enlighten the mind, nourish the spirit, and challenge the conscience. The publishing arm of the Maryknoll Fathers and Brothers, Orbis seeks to explore the global dimensions of the Christian faith and mission, to invite dialogue with diverse cultures and religious traditions, and to serve the cause of reconciliation and peace. The books published reflect the views of their authors and do not represent the official position of the Maryknoll Society. To learn more about Maryknoll and Orbis Books, please visit our website at www.maryknollsociety.org.

Library of Congress Cataloging-in-Publication Data

Names: Schenk, Christine, author.
Title: To speak the truth in love : a biography of Theresa Kane, R.S.M. / Christine Schenk, C.S.J.
Description: Maryknoll : Orbis Books, 2019. | Includes bibliographical references and index.
Identifiers: LCCN 2019020128 (print) | LCCN 2019980667 (ebook) | ISBN 9781626983458 (print) | ISBN 9781608338092 (ebook)
Subjects: LCSH: Kane, Theresa. | Sisters of Mercy—Biography. | Nuns—United States—Biography. | Women in church work—Catholic Church. | Women in Christianity.
Classification: LCC BX4705.K21966 S34 2019 (print) | LCC BX4705.K21966 (ebook) | DDC 271/.92092 [B]—dc23
LC record available at https://lccn.loc.gov/2019020128
LC ebook record available at https://lccn.loc.gov/2019980667

To the Sisters of Mercy of the Americas,
the Leadership Conference of Women Religious,
and the women and men throughout the world
who persist in speaking the truth with love.

To Theresa, knowingly:
Someday, someplace
there will be a monument
to those who
in this time
showed a kind of courage
that gave courage to others;
told a kind of truth
that kept others honest;
had the kind of power
that empowered the powerless.
Your name will head the list.
My love will burn it in.

 —Joan D. Chittister, OSB
  (May 24, 1984, tribute at gathering of
  LCWR presidents who convened
  to honor Theresa Kane)

Contents

Acknowledgments

No book ever comes into being because of the efforts of the author alone, and this one is no exception. I am indebted first and foremost to Sister Theresa Kane, who patiently sat through many hours of interviews as I mined her remarkable memory about her even more remarkable life. Sister of Mercy Helen Marie Burns patiently read each chapter and was an invaluable source of information and balance as I sought to understand this challenging time in Mercy history—indeed in the history of US women religious. Dominican Sister Diana Culbertson once again guided me with her wise and skillful edits to my initial manuscript.

Mercy leaders Sisters Pat McDermott and Pat Vetrano graciously offered their open-hearted support as well as access to congregational archives. Kat Oosterhuis, Emily Reed, and the rest of the amazing staff at the Mercy Heritage Center in Belmont, North Carolina, patiently pulled hundreds of files containing years of correspondence, media stories, photographs, video footage, newsletters and other internal communications. Mercy Sister Margaret Farley generously shared her personal papers—and her wisdom—about the historic events of this time period. I also wish to posthumously acknowledge Mercy Sister Emily George. Her detailed notes about meetings between the Mercy leadership and bishops, theologians, and canon lawyers were invaluable to chronicling a remarkable period in Catholic history. I am grateful to Immaculate Heart Sister Ann Marie Sanders at the Leadership Conference of Women Religious and William Kevin Cawley and the staff at the Archives at the University of Notre Dame for their kind research assistance. While I was blessed with access to privileged files and wise guides, errors can sometimes happen. These are mine alone.

Special gratitude is owed to Emmaus House in Ocean Grove, New Jersey, the Mercy Sisters at Marian Woods in Hartsdale, New York, and the Medical Mission Sisters in Philadelphia, Pennsylvania, for graciously providing episodic hospitality over two years of interviews. Likewise, my gratitude to Robert Ellsberg and Mike Leach at Orbis Books who supported this effort from the beginning. Where would we be without our courageous brothers?

Last, my thanks to my housemate, Saint Joseph Sister Jeanne Cmolik, who once again patiently tolerated weird writer hours and occasional unsolicited outbursts of "Can you believe this?" as I slowly pieced together both the trials and the grace that accompany those who speak hard truths with love.

Introduction

The daughter of Irish immigrants and the fourth of seven children, Theresa Kane rose from humble origins in an economically poor Bronx neighborhood to lead the four-thousand-strong Sisters of Mercy of the Union from 1977 to 1984. She would eventually represent more than one hundred and thirty thousand US sisters as president of the Leadership Conference of Women Religious (LCWR) from 1979 to 1980. When she respectfully asked Pope John Paul II in 1979 to open "all the ministries of our Church" to women, both groups of sisters had already passed—by wide margins—their own resolutions in favor of women's ordination. Just four years earlier, the first Women's Ordination Conference in Detroit had attracted an overflow crowd of twelve hundred people including sisters, laywomen, theologians (both female and male), laymen, and priests. Far from being the one-woman "protester" belittled by her detractors, Kane in making her request was expressing the faithful discernment of thousands of the church's most committed believers.

On October 7, 1979, more than five thousand sisters were present as Theresa Kane greeted the pope during a nationally televised prayer service at the National Shrine of the Immaculate Conception. She urged him "to be mindful of the intense suffering and pain which is part of the life of many women..." and said, "Our Church, in its struggle to be faithful to its call for reverence and charity for all persons, must respond by providing the possibility of women as persons being included in all the ministries of the Church." Her request was greeted with thunderous applause, even though only three days earlier in Philadelphia the pope had reiterated his opinion that women could never be ordained. Video of Theresa Kane's greeting ran repeatedly throughout the day's TV coverage, and photos of her kneeling humbly to receive the papal blessing graced front-page stories in newspapers all over the country.

Hers was the first and only voice to speak frankly and publicly about painful issues in Catholicism during the 1979 papal visit. Her widely publicized remarks became a media tipping point that galvanized the women's movement in the Catholic Church for decades to come. She sparked a public dialogue that gave voice to the aspirations of thousands of Catholic women and men. This is the heart of Theresa Kane's genius. Throughout her long and productive life, she has passionately pursued the right of every person to have her or his voice heard, even those with whom she disagrees. Far from avoiding confrontation, she actually seems to relish it—but she names unpopular truths in a way that respects the dignity of those present. Her concluding address as LCWR president, "To Speak the Truth in Love" is, therefore, a fitting title for this book about a life filled with love, controversy, and no small measure of joy.

Yet Theresa Kane would suffer for "speaking truth in love," especially when those with whom she was in dialogue were conservative members of the Roman Catholic hierarchy. During her seven-year tenure as president of the Sisters of Mercy of the Union, she negotiated numerous conflicts with the Vatican while her sisters sought to implement the community's prophetic 1977 Chapter directives addressing women's equality, political advocacy, and moral decision-making. The Mercy sisters' innovative efforts were strongly resisted by conservative Vatican prelates, including Pope John Paul II himself. Because she would not desist from speaking her sisters' truth—and her own—the Vatican tried to remove her from office. But still, Theresa Kane persisted. Her persistence has as its source a filament of pure gold that threads its way through the tapestry of her life—a deep and persevering faith. Hers is a straightforward, down-to-earth spirituality that—perhaps unsurprisingly—occasionally involves experiences that most would call mystical, but that she describes as "receiving a message." Her "messages" brought strength, consolation, and a sure confidence that God is present in the midst of painful challenges that would appear overwhelming even to the most disinterested atheist. Theresa Kane's Irish heritage, her gregarious love of people, and her blithe spirit balance a steely determination never to be deterred from "speaking the truth with love," even to the present day.

In September 2015, she proclaimed a public message to Pope Francis at the Women's Ordination Worldwide Conference held in Philadelphia prior to the pope's arrival. As she had done thirty-six years earlier, Theresa Kane called for the eradication of gender inequality and urged Pope Francis "to listen to the women of our church and world who cry out in anguish as women throughout the ages have done. Only radical (at its roots) gender equality in church and in society will begin to diminish the violence, hatred, and other forms of inhumanity in our world today."

While this book is a biography of Sister Theresa Kane, it is also a story about the Sisters of Mercy, and it resonates with the stories of many other US communities of women religious. The sisters' courageous embrace of the visionary reforms of the Second Vatican Council led them to new understandings of how authority is meant to operate within a community of believers. Since Vatican II had affirmed that each believer is gifted by the Spirit of God, the sisters came to see that leadership no longer meant simply telling each sister what she was assigned to do. Now the function of leadership was to support careful discernment—by individuals and by the communal body—as to where the Spirit of God was leading.

The decision-making chapters of the Sisters of Mercy became an important means of discerning directions that were emerging from the sisters' lived experience rather than—as had previously been the case—having decisions imposed from on high. This evolving understanding of authority and mission led Theresa Kane and the Sisters of Mercy to embrace ministries on behalf of justice in the church as well as justice in society. It did not take long for the sisters to run afoul of an all-male Catholic hierarchy more accustomed to nuns quietly taking orders rather than asserting their right to help make them. This was especially true with regard to church policies and customs that directly affected the sisters' lives and the lives of those they served, especially women. This reality is at the root of Theresa's respectful request to include women in Catholic decision-making structures. It is also at the root of the vehement Vatican pushback that she and the Sisters of Mercy suffered in the ensuing decade.

The Sisters of Mercy years-long saga is chronicled in considerable detail in this book. In addition to Theresa's personal story, I am gratified to have been able to document an important period of contemporary Catholic history. It is a period in which Theresa—and so many of her sisters in her own and other communities—exercised unparalleled leadership in the Catholic Church. They did so by speaking truth to power—with love, wisdom, and grace.

Unless otherwise indicated, all quotations from Theresa Kane in the chapters that follow are from more than 160 hours of audiotaped interviews with the author now stored at the Mercy Heritage Center Archives, Belmont, NC.

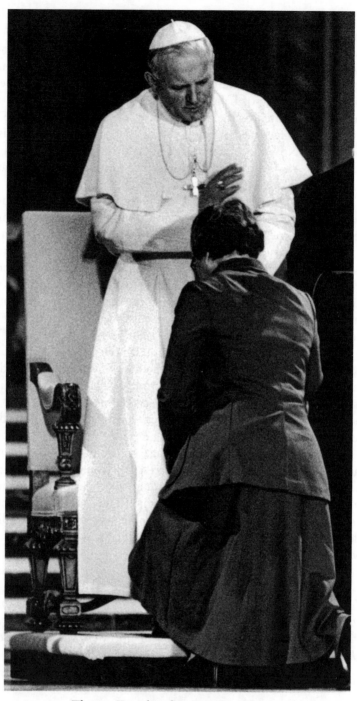

Theresa Kane kneels to receive a blessing
after greeting Pope John Paul II on October 7, 1979. (CNS)

CHAPTER ONE

The Elephant in the Sanctuary

On the morning of October 7, 1979, Sister Theresa Kane sat nervously in the sanctuary of the National Shrine of the Immaculate Conception awaiting the arrival of Pope John Paul II. The pontiff would soon speak at a prayer service for Catholic sisters on the final day of his first visit to the United States. He had been elected to the papacy just one year earlier. As president of the Leadership Conference of Women Religious (LCWR)—an organization representing more than 130,000 American sisters—Theresa had been invited to present a brief greeting. She had pondered a long time about what to say, and ultimately decided to include the elephant in the sanctuary— the need to open all the ministries of the church to women.[1]

Now that the moment was at hand, however, her anxiety was mounting. It didn't help that four days earlier the pope had reiterated that women could never be ordained. And now he was more than an hour late—a lot of time to consider changing her mind. "I had written it, but I sat there saying to myself: 'I don't have to say it. Nobody has seen it.'"[2]

Then the woman next to her asked, "Are you the sister who's giving the greeting?" When Theresa replied that she was, the woman inquired, "Are you going to say something about women?"

"Oh my God, I don't need this now," Theresa thought. "Supposing she doesn't want me to do it?" But she told the woman, yes, she planned to say something about women.

"Good, I'm glad," said her neighbor. "I'm an attorney, and when I wanted to go to law school, I got no support at all from the Catholic Church. The only support I got was from my husband." As it happened, the female attorney was accompanying Bishop Bernard Law's mother—who was in a wheelchair—to the prayer event.[3] "Helen, this sister is going to speak about women in the church," the lawyer said. "Isn't that wonderful?"

"Good luck, Sister," Helen responded.

For Theresa, the serendipitous conversation was deeply affirming: "That was almost like God speaking to me. I felt the presence of God saying, 'Yes this is right. You need to do this.'" Oddly, she would later remember a mysterious "message" she had received in February 1971. While praying at the tomb of John XXIII, she was given to understand that she would have an encounter with the pope. It was one of many "messages" this down-to-earth woman would experience as she struggled to "speak the truth in love" to a hierarchy that didn't want to listen.

WHY THERESA KANE HAD TO SPEAK

While her critics delight in depicting Theresa Kane as a nun-gone-rogue, nothing is further from the truth. Both her religious congregation and the LCWR had already spoken publicly about ordination and women's equality in the Catholic Church. At their 1977 Tenth General Chapter, the Sisters of Mercy of the Union overwhelmingly approved a "statement of concern" about the 1976 Vatican declaration, *Inter Insigniores,* that said (among other things) that women could not be priests because they do not resemble the maleness of Jesus.[4] The Mercy chapter directive said (in part) that the Vatican declaration had "failed to deal adequately with the meaning of tradition...the nature of the charism of authoritative teaching in the Church...the values of equality and mutuality...and the suitability of persons as persons to represent Jesus Christ."[5]

The chapter then "authorized the administrator general and provincials to convey its concerns to the secular and religious press, to the National Conference of Catholic Bishops, and to bishops in whose dioceses the sisters served."[6] The Sisters of Mercy joined other groups in urging the World Synod of Bishops—which was scheduled to meet in 1980—to reconsider the conclusions of the Vatican declaration.[7]

While in session, the chapter body is the highest governing body of any religious order. For Catholic sisters, the Holy Spirit is especially present in the chapter to inspire and lead their discussions. Theresa Kane had been elected administrator general of the Sisters of Mercy at that same chapter. She and her elected administrative team were canonically bound to implement the decisions made there. Her decision to ask the pope to provide "the possibility of women as persons being included in all the ministries of our Church" was consistent with the chapter directives entrusted to her by her religious congregation.

In 1975, the Leadership Conference of Women Religious was one of forty-nine groups and individuals that publicly endorsed the

Detroit Women's Ordination Conference, which had attracted more than twelve hundred Catholics, including priests, sisters, theologians, and laity. Twenty religious communities were among the endorsers,[8] and more than five hundred Catholic sisters had already indicated they had experienced a call to the priesthood.[9] In May 1976, the Ecclesial Roles of Women committee of LCWR approved a meticulously researched paper—*The Status and Roles of Women*—that called for women's ordination. That document said, in part, "...only participation of women in the full ordained priesthood will begin to create a Church in which men and women can live together as equal partners in Christ...When we bring our experience as women to bear in theological reflection...we know the urgency of the Church's call to now open its ordained ministry to women."[10]

For many years, LCWR committees had sponsored workshops—and created materials for sisters themselves to sponsor workshops—on women in the church. "We were all just eating it up, every bit of it," recalls Theresa. "We loved it." At the time of her papal greeting, many thousands of ordinary Catholics, priests, sisters, theologians, and even a few bishops, had already publicly voiced support for women's ordination. But the issue had yet to hit the national media.

That was about to change. By year's end, the Catholic news editors of America would name Sister Theresa Kane among the top four newsmakers of 1979, and she would receive the *U.S. Catholic* Award for "furthering the cause of women in the church." For Women's Ordination Conference leader Ruth McDonough Fitzpatrick, Theresa Kane "brought the women's movement in the Catholic Church out of the shadows and into the light."[11]

But it did not start off that way. In fact, Theresa initially expected minimal media attention, since her greeting would occur early on a Sunday morning at the end of the papal visit. She had vigorously pursued a private meeting between LCWR leadership and John Paul II, but this request was denied. After observing the pope speak to women religious in Mexico, LCWR leaders were concerned that he seemed unaware of the extent to which Vatican II renewal had changed the lives of US sisters: "He was very much highlighting cloister, their prayer life, and their religious habit. And that had us concerned that, if he were to continue that message when he came to the United States, he was going to cause some real tensions among our sisters and between us and him."

This was why Theresa had called the general secretary for the bishops' conference, Bishop Thomas Kelly, to see if a meeting could be arranged.[12] She and the other LCWR leaders wanted to help the pope understand that "we were not cloistered communities, we were apostolic communities...and we had moved into contemporary dress. We were not requiring it, but it was certainly an option for the sisters."

Close Encounters of a Papal Kind

Several weeks before the pope arrived, Theresa received an unexpected telephone call from Monsignor John J. Murphy, director of the National Shrine of the Immaculate Conception. Murphy was preparing the worship aid for the October 7 prayer service and needed her official title. Theresa loves to tell the story.

> I said to him, "May I ask why you want it?" He said, "Yes, you're giving the greeting to the Holy Father in the Shrine on Sunday when he talks to the sisters."
>
> I said, "Monsignor, this is the first I've heard of it. Now, how long is the greeting supposed to be?"
>
> "Oh, very short, Sister. They're not coming to hear you. They're coming to hear the Holy Father."
>
> And it was right in my heart to say, "I know that. I'm not stupid." So I said, "Monsignor, when is this?"
>
> He said, "Sunday, October 7th."
>
> I was so tempted to say to him, "Well, I'll have to check my calendar." But I thought that if I did he would have hung up on me.[13]

Days later, Murphy called again. He had heard that some sisters were planning a prayerful witness on behalf of women's ordination at the time of the papal prayer service and wanted to know if Theresa knew anything about it. She told him that, while she knew some of the sisters, she "wasn't part of that activity." Whereupon Murphy asked her to do him a favor and "tell the sisters not to do it." Theresa replied that she was willing to call them up, but she didn't believe it would dissuade the sister-activists. Instead, she suggested that Murphy call and meet with them himself. Apparently, the monsignor was worried about security if the sisters all stood together at the Shrine. The surviving organizers of the silent witness have no recollection that anyone ever met with Monsignor Murphy, but they do recall deciding themselves to stand separately throughout the cathedral so as not to block the view of others.[14]

Women and men from three organizations whose national offices are in Washington, DC, had been diligently organizing in advance of the pope's visit: Adrian Dominican Sister Carol Coston, founder of

NETWORK, a Catholic social justice lobby; Mercy Sister Maureen Fiedler[15] and Ms. Dolly Pomerleau of the Quixote Center, a multi-issue justice organization; and representatives from the Women's Ordination Conference began to meet and strategize.[16]

It was not difficult to find activists who wished to participate. Progressive Catholics were concerned about the unrestrained papal adulation evident in the media with little recognition that very many Catholics disagreed with the pope about issues such as birth control, mandatory celibacy, and women's ordination. Coston and the others felt they "needed to do something public to witness to their support for women's equality in the church, and to provide some public manifestation of Catholic sisters' views."[17] Many in the group were already trained in nonviolent protest, having participated in demonstrations against war and on behalf of women's rights.

After the pope's Philadelphia homily, "we began prayerfully preparing for the Shrine event. We spent two and three hours a night praying for what we were going to do," Coston later told the *New York Times.*[18] The group decided on a simple witness in which they would wear a light blue armband (in honor of Mary) and stand in silence while the pope spoke. Organizers planned to distribute armbands and explanatory flyers inviting others to join their "Stand Up for Women" witness as they entered the Shrine. Created by the Quixote Center, the flyer identified many reasons to stand up, including challenging the church's "exclusion of women from major decision making" and sexist structures that "legitimate and reinforce discrimination."[19]

Neither Coston nor Pomerleau had ever met Theresa Kane before, but when word trickled out that she would address the pope, the activists asked Fiedler to reach out to her and see if she would join them. Theresa remembers Fiedler calling to say, "The petition is all finished, we're attaching a blue armband... Would you be willing to give the pope the petition and wear a blue arm band?"

Theresa responded with her usual diplomacy: "Maureen, I really appreciate what you're doing. I respect it, but I really don't think I should do that."[20]

Bishop Kelly finally got back to Theresa about her request for a private meeting: "Theresa, I'm really sorry, I've done my best. The pope is over-scheduled. He's doing a lot with the apostolic delegate, he's doing a lot with bishops' groups, and there's no way at all that he can see you." Instead, Kelly suggested that if LCWR leaders would sit in the front row he would make sure to bring the pope over to meet them and shake their hands.

"Tom, thank you very much," replied Theresa. "But they don't really want to just shake his hand. They want a conversation."

Somewhat exasperated, the other LCWR leaders agreed: "You've got to be kidding... Go all the way from Iowa to Washington to shake his hand?" objected Blessed Virgin Mary Sister Joan Doyle."[21] Besides Theresa, the only other woman to publicly address the pope was first lady Rosalyn Carter, who greeted him in Boston.[22]

In the two weeks she had to prepare her greeting, Theresa carefully considered what to say. She consulted with other LCWR officers, past presidents Saint Joseph Sister Mary Dooley and Blessed Virgin Mary Sister Joan Doyle; and president-elect Claire Fitzgerald, who was a School Sister of Notre Dame. She also consulted her own Mercy Administrative Team, especially Sister Doris Gottemoeller, who had worked for years on LCWR's Ecclesial Role of Women Committee (EROWC). This committee had recently identified three major goals: "Cooperation with others to demonstrate the relationship between sexism and social evils; study and action relative to women and ministry; [and] solidarity with marginalized women." It had also completed a multi-year Women and Ministry study that supported removing sexist language from the liturgy, sought representation at the UN World Conference on Women in Copenhagen, and promoted action on Women's History Week.[23]

When Doris asked Theresa if she planned to say anything about women, Theresa responded that she did and inquired if Doris "thought it was all right."

"Oh yes," Doris replied. "I think it's great."

But, for the first time, Theresa began to wonder if everyone would agree with what she planned to do. As she worked on her remarks, she remembered with gratitude suggestions from Mercy Sister Elizabeth (Betty) Carroll, and Peter Henriot, SJ, of the Center of Concern.[24] Carroll—a former LCWR president whom Theresa deeply admired—was "delighted" that Theresa would include women's equality. She also told her, "Oh I wish you would include solidarity with the poor."

Fearing that her original text might sound judgmental, Theresa asked Henriot for his opinion. He suggested shaping the language about "opening all the ministries" so that it would reflect church teaching and faithfulness to the Vatican Council's call for reverence and dignity for all persons. "He turned it around for me. And it was absolutely perfect," recalls Theresa proudly.

While Theresa was determined to include Catholic women's equality in her greeting, she spent a lot of time mulling it over. She was surprised that no one had asked to see the greeting ahead of time. If they had, she would have given it to them, but she reflects, "I wouldn't have felt obliged to do what they said after they got it. After all, it was my greeting." At one point, she even found herself thinking, "If I get a sense that the group [at the Shrine], is not receptive, I may not say it." It felt good to her, knowing "that I had that freedom. I could say it or not say it. But I knew I wanted to."

She was blessed with a discerning sounding board in Mercy Sister Della Mae Quinn, her lifelong friend and companion. Della Mae supported raising the women's issue, but worried about repercussions. When the pope's Philadelphia homily prohibiting women priests made the evening news on October 4, she summoned Theresa to watch: "What do you think? Do you think you should still say it?"

"I do, Della Mae," Theresa replied. "I know that's his feeling, but this is an important issue. We feel strongly about it."

Della Mae later told her, "When I asked you that night, the image I had was of Jesus in the garden. I felt you were agonizing over it, but you still felt strongly it was important to do."

Everywhere he went during his US tour, the pope was greeted with massive crowds and adulatory media coverage. An estimated four hundred thousand people stood in the teeming rain on Boston Common to pray at a papal Mass. After addressing the UN, John Paul celebrated Mass for seventy-five thousand people at Yankee stadium, and on October 3 in Madison Square Garden tens of thousands of teenagers held a love-fest with the youth-savvy pope, loudly chanting "John Paul II, we love you." A laughing pope replied "*Woo hoo hoo*; John Paul II, he loves you." In Philadelphia, the pontiff met with seminarians and celebrated an outdoor Mass with over one million people. The next day, in a Mass with priest leaders, John Paul's homily reiterated "the Church's traditional decision to call men to the priesthood, and not to call women."[25] Large crowds greeted the pope in Des Moines and Chicago on October 4 and 5, before he flew east for an October 6 reception with President Carter and six thousand guests at the White House. On October 7, the pope was late to the sisters' prayer event after meeting with theologians at Catholic University and then interacting with enthusiastic students. A papal Mass with two hundred thousand people on the national Mall closed out the pope's immensely successful US visit. Small wonder that *Time* magazine dubbed him "John Paul Superstar."

In George Weigel's view, the massively attended and widely publicized papal appearances left "powerful memories and a fixed media interpretation of the Pope."[26] The resounding success of John Paul's triumphal tour, with nary a critical word spoken, undoubtedly heightened the unprecedented media coverage of a simple nun's courteous challenge on the last day of his visit. It was the first time anyone had suggested that not everything was perfect in Catholic-land. Some things needed to change.

Theresa already had a busy schedule planned for the weekend of the pope's Washington visit. The Mercy Administrative Team was hosting a community-wide justice workshop and, in addition to Sunday's greeting, she had been invited to a White House reception honoring the pope. When her mother Mamie, her sister Rose, and her niece Mary Beth accepted an invitation to come for the weekend, Theresa called Monsignor Murphy who sent extra tickets for the papal prayer service and White House reception.

Theresa remembers that by Saturday evening she was hoarse and worried that she would lose her voice before Sunday, but she awoke the next day in good health. A New York sister had telephoned on Saturday to say that the TV guide had a listing for the sisters' papal prayer service. CBS's David Brinkley would cover the event. Theresa remembers thinking: "Oh God, that means it's going to be televised in Washington and New York...I knew now for sure that there would be a bigger audience than just the sisters in the Shrine." She wondered if all LCWR members across the country would agree that this was the time to raise the women's issue. Having no way of finding out, she reminded herself that the 1975 LCWR resolution had "passed overwhelmingly" and that her greeting "included almost the same wording." She quickly notified the other LCWR officers that her presentation would be nationally televised. They stood by her.[27] There was nothing to do but move forward, especially since Theresa was, in her words, "permeated with the issue of women in the church at this point."

Very early Sunday morning, Theresa, Mamie, Rose, and Mary Beth joined Della Mae and about seventy other Sisters of Mercy on a bus that would take them to the Shrine. They had been told to arrive by 6:30 AM, even though the service wouldn't begin until nine o'clock. Upon entering the enormous church, they were met by sister organizers already passing out blue armbands and flyers. Theresa was struck by their creativity: "Anyone who walked into that shrine, if they felt strongly about it, could have put a blue armband on." After Theresa's party accepted both armband and flyer, Mamie asked Rose, "Do you think I should put this armband on? All the sisters are wearing it." Rose replied: "Mom, I don't think so, maybe let the sisters do it. I don't know if they want you to be doing it." Rose later told Theresa: "I was so afraid we'd go out on the steps and they'd take our picture with the armband on."

Several weeks before the service Theresa had received a third call from Monsignor Murphy, who, because of his concern about the silent witness, was thinking of having the rosary prayed aloud before the service. Theresa advised against it, "I don't really think it's appropriate to just throw in a rosary to keep people quiet. Why don't you play some music?" The monsignor "loved that idea." For three hours, more than five thousand sisters listened to liturgical and/or classical music as they patiently waited for the pope. Later, media reported that although there were many sisters in habits; it was difficult to say whether they were the majority.[28] Theresa estimated that about one third of the congregation wore habits. The cloistered sisters were seated in front in their habits and veils. While she waited, Theresa quietly reread her greeting from her seat in the sanctuary.

Just before the service, a young priest approached: "Sister, when you finish, you'll bow to the Holy Father and go back to your seat."

Theresa answered, "Father, I would like to approach the Holy Father and just shake hands with him."

"That is not allowed, Sister," the young cleric replied.

Theresa gazed at him and held her peace.

Accompanied by myriad bishops, priests, and male acolytes, the pope at last made his triumphal entry into the Shrine of the Immaculate Conception. He was met by cheering sisters who enthusiastically snapped pictures as he entered. But other sister-activists were preparing to help him "understand that while they loved him, they disagreed with his views on the proper role for women in the church."[29] Theresa does not remember seeing any women in the entrance procession, but she did see organizers of the silent witness milling about at the back of the church. After Cardinal William Baum made brief welcoming remarks, Theresa stood, bowed to the pope, and was escorted to the podium by a young priest, who, she recalls, never left her side.

When she noted that "it is appropriate that a woman's voice be heard in this Shrine," the congregation responded with whole-hearted applause. There was lengthy applause again when she pledged solidarity with the pope in his "efforts to respond to the cry of the poor" and spoke of the contributions of sisters to building the church in the Americas. She then said:

> As I share this privileged moment with you, Your Holiness, I urge you to be mindful of the intense suffering and pain which is part of the life of so many women in these United States. I call upon you to listen with compassion and hear the call of women who comprise half of humankind. As women we have heard the powerful messages of our Church addressing the dignity and reverence for all persons. As women we have pondered upon these words. Our contemplation leads us to state that the Church, in its struggle to be faithful to its call for reverence and charity for all persons, must respond by

providing the possibility of women as persons being included in all the ministries of our Church.

At this juncture, Theresa remembers the sisters responding with "sustained applause." Veteran Vatican correspondent Peter Hebblethwaite characterized the applause as "thunderous, although by no means universal,"[30] and some sisters—many older and dressed in habits—"pointedly refrained from applauding."[31] According to Hebblethwaite, for the first time on his US visit, John Paul II "looked nonplussed... The hands that were all set for the customary modest acknowledgment of flattery, moved into a deprecating gesture." As applause reverberated throughout the cavernous church, the pontiff, "looked faintly grim, and for a moment hid his face in his hands."[32] Bad acoustics and his relative unfamiliarity with English, however, make it unlikely that the pope had completely understood Theresa's unprecedented plea.

Congregation of Jesus and Mary Sister Helen Scarry was secretary to Saint Joseph Sister Margaret Culbert, the vicar general associate for women religious in the Archdiocese of Washington at the time. Seated in the sanctuary directly behind Theresa, Scarry remembers her speaking "very beautifully in a strong feminine voice," and that there was a "very light but audible gasp" when the pope put his hand to his face. Scarry had been told that Pope John Paul II often put his hand to his face when he was trying to listen closely. She believes that the pope's gesture triggered much of the speculation that Theresa had "spoken out of turn."[33]

Immediately after the service, Theresa remembers Archbishop John Quinn, who was president of the National Conference of Catholic Bishops at the time, approaching her to say, "I'm not sure the pope heard everything that you said, but I know he'll be getting a copy of it." Of course, the pope had received no advance copy because Theresa had not shown it to anyone outside of her immediate circle. She had the only copy, and Archbishop Quinn did not take it from her. (She would later give it to her mother, who wanted to show it to her friends.)

The only copy of Theresa's greeting that the pope would receive was one retrieved from television footage. What church officials had received beforehand was a copy of a statement drafted by Catholic Advocates for Equality and signed by thirty-nine sisters. It asked the pope "to listen to the particular concerns of Catholic women in the United States."[34] This effort, like the silent witness, was completely separate from Theresa's greeting. Between the petition and the obvious activism of sisters with blue armbands as he processed in from the back, the pope must have had more than an inkling that all was not going to go completely as planned.

Theresa remembers that, by the end of her greeting, her young priest escort had become "really jittery," because what was to have been a four-minute greeting had gone on significantly longer owing to so much applause. "Sister, you'll go to your seat," he said, only to watch helplessly as she left him standing at the podium and walked straight over to the pope. "And they weren't wild about that, I tell you," Theresa wryly recalls. She continues:

> I just went right over to him. He stood up. He was gracious. I said, "Hello, Holy Father." I took his hand and I shook hands with him. He said something to me, and of course I didn't understand him because he wasn't speaking English that well at that point. He didn't understand me, I don't think. So, with that, I just automatically said, "May I have your blessing?" And I knelt right down in front of him. He put his hand on my head. I got up, he thanked me—at least I think he said something—and I walked back to my seat.

Enthusiastic applause accompanied Theresa back to her seat, where Scarry gently placed her own hand on Theresa's shoulder, "because to me Theresa Kane was, and is to this day, a sign of hope." Sisters inside and activists outside the Shrine were ecstatic. They had had no advance notice of what Theresa would say. "All we knew is that she was praying over it really hard," recalls activist Dolly Pomerleau, who was outside listening to the service on loudspeakers. "So of course, when she spoke in such a deliberate but gentle way that was clearly saying "ordain women," but did not use those words, I thought it was absolute genius on her part. I was just so happy. I was also grateful. It took a huge amount of courage and humility to speak to the pope the way she did."[35]

Inside, Sister Carol Coston—who had decided to wear red and sit in the front so that she would stand out—remembers being "so delighted that I just clapped and clapped." Theresa's action was a "huge boost to the women's movement," Coston believes. For the first time, someone in institutional Catholic leadership was speaking out. This allowed other women's organizations to "see that we were potential allies in the Equal Rights Amendment [effort] and other women's issues."[36] Pomerleau echoes Coston's take on the importance of having support from someone closely aligned with the institution: "Up until that moment, I would say that [women's ordination efforts] felt more like a fringe movement and that nobody in an institutional position would take a stand that forcefully on behalf of women. And so [Theresa's greeting] was a very strong validation."[37]

Many of Theresa's own Sisters of Mercy heard her address from a distance. Sister Helen Amos—who would succeed Theresa as administrator general—remembers watching on television with her small community in Baltimore: "We unanimously cheered and were very proud of her. It wasn't until later that it dawned on us that everybody didn't think it was wonderful—that part was surprising to me—how intensely some people felt so negative about it."[38]

Sister Margaret Farley—who had earlier attended the papal meeting with theologians—heard it on the radio as she was driving home: "I actually was astonished...When I talked to Theresa later (it's shameful when I think of it now), I said, 'Theresa, I didn't think you had it in you to do that.' And she just laughed and said, why not?"[39]

Sister Doris Gottemoeller recalls that sisters returning from the Shrine were "full of the news but no one really understood the tremendous impact it [would have]." For the rest of the day, she relates, "the phone rang off the hook and news media of all kinds were bombarding us for speeches and interviews. It took everybody's breath away, including Theresa's. I don't think she had any idea." For Doris, Theresa was "the ideal person to address those words [to the pope], and she addressed them with humility, candor, and courage."[40]

Now it was time for the pope to speak.[41] Sister Maureen Fiedler remembers feeling nervous, and later told the New York Times: "I thought about what the Holy Father has been telling us about the resurrecting power of Christ. I thought about the power and strength of Christ, and I came out of my nervousness."[42] Fifty-three Catholic sisters clad in light blue armbands rose from their seats, and stood silently for the next forty-two minutes as the pope laboriously read his remarks in thickly accented English. Sister Theresa Anderson told Newsweek, "First I wanted to rise, then I didn't." But when the pontiff spoke of the need for "public witness," Anderson—a Benedictine nun who wanted to be a priest—took heart and decided to stand.[43] As Coston remembers it, the pope's presentation "wasn't personalized or geared to US sisters' experience. It wasn't interesting."

Peter Hebblethwaite's astute analysis of the papal address reveals key differences between the pope's understanding of religious life and that of Theresa and many other sisters. The pope defined religious life in traditional terms: consecration, intimacy with Christ, faithfulness to prayer, and the vows of poverty, chastity, and obedience. While not denying these core elements, Theresa "added another factor which changes the emphasis. She defined religious life as a *response* to the needs of the world."[44] In this way she aligned sisters with the pope's own words, calling on Catholics to be in solidarity with the poor and oppressed. In fidelity to Vatican II renewal, many sisters were now pursuing ministries among those made poor and working to change the structures that kept them poor. Yet the pope referenced only one apostolate—teaching in Catholic schools—and equated educating largely middle-class and wealthy children with the founding charism of most religious orders. But most founders—such as Theresa's Mother Catherine McAuley—began teaching poor children (often girls) as a way to counter the ignorance that trapped them in a life of poverty. The pope did not mention other important apostolates such as health care and care for orphans and the poor. Most founders began health ministries primarily to serve poor people who were dying for lack of access to care. The common denominator for sisters' communal charisms, whether in the seventeenth century or the twenty-first century, has always been responding to the needs of the world—and especially the needs of those made poor by income inequality.

At the Shrine on October 7, the pope seemed mainly concerned with communicating that all sisters should wear religious garb and return to the corporate ministries that he interpreted as their "original charism." In what some deemed a veiled response to progressive Catholics urging ministerial equality for women, he carefully pointed out that Mary "is honored as queen of the apostles without herself being incorporated within the hierarchical constitution of the church ... Yet she makes all hierarchy possible."[45] While the pope undoubtedly intended to be inspirational, it didn't fly among Catholics whose consciousness had been raised by feminist analysis. In Hebblethwaite's felicitous phrasing: "The chains are of gold, but they are nonetheless chains."[46]

Still, the pope received as much applause as Theresa did. In 1979 some 40 percent of all teachers in parochial schools were Catholic sisters,[47] and an Associated Press (AP) poll had found that Catholic laity were "equally divided in their feelings on the ordination of women."[48] The sisters at the Shrine were also laity, and their opinions likely mirrored the AP poll. They valued their religious consecration to Christ, teaching in Catholic schools, serving the sick, and activism on behalf of the oppressed. Yet not all saw themselves as marginalized in the institution within which they lived out their lives. For some, blind obedience to religious authority was still a seminal value. They willingly embraced chains of gold.

Rather than processing back down the long center aisle, the pope exited from the side to visit the Black Madonna in the chapel of Our

Lady of Czestochowa, donated by Polish American Catholics. Theresa had been handed a note that CBS wished to interview her on the front steps of the Shrine. But she also needed to hurry to get over to WETA, the PBS studio in Alexandria where she was scheduled to help cover the papal Mass. After finding her family, she exited the Shrine only to be deluged with "about fifteen microphones in front of my face," and many sisters—both in habits and in lay clothes—who wished to shake her hand.

Best of all for Theresa was seeing her friend and mentor Mercy Sister Betty Carroll at the bottom of the steps: "She was so thrilled. She embraced me and said, 'Oh Theresa, it was beautiful and wonderful ...I never thought I would live to see such a day.'" A former president of LCWR, Carroll had herself jousted skillfully with church hierarchy. In the early 1970s she successfully defended the right of sisters to choose their own clothing when the prefect of the Congregation for Religious, Cardinal Ildebrando Antoniutti, insisted that sisters return to wearing the habit.[49] Theresa still tears up when she remembers Betty's strong support. "It was the best thing in the world ...It was so affirming. [It felt] like I was continuing her work ...and she was very proud that it was a Sister of Mercy that had done it, too."

Although besieged by reporters, Theresa tactfully told them that she was unable to give interviews because she was due immediately at the PBS studio. But there was another reason. Theresa felt it inappropriate to "come out from talking to the pope and then all of a sudden take on this whole group of press people." She had said what she needed to say, and her statement stood on its own. She experienced a deep sense of peace after finishing her greeting because, she says, "It is no longer mine. It belongs to the public. It belongs to anyone who wants to hear it and to react to it. If anybody reacts positively, thank you. If they don't react positively, thank you also ...It was bigger than I was at that point." It was enough for her to have put women's full equality in the Catholic Church squarely on the public table.

While she declined to feed the media's appetite for sensation, the *Washington Post* did manage to get one brief quotation: "I said I don't speak for every woman. I am not challenging the Pope's right to say what he wants to say. I merely hoped to offer a challenge to him to hear the suffering and pain of women." The same article quoted sisters who were dismayed by what had just happened: "What she said is biased and inappropriate," said Sister Joan Marie. "It disturbs me that she says we have all this pain and agony because we can't be priests," said Sister Mary Dennis. "I am perfectly happy. I don't want to be a priest, and I don't think women should be." Yet another sister wisely noted: "This debate here is a microcosm of the whole church."[50]

But for now, Theresa, her mother, her sister, and her niece were en route to Alexandria for the WETA-PBS telecast. Della Mae—who had returned to the motherhouse for a car to ferry the group to the TV studio —had learned from a repeating radio segment that Theresa's greeting had become a major media moment. The lead-in to the sensationalized story was something along the lines of, "Nun from New York Defies the Pope." In subsequent years Della Mae loved retelling the story: "You were sitting in the front combing your hair, checking to see if you needed powder on your face, and this story "Nun Defies the Pope" comes on the radio. Your mother says from the back seat, 'Did you do that?' and you say, 'No, I don't think so, Mom.'"[51]

At PBS, Paul Duke hosted a panel of Catholic commentators including Fr. Kenneth Baker, SJ, the new editor in chief of the conservative *Homiletic and Pastoral Review*; Father Bryan Hehir, a progressive and a key policy advisor for the National Conference of Catholic Bishops; Peter Hebblethwaite with the *National Catholic Reporter*; and Theresa. Baker and Hehir explained various parts of the Mass to the viewing audience. At other times—Theresa estimates "at least five or six times"—Duke would say "Now, we have with us today Sister Theresa Kane who just finished greeting the pope at the Shrine, and we have to show you the clip, because it's really quite remarkable."

At one point the conversation turned to women in ministry. Theresa recalls that both Hebblethwaite and Hehir "were excellent" on the issue, saying women have a high educational level—not only in the United States but also in other parts of the world—and should be granted equal opportunities in society and in the church. At no point did any panelist, or Duke himself, seek to interview Theresa on what had just happened, nor did she offer to expand on what was already on the airwaves.

That said, both Hebblethwaite and Duke privately offered valuable advice. Hebblethwaite—whom Theresa found "so very gracious and kind"—told her: "What you did today would be equivalent to what Catherine of Siena or Teresa of Avila did in their day. But I also will tell you that you probably could have been burned at the stake like Joan of Arc." He warned, "The press can crucify you. They can be harder than the church on you. You have to be very wise, and very discerning about how you want to deal with them, because you're going to get a tremendous amount of press on this. Just be very careful of the press, because they can kill you." Duke even suggested that she hire a press manager. But Theresa chose not to do that, mainly because "we didn't have time, and I wasn't going to spend all my time talking to the press."

Hebblethwaite proved prophetic. When Theresa returned to her office at the Mercy generalate on Monday morning, Della Mae (who served as her secretary at that time), wanted to know what to do with the hundreds of messages that had come in, as well as "a million and one calls from this press and that press." Theresa quickly conferred with the other four members of the Mercy Administrative Team. They suggested seeking advice from experienced media people and consulting with allies in the clerical system for how to manage what was becoming a politically fraught situation.

Theresa then called her mentor, Sister Betty Carroll, who said to her, "Oh if I were you, I wouldn't do anything right away. This story is going to be around, and it's going to be very time-consuming." A priest friend in New York who had astute insight into clerical politics suggested, "I would just make a short statement saying, 'I have spoken to the pope, I said what I had to say, and at this time I don't have any more that I want to add to it.'" Another trusted priest friend—Father Joseph O'Keefe, who was Theresa's former spiritual director and would later become the bishop of Syracuse—told her: "Basically, the guys I spoke to said not to prolong it, and not to exploit it. You had a message, you delivered your message. Let it cool for a while."

On Monday, October 8, Della Mae and her staff distributed Theresa's brief communiqué to members of the media seeking interviews:

> I appreciated the opportunity to greet the Holy Father, and it was his openness that encouraged me to express a concern experienced by me and many other women across the country. It is my hope that such opportunities will increase when women can dialogue further with the Holy Father about such concerns as I expressed yesterday. I reaffirm my respect for and fidelity to the Holy Father.[52]

Theresa decided she would refuse press interviews and speaking engagements for the foreseeable future. Aside from the need to allow her greeting to marinate in the public discourse, she had severe time constraints. She was president of LCWR, and the Sisters of Mercy had just sold the generalate property. The sale required daily attention to the many administrative tasks involved in closing the building and relocating generalate offices. She was, moreover, at the end of her three-year term as administrator general and wished to avoid additional high-profile media attention before her community's upcoming April elections.

Her decision prompted several feminist theologians, including Margaret Farley and Elisabeth Schüssler Fiorenza, to ask her to reconsider. In light of the intense media interest they felt that she really should be speaking publicly. But Theresa disagreed. "Before we start dissecting it again, everybody needs a little bit of time and space to take it all into perspective." The Quixote Center's consummate church reform activist Dolly Pomerleau admits that, while she was initially disappointed by Theresa's media silence, she eventually understood its strategic wisdom: "It made her Shrine statement all the more powerful because she wasn't doing it for self-aggrandizement, you know, to be a famous media star,... she did it purely out of conviction and out of love for the church and the people in the church."[53]

A MEDIA FIRESTORM

Despite Theresa's decision to refuse interviews, media people camped out at the entrance to the Mercy generalate for a week. Her prescient realization that her statement now "belonged to the public" was soon validated with a vengeance. It ignited a media firestorm of praise and blame that would continue for months—indeed years—to come. Across the United States both Catholics and non-Catholics weighed in on the propriety of female priests, and of the woman who dared give voice to the possibility. Newspapers from coast to coast wrote editorials and ran feature stories about the widely differing views of local Catholics. Letters poured in to LCWR and to the Sisters of Mercy either bitterly opposing or passionately affirming Theresa's papal greeting. Priests, sisters, laity, and even some bishops publicly opined on her action.

Mother M. Sixtina of the Sisters of St. Francis of the Martyr St. George paid thousands of dollars for an October 12 quarter-page ad in the *Washington Post* to publicly apologize to the pope for what she called Theresa's "rudeness." The ad also accused Theresa of being "impertinent" and offending "millions" of others.[54] The *Philadelphia Inquirer* published an op-ed from the superior of the Immaculate Heart of Mary Sisters, Mother Mary Claudia, who felt the need to support Pope John Paul's views on the habit and to "clarify" her more traditional style of religious life.[55]

In an Associated Press column published in papers throughout the nation, religion writer George Cornell wrote that Theresa was being hailed as "a new Joan of Arc." School Sister of Notre Dame Sister Margaret Ellen Traxler told him: "Like Joan of Arc, she spoke the truth in high places... When you love something or someone very much, when you love the church very much, you owe it the truth." In the same piece, the national bishops' conference general secretary Bishop Thomas Kelly praised Theresa: "She had a responsibility to make the truth known to the Holy Father as she saw it and to represent the membership. She expressed herself with great respect and devotion to the Holy Father personally, and I'm full of admiration for that."[56] Over the next week, the *Washington Post* published multiple letters to the editor, most of them negative. These were soon counterbalanced by other letters strongly praising Theresa's intervention.

Some diocesan publications were openly critical of the greeting. One example is this remark from the *Southern Cross*: "Sister Kane, in her direct confrontation, has left no room for negotiation... [her] action lacked class and respect."[57] Other diocesan papers viewed the moment more positively. Catholic columnist John F. Kavanaugh, SJ, evoked Teresa of Avila and Catherine of Siena:

> Catherine of Siena realized that to be a Catholic was to be a free person who could dissent and who would yield—but yield only because of the faith itself... [It has been] a long time [since] a Pope has been spoken to with such simplicity, forthrightness and fidelity in word and gesture. It's a sign of John Paul's great soul, the courage of this woman. Saints Catherine and Teresa may well have smiled.[58]

The *St. Cloud Visitor* wrote, "It took a lot of stamina and guts for Sister Theresa Kane to get up and let be said what she did... The best dissent is not coming from the rebellious, but from the loyal sons and daughters of the Church..." The same editorial lamented that "many an ordinary person still prejudiciously resents women lectors, women ministers of the Eucharist, women in any leadership capacity."[59] An editorial in *The Davenport Catholic Messenger* quoted Archbishop John Quinn of San Francisco, who found Theresa's greeting "a bit lacking in good form." Nevertheless, it suggested, "Surely if this Pope is as strong a man as he appears to be, he is not going to be offended by what Sr. Theresa Kane did. In fact, if he really is a strong man, he will grow to appreciate it, even learn from it."[60]

Quinn was the only bishop to publicly express doubts about propriety. In addition to Bishop Kelly, two other bishops, Frank J. Rodimer of the Paterson, NJ, diocese, and Denver Archbishop James V. Casey spoke more positively. Quoted in an article in the *Denver Catholic Register* and subsequently distributed nationally by the National Catholic News Service, Casey said, "I feel that what she said was reverent, kind and loving—and I applaud her. Both in the church and society, women have been denied offices, responsibilities, and positions they could easily fulfill... They have reason to be impatient—but not angry... Women enthusiasts could learn a great deal from her approach." Casey expressed pride that his archdiocese was a pioneer in welcoming sisters into pastoral ministry. Because of the priest shortage, he said, "I must find ways to open new parishes without pastors being in residence."[61]

Bishop Rodimer wrote a thoughtful column for his diocesan paper—the *Beacon*—suggesting that the issue Theresa raised "went beyond that of ordination," and called on the whole church "to face the question of justice as it applies to our teaching about the equality of men and women." Catholics who believed only a few "disgruntled and unduly vocal" women were raising the issue "are mistaken," he said, since the place of women in the church is "much more serious" than many realize. He praised Theresa's remarks as "respectfully made" and concluded with this prescient observation: "Perhaps it was not the Pope's sensitivities but our own that our sister touched last week in Mary's Shrine."[62]

Biblical scholars and theologians also weighed in. The *Catholic Messenger* in Davenport, Iowa, printed the Religion News Service's coverage of a presentation by renowned biblical scholar Father Raymond Brown to several hundred priests and bishops at a fiftieth anniversary commemoration of the founding of St. Mary's Seminary in Roland Park, Maryland. Brown carefully explained that the term "priest" was not applied to the ordained priesthood until several hundred years after Christ's death and resurrection. A member of the Pontifical Biblical Commission, Brown reiterated the commission's findings, published in April 1976, that scripture alone does not exclude the ordination of women. In contrast to *Inter Insigniores* (which was published later that same year), the biblical commission had concluded by a 12–5 vote that the church could ordain women to the priesthood without going against what Christ originally intended. Further, Brown pointed out that the notion of Mary as a priest has a strong biblical foundation, since "she is first among Christians... In terms of the priesthood of all believers, Mary, the Mother of Christ is the greatest of priests."[63]

The *Milwaukee Journal* published an interview with theologian and Immaculate Heart of Mary Sister Sandra Schneiders of the Jesuit School of Theology in Berkeley, California. "The Pope was operating from a hierarchical model where he demonstrated that his view was to tell people what to do," Schneiders commented. "Theresa Kane was operating from a participatory model, where she showed that we have to listen to each other... We in America come from a position of participation and equality."[64]

National Catholic publications were predictably divided according to their ecclesial perspectives. The progressive *National Catholic Reporter* wrote: "Sister Theresa Kane served as a model for respectful dissent," and published a sympathetic analysis by respected Vatican correspondent Peter Hebblethwaite. *The Wanderer*, a conservative tabloid, published an editorial by Joseph T. Gill describing Theresa's greeting as a "harangue" and saying she had "defied the Pope."[65] A letter to the editor of *Our Sunday Visitor* from a priest found Theresa's action "a gauche breach of ordinary etiquette."[66] The National Catholic News Service reported on Mother Sixtina's *Washington Post* advertisement and quoted the vice president of LCWR, Sister Clare Fitzgerald, with whom Theresa had shared her statement beforehand: "I read it quietly and prayerfully," said Fitzgerald, "and I thought it was fine."[67] The Spanish language *El Visitante Dominical* published an in-depth feature story quoting those who admired Theresa's action and those who decried it.[68]

Influential weekly news magazines such as *Time* and *Newsweek* published full-page stories and analyses of Theresa's unprecedented greeting. *Time* observed that John Paul had "come down hard on the conservative side of issues that divide the American church... no artificial birth control, no married priests, no women priests..." and quoted moral theologian Father Charles Curran, who remarked: "Most American women thought [the habit] issue had been settled years ago."[69] *Newsweek*'s Kenneth Woodward and Mary Lord opined that papal handlers may have unwittingly invited US nuns to publicly voice their concerns by refusing to grant an audience to LCWR leadership beforehand and by instructing US priests to cancel their own Sunday Masses so there would be no need for laywomen and laymen to distribute communion at papal Masses. *Newsweek* also reported that many sisters felt the pope had spoken "like a condescending patriarch" in rejecting women's ordination at his Philadelphia address. This was amplified when young seminarians and priests responded by standing up and clapping. "I saw all those priests get up and clap," said Sister Jacqueline Merz, who was a member of the Women's Ordination Conference. "They didn't have to stand and applaud. They could feel a little something for us."[70]

In addition to the *New York Times* and *Washington Post*, diverse dailies such as the *Los Angeles Times*, the *Tennessee Register* and the *Sacramento Bee* published editorials and letters to the editor and reported on local response. The *Chicago Catholic* recorded differing reactions in that Midwest heartland. Kathleen Valenta of the Chicago archdiocesan Daughters of Isabella found Theresa "out of order, brazen," and wondered "why they let her talk." Patricia Hughes, a campus minister at Mundelein College, sent Theresa a telegram because "I felt hers was the finest gift offered the Pope during his trip." Several Chicagoans acknowledged that while Theresa's greeting was respectful, they had difficulty with the public timing, while others pointed out that requests for a private meeting had been denied. Reading from a media release, Patricia Spencer, chairperson of the National Institute of Religious Life, an organization claiming to represent ninety orders of US sisters, stated the greeting encouraged "open dissent," and questioned Theresa's fidelity to the pope.[71] An inspiring—and perhaps a bit more objective—perspective is found in a self-described "outsider" editorial published in the *Sacramento Bee*:

> As outsiders...we were moved by the style in which the message was delivered, by the faith which gave it meaning and by the powerful protest that those gentle tones managed to convey ...We have rarely heard such quiet, measured language of such force, nor have we often seen a declaration as telling as that of the nuns who applauded Sister Theresa's words or who stood with her the other day. Together they honored both the traditions of the church and the women within it.[72]

In coming months Theresa would repeatedly encounter people in airports who recognized her: "Are you the sister who spoke to the pope?" One Iranian woman told her. "I want to thank you. Women are having an awful time in Iran right now." Another woman said, "You know, I was in Australia the day you spoke to the pope. And every bit of it was live." Theresa warmly remembers that, along with being deluged with media requests and other communiqués, she received a beautiful arrangement of a dozen red roses with a loaf of bread in the middle sent by Sonia Johnson, the Mormon feminist who was first divorced by her husband and then excommunicated for her advocacy for the Equal Rights Amendment.[73]

COMMUNICATING WITH HER SISTERS—AND THE HIERARCHY

On the Monday after her greeting, Theresa met via conference call with other LCWR officers. The leadership decided to seek immediate in-person meetings with all US cardinals who, as it happened, were scheduled to be in Rome for a November 5–9 plenary assembly. This would simultaneously provide an opportunity for prelates to raise any concerns they might have about Theresa's papal greeting and to explain why it was necessary. Each sister-leader then selected the cardinal or cardinals with whom she was already acquainted in order to telephone for an appointment. There were some cardinals with whom national LCWR leaders had no connection. But there were certain regional LCWR leaders who knew them well.

The national office reached out to local leaders, asking them to request appointments with cardinals known to them. To their credit, every US cardinal agreed to meet with LCWR leaders. Theresa met with Cardinal William Baum, of Washington, DC; the papal nuncio Archbishop Jean Jadot; and Cardinal Terence Cooke of New York. Theresa found Cardinal Baum, "most gracious." After her introductory remarks, Baum told her: "Well, I know...I know it's a concern to many, many sisters, but I don't know if that was really the time." He then informed Theresa that Monsignor Murphy was "very, very upset" and asked her to meet with him. Theresa agreed to do so.

When she met with a visibly angry Murphy, he reminded her how "very closely" he had worked with her before issuing this rebuke: "You walked away from my assistant. That was a serious breach of Vatican protocol, and to me that was more serious than what you said." A puzzled Theresa quickly apologized. A year later Murphy would complain to journalist Paul Wilkes:

> Why did *she* have to do what *she* did *here*?...A man would have called me up beforehand and said he was going to do it. Not her. She might have felt divinely called to say what she did, but in the Catholic Church we believe in authority and discipline. The will of God was clearly reflected in the organizational rubric that she take two minutes for her welcome and then return to her seat.[74]

Next Theresa visited the papal nuncio. "Archbishop Jadot," she said, "we know the cardinals are going to Rome and LCWR wanted to speak to each cardinal and to you because you represent the pope here. So if you have any questions or any concerns about what was in my greeting, or the greeting itself, I just wanted the opportunity to speak to you about it." Jadot replied that he felt Theresa's greeting had been respectfully done, but he added, "If you had asked my opinion, I would not have advised you to do it."

Theresa replied: "Archbishop Jadot, with all due respect, I would not have asked you." A startled Jadot asked why. "Well, if I had asked you, and you said yes, then it would have caused you difficulty.

And if you said no, then I would have had to go against what you asked me to do. That would have been bad for both of us. So it was wiser not to ask."

"Oh," said Jadot, "I guess that's true."

Cardinal Cooke, who knew Theresa very well since she was from New York, first acknowledged his appreciation for how respectfully Theresa had delivered her greeting. He then asked if she had decided to raise the issue before the pope's speech to Philadelphia seminarians, when he had stated his opposition to female priests. Theresa replied she had prepared the speech days earlier, saying she recognized that the pope is "not in favor of [women's ordination] and it's not something that we can do now. But my understanding is that it certainly could be thought of for the future."

On October 19 and 22, Theresa wrote similar letters to all members of LCWR and to her own Sisters of Mercy community, sharing vital information about why she spoke as she did, the aftermath of her greeting, and future planning. She enclosed copies of the greeting and of the pope's presentation. Her letter expressed a "deep sense of peace and tranquility" as she pondered the events "before, during, and after the experience." To LCWR, she wrote that she was "in dialogue personally with every member of the National Board in an attempt to share fully the spirit which prompted me to speak," and she shared plans to meet with officials in Rome in November as well as hopes for a personal meeting with Pope John Paul II. She included her October 8 media statement with her letter telling both groups of her conviction that "dialogue within our Church must proceed immediately, and I must give priority to furthering such dialogue"[75]

Even though Archbishops Quinn and Casey and Bishop Rodimer publicly vouched for the graciousness of Theresa's greeting, the first reaction of LCWR member groups was mixed: "Many applauded her courage, many agreed with her statement, a handful were offended."[76] Even though five communities of sisters dropped their membership in LCWR, the leaders of most orders were supportive. When sister-leaders were able to reflect together at subsequent regional gatherings, the prevailing sentiment was one of acceptance and support: "There was recognition that what she had said was, in fact, truthful and that the church must confront its systemic exclusion and depreciation of women."[77] LCWR region VI (Ohio-Kentucky-Tennessee) publicly praised Theresa for her "professional, prayerful response fulfilling a responsibility she felt was hers as a leader."[78] On February 9, 1980, the Dominican Leadership Conference issued a statement of support signed by ninety-four male and female leaders commending Theresa's statement. The Dominicans sent copies to Archbishop Jadot, Archbishop Quinn, Bishop Kelly, officials at the Vatican's Sacred Congregation for Religious and Secular Institutes, and Pope John Paul II.[79]

A LIGHTNING ROD FOR CATHOLIC FRUSTRATIONS

In the meantime, a "flood of letters" was deluging LCWR offices and the Mercy generalate. Initially, LCWR staff found "the vast majority" of responses to be favorable.[80] As the media drumbeat continued, however, more negative, mean-spirited, and vitriolic letters arrived. Within the next six weeks, more than five thousand letters from the United States, Canada, and Western Europe would pour in. Judging it inadvisable—if not impossible—to reply personally, the LCWR executive committee decided to analyze the correspondence with view to discovering what could be learned from this uniquely Catholic phenomenon.

LCWR's admittedly "non-scientific" analysis supports Bishop Frank Rodimer's prediction that Theresa's Shrine interaction revealed more about US Catholic sensitivities than those of the pope. Every letter focused on just one paragraph—the request relating to the inclusion of "women in all the ministries of our Church." Of the 2,917 letters from sisters, 2,105 were positive. Among the 463 clerics, (including at least one bishop), 375 affirmed Theresa's action (the bishop did not). The 1,879 lay correspondents were the most evenly divided, with 965 positive. The remaining 29 letters were from other denominations and overwhelmingly positive, with 28 affirming. Thirteen of these were ordained women from Protestant denominations.[81] Overall, two thirds of letter writers responded positively and one third were disapproving.

For those who wrote in praise of Theresa, the word "courage" stood out most clearly, as well as the words "sensitive, gentle, respectful, honest, dignified, strong, articulate, and loving."[82] Sisters wrote to say Theresa was a loyal daughter of the church, living in the spirit of Mercy founder Catherine McAuley, and Frances Warde, who, with six other sisters, established the first Mercy foundation in the United States. One writer compared the Shrine encounter to "early civil rights leaders speaking on behalf of blacks." Others cited "the courage of the first disciples of Jesus who persisted in public proclamation of the Gospel even after being silenced by established religious leaders." Theresa was said to have "started a dialogue in search of truth," to have spoken "the heart of the gospel message," and to have "challenged the church regarding justice and human dignity." Clergymen agreed that she "used her available time well to speak about the church."[83]

Three dominant themes emerged from writers who approved. Her words and behavior were (1) courageous, (2) attuned to the situation, and (3) empowering for others.[84] Since many writers from all Catholic categories contrasted Theresa's courage with their own inability to act, the LCWR analyses suggested that "Implicit in their remarks is an acknowledgment of fear...To represent oneself and others openly to powerful persons is perceived as dangerous." This led the LCWR analysts to suggest: "The persistence of the [fear] themes is an invitation to the Church leadership at every level to reflect on the tendency of all institutions to coerce and oppress those they exist to serve."[85]

Among the one third "disapproving" correspondents, a severe criticism came from a priest who compared Theresa to Madalyn Murray O'Hair, the woman who founded American Atheists and won a Supreme Court case that ended official prayer in public schools. One lay person called her "*Miss* Kane (you don't deserve the title Sister)." Others called her a "women's libber," comparing her to Gloria Steinem and Bella Abzug. Other dubious phrases from the disapproving lay lexicon characterized her as an "ungracious militant, the foolish virgin, the apostate: 'equal to one man—Judas Iscariot'; like Luther (found your own church); and a spreader of Marxism." Some descended to name-calling: "narcissist, undisciplined selfish brat, child having a temper tantrum and educated beyond your intelligence."

Three dominant themes emerged from the "disapproving" group. Theresa's behavior was perceived to have been (1) dangerous, even sinful, (2) defiant, and (3) embarrassing. She was said to have "talked back," "argued," and "given serious scandal." Because she had "upstaged the Pope," new vocations were harmed, and this jeopardized the future of the Catholic school system. One writer asked, "Shouldn't the religious, Christ's spouse be more subservient than anyone else in the Church?" Another said Theresa had "promoted lesbianism by challenging the tradition that the church as the Bride of Christ needs male priests." Since disapproving writers saw Theresa's behavior as sinful, they freely prescribed acts of repentance such as confession, public submission and apology, wearing a habit, and accepting her proper place as a sister by teaching catechism *gratis* to children. She was advised "to resign from her public responsibilities...to leave the church, indeed to found her own."[86]

Generally, those who wrote to express their disapproval vented frustrations about the changes in religious life since Vatican II. They spoke negatively about hair, clothing, change of ministries, and accused sisters of abandoning their vows and "proper" roles in the church. This led to the question, "How can we [LCWR sisters] enjoy evangelical freedom and remain accountable to one another?"[87]

While not all letters had arrived by the time Theresa wrote her mid-October communiqués to LCWR members and the Sisters of Mercy, enough had been received to recognize that Theresa's greeting had become a lightning rod. Theresa shared her thoughts about how to respond:

> Both positive and negative responses have been received as a result of my greeting; these I accept with reverence. The hostile, unchristian, and uncharitable expressions which have come forth from so many of the faithful—clergy, religious and laity are a deep source of concern to me ... our response must be one of compassion, of charity and an awareness of both the sinful and redeeming nature of our humanity.[88]

She also expressed heartfelt appreciation to her sisters: "I want you to know that I am humbly grateful for the tremendous sisterly support [which has] been a source of grace and strength to me. For those of you who have expressed concern and disapproval because of what you judged to be an 'inappropriate time' I welcome, reverence, and respect your responses." Even though some disagreed and disapproved, Theresa remained firm in holding "a deep conviction that it was a grace-filled moment; a sacred moment. I exercised a prudential judgment and it was the inspiration which I have received from so many of you that compelled me to speak with courage, with conviction—to speak the truth in love and with fidelity."[89]

The Vatican Wants Clarification

LCWR leaders would themselves soon journey to Rome for their customary annual meeting with officials from the Sacred Congregation for Religious and Secular Institutes (SCRIS) scheduled for November 6–9. Shortly thereafter, Theresa attended the International Union of Superiors General (UISG) council meeting, a gathering of sister leaders from all over the world. Theresa and LCWR leadership hoped to schedule a meeting with Pope John Paul II while they were in Rome. They quickly received promises of support from Archbishop John Quinn, Archbishop Jean Jadot, and SCRIS prefect Cardinal Eduardo Pironio. The cardinals' plenary assembly made a November meeting with the pope impossible, however, so it was decided to try again after the first of the year.

LCWR always sent their proposed agenda ahead of time. For this meeting it included: (1) processes for preparing and approving new constitutions,[90] (2) reports on ongoing dialogue about two LCWR studies, *Patterns in Authority and Obedience* and *Women and Ministry*, and (3) discussion of "significant directions" in US religious life.[91] When SCRIS secretary, Archbishop Augustin Mayer, OSB, wrote back, he informed LCWR that because of the pontiff's recent reiteration of the traditional teaching on female ordination, SCRIS had removed the *Women and Ministry Study* as an agenda item. The congregation also added a new agenda item, requesting that Theresa clarify her greeting to the Holy Father.

Theresa tactfully replied October 25 with a request to reinstate the *Women and Ministry* agenda item, since this study was about "the involvement of women in the ministry of the Church as already effected and of women as recipients of the Church's ministry." Further, she wrote, "The word 'ministry' as used increasingly here in the United States...is not synonymous with ordination but rather implies the broader area signified by the word 'apostolate.'" She informed SCRIS that she would also be "most happy" to share her "observations of clarification" about the Shrine event at the November meeting.[92]

In light of the agenda change, the LCWR executive committee met beforehand to strategize ways of approaching a potentially difficult meeting. Since it was likely that Rome had received only negative letters about Theresa's greeting, they decided to select one hundred of the positive letters they had received from clergy, laity, and religious leaders to present to SCRIS. Sympathetic clergy were notified and given the opportunity to request that their letters not be included. LCWR past president Saint Joseph Sister Mary Dooley suggested inviting Mother Alice Anita Murphy, of the Sisters of St. Joseph of Philadelphia, who was already planning to attend the UISG gathering. Although a member of *Consortium Perfectae Caritatis*—an organization of more conservative sisters—Mother Alice Anita was known for her dialogic approach and respect for diversity. She agreed to attend. Other LCWR members who attended were Sister Mary Dooley, Blessed Virgin Mary Sister Joan Doyle, Carondelet St. Joseph Superior Mary Kevin Ford, and Sister of Charity Barbara Thomas. Congregation of Divine Providence Sister Lora Ann Quiñonez—who was the executive secretary of LCWR and fluent in Spanish—completed the delegation.

Archbishop Mayer was not able to attend, and, because of the cardinals' assembly, Cardinal Pironio could not be present for every session. The three-day meeting was therefore chaired by the Rev. Basil Heiser, OFM, an American who had served as undersecretary to SCRIS until 1984. Other SCRIS attendees included three sisters—one

British and two Americans—and two more religious order priests, one British and one French Canadian.

Sisters Mary Dooley, Lora Ann Quiñonez, and Theresa had been asked to arrive three days early to meet privately with Cardinal Pironio and discuss a possible meeting with the pope. Upon their arrival, however, the meeting was summarily cancelled, not once but twice. The sudden change of plans prompted Theresa to reflect wryly on the differences in "the culture, style and approach" of the Vatican compared to what was customary in the United States. In her communiqué to the LCWR National Board she wrote: "We succeeded in letting our sense of humor overshadow our sense of frustration and discouragement at the inefficiency, or perhaps even thoughtlessness in how much was involved in adjusting schedules for three of us to be there several days in advance."[93] Fortunately, the trio had "an excellent conference" with British Sister of Notre Dame de Namur Mary Linscott of SCRIS in the interim.

Sister Mary Dooley was able to arrange for a large apartment that would accommodate the seven LCWR sisters during the week they were in Rome. Before the first meeting, Theresa proposed two strategies to enhance their sense of mutuality and empowerment. "I don't think we should go in and have them lead the meeting, and tell us everything," she said. "Why don't we set this up? I will co-chair with Father Heiser. The two of us will then work with everyone around the table to look at the different issues."

The other LCWR members "loved the idea," as well as her proposal to intersperse group members around the table rather than having SCRIS sit on one side and LCWR on the other. Having attended this meeting previously as president-elect, Theresa knew she wanted a different dynamic. Fr. Heiser had no idea this request was coming. On hearing no objections from other SCRIS staff, he agreed to it.

After the opening prayer, Theresa inquired if Cardinal Pironio was coming or if they were to start without him. She was assured that he would be coming, although at present he was unavoidably detained. Theresa then wisely gave Fr. Heiser control of what was potentially the most contentious issue: "Now, before we start, you wanted the greeting to the pope to be clarified. It's on the agenda, but I'm going to leave it up to you, Fr. Heiser, to let me know when you want me to clarify it."

The priest thanked her saying, "Now we want to hold that until Cardinal Pironio's here." Theresa nodded, "Fine. Then, I won't bring it up again. You'll bring it up when you're ready." She remembers thinking to herself, "If you never bring it up, I'll never bring it up."

At evening meetings held on Monday and Tuesday, the group addressed the other agenda items. Cardinal Pironio did not attend either of those days. The next meeting was to be held for two hours on Friday morning. On Thursday, however, Cardinal Pironio was finally able to meet privately for ninety minutes with Sisters Lora Ann, Theresa, and Mary Dooley.

On Friday morning, Fr. Heiser announced that he had just received word that Cardinal Pironio "is very sorry he's unable to be with us today." The undersecretary then moved to the issue of the greeting at the Shrine. He first noted that SCRIS had received newspaper clippings and a number of negative letters, characterizing them as "information that led the Sacred Congregation to the formation of a judgment." He then asked Theresa to offer her clarification. Theresa agreed, but first. she said, "I would like to give my clarification in full, from beginning to end, without any questions. I will take any questions you have after I finish. Is that acceptable to you and to your staff?" After looking around Fr. Heiser agreed.

Theresa then recounted LCWR's fruitless requests for a private meeting with the pope when he was in the United States. She addressed why a private meeting was important in light of the pope's public presentations about "a much more traditional view of religious life, which we appreciate and respect, but which [because of Vatican II directives] many active orders of apostolic sisters are no longer following." She reiterated the four points of her greeting, (1) to welcome the pope to the Shrine, (2) to speak about the lives of the sisters, (3) to express solidarity with the pope in advocacy for the poor, and (4) to speak about women in the church. She then reprised the history of LCWR on women's issues, noting that "all through the '70s every assembly was about women in church and society," and referring to LCWR's 1975 "overwhelming endorsement" of a conference on women's ordination. She closed by explaining they had received a great deal of positive publicity and thousands of letters, which were in the process of being analyzed. She presented a hundred positive letters from clergy, laity, and religious and promised to send a summary of the analysis to SCRIS when it was completed.

After Theresa finished her presentation, a SCRIS member—who was a sister—acknowledged that she hadn't realized that people were actually affirming what Theresa had said: "We just received all negative publicity." When Lora Ann asked the source of the negative publicity, the sister admitted that everyone had been given free subscriptions to *The Wanderer*, and that everything there was negative and so, she said, "we really didn't have any positive impressions." As Theresa recalls,

Lora Ann's Latin temperament emerged with a vehement response: "I am scandalized, I am totally scandalized that I am sitting here, the highest echelon of the Catholic Church and you tell me that you made a judgment about some sister based on *The Wanderer*? I think that is a disgrace. Period."

Silence briefly ensued. Then another SCRIS member, who had freely admitted to forming views based on the newspaper articles and negative correspondence, singled out the sentence in the greeting that referred to the inclusion of women in all church ministries. He said it was inopportune to raise the issue, since the pope had explicitly stated that it is not in the tradition of the church to ordain women. He criticized bringing a "matter of that nature to public attention," saying that such discussions should take place "at an opportune time and place."[94] He added that in her position as president and as official representative of women religious, Theresa should not have taken such a stand.[95]

Theresa vividly recalls a sister member of SCRIS who then asked if she was familiar with *Inter Insigniores,* the 1976 papal encyclical opposing the ordination of women. "I've read that document very carefully," Theresa replied. She mentioned Cardinal Terence Cooke's invitation to New York LCWR members—before the encyclical was publicly announced—to meet with diocesan theologians. "In section five it says that ordination is a mystery of the Church that requires continued dialogue as we move into the future. That's my understanding and therefore I am concluding that you want to continue dialogue on that issue," she said firmly.[96]

But the sister replied, "We wanted to make sure we clarified that you didn't include ordination. You didn't include ordination, did you Sister Theresa?"

Theresa well remembers her heated reply: "So I answered, 'Excuse me. I want everyone in this room to know and please put it in the minutes, that I included the ordination of women in my greeting. And I want it included. Period.'"

Recalling the interaction Theresa suspects that "what they wanted was to walk out of the room and say, 'Sister Theresa clarified her greeting and she did not include ordination.' So I was very strong on that point and that's how we ended."

When the meeting finally concluded, she felt "great, great peace with it all." From the distance of years, she seems to have actually enjoyed the spirited exchange. Most of all she remembers feeling "obligated and responsible to LCWR. This was the direction we had taken, and we didn't apologize for it. It had come from seven or eight years of work on women in church and society, and I knew the others were very much with me on it." Mother Alice Anita SSJ—who was wearing a habit at the time—graciously told SCRIS how respectful she found Theresa's greeting at the Shrine and affirmed that the ordination issue was of great concern to many women in the United States.[97] She quietly helped SCRIS understand that significant unity existed among US sisters on this issue, despite their diversity of dress and lifestyle.

Theresa's spirited response at Friday's meeting may have been aided by Cardinal Pironio's sympathetic reception the day before. Lora Ann, Theresa, and Mary Dooley had told him of their frustrated attempts to meet with the pope and explained why the women's issue was so urgent in the US church. For many Catholics, they said, Theresa's action was "a ray of hope that perhaps the Church can be moved toward justice to women." They spoke of the pervasive sexism in language, symbols, and rites in the church that presented obstacles to very many women. They were at pains to explain that, therefore, "we are not referring simply to the ordination question when we make this statement."[98]

The cardinal inquired whether Theresa would not have preferred a different channel to express her concerns. If she had asked his opinion, he said, he would have replied, "Let's try another avenue." It was the first time Pironio had heard of LCWR's efforts to arrange a meeting with the pope beforehand.[99] The LCWR women patiently explained that "other channels are just not accessible to women in the Church," and suggested that, as a member of the hierarchy, the cardinal had a serious responsibility to address women's non-involvement. The three later reported that they found Cardinal Pironio open, nonjudgmental, and willing to hear their ideas without becoming offended or defensive.[100] He told them it was "very important for the pope as well as himself to hear [their] concerns and strongly endorsed the pursuit of an audience."[101] He also promised a letter of support that would urge the pope to grant them an audience, and he directed them to the functionary who handled such meetings.

After returning home, LCWR leaders sent a formal request via Archbishop Jean Jadot's office asking the pope for a three-hour meeting to address the topics of religious life in the US, women in ministry in the church, and religious dress.[102] It would be the first of many formal requests Theresa would make asking to meet with Pope John Paul II. Although she was dogged in her pursuit of dialogue with the highest authority in the church, none of her requests would ever be granted.

At the close of her Shrine greeting, Theresa had prayed a *Magnificat* blessing for the pope: "May Your whole being proclaim and magnify the Lord; may your spirit always rejoice in God your Savior; the

Lord who is mighty has done great things for you; holy is God's name."

But Pope John Paul II was not ready to receive the woman who blessed him. Over the next three years, US bishops, at the behest of the Vatican, tried to silence Theresa Kane by plotting to remove her from office. Although never an activist herself, in the coming decades she would become a living symbol of female priestly ordination. This came about because thousands of women (and a few good men) were willing to act, to educate, and to raise consciousness within the family of Catholicism.

Who is the woman who inspired so many Catholics to exercise their own spiritual authority on behalf of women's equality in the church?

The Kane family in 1938. (From left) Margaret (Sr. Theresa) age 3, Mamie, Catherine (Honey), Nancy (Sr. Ann), Mary, Phil, and Patrick. Theresa's two youngest sisters, Rose and Barbara, had not yet been born.

CHAPTER TWO

Daughter of Immigrants

On September 24, 1936, the feast of Our Lady of Mercy, Margaret Joan Kane came into the world. She was the fourth of seven children born at home to Mary Theresa ("Mamie") and Philip (Phil) Kane. Eighteen years later, Margaret would enter the Sisters of Mercy, taking her mother's name as her own in religion. From that day forward, Sister Mary Theresa Kane would celebrate her birthday on "Mercy Day," the Mercy sisters' foundational feast. But to her family, Theresa would always be "Maggie," "Margaret," or "Aunt Margaret."

Theresa's oldest sister, Mary (later also known as Mamie), remembers her as "a cute little girl with black curly hair" and recalls that her three older siblings, Mary, Nancy (who would also join the sisters of Mercy), and brother Patrick (the only boy) all had the mumps on the day she was born. (Thankfully, baby Margaret never got them.)

A good Catholic couple, Mamie and Phil had seven living children roughly two years apart. Mary, the oldest, was born in 1931 and Barbara, the youngest, in 1943. The couple's first child—a boy named Joseph—had been born in a hospital and died of pneumonia one week later. After that heartbreak, Mamie chose to birth all of her children at home.

The family lived in a three-bedroom, one bath apartment in the Bronx. When Barbara was born, Margaret's sister "Honey" (next in line after Margaret) recalled that her mother had gotten a burst of energy the previous day and baked a batch of Irish soda bread.[1] When the doctor arrived, the older children were sent to the front bedroom, probably to muffle any scary sounds coming from their parents' room. When Barbara entered the world at last, Theresa recalls, "Dr. Lang came out holding soda bread and the black bag. Someone in the room—I don't know if it was Nancy or Pat or me—said 'that's how the baby came, he brought the baby in his black bag and then he went out with the Irish soda bread.'"

PARENTS, FAMILY, AND EARLY CHILDHOOD

Both Mamie and Phil Kane had emigrated from Galway Bay, Ireland, in the early twentieth century. As a youngster in Ireland, Phil worked as a lobster fisherman to help his family who were too poor to eat lobster themselves. "Once in a while we used to take the claws from the lobster and suck on them," Theresa recalls her father saying. Seeking a new life, Phil sailed for the United States around 1918 and went to live with a sister and brother in Boston. Tragically, his brother died in 1919, possibly of the Spanish flu. After a stint in Johnstown, New York, where jobs were more plentiful, Phil, his cousin, and another brother, Mike, moved to the Bronx where they lived in a boarding house, as was customary for male immigrants.

Soon Phil found employment rolling cable for Consolidated Edison, a job he would hold for thirty-five years until he retired with a modest pension and a gold pocket watch. Phil also worked four nights a week cleaning offices in Manhattan. "We needed the money and, you know, he didn't make that much; he got about sixty-five dollars a week take-home pay," remembers Theresa. Not completely comfortable in retirement, Phil would sometimes work part time cleaning offices at Bloomingdale's.

Because he had had to quit school at the age of ten, Phil had never learned to read, something he skillfully hid for many years. "Every night when he came home we had supper and then he'd go in and read the daily news," Theresa recalls. "But my sister told me years later, 'You know, Daddy couldn't read. He just looked at all the pictures.' He never learned to read but we never knew it."

In 1914, Theresa's mother, Mamie Faherty, was just sixteen years old when she booked passage to New York City with a male acquaintance from her home in Galway Bay. She had grown up in a small house in a rural area. Like most houses in the region, hers had a dirt floor and no indoor plumbing. Water had to be carried in from the outside. Mamie's own mother was a teacher and there was a school nearby that Mamie attended faithfully.

When Mamie disembarked in New York, a cousin from Brooklyn met her and took her via subway to a three-family house in Brooklyn. The closely-knit Irish community would often find someone from Brooklyn to greet immigrating family members at the docks and, after a few days, connect them to extended family living elsewhere.

Mamie's first impressions of America would be a source of amusement to her children for years to come. As she walked along the street, her cousin inquired, "Mamie, what are you looking for? What are you looking for? You keep looking around."

"Well," Mamie said quite seriously, "I'm looking to pick up some of the gold that you have here on the street."

"Oh, Mamie that's not true," her bemused cousin said. "There's no gold on the street."

In her simplicity, Mamie had believed all the stories she had heard about America. The apartment house amazed her because she had never seen one and had certainly never walked up steps before: "You know," she would later tell her children, "I was in that house twenty-four hours before I felt myself getting comfortable and feeling that these were the right people I was supposed to be with."

Soon Mamie moved to Jersey City to stay with her Aunt Jo (her mother's sister), who quickly found her a position as live-in help for a wealthy Manhattan family. Two years later, Mamie's sister, Katie, also emigrated and found employment with another Manhattan family. "They were very good people. Very well off and they were good to the help..." Theresa recalled her mother saying. She adds that "they taught them everything: how to cook, clean, and sew. My aunt particularly learned how to be a great baker."

After four or five years, Mamie went through a difficult time when her mother became ill back home. Over her sister's objections, she returned to Ireland. She had become very nervous and Katie feared she was on the verge of a breakdown. But after two years in Ireland, Mamie recovered, returned to New York and started back to work.

On Friday nights for entertainment, the young Irish maids would visit a Manhattan dance hall to meet people from home who gathered to socialize. Mamie met Phil Kane there and the couple fell in love. In the meantime, Katie also met an Irishman named Phil Smith. Both couples were married in 1929, the year of the stock market crash. The sisters were maids of honor in each other's weddings. The families remained close, frequently visiting back and forth and helping to care for one another's children. Initially both couples moved to Queens, but since Phil Kane's job with Con Ed was in Manhattan, he and Mamie moved to the Bronx where a number of relatives from both sides had also relocated.

After losing their firstborn to pneumonia, Mamie gave birth to their oldest daughter, Mary, who was born in 1931. In 1933 the family moved to 415 Brook Avenue, near Third Avenue in the Bronx, an eighteen-apartment complex that at one time was home to about eighty children. It was here that Mamie would labor and give birth to her seven remaining children, Mary (1931), Nancy (1933), Patrick (1935),

Margaret (Theresa, 1936), Catherine "Honey" (1938), Rose (1940), and Barbara (1943).

Theresa remembers the family's sleeping arrangements, which were probably similar to those of many immigrant Irish families. Older sisters Mary and Nancy shared a bed in the front room. In the back, Theresa, Honey, and Rose shared a bed while baby Barbara had her own crib. Mamie and Phil were in the large middle bedroom where Patrick slept in a cot placed on one side of the room until his youngest sister Barbara left home, when he finally got his own room. When Nancy entered the convent, Theresa moved in with Mary, leaving the front room to the three younger girls. Honey recalls how challenging it was to negotiate bathroom time: "Six girls and my father trying to get in the bathroom—that was tough...We were always in there. Teenagers, you know." Honey, Rose, and Patrick would live with and care for their parents for much of their working lives.

By all accounts, Mamie was the heart of this large Irish household. Once the children were old enough, she attended daily Mass at the nearby St. Pius V parish and made sure the children also went on first Fridays and daily in Lent. "We were going to seven o'clock Mass every morning before school. We came home, ate, and went back to school. I was eight or nine I think," recalls Theresa. "The parish church and school were right around the corner."

Mamie wanted her family to pray the rosary together during Lent. "We'd be in the living room and we would all kneel down, but we didn't ever face each other. We had a couch, and three of us knelt facing the couch...and then we'd start laughing," remembers Theresa. "My mother would say, 'Don't be laughing. We're trying to say the rosary here.' We had the rosary every night."

Mamie was very devout: "She was a holy woman, really," Theresa remembers. Her father went to Mass every Sunday and served as an usher: "He always dressed up nicely, and he took up the collection. He used to stand at the back door. You put a quarter down, I guess for the seat, and then of course they took up a collection after you sat down. He loved doing it."

Theresa's first vocational leaning took place during Mass. Her brother Patrick was an altar server and had to memorize all the Latin responses. "He wasn't that good at it either," says Theresa. "I would always sit in the front pew so I could help him. One day I was in church and I saw him up on the altar and I saw the priest and I thought, 'Oh, I wish I were a boy, so that I could be a priest.' It never occurred to me to wonder why girls couldn't be priests."

Mamie and Katie had high educational expectations for their children. Their own mother had been a teacher who would invite people from their small village to sit in their living room while she read them the newspaper. To help their own children learn, the two sisters purchased encyclopedias. "They didn't have two pennies to rub together, but they bought those encyclopedias and wanted you to read the whole set," Theresa recalled. "There were twelve of them, so you got educated." Mamie always kept a shelf filled with books and Theresa loved to read the Nancy Drew mysteries.

Theresa's oldest sister Mary remembers how hospitable her mother was. "You could bring any friend to the house and she'd welcome them. Any time you wanted to come in, whoever you had with you came along." Mamie also helped relatives recently off the boat, just as she had been helped: "They'd end up staying in our house overnight. Where they stayed I don't know, maybe on a couch," says Mary. "They squeezed in for a few days and Mom took them someplace downtown to find jobs." Mamie was frugal and a good money manager. "We had an enamel table. She'd have a pencil and she'd be writing down what had to be paid with the money that my father brought home," said Mary. "The rent or a couple of different things were mandatory, those had to be paid."

Mamie kept a jar on the second shelf in the kitchen for loose change to save up for the children's Catholic school tuition and other necessities. Theresa frequently added her own babysitting money to the stash, although her sister Honey remembers, "I always kept mine."

Around the neighborhood, Mamie was known for her kindness and generosity. One time a neighbor's child needed hospitalization, but his mother had no money. Mamie came out with "a little wad of bills" and said, "Here take this. Don't wait any longer." Later Theresa remembers that the child's mother, Kathleen O'Shea, would say, "Your mother, that was probably all she had to her name, and she turned it over to me." As Honey sees it, "She may not have had a lot of money, but she seemed to take care of everybody in the neighborhood. One time there was a man down the street looking for help to wrap up his arm. The neighbors must have said 'Go upstairs to apartment 2A,' because I opened the door and here's this man. I said 'Ma, come on out.' She wrapped him up with a sling. They knew on our street that if you needed help you went to Mrs. Kane's house."

While the family always had food, Mamie sometimes needed to stretch the budget just before payday. Theresa recalls her mother instructing the butcher to put bread into the ground beef when money was scarce. Mamie was a good cook. "She could even make hamburger taste good," remembers Honey. She always had a hot meal waiting for Phil at the end of his workday: "My mother knew what he wanted . . . He had a bottle of beer and a bottle of ale and then he had to have boiled potatoes with the skins on them every night. She'd make him at least four boiled potatoes, right? Put them right next to him in a bowl," adds Theresa.

All of the Kane children were industrious and began doing odd jobs at an early age to help out with family expenses. In middle school Theresa remembers stocking shelves in the grocery store beneath their apartment for twenty-five cents an hour. Fourteen-year-old Mary worked for ten cents an hour folding a newsletter published by a local missionary priest from Portugal. Honey and another grammar school friend earned twenty-five cents every time they replenished the votive lights at the parish.

After reaching the official working age of sixteen, Mary got a job at the five-and-dime store before being recommended for work at New York Life Insurance by the counselors at Cathedral High School, a common practice at the time: "You had like some sort of guardian or person at Cathedral who steered you to different jobs." Mary turned most of her earnings over to her mother but began putting away some for herself when she needed the $150 fee to attend nursing school at New York's Bellevue Hospital. On Friday nights, Mary brought home strawberry shortcake from the local bakery as a family treat. "And we were so thrilled," reminisces Theresa. "Oh my God, here comes Mary with the cake."

Theresa got her own early working papers at age fourteen as did Honey two years later. Both helped out with the food service at St. Francis Hospital after school from 4:00 PM to 7:00 PM and from 7:00 AM to 7:00 PM on weekends. "You'd take the trays to the rooms and then collect them, put them on the huge cart, and take it down to the basement," recalls Theresa. She was paid twenty-five cents an hour, but by the time Honey arrived, the wage had increased to fifty cents an hour.

Once the girls turned sixteen they were steered to better paying after-school jobs in the city. Theresa actually held two jobs while in high school. She worked from 4:00 PM to 7:00 PM at Metropolitan Life Insurance: "We were filing cards in big filing cabinets. Boring as could be." On Thursday evenings and Saturdays, she worked at a religious articles store in Manhattan. When the girls returned home, Mamie made sure there was a hot meal waiting for them. "She appreciated her children out working," recalled Theresa. "Every time you were working late, when you came in, your dinner was there ready and waiting for you," says Mary. "That was one thing. You never had to worry about whether you'd have to go make yourself dinner. There was always something left for you and it was warmed up."

But it was not all work and no play in the Kane household. On Saturdays Phil took the younger children to see cowboy shows at the local movie theatre. The children loved playing at nearby St. Mary's Park, often paying twenty-five cents to rent a bike for an hour's ride. In the summer, there were visits from cousins and trips to the beach. Phil usually took the children to Pelham Bay Park. "He loved walking on the rock-strewn shore," reminisces Theresa. Often, the children would beg, "'Daddy, we want to go to Orchard Beach.'"[2] But Phil would reply, "No, no, no. I don't want you going to that beach. It's too expensive." Theresa says, "This was because he had to pay two cents for the transfer for each child." One wonders if Phil preferred Pelham Bay because it reminded him of the rocky coast of his childhood.

During the week, however, Mamie would take the children to Orchard Beach—and she would take not just her own family: "She'd bring about fifteen kids with her—the Sullivans, the Bradleys, and the Kellys. Then, when we got up to Pelham Bay, she would get the transfers for two cents and go bring us to the beach," says Theresa. She and her siblings were great swimmers after having been taught by their father, who loved the water.

One favorite family memory that Theresa enjoys sharing is of the weekend evenings when Phil's good friend—Jim Brennan—came to visit:

We'd be standing on the stoop. We'd see Jim. We'd run upstairs and say, "Ma, Mr. Brennan's coming." Jim would take out his accordion and he'd play, and he'd sing, so the next thing you know, the Sullivans would come in, then the Kellys, then the Rutledges, O'Sheas, and Bradleys came too. Then Mrs. Sullivan—who had a beautiful singing voice—would sing with him, but she wouldn't sing one verse, she'd sing about fifteen. Old Irish "comallyas" we called them. Everything started off with "come all you young people," so we called them "comallyas."

Mamie recruited her daughters to help out in the kitchen preparing tea for her guests, as well as sandwiches, and the ever-present Irish soda bread.

The Kane children all became hardworking, successful adults. After graduating from Cathedral High School and working for a time, Mary attended nursing school and worked as a nurse until she met her husband David Gillen. She stayed home until their three children were in school and then returned to nursing, retiring at age sixty-five.

After four years at Cathedral High School, Nancy joined the Sisters of Mercy, where she was known as Sister Mary Eucharia before changing her name to Sister Anne, a version of Anna, which was her baptismal name. She worked for many years with newer members as formation director—a position only slightly less influential than that of superior. After receiving a second master's degree in pastoral counseling (the first was in education), Sister Anne became a beloved giver of retreats and a spiritual director. During the final ten years of her life she suffered from a rare form Alzheimer's disease. Theresa and her dear friend Sister Della Mae Quinn helped care for her before her death in 2004.

Patrick had difficulty in school after suffering a head injury and the loss of one eye from a stickball accident at age twelve. He left school early and was drafted, serving as an Army medic during the Korean War. After his discharge, he worked at a large department store in Manhattan. Patrick cared for his parents at home until they died and continued to live in the family home until his own death in 2006. He had many friends but never married.

Honey (Catherine) graduated early from Cathedral High School, having completed four years of study by the age of sixteen. She was accepted at Grace Institute, a well-known secretarial school founded in 1897 by W. R. Grace, an immigrant turned shipping magnate and two-time mayor of New York City. The institute created a tuition-free program so that low-income women could learn the typing, bookkeeping, and stenography skills greatly needed in New York's rapidly growing business community. Originally staffed by the Sisters of Charity, the Grace Institute is dedicated to this day to helping low-income women achieve career independence.

After finishing at Grace, Honey worked at a bank and then as a legal secretary at a successful law firm for the remainder of her career. In her early fifties she met and married a man from Brooklyn, Joe Hartdegen. Sadly, Joe would die of cancer some twelve years later. Today Honey lives in a downstairs duplex in Queens while her older sister Mary lives in the upstairs unit. Mary's husband Dave died in 2017.

Rose Kane did not attend Cathedral High School as her older sisters had but—thanks to her now–Mercy sister Nancy (Eucharia)—received a full scholarship to a Mercy high school, St. Catherine's Academy in the Bronx. After graduation Rose initially worked for a bank but eventually took a more promising position with a company in upstate New York. "She did extremely well," says Theresa. "She worked her way up to be an administrative assistant to the president and founder of the company." Rose would accompany Theresa's mother on that memorable October day in 1979 when Theresa greeted the pope and shocked the world.[3] Rose also lived at home with her parents until her company moved to Stamford, Connecticut, and she purchased a nearby condo to be closer to work. "My sister Honey always teased that Rose had half a bedroom for all her life and then she went to a whole apartment," Theresa joked. Rose had a lifelong boyfriend, Edward Bopp, but the couple never married.

"She and Ed were very close, did everything together for years, went on cruises together, went on ships, went on flights, but never married—to my mother's great disappointment," recalls Theresa. Rose died in 2002 after a yearlong fight with pancreatic cancer. Her death was a great sorrow to Theresa, who would herself suffer a serious illness shortly thereafter, which her family attributed to the loss of a beloved sister.

Like her older sister "Maggie" (Theresa), Barbara Kane attended St. Pius V High School, graduating after four years of business training. The following September Barbara entered the Dominican sisters but left at Thanksgiving. Later, her four children loved to shock their friends by announcing, "Did you know my mother was a nun?" After leaving the Dominicans, Barbara moved back home and quickly found a good business position in Manhattan. Over a weekend with friends in the Catskills, she met her "totally Italian-American" husband, Nick DiMaria from Germantown, a neighborhood in Philadelphia. The couple settled in Philadelphia where they would raise their four children.

Barbara and Nick were happily married for thirty-four years. Both Mary's and Barbara's children are very attentive to their mothers as well as to the remaining Kane "aunties," Aunt Honey and Aunt Margaret, of whom they are very proud. After her husband died in 2002, Barbara would grow even closer to Theresa and her lifelong friend, Sister Della Mae. The trio loved an occasional visit to the casino in Atlantic City, where Della Mae almost always came home a winner.

EARLY EDUCATION

Like all the Kane offspring, Margaret went to the Catholic grade school in her local parish, St. Pius V, just two blocks from home. There were about sixty students in her first and second grade classes, and the children had to sit two in a seat. Unlike today, Catholic schools were "cheap as cheap could be" and, as Theresa remembers, "I'm not sure if my parents even paid parish elementary school tuition because we belonged to the parish. If they paid anything it was about fifty cents a month."

High school was more expensive, however, at five dollars a month: "Well, that's why we went out to work, so we could help pay for our tuition," Theresa reminisced. "Then we brought the money home and put it on the jar on the shelf in the kitchen. Everybody dropped their money in and if you needed it, my mother would give you whatever you needed for school—quarters, nickels and dimes— whatever it was."

Throughout her school years Margaret's best friend was Nora O'Connor, who lived two blocks away and was also one of seven. The two met in second grade and went on to become lifelong friends.

> We were very, very close. We went to everything together. We went to parties together. And we talked for hours and hours and hours with each other. Then eventually when we got phones we went home and called one another. My mother said, "You just spent the whole day with Nora. What are you calling her on the phone for?"

From the time Theresa entered until Nora's death in 2014, the two stayed in close touch. After her marriage Nora brought her four children to see Theresa in the convent: "She was very faithful. She'd bring them over to visit saying, 'You never come to see me, and I want my kids to know you as they're growing up.'" When Nora's husband died, Theresa made it a point to visit frequently, staying overnight just to be there for her.

Dominican sisters taught all twelve grades at St. Pius Elementary and High School. The Sisters of Charity taught at Cathedral High School, which Mary and Nancy had attended. Margaret went to Cathedral for two years of high school but then returned to St. Pius V for commercial courses because she liked business courses. "I remember thinking when I graduated that I'd like to be able to teach high school and teach business subjects because I was good at them and they were so easy for me."

Theresa relates that a sister at Cathedral called her mother Mamie to object: "Mrs. Kane, we really want you to encourage your daughter to stay in the academic curriculum at Cathedral, because she's a good student. We think she'll do well, and she should stay here for the four years." Mamie couldn't convince the sixteen-year-old Margaret to stay, "so she was very disappointed because she knew the nun wanted me to stay at Cathedral. I went to the commercial high school and I loved it. It was a breeze. I didn't do any work, so I guess I wasted my IQ." Although St. Pius V focused on business skills, the young women also took classes in English, history, a foreign language, algebra, and geometry—but no science courses.

Theresa remembers herself as a pious child. "Like not really fanatical, I don't think, but church meant a lot to me, and going to Mass meant a lot, and so did the devotion connected with it." She remembers that from approximately five to ten years of age she made frequent visits to the Blessed Sacrament at St. Pius V, her parish church. At her first communion she had "a very clear experience of being in the presence of and in conversation with Jesus."[4] She also had an early appreciation for the sacrament of penance, finding there a "sense of grace, strength, and consolation received—always an occasion for beginning again."[5] She remembers avoiding "loud, harsh men who scared me," and would even travel to other churches to seek out understanding priests who were kind.

She recalls that at the age of eleven or twelve she felt she would like to do something different with her life and wondered what it would be. Before graduating from elementary school she recognized "a persistent urge to dedicate my life to God." For her, "religious life seemed the only way to express that total dedication, but it was always secondary to the urge for total dedication of my life, years, and my very being to God." She remembers being attracted to becoming a sister while watching the Dominican sisters process two by two into Mass every morning: "They walked up the middle aisle and they bowed, the whole crowd of them, and went into the pews... Watching those women... they were very prayerful.

"That was an experience that stays with me, because I think it's when I began really thinking about doing something with my life." Even though she had a very good family and many friends, she says, "I didn't want to spend my life just having a lot of kids and no money." She adds that it sometimes "came up flat in front of your face that money wasn't there."

When she was in second grade her school put on "My Sweet Little Alice Blue Gown," and her classmates were very excited about it. The sister asked little Margaret if she wanted to be in the play and she answered that she couldn't, because there was no money for the costume. Theresa explains,

Now, maybe the costume was two dollars or something. The next thing I knew, the sister called me up and said, "We have an extra costume. Ask your mother if you could be in the play." My mother said, "Oh! Isn't that nice? Oh, that's very nice...Yes, sure. That'd be great." So, I was able to be in the play after all, even though initially I couldn't, because I didn't have the money.

Looking back, Theresa still finds it surprising that she felt no resentment over her family's lack of money. While she was sad about it, she says she knew that "my mother would not hold back on anything from me. If we really needed something, she'd say, 'Well I don't have the money for it now, but I'll get it if I can,' or something, you know?" In high school Theresa noticed that most of her girlfriends wanted to get married as soon as they graduated. "They thought that would get them out of their family's life, and then whoever they were marrying would be better off, and then they could start having children.

"But I wasn't for that," says Theresa. She wanted something more. She remembers with gratitude the conversation she had with her father. "You know, I think I'd like to be either a teacher or a nurse," I said. 'Oh, I'm glad,' he answered. 'That's wonderful, Margaret. That would be very good. Now, you know, I don't have any money for you. I'm sorry, but I'll help you however I can.'" Her father's encouragement about having a career meant a great deal to Theresa at the time, and even to this day. "So it was a beautiful story. He was supportive of me and promised to help, even though he couldn't support me financially."

Theresa recalls several experiences of feeling close to God as she was growing up.

> I remember going to church just as a young girl, nine, ten, and eleven, and the thing that struck me was I felt like I knew God or that I felt very close to God, and almost as if I was talking to God...I felt like I was really in the presence of God, and I used to find myself thinking God was asking me to do something or asking something of me. That's as clear as I could be, but it stayed with me from the time I was young, say from nine years of age until when I entered [the Sisters of Mercy]—that sense that somehow God was calling me to something, but I didn't know what it was.

Once on the subway she noticed how worn out and unhappy some fellow passengers seemed. "And I thought, 'I don't want to live my life like that.' They didn't seem to have joy in their life. I knew I wanted something. It wasn't clear that it was religious life, but it was clear that I wanted to do more with my life...I wanted to make my life worthwhile."

When she was a sophomore in high school one of the sisters, "a quiet, holy teacher," asked her, "Do you ever think about becoming a nun?"

"Sometimes I do," Margaret answered.

"Well, think about it," the nun replied.

Theresa continued to have "some very close experiences with God" during high school. Some of these she describes as "very intimate—almost mystical." But others were "very angry, negative experiences. At times, I didn't want to dedicate my life to God—but I always knew that that's what God wanted for me."[6]

As a teenager, despite her heavy work and school schedules, Margaret had an active social life—so much so that her friends were shocked when she chose to enter the Sisters of Mercy. They only knew one nun and that was Margaret's sister Nancy. She had been quiet and very pious, and she had never gone out to parties. No one was surprised when she entered the Sisters of Mercy. "Maggie," on the other hand, loved parties, and the bigger, the better. Her niece Mary Beth Burke (Mary's daughter) relates a story her Aunt Margaret once told her.

> She'd go to bed, fully dressed until her father went to bed. Her bedroom was near the front door, so she would go to bed early and then she'd slip on out. I think he thought everybody should be home in bed by eight o'clock. So, they said she was the least likely to go in the convent because she liked to socialize.

Theresa recalls her high school social life in considerable detail, including ways to get around the legal drinking age, which at the time was eighteen:

> We had a nice crowd in high school...We went to school together, went to work together, most of us, and then on Friday night we always went to the pizza place and sat with the guys. Then when we were sixteen we used to get on the subway and go down to Manhattan to the Yorkville Casino, which was all dancing. We would hang around there and dance with the guys and have our drinks. You weren't allowed to drink until you were eighteen, but we had forged our birth certificates, so it looked like we were eighteen.

While Margaret dated several young men, she never became serious with anyone. Her description of dating typifies teen-age Catholic beliefs and social mores of the 1950s, including fuzzy notions about human reproduction:

> We went out to the movies, but it was usually four, six, or eight of us together. We never went just alone. And we went to the dances. You would dance with a guy and he would walk you home. But I don't think we did a lot of kissing. Maybe once or twice. You know, we weren't heavily into it, because there were all these stories that you could get pregnant if you kiss a guy.

In June of 1954, Margaret graduated from St. Pius V Academy for Girls with excellent secretarial, business, and accounting skills. Although it was "pretty clear" to her that she wanted to be a nun, she first needed to earn $350 for the dowry required at the time. Sister Ruth, who was the principal at St. Pius V, encouraged her to apply for a newly opened position at the R. J. O'Leary Company, a small public relations firm in the Bronx: "They want somebody who's really good, so I think you should interview," said Sister Ruth. Theresa recounts: "I went up and I was hired immediately. My friends were like 'Oh, my God. How'd you get that job? You're getting much more money than we are...' They were all making twenty or twenty-five dollars [a week] and I was making thirty-five dollars."

It was a small office with six employees including Margaret, who was the secretary for everyone. She was alone in the office for much of the summer and found herself with a "great deal of time to think...That was probably good solitude for me," she recalls, "because it gave me time to really consider what I wanted to do." Then, one afternoon, "I went down on my knees and I prayed and said, 'God, I really want to know what's the thing you want me to do. What's the best thing for me to do?' It just became very clear that I was to go to the convent and be a sister."

During her colloquy with God, Theresa remembers, "The only thing I felt a little sad about was that I wouldn't have children...It would be a big loss in my life, not to have a child...I was one of seven, so you would think I had probably had enough 'family' and I wouldn't want any more. But I didn't feel that way. That was my sad moment." At the same time, she felt no sense of loss at not being intimately involved with a man or not having any desire to marry. "The men that I knew in our neighborhood were very hard workers, but a number of them were drinkers. They were Irish...I used to be a little afraid of them...they were too rough." One young man who lived in her building had even accosted her at a party: "I knew he was getting at me, so I just pushed him away. That was somewhat of my impression of men sometimes..." Like most men of that era, Theresa's father did occasionally binge drink, but he was never rough or violent with the children.

Theresa remembers "a couple of nice fellows," one of whom was Chris Farley who volunteered for the army after high school. He was leaving for the military at the same time Theresa was leaving for the convent. "He gave me his rosary beads. They were Irish rosary beads, and he said, 'I want you to have these and I want you to pray for me.' Isn't that beautiful?"

In retrospect Theresa believes her spontaneous prayer that summer afternoon at the office "was like somehow, I said that day to God, 'Yes, this is what I believe you want me to do, and God, I accept it.' I chose it. I didn't just accept it, I made that choice. That was my decision."

Once the decision was made, Theresa swore Mamie to secrecy because she didn't want everyone talking about it: "For some reason I guess I didn't want to be the center of all this attention." But Mamie insisted that she tell her father herself, so one evening Theresa approached him. "Daddy, I want to tell you something. I'm going to go to the convent."

"What do you want to do a thing like that for?" her father replied.

"Nancy did it and that was all right with you," Theresa said artfully. "I just feel like I'd like to do something like that. It just appeals to me."

Her father said to her, "You'd be scrubbing floors for the rest of your life."

That ended the conversation, although Theresa recalls with relish: "My sisters, to this day, laugh and say, 'You're the only one who didn't scrub floors all your life.'"

Theresa initially applied to enter the Dominican sisters who had taught her at St. Pius V. But her old friend Sister Ruth (a Dominican) said, "Oh, no, no, dear. You don't want to go to the Dominican Sisters" and redirected her to the Sisters of Mercy. Three of Sister Ruth's blood sisters were also Dominicans and they loved being able to see each other on a regular basis. "If I didn't go to the order where my sister Nancy was, I wouldn't get to see her," recalls Theresa. So, she applied and was accepted for February 1955 admittance into the Sisters of Mercy in Tarrytown, New York.

Still, she didn't tell any of her close girlfriends about her plans until December and then the news spread like wildfire. It was hard for them to believe this fun-loving, gregarious woman would ever want to be a sister. As Theresa recalls,

> They were surprised because I wasn't the type to be a nun. They thought you should be quiet and going to church all the time and pious. You certainly didn't go out dancing and drinking and enjoying yourself and having a big social life. Every weekend we went to Rockaway for the weekend, all the girls went. We rented one room, and we sat out on the beach all day with these guys, and then we met them at night and went out to big Irish pubs they had down there in Rockaway. It was all Irish people. We danced for hours. They couldn't imagine me in a convent.

Margaret's friends decided to throw a going-away party and wanted to know what they could give her. She told her best friend Nora O'Connor, "Nora, I just need the money. I need $350." Although she had a well-paying job, Margaret wasn't earning enough to help with expenses at home and at the same time cover her dowry. Even the raise the R. J. O'Leary Company had given her in September (after only three months' employment) would not be enough. Plus, Mamie worried, "Wait till they hear what you're doing. They're going to take away that bonus from you." But an amused Theresa remembers: "They were all Catholic [at the company]. In no way would they do anything. They just were so thrilled that I was entering."

Margaret had a huge send-off. "They must have had seventy-five kids there that night, boys and girls," she recalls. "From then on Nora always said, 'God, we talked about that for years. Remember Margaret's beer party that we had?'" Her friends raised between five and six hundred dollars, more than she needed. In characteristically generous fashion, she gave the extra money to Mamie: "You keep that because I don't need it," she said.

And Mamie promised: "When you need things in the convent, you tell me, and I'll get you things, whatever you need."

On February 2, 1955, the party girl whom "no one could imagine in a convent," left the Bronx for Tarrytown to become a Sister of Mercy.

CHAPTER THREE

Catherine McAuley and the Sisters of Mercy

The community of sisters with whom Margaret hoped to pledge her life was founded in the early nineteenth century by Catherine McAuley. A single woman who had unexpectedly inherited a large fortune, Catherine quickly put her newfound wealth at the service of poverty-stricken children and young women.

Born on September 29, 1878, possibly in the Fishamble neighborhood of Dublin, the young Catherine was only five years old when her father, James McAuley died. She and her two siblings, James and Mary, were left in the care of her mother Elinor, who was twenty-five years younger than her deceased husband. Although Catherine was only five years old when her father died, her childhood memories "are said to have clustered around his religious instructions and charities to poor children in the Stormanstown and Fishamble neighborhoods," despite her mother's "frequent complaints about his unreasonably generous gift of his time and resources."[1]

Her father's example would stay with Catherine always. Until his death, the family was relatively well to do, as James owned a number of properties in Dublin and worked as a building contractor and woodworker. But the young Elinor had little experience handling financial matters, and the bereaved family quickly fell on hard times. Catherine's siblings eventually moved to the home of William Armstrong, a distant relative who was Protestant, while Elinor and Catherine moved in with Elinor's brother, Dr. Owen Conway, who was Catholic. Here Elinor's health began to fail, and Catherine spent three painful years nursing her mother until she died in 1798. As she was dying, Elinor was tormented by the thought that she been a lukewarm Catholic, having "neglected the full practice of Catholicism and offered little resistance to the sharp criticism of her faith offered by Anglican and Protestant friends and relatives."[2] This soul-wrenching experience would stay with Catherine for many years.[3]

When her uncle's fortunes began to decline, Catherine briefly joined her siblings at the Armstrong home where she was encouraged to convert to Anglicanism as her brother and sister had done. Since most high-status families in eighteenth-century Dublin were Protestant, the well-meaning Armstrongs wished to advance the social standing of their orphaned relatives. In Catherine's case, this would increase the likelihood of making a beneficial match. But, perhaps remembering her father's religious devotion and her mother's recent agony, Catherine chose to remain Catholic. Throughout her life she remained close to her family, despite the "painful gulf" that existed because of religion. When she died, her brother James and his wife were at her bedside.[4]

When Catherine was twenty-five, William Armstrong helped her obtain a position with a well-to-do couple, William and Catherine Callaghan, who were "attracted to Catherine's vivacity and graciousness."[5] The couple had just moved to the expansive twenty-two-acre Coolock estate outside of Dublin and required a companion for Mrs. Callaghan, who suffered a chronic illness. The duo, moreover, needed help managing both their large household and the largess to the poor that Catherine Callaghan's Quaker upbringing had inspired. In fact, biographer Mary C. Sullivan observes,

> A great deal of Catherine Callaghan's Quaker faith and spirit can be found in the early biographical manuscripts about Catherine McAuley, especially the references to Mrs. Callaghan's charity and her appreciation of silence. As a Quaker she would also have been profoundly devoted to reading the Christian Scriptures.[6]

Catherine McAuley spent twenty years tending to William and Catherine Callaghan. In the process, she herself would be deeply formed in the unassuming Quaker values of love and care for the poor, especially impoverished women and girls. She visited the homes of poor families, gave religious instruction to children, and taught young girls from the neighborhood how to do needlework, even going so far as to set up a small shop where they could sell their creations. Along the way, she developed a love for music and for dance as the Callaghans enjoyed hosting festive candlelit dinners that included music, singing, and dancing.

As William and Catherine Callaghan aged, more and more of the business of running Coolock House fell on Catherine McAuley's capable young shoulders. She proved herself up to the task, and soon developed significant organizational and financial management skills. She had great love for the children, eventually adopting six orphans, two from the Coolock neighborhood and four orphaned children of a beloved deceased cousin, Anne Conway Byrn. Anne's daughter, Catherine Byrn, would later join Catherine as one of the first Sisters of Mercy.

But even with the greater security her position as a much-loved companion to the Callaghans afforded, Catherine was troubled in spirit. She was reluctant to openly practice her Catholic faith because it was so frequently belittled by upper-crust Dublin society. Her integrity and inquiring mind also sought answers to the critiques of Catholicism brought by her family and those in her social network. Although the Callaghans were good Christians and respectful of her religious beliefs, they could not offer the guidance she needed. Catherine wanted to avoid upsetting family and friends believing that "an overt decision ... to attend Sunday Mass and participate regularly in the sacraments would not have been without pain and confusion on all sides."[7] She sought counsel from several priests, especially Fr. Andrew Lube, who "never failed" to comfort her, and Jesuit Fr. Thomas Betagh, from whom she "learned not only theology but also something of his deep commitment to the plight of poor children, especially their desperate need for food, clothing, and schooling."[8]

One day she took courage and inquired at the priest's residence at St. Mary' parish in Dublin, the very parish her own father had helped build and then adorn with a carefully crafted oaken pulpit. She was introduced to the curate, Fr. Daniel Murray, who, as the ways of God would have it, later became the archbishop of Dublin and instrumental in the foundation of the Sisters of Mercy. But on this day, Fr. Murray listened carefully to Catherine's experience, answered her earnest questions, and provided wise counsel. He suggested a possible time when she might visit again to prepare for a return to the sacraments.

Although now much at peace, Catherine did not at first tell the Callaghans about her renewed Catholic practice. When she did tell them, she discovered that they respected her decision, even allowing her to take their horse-drawn carriage to Mass. Still, she refrained from using a crucifix or any external sign of Catholic devotion, as the couple found these objectionable. Instead, she came to see that the mystery of God is everywhere: "As a young woman at Coolock House, she used natural objects to lift her heart to God: the cross in the branches of trees, in the window frames and in door panels of the house."[9] Her Celtic heritage also gave her a facility for apprehending the divine in the midst of the commonplace. Such experiences of contemplation in the midst of activity would become bedrock spiritual realities for Catherine and her spiritual daughters.

In light of the Callaghans' aversion to Catholic devotionals, it is ironic —and a sign of God's sense of humor—that Catherine McAuley's gentle ministrations would lead each of them to be baptized as Catholics on their deathbeds. To her great surprise, William Callaghan named Catherine as the couple's sole heir, leaving her a fortune of roughly twenty-five thousand pounds, estimated to be about three million US dollars at 2007 exchange rates.[10]

And so began a new chapter in Catherine McAuley's life, one for which she was well prepared after having served for twenty years as nurse, teacher, spiritual guide, social worker, and administrator at Coolock House. Within five years she would open the first House of Mercy in 1827 on Baggot Street in southeast Dublin, Ireland. She was forty-nine years old. Later biographers would write that "[Catherine] was convinced that Almighty God required her to make some lasting efforts for the relief of the suffering and instruction of the ignorant."[11]

Undoubtedly her conviction derived from the vivid dreams she had while sleeping in Catherine Callaghan's room as she cared for her friend and employer in her final illness. Catherine would often awaken and burst into tears after dreaming of orphan children, of destitute and deserted women, and a "crowd of young women" learning employable skills.[12] The sick woman told her, "I almost wish you never went to sleep, you frighten me so much, and seem to suffer such agony."[13] Such was the passion and vision that drove Catherine McAuley in the next chapter of her life.

First, she expanded her ministries beyond Coolock House and founded the Baggot Street House to "serve as a shelter and educational center for young women from poorer neighborhoods of the city."[14] Her adopted daughter Catherine Byrn and an acquaintance, Anna Maria Doyle, were the first to move in to Baggot Street and serve the young inhabitants of the House of Mercy. Catherine herself delayed moving in because her sister Mary was dying and needed help in caring for her family. Other women quickly joined the Baggot Street community—so many that Catherine later recalled:

> In a year and a half we were joined so fast that it became a matter of general wonder... Seeing us increase so rapidly and all going on in the greatest order almost of itself, great anxiety was expressed to give it stability. We who began were prepared to do whatever was recommended and in September 1830 we went with Dear Sister Harley to George's Hill to serve a novitiate for the purpose of firmly establishing it.[15]

Catherine's original idea seems to have been to gather a community of lay co-workers to shelter and educate poor women, but their activities at the Baggot Street House would soon receive severe criticism. Financially comfortable neighbors weren't particularly happy about attracting poorer people to their neighborhood. Sexism also reared its ugly head. Fr. Matthias Kelly, in whose parish the House of Mercy was located, called Catherine an "upstart," saying he had "no great idea that the unlearned sex could do anything but mischief by trying to assist the clergy."[16] Kelly was also a good friend and patron of another community of sisters and may not have looked kindly upon women viewed as "competition."[17]

To quell criticism and protect and stabilize this desperately needed ministry, her old friend Archbishop Daniel Murray recommended that Catherine found a religious order. At age fifty-two, after taking three years to carefully consider the archbishop's suggestion, she agreed to become the founder of the Sisters of Mercy. But first, she and two companions—Anna Maria Doyle and Elizabeth Harley—were required to complete a year's novitiate with the Presentation sisters in Dublin. On December 12, 1831, the trio returned to Baggot Street, which became the first convent of Mercy. After resisting the idea of adopting the title "Reverend Mother," Catherine reluctantly agreed to be called "Mother Catherine," but only after Archbishop Murray insisted.[18]

Over the next ten years, Catherine and her sisters founded thirteen more Houses of Mercy, including two in England. When Catherine died of tuberculosis on November 11, 1841, there were approximately one hundred Sisters of Mercy. Fifteen years later there were three thousand sisters in foundations in the Americas as well as in the British Isles. One hundred years after Catherine McAuley's death, there were twenty-three thousand Sisters of Mercy all over the world.[19]

MISSION TO THE AMERICAS

Within six months of Catherine's death, Frances Creedon, Mary Ursula Frayne, and Rose Lynch established the first Mercy foundation in North America in St. John's, Newfoundland. Between 1843 and 1890, an additional sixty-two women journeyed from convents in Ireland and England to found nine different Mercy communities in the Americas. Six of these "colonies," as they were called at the time, were in the United States. The other three were established in Argentina, Jamaica, and British Guiana.

In 1843, Frances Warde and six sisters journeyed from Carlow, Ireland, to Pittsburgh, and in 1846, Baggot Street sent Agnes O'Connor and seven sisters to New York City. Other US "colonies" included Little Rock, Arkansas (1851), San Francisco, California (1854), Cincinnati, Ohio (1858), and Meridan and Middletown, Connecticut (1872). By 1929, there were 9,308 Sisters of Mercy in the United States in sixty independent motherhouses.[20] In August 1929, thirty-nine of those houses established a new governance structure—The Sisters of Mercy of the Union. Delegates chose a mother general and a six-member council and set up six provinces: Chicago, Cincinnati, Omaha, Providence, St. Louis, and Scranton. In succeeding years new provinces were created and smaller groupings incorporated into existing provinces. The goal was to keep the numbers of sisters in each province at manageable levels while providing a central coordinating structure that would address issues common to all the provinces.

In 1991, after a ten-year process, all of the Mercy congregations in North, South, and Central America joined together under one governance to become the Institute of the Sisters of Mercy of the Americas, one of the largest English-speaking congregations of women religious in the world.

In 1959, just four years after Theresa's entrance, there were 6,936 Sisters of Mercy of the Union in nine provinces in the United States. Her New York province was the smallest, with 423 sisters, while Chicago was the largest with 1093 sisters.[21] The sisters' institutional ministries were—and still are—more or less evenly divided between health care institutions (1/3), educational institutions (1/3), and social services and pastoral settings (1/3). A press release in February of 1960 reveals the sisters' involvement in US health care, listing eighty-four general hospitals, four psychiatric facilities, one tuberculosis sanatorium, and five convalescent homes. Ministries outside the United States included a leprosarium and general hospital in British Guiana, a school of nursing in British Honduras, and a clinic for the poor in that country. Fifty-seven schools of nursing were under the auspices of the Sisters of Mercy of the Union. All told, two million people annually received health care in their institutions.[22]

The Sisters of Mercy were also respected educators who taught in Catholic parishes and even some public schools in the West. In 1953, the Mercy Educational Conference was formed to address common concerns of Mercy colleges, secondary schools, and elementary schools. An important subcommittee addressed the need for educating the sisters themselves in nursing, teaching, business, and social service.[23] The sisters also ministered to homeless children. In 1962 at least 118 Sisters of Mercy of the Union in seven provinces cared for two thousand children in fifteen homes.[24]

At the time Theresa entered, the sisters in her New York province were probably best known as educators, although they were also involved in health and child care. Today, Sisters of Mercy and their associates remain deeply involved in health care, education, pastoral and spiritual care, and work with the poor—particularly women and children.

MERCY GOVERNANCE, SPIRITUALITY AND EMPOWERMENT

Despite the hierarchical authoritarianism of her times, Catherine McAuley wished each of her new foundations to have independent governance, so that the sisters' connections "relied less on regulation than on the bonds of love."[25] She also favored appointing, "young and inexperienced Sisters as superiors, trusting that challenging circumstances would draw out their fullest potential."[26] An oft-quoted letter to Mary Ann Doyle displays her desire to empower her sisters: "Do not fear offending anyone. Speak as your mind directs and always act with courage."[27]

When she was dying, Catherine was asked to name her successor, but she refused, saying, "The Constitutions give the Sisters the liberty of choosing for themselves, and I will not interfere by directing their choice."[28] Always solicitous of those around her and apparently fearful that she would die after nine PM when grand silence began, she asked the sister tending to her, "Will you tell the Sisters to get a good cup of tea—I think the community room would be a good place—when I am gone and to comfort one another—but God will comfort them."[29]

Catherine's spirituality was both practical and profound. In coming centuries, each Sister of Mercy would be deeply influenced by her love of God and of God's people. Mercy Sisters Helen Marie Burns and Sheila Carney suggest that "perhaps Catherine's greatest contribution to the church is not the congregation itself as much as the spirituality that enlivened it—a fresh and fertile blending of the contemplative spirit and compassionate heart."[30] Official documents petitioning the Vatican for her canonization tell us,

Her spirituality was marked by her ability to create and maintain inner spiritual space, to be constantly aware of the mystery of God and to be able to find his touch everywhere in the

world of people, of their occupations and of their miseries
... Her apostolic spirituality may be said to have effectively
translated the Gospel into the idiom of her time and to have
conveyed this ideal to others.[31]

Along with other women founders of the eighteenth and nineteenth centuries, Catherine McAuley struggled to free her sisters of
monastic enclosure, from medieval times a church requirement for
women religious. But because society at large was not yet ready for independent females in any work, let alone ministerial work, passionate
Gospel women such as Catherine could live the ministry to which they
were called only by agreeing to become members of a formal religious
order. In consequence, they were often obliged to serve at the behest of
male clergy. As the official church saw it, to be true religious sisters,
the new communities needed to adopt quasi-monastic practices that
did not always complement the apostolic dynamism of their charism.

When the Second Vatican Council asked women's religious orders
to "return to the spirit of their founders," many communities discovered the historical context and the essence of their founders' original
intent for the first time. But now, that original vision could be lived in
a society that—at least in the West—increasingly valued female initiative and independence. The dramatic changes of the past fifty years
among women's religious orders have arisen from the sisters' desire to
be more faithful to the original charism of their communities. Such
changes are not, as some have suggested, a deviation from their original graced call to be, like Jesus, totally given to bringing about God's
just reign "on earth as in heaven." Perhaps biblical scholar and IHM
sister Sandra Schneiders describes it best:

> In fact, the removal of major (mostly monastic or purely cul-
> tural) barriers of all kinds made possible the full emergence of
> a new form of Religious Life that had been developing within
> and around those barriers for nearly four centuries, namely,
> non-monastic ministerial Religious Life for women... A major
> transition was under way, from ecclesiastically delegated and
> controlled apostolates of caring for Catholics in large Catholic
> institutions attached to monastic-style convents to more indi-
> vidualized ministries in situations of need regardless of the de-
> nominational affiliation or lack thereof, ability to pay, or
> respectability of the recipients.[32]

Theresa Kane entered the Sisters of Mercy at a time of "monastic
and cultural barriers," but lived to see and to lead the major transi-

tion to "non-monastic religious life for women." Yet the seeds of this contemporary expression of the Mercy charism are found first in the spirit and spirituality of Catherine McAuley, whose daughters carry forward her vision of combining action and contemplation outside convent walls. Catherine's 1833 petition to Rome summarizes the principal aim of her fledgling Congregation: "to educate poor girls, to lodge and maintain poor young women who are in danger... and to visit the sick poor."[33] Her spirit and spirituality—especially her advocacy for women—is mirrored in the life of Theresa Kane. It is mirrored in the chapter directives of the Sisters of Mercy as, in the years immediately following the Second Vatican Council, they fought to address systemic issues that disadvantage women—a struggle that continues to this day. Alongside a myriad of Mercy sisters, Theresa would drink deeply of Catherine's spirituality even as she formed her own.

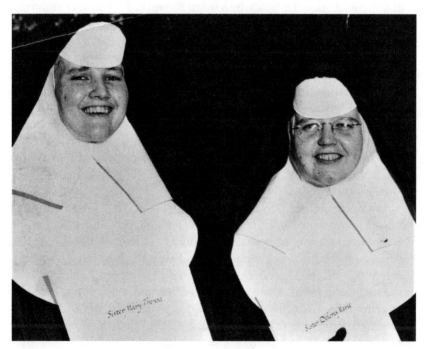

Theresa (left) graduates from Manhattanville College in May 1959. Pictured with Mercy Sister Dolores Marie, who left the Sisters of Mercy but remained a lifelong friend.

CHAPTER FOUR

"My God I Trust in You"

On the day she entered the Sisters of Mercy, Margaret Joan Kane awoke to a cold rain that soon turned the snow on the ground to slush. She dressed quickly and attended morning Mass with her two best friends, Nora O'Connor and Helen Sweeney. "Afterwards we had a cup of coffee then they had to go to work. I remember standing on the corner talking to them, and they were feeling so sad. I wasn't feeling sad, but the weather was terrible. It was a dull, dark day."

With everything packed, she prepared to journey from the Bronx to the Mercy motherhouse in Tarrytown, New York. A large contingent of family and friends accompanied her to Tarrytown to bid her farewell. "My sisters and my brother and my cousins and my aunt— they all came on the train. I probably had about twenty people come to the motherhouse...The whole neighborhood came," she recalls with a smile. Although her extended social network would journey by train, a neighborhood friend had offered to drive Margaret, Mamie, and Phil in his car.

As she left home, Theresa always remembered her father's advice, "Now, I want to tell you, if you're ever not happy and if it doesn't work out, you know to come right home." Theresa never forgot her father's counsel: "It was giving me permission to come back home if I wanted to." While Theresa's mother would have been "really upset" if she had come home, there would have been no sense of disgrace. As first-generation Irish immigrants, Mamie and Philip were somewhat inoculated from the shame American Catholics sometimes experienced in the 1950s if a daughter or son left religious life. "They had never known nuns in Ireland. They had never met any nuns at all until they started having kids."

It meant a great deal to Theresa that her mother was happy that a second daughter had chosen to become a sister. "I wanted to be the mother of a priest, but I'm the mother of two nuns," Theresa recalls her mother saying. She adds, "I never forgot that. It was like giving me a million dollars for her to say that."

ENTERING THE POSTULATE

In the weeks before leaving, Margaret had gathered together everything she would need as a Mercy postulant:

> Everybody was supposed to bring a trunk, and they gave you a whole list of things to bring. You had to have white slips. You had to have black stockings. You had to have a pair of oxfords, black shoes...Johnson deodorant and no smelly things—and Johnson powder you had to use. Nothing could be cosmetic. It was the weirdest list, when I think of it.

When Margaret's extended entourage—and the trunk—arrived at the Tarrytown motherhouse, a friendly sister welcomed everyone and invited them to enjoy tea and cookies in the parlor. Margaret was escorted upstairs, where she donned traditional postulant garb consisting of a simple black dress with a short cape, long sleeves with white cuffs, and a gauzy, see-though veil. She descended the stairs and was presented to her waiting retinue: "Now, this is Sister Margaret," said the sister who had first greeted them. "They stood around looking at me," recalls Theresa, "and then it was time to go to church."

Soon it was time for everyone to leave. "I said goodbye to them. I wasn't feeling bad that day, but they told me that when they went outside, they felt like these big doors were closing forever and they'd never see me again."

Yet for the next six months Theresa and seven other postulants in her group would be able to receive visitors every month. Her friends and her family were "very faithful" about visiting. "They never missed a visiting Sunday. It was like a religious holiday or something." Theresa and her postulant sisters shared a large dormitory room with nine novices who had entered the year before. Each young nun had a bed, a nightstand, and a chair surrounded by a curtain to provide a modicum of privacy. Four dressers with four drawers each graced each end of the dormitory. Each of the sixteen women had two drawers in which to place her worldly possessions. The day began at 5:15 AM when the sisters rose, dressed, and were expected to be in the chapel by 5:40 AM for morning office. This was followed by thirty minutes of meditation, Mass, and breakfast.

The postulants then attended regular college classes all day at Mercy College, conveniently located right on the grounds. "It was the first time I did very much science," Theresa recalls. "We had anatomy and botany and biology as well as English and history." The postulants also had special classes in religious education and Bible study. Work in the laundry and kitchen as well as other household chores rounded out the week.

But after four or five days, the young Margaret found herself getting terribly lonesome:

> I would cry, and cry, and cry, and cry. I cried at night, I cried during the day, I cried in chapel. They would send for my sister Nancy [Sister Eucharia]: "Tell Sister Eucharia to come over here, because her sister is really in terrible shape." She'd come over and we'd talk for a while, and she'd leave, and I'd cry some more.

These expressions of grief continued for six months. Margaret missed her mother and father more than she could ever have imagined, more even than her friends, her social life, or even her sisters and brother:

> I just did not want to be away from them. It was strange, because we weren't terribly affectionate...we weren't running around kissing each other or hugging all the time. But it was like the stability was there and they were always, always there, and I guess that was gone from my life all of a sudden.

Although Margaret quickly made friends with the other postulants, she grieved over the loss of her family. While she was comforted by Nancy's visits, her overwhelming sense of loss continued, and her tears flowed daily. Yet no one viewed her grief as a sign that perhaps she should not become a sister. Despite everything, "I was peaceful in the life," remembers Theresa. "But I was just terribly lonesome." She talked to her postulant mistress, Sister Teresa Marie Conway, who told her, "This takes time. It is a big change in your life. It takes a lot of time and you need to be patient." Then, about a month before being received into the novitiate, something shifted:

> I remember feeling that I had passed through it, I had gone through it...It wasn't that I didn't miss them anymore, but it wasn't that overwhelming grief either. By the time I had to

sign a paper about the novitiate, I felt very much at peace. A peace came over me and I felt this was where I belonged.

THE NOVITIATE

On September 8, 1955, Margaret Kane was received into the Mercy novitiate and given the name Sister Mary Theresa, her second choice. Her first request was to be named Philip Marie for her father: "My initial response was disappointment, because I wanted my father's name. I thought that would mean a lot to him—although in the end the new name meant a lot to my mother too." The reception ceremony was open to her family. "They all came, and we went in as postulants and then put on the robe and the habit and the white veil and processed down the aisle...I always remember my family saying, 'We kept looking and looking and we didn't know you because you all looked alike.'" As part of the ceremony, the new novices prostrated themselves in front of the altar, and Theresa "found that a beautiful experience—prostrating. It was like totally giving myself over to God."

The novitiate lasted two years, with the first year designated the "canonical novitiate" during which, by church law, no outside work, classes, or ministry could take place. Canonical novices did take college level offerings in biblical studies and spirituality, but they could not receive credit. This special year would be devoted exclusively to prayer and spiritual practices designed to deepen the novices' understanding of Mercy spirituality and the community's way of life. Foremost among the spiritual practices of any sister-in-training is further development of a life of prayer. Theresa liked to pray and she entered into community prayer times with characteristic gusto:

> I liked the time for spirituality. I really never had a problem going to chapel for meditation and for prayers. It was something I really relished. I looked forward to it. The prayers were, for me, very important. I wanted to be a *pray-er*. I wanted to be a praying nun, I guess.

Once she had decided to be a Sister of Mercy, Theresa gave herself fully to her new life. Above all that meant becoming a "praying nun." She says, "I felt I was here, I'd made a decision to live this life, so I wanted to do the best I could and contribute to it and receive back from it and live it to the fullest." She recalls a conversation with her fellow novices:

"I think we all feel really zealous right now." I said, "I hope we always feel like this, because this is really what we're supposed to be about as religious, to be zealous women and to be, I guess, dynamic in terms of being spiritual." I think they agreed with me. Years later, someone said to me, "You were always a good nun, even from the beginning."

In addition to daily Mass and performing necessary household chores, meditation and spiritual reading were important in the life of each novice. Aspiring sisters did not receive training in any particular method of meditation, such as the Ignatian practice of envisioning themselves within a particular biblical scene. Instead, each sister's personal prayer style was developed more or less organically through the spiritual books she chose to read: "So I'd go into spiritual reading, and the spiritual reading became food for meditation," reflects Theresa. She remembers appreciating books by Thomas Merton, and adds, "We certainly did Catherine McAuley over, and over, and over again."

Her favorite book for spiritual reading was *The Virtue of Trust* by Paul de Jaegher. "I always remember reading that book...I remember thinking that the virtue I wanted most was the virtue of trust. Trusting God, primarily trusting God, really, and that's where I chose my [final vow] motto from." In his book, de Jaegher offers many reflections about the benefit to be had from trusting God in all things: "For it is trust that enables us to live as true children of God," he writes. And further,

> The charge of my body and the material needs which concern it I must leave to God. Still more must I leave to [God] the charge of my soul: that is axiomatic. If God makes our physical needs his circumstantial concern, how much more lovingly must [God] make my soul...his constant care. Each tiny flower is the object of [God's] loving solicitude...Each of our good inclinations is like a flower-bud, whose blossoming [God] lovingly watches and whose ripe fruition is [God's] heart's desire.[1]

Unlike some other religious orders in the 1950s, the Sisters of Mercy never had the custom of engaging in harsh penitential practices such as the use of a discipline or the public humiliation of sisters for minor infractions such as breaking a glass or a dish. The sisters were required to attend a monthly "chapter of faults" in which they publicly acknowledged small failings in charity toward one another or carelessness with household items. This practice was discontinued in

1959, however, four years after Theresa entered. She comments: "It didn't really have any meaning for me...I think all of us took it very lightly. It was almost something you had to do—like doing the dishes after meals." In the second year of the novitiate, even as they continued deepening their spiritual practice, the senior novices again attended college classes—this time for credit—at Mercy Junior College. As the time for first vows approached, Theresa recounts,

> I do remember taking it very seriously and knowing that this maybe wasn't the final decision. I was very peaceful about it...At nighttime, quite often, when I was in novitiate and juniorate, I would get out of bed, kneel down, and pray for about an hour or so, then get back into bed. If I woke up, I just felt I wanted to pray.

During her nightly vigils and at other times, she employed various prayer forms: "I said the rosary. I appreciated the psalms, and we prayed them three times a day...A desire to be close to God was what I was always looking for." Theresa loved chanting the psalms in Latin, although she found herself "always reading the English side. I wanted to know what I was praying. If I didn't know what I was praying, I didn't feel that I was praying. When we finally got everything in English, there was nobody happier than I was."

Theresa's experiences of prayer during her formative years point to the deep roots of her call: "Being in chapel was very important, attending Mass was very important...whatever I did, whatever brought me closer to God was what I wanted to do. I didn't feel that I was working hard at it, or that I was wearing myself out. It gave me great pleasure...It was very satisfying for me."

As she prepared for her first profession Theresa recalls feeling "very peaceful—there was no hesitation about asking for first vows." On August 15, 1957, with their families in attendance, the eight novices processed into the motherhouse chapel in white veils and processed out in the black veils of fully professed Sisters of Mercy.

JUNIORATE

After first vows, Theresa and her companions became "junior professed" and were now permitted to attend upper-level classes away from the motherhouse. Theresa's provincial superiors suggested two future ministerial possibilities for her: teaching accounting and business at the high school level, or working in the business office of a hospital. Although she preferred teaching high school, Theresa said she would "be fine" doing either ministry.

Soon she and three others were sent to Manhattanville College. Theresa was to pursue a degree in economics. For the next two years, she followed a hectic schedule of community and academic responsibilities that included being chauffeured each day to Manhattanville in Harrison, a thirty-minute drive from the Tarrytown motherhouse. The four arose at 5:15 AM for morning prayers, followed by Mass, breakfast, and household chores—all to be completed before the 8:00 AM departure for Manhattanville. Once in the classroom, "We would fall asleep, we were so tired," Theresa ruefully recounts. This was because, after they arrived home at 5:00 PM, completed their prayers and had supper, the young professed would have to sit through a lengthy lecture, often lasting until 9:00 PM, given by the juniorate mistress. "She was convinced we weren't getting enough religious life because we were out in the world with other students, . . . so she was going to make up for it," explains Theresa. Finally, at 9:00 PM the sister-students could begin doing their homework, which frequently was not completed until midnight. This made rising at 5:15 AM difficult indeed.

Even though she had little time to study, Theresa appreciated Manhattanville: "We had wonderful, wonderful Religious of the Sacred Heart sisters there. It was an excellent academic environment." Although time was at a premium, Theresa remembers, "I didn't need a lot of study time. I was fortunate . . . Some of it was osmosis, like theology, I just ate it up . . . I also loved the history courses." But she did not find her economics classes interesting: "They were dry, and I really wanted accounting more than anything. There was very little accounting in economics. Economics was a great deal of theory."

Later, when she became the financial manager for St. Francis Hospital in Port Jervis, New York, she found her economics degree hadn't really prepared her for her responsibilities in the business office.

In 1959, Theresa's mother and sister came for her graduation from Manhattanville. "It was nice. We could have family members at the graduation, and they were so thrilled. To see someone from our family graduate from college was wonderful."

Theresa and her sister Nancy (who would become Sister Anne after Vatican II) were the first in the Kane family to earn college degrees.

Administrative Prodigy

From her earliest days with the Sisters of Mercy, Theresa's business and administrative gifts were recognized, nurtured, and well utilized.

She found herself singled out even in the postulate:

> I had unusually good business skills. I was an excellent typist.
> I took shorthand. I was very good at office practice and all of
> that...They identified me as someone who could do the sec-
> retarial work, so the dean asked, "Could Sister Margaret
> come over and help us out with the secretarial work?" Of
> course, they had to say yes. They had no choice, so I went
> over.

Her preferential treatment led to understandable complaining from
some of the other sisters whom Theresa remembers saying, "You get
special treatment...when we're not in school, we have to do the bath-
rooms and we have to do this and that." But she gently observes,
"That [office work] was like my job. They were right. I didn't have to
do some of the manual labor. I didn't have time." Despite her father's
prediction, Theresa rarely scrubbed floors.

The seeds of Theresa's rapid rise through the administrative ranks
of the Mercy community were probably sown during these early years.
From the time she entered the postulate until she was missioned to
Port Jervis Hospital in 1959 she worked on weekends and/or up to
four hours a day in the administrative offices of Mother Jeanne Ferrier,
the president of the college. Ferrier, who was also the provincial of the
New York Province, quickly came to appreciate Theresa's skill, even
asking her at times to assist with her own work. Theresa became such
a mainstay in the Mercy College administrative offices that her novice
director expressed concern that she was being exploited. The director
felt Theresa didn't have enough quiet time and was concerned that she
sometimes missed daily recreation with the other novices because of
her work. After the monthly chapter of faults, Mother Jeanne asked to
see Sister Mary Theresa. "I was dying," recalls Theresa:

> You had to first kneel down, but she had me sit next to her
> and said, "I want to ask you how you are. Do you feel you're
> working too much?" I said, "No, I don't." Then she asked,
> "Do you feel that you're neglecting your religious duties,
> you're doing so much over in administration?" "No, I don't,"
> I said. "I don't always make recreation, but I'd rather make
> sure the work is finished and then I can recreate after that."

Theresa's work continued as before, even during the hectic junior-
ate years when she worked weekends. In addition to assisting Mother
Jeanne, Theresa loved working with the dean of Mercy College, Sister
Gratia Maher, whom she describes as "a brilliant lady...I learned

more from her than I ever learned from anyone." Maher was preparing Mercy College to become a full four-year academic institution, which entailed charter changes and a great deal of work with the state government. Until now, the junior college had been an extension of Fordham University, "So [Maher] was in communication with both the state and Fordham. I learned how she negotiated with people and how she communicated with them."

Theresa did all of Maher's secretarial work as well as some for Ferrier. She found both of them to be "very intelligent women," who were also very kind. "They appreciated me and what I did for them, I guess...So it was a good experience." From the beginning, Theresa's superiors seem to have recognized her leadership skills. While the novitiate had its challenges, Theresa was fully engaged.

> I was very responsible. I participated, and I know I was exerting leadership, even then...It wasn't a deliberate thing, but I knew that at times other sisters would turn and ask me different things, and then even the people in authority would say, "What do you think about that, Theresa?" I was aware they saw me as someone they could depend on.

Because she had taken on so much responsibility while growing up, Theresa, although young in years, was quite mature. Life in the convent was fulfilling her long-held wish to have a life that would "be worthwhile," and she took her administrative work seriously: "Even with the fact that I had such a different job for the first three to five years of my community life, I felt that somehow God was directing me to use my skills and my gifts for the good of the community."

After completing the juniorate, each sister was assigned to a mission away from the motherhouse to engage in ministry for at least a year before making final vows. When she graduated from Manhattanville, Theresa was told she would teach at the all-girls high school on the motherhouse grounds. But instead, she was assigned to work as a financial manager at St. Francis Hospital, a small facility in Port Jervis, New York. It was a remarkably responsible position for a twenty-three-year-old woman. After having worked with her for five years, Mother Jeanne Ferrier knew Theresa was up to the job. Looking back, Theresa recognizes how valuable the Port Jervis experience was for her later responsibilities in administrative leadership:

> What was very good is that I was immediately put into administration. At the time it was a very small hospital with only fifty beds. They later increased it to seventy-five. The

advantage of a small facility is that you learn to do everything, and you learn to know every department—so as the business manager, I was familiar with the emergency room, with the outpatient and OB departments and how they work, and how the income and expenses work. You had a really good picture of the whole institution. It does prepare you for administration.

There was one downside: "I knew next to nothing about finances except for my accounting classes in high school." Thankfully, the savvy hospital administrator, Sister Michelle Ayotte, recruited a certified public accountant from the Archdiocese of New York to help: "He came up and worked with me for weeks at a time. I caught on...It was really like accounting again, so it didn't take me too long...I thoroughly enjoyed doing it."

The biggest concern during her first year was the many patients who owed the hospital money. There were numerous open files with unpaid balances despite many fruitless attempts to collect.

So, I remember bringing boxes of files over to my room...
And I would go through them for about two hours at night.
And I made the judgment on my own—that this was twenty dollars, or this was twenty-five dollars, or it may have been five dollars, and I would just write that bill off. And then I had to go back the next day and take it out of the system.

Theresa found the write-offs challenging, "because I knew I was actually erasing money that was owed to us. And yet, we had made the judgment, rightly so, that these small bills weren't worth pursuing anymore."

Final Vows

Nine months after her September arrival at St. Francis Hospital, Theresa returned to the Tarrytown motherhouse to prepare for final vows. She already knew she would be returning to Port Jervis as financial manager, because the woman she would replace had been asked to serve as treasurer of the New York Province. As in all religious communities then and now, canon law requires that each sister be given sufficient leisure and prayer time prior to final vows so that she is as sure as anyone can be about making a commitment that will last a lifetime. For the Sisters of Mercy, this entailed six weeks of enhanced prayer and meditation. Theresa found herself revisiting her favorite book, *The Virtue of Trust*. It helped lead her into contemplation— and set the stage for prayer: "I always liked meditation. I always liked spiritual reading. I still do. I think most of my day is spent in meditation and contemplation. If I'm not reading something or working with something, I just spend the time in prayer."

And then of course there were the daily talks—something Theresa's group didn't really enjoy: "We had the same mistress we had as juniors. Very lovely woman, she was very kind, but she would talk forever— about an hour or an hour and a half—they were like spiritual nosegays. We didn't appreciate them very much."

Overall however, Theresa found the six weeks "relaxing" and says, "I was very peaceful about my final vows. Very much so. We had seven days of retreat right before the vows, and I remember thinking a great deal and being very peaceful about what I was doing." Her peace derived from knowing that she was valued in her ministry at Port Jervis and feeling grounded in her prayer life. "I felt very content, realizing that this was where I belonged and where God wanted me to be, and where I wanted to be also. I was aware also that I was doing something worthwhile, which was important to me." Theresa recalls the August 15 ceremony:

> This one was very early in the morning. We went in our church cloaks. I think we prostrated again, and then we went up and pronounced our vows, and that's when we received our ring. I remember very clearly what I wanted as my motto. "My God, I trust you." Of course, I had been praying it for a couple of years, so I was very clear on that!

And so, with great trust in the God who had led her this far, Sister Mary Theresa Kane professed lifetime vows with the Sisters of Mercy.

EARLY MINISTERIAL AND COMMUNITY LIFE AT PORT JERVIS

In 1955, the Archdiocese of New York had asked Mother Jeanne Ferrier to take over St. Francis Hospital in Port Jervis, New York, from an order of sisters who wished to move on to other ministries. In the fall of that year, Mother Jeanne received permission from the administrator general, Mother Maurice Tobin, for the New York Province to assume ownership of the fifty-bed hospital. St. Francis served predominantly low-income and middle-class people as well as a few wealthier families who had summer homes in Port Jervis or nearby Milford, Pennsylvania.

When she first arrived in Port Jervis, Theresa learned she would live in a "very nice" wooden building adjacent to the hospital. Originally a private home, it had been remodeled into a convent for the sisters. She recalls a "big crowd" of eight or nine sisters, mostly nurses, who normally worked seven days a week in all departments of the full-service hospital that included surgery, medicine, labor and delivery, and an emergency room. The "cracker jack" administrator, Sister Michelle Ayotte, was also a nurse.

Unlike some all-medical communities, conversation around the dinner table did not necessarily dissect the latest surgical or medical case over the evening meal. Instead, Theresa recalls the conversation centered mostly on the patient census: "We were always asked to pray for more patients. And I remember thinking, 'Isn't that a terrible thing? We are praying for people to get sick because we want to fill the hospital.'"

Even though there were occasional census concerns, the hospital was often completely filled. This happened so frequently that Sister Michelle wanted to undertake a building project to increase the hospital's capacity to seventy-five beds. She worked closely with a predominantly male board of advisors and frequently asked Theresa to present the financial report at these meetings: "I remember being so nervous about it because here I was talking to this crowd of doctors … it seemed like such an elite group. And yet I was very well prepared and knew what I wanted to say. They were significant moments, because it was my first time going into a public arena."

In 1961, Sister Michelle moved to Lake Placid to build a state-of-the-art nursing home. Sister Cyril Barry—a nurse who had previously worked with tuberculosis patients and in obstetrics—was appointed the new administrator. Theresa describes her as "a very lovely woman," who nevertheless felt somewhat inadequate because she had never been a hospital administrator before. In her late fifties, Barry also had health and mobility issues. Consequently, she relied on Theresa to attend some meetings in her stead, and always had Theresa accompany her to her own meetings.

When new assignments were announced in 1962, Theresa was shocked to discover she had been named assistant administrator at St. Francis. She remembers Cyril telling her: "I asked for that, Theresa. You do so much around here and I need and depend on you. If you are willing, I want you to do it." Theresa said yes, although she was dismayed to learn that she had also been appointed first councilor at the convent. At age twenty-five, she was one of the youngest sisters, and this could have created an awkward situation. But she recalls that the other sisters "were absolutely wonderful . . . It didn't really amount to much, because Cyril was a very easy administrator and an easy superior."

After John F. Kennedy was assassinated, Theresa and four other younger sisters wanted to drive to Washington, DC, to view the eternal flame memorial. At the time, sisters were never permitted to stay anywhere overnight. Therefore, they would need to make the round trip to Washington in one day. The sisters came up with a plan: "We would leave at four o'clock in the morning. Be there by nine. Go to Mass at the shrine. Go over and see the flame. Have some lunch someplace and then start back. And probably get home by nine or ten o'clock at night." Although Cyril was initially apprehensive ("If I don't tell the provincial and you have an accident, there could be a problem!"), she finally relented. "She was up at four o'clock in the morning," Theresa gratefully remembers. "She gave the five of us money for the trip. It was a long ride for five people in habits. We had a wonderful time."

Cyril also made arrangements to rent two cabins in the mountains every July and August, "She wanted us to be able to get away someplace. We were normally allowed only one day off a week. There was room for about eight of us. We took turns going up for a few days of vacation and then coming back," Theresa recalled.

But in 1964 tragedy struck. Theresa was taking a short vacation in the mountains after the dedication of the new wing of the hospital when she received a telephone call. Cyril had suffered a stroke. Theresa hurried home only to have the cardiologist tell her that Cyril's stroke had been massive, and that she needed a specialty hospital. Cyril was sent by ambulance to St. Vincent Hospital in Manhattan. Although there were other suitable facilities closer at hand, it would have been unthinkable at the time for a Catholic sister to be admitted to a non-Catholic hospital.

Theresa was now responsible for running the entire hospital. A month later, Cyril died. Theresa always regretted that she was never able to go to St. Vincent's to see her. It would have been a violation of protocol to leave her work: "It was just not something you did. You didn't leave the hospital."

Very many people from Port Jervis, including hospital staff, doctors, board members, and friends made the two-hour drive to the sisters' new motherhouse, which was now in Dobbs Ferry to attend Cyril's wake and funeral. Afterwards the New York provincial, Mother Regina Haughney, asked Theresa to serve as acting administrator until she could find someone to fill Sister Cyril's position. Having been tipped off earlier that she would be asked, Theresa made a counter offer:

> I told her I wanted to be the administrator. An acting administrator doesn't really have authority, and I do not think that is good for the institution. I said, "Mother Regina, I don't care if it's one month, six weeks, or what, but make me the administrator and tell everyone that this is a transition until we get someone else."

And so it was that Sister Mary Theresa Kane became the administrator of St. Francis Hospital in Port Jervis, New York. She was twenty-eight years old.

During the challenging events surrounding Cyril's final illness Theresa received a great deal of support from Sister Della Mae Quinn, a woman who would become her lifelong friend and soulmate. Theresa first met Della Mae through mutual friends during her juniorate years at the Tarrytown motherhouse. Three of Theresa's closest friends—Sisters Ellen Duffy, Roseanne Lisanti, and Mary Ann Marrin—frequently socialized throughout the postulate, novitiate, and juniorate:

> We would go for walks together. We would sit and chat together. Ellen Duffy's mother insisted always on bringing dimes for her to use in the Coke machine. So, we would go down behind the barn where there was a Coke machine ...We had a great time having our Cokes. And every once in a while, her mother would bring a little beer. So, then we would each have a can of beer. I can't believe that we went down behind the barn and had beer!

Each year, sisters from outlying communities came to the motherhouse to celebrate the mother provincial's feast day. In 1959 about two hundred sisters were in Tarrytown for the party. Ellen Duffy's sister, Madeleine, was also a Mercy sister and a good friend of Della Mae's. Both Madeleine and Della Mae had already professed final vows. At this time, sisters in formation were not permitted to speak to the finally professed, although exceptions were made for blood sisters. When the provincial's feast day arrived, Ellen convinced Theresa to go with her to see her sister Madeleine. Although Theresa had reservations, she went with her friend and met Della Mae for the first time:

Off we went downstairs, over through the corridors, and down to the kitchen area in another building. Out in the hall were Madeleine and Della Mae, having snacks. I hadn't met Madeleine and I hadn't met Della Mae. So, Ellen introduced me. That was in 1959.

The following year, Theresa was appointed to Port Jervis, and Della Mae was appointed to serve the new provincial, Sister Regina Haughney, as secretary to the governing council of the congregation. Because of the hospital building fund, Theresa occasionally communicated with the office of the provincial, which had recently relocated from Tarrytown to Dobbs Ferry. She sometimes spoke with Della Mae on business matters.

Cyril and Mother Regina were good friends, which probably accounts for Cyril's success in having Theresa appointed assistant administrator despite her youth. Mother Regina's assistant, Sister Bernadine Bond, was also a friend of Cyril's and would sometimes come to visit on weekends. Bernadine frequently brought Della Mae along with her, since sisters were not permitted to travel alone. Theresa recalls the early days of their friendship:

So, she and I began chatting and talking away and we just clicked. I mean, that's all I can tell you. And she'd be there for the weekend. I remember being in the laundry one day ironing my veil...I was very fussy about it. And she stopped in to see me. "My God, you are fussy, aren't you? I didn't think you were that fussy!"...I always remember that comment, because I'm not that neat all the time.

In 1964 Theresa invited her sister Nancy (Sister Anne), Nancy's friend Sister Kathleen McGovern, and Della Mae to join them for a week's vacation at the mountain cabins in Pennsylvania. Della Mae was present when Theresa received the fateful call about Cyril's stroke. She accompanied her back to Port Jervis and stayed the rest of the week to support her until Cyril was transferred to Manhattan.

Theresa loved Cyril, and Theresa's family also loved her. "My family used to come over to Port Jervis to visit me. Cyril could not have been kinder to them. She opened up the dining room. She had them served everything. My family felt like millionaires over there."

During Cyril's month-long decline, Theresa received numerous calls every night, often from Cyril's good friend Sister Mary Daniel Brackett, who lived near St. Vincent's and visited Cyril every day.

Theresa remembers feeling overwhelmed, "I got a phone call from Mary Daniel about Cyril. I was standing in the hall and all of a sudden, I sat right down on the floor because I was just overwhelmed by the whole thing." Theresa remembers gratefully the sensitive attention Della Mae offered throughout this ordeal.

> She was there for everything. And then when Cyril died, I went to Dobbs Ferry and stayed there for the wake and funeral. Della Mae was around the whole time. And she was just so kind to me, so understanding and sympathetic. I was very young when I went through this, and Della Mae was a big support.

Despite such a painful start, Theresa enjoyed her new role as hospital administrator, recalling now that she "learned a lot." She created and met faithfully with a personnel committee made up of representatives from all the different departments. She was careful "to be open to everything they wanted to say," and found committee members had a "very good spirit, knowing that they could speak up and be listened to." She persuaded the committee to conduct an anonymous survey of all staff members, asking them "to be very honest and tell us what their problems were." After receiving a nearly 100 percent response, the committee published its findings. "And I think we responded to most of [the survey requests] in a positive way if we could," recalls Theresa. "And what we couldn't, I think we said to them we would respond eventually...so it caused a lot of very good feeling in the hospital."

Throughout her years as administrator at Port Jervis, Theresa's friendship with Della Mae continued to blossom, albeit slowly, "She always said, 'I became your best friend in 1963. But you didn't become my best friend until 1964'...I was very busy, and she wasn't getting the sense that the friendship was reciprocal." Between 1964 and 1966, a relaxation of certain rules—probably in the wake of Vatican II—allowed the two to drive back and forth and visit one another, although, between the habit and little access to personal spending money, this meant visiting in private rather than in a coffee shop:

> If she didn't come here, I would drive over and see her. All we actually did was get in the car, drive to the shopping center, sit in the car for two hours or so, and talk. I don't even remember ever going in for tea. And then I'd drive her back and go home. But it was a wonderful way to deepen the friendship.

It was also a wonderful way for Theresa to debrief outside of hospital circles and receive support for her demanding job.

As hospital administrator Theresa frequently attended meetings of the Orange County Hospital Association. She vividly remembers "an entire room of men and four women who were hospital administrators —and the four women were all nuns. And I was still young and asking myself, 'What is this, that all the hospital staff are women and all the administrators are mostly men?'"

While at Port Jervis, Theresa sought to upgrade her professional qualifications by taking classes at Columbia University to obtain a certificate as a hospital administrator. Since other hospital administrators had master's degrees, she also pursued a master's in public administration at New York University. But since her hospital responsibilities allowed time for just one course a semester, she would not complete the master's degree until much later. After two years at Port Jervis, Theresa would soon be called to another kind of leadership—this time within the community of the Sisters of Mercy.

CHAPTER FIVE

Innovative Provincial

Implementing Vatican II

In 1966, Mother Regina Haughney's term as provincial was ending. This occasioned speculation among the older sisters in the New York Province about who would be their new provincial leader. Theresa remembers that she was not "really into that kind of conversation then, because I was too young." But her friend Della Mae—who always had her finger on the pulse of happenings at the Dobbs Ferry mother-house—told her "I think you will be appointed secretary to the council." Theresa responded: "Oh, I don't want to do that. I want to stay right here in Port Jervis. I'm enjoying it. I'm just starting."

In 1966, each of the nine US provinces were served by a provincial, her assistant, three councilors, a secretary, and a treasurer, all of whom were appointed to a four-year term by the mother general (as she was called at the time) and her council. There were no elections. Instead, the mother general sent a highly confidential communication to certain sisters in each of the nine provinces, inviting these sisters to suggest names for the new provincial and councilors. The list was sent back to the mother general for a final decision. The sisters chosen for service then received an appointment letter but were enjoined to tell no one about it.

Theresa recalls, "So I got a letter in Port Jervis that said, 'You have been appointed to be a Councilor Provincial and Secretary Provincial effective on [a specific date in June]. Please report to the provincialate on that date.'" Theresa remembers being quite surprised, and went immediately to the chapel, "I just knelt there. I didn't cry or anything. I was sorry I would have to leave. But it almost seemed as if God was calling me to do this. And I remember being very peaceful and saying, 'God, if this is what you want me to do,' and then I prayed as I always did, 'Into your hands, I commend my spirit.'"

The letter instructed Theresa to not, under any circumstances, share the news of her appointment with anyone. To Theresa this injunction "made absolutely no sense." She did not want the assignment, but neither would she think of refusing it. She wrote and told Mother Regina that she accepted the assignment but stipulated, "I don't think I can leave Port Jervis without people knowing that I'm resigning as administrator. We have a responsibility to tell them who their new administrator is." Mother Regina agreed, and Theresa was able to announce that Sister Jeanne Ferrier—who had been Theresa's provincial when she entered—would become the new administrator. "We had a very nice transition," recalls Theresa.

> They gave me a big party, sponsored by the Medical Society. My three sisters came from New York...I have a picture and each one of us is wearing a beautiful corsage. It was a very nice sendoff for someone who had been administrator for only two years. You'd think I had been there twenty-five years.

While Theresa willingly accepted her new assignment in Dobbs Ferry, she recalls feeling less than enthusiastic about it because she was just beginning to get the feel of Port Jervis. "But it was part of the life I had chosen," she remembers. "It never dawned on me to say to them, 'I won't take it.' It just would never cross my mind. So, I had a wonderful farewell party sponsored by the medical staff, went to Dobbs Ferry, and started a new life." She was thirty years old.

Theresa's appointment as councilor and secretary was a new position for the New York Province. Previously the secretary had been non-voting, but now that it was combined with the councilor position, only the treasurer was a non-voting member. The total leadership cohort had been reduced from seven to six. After Theresa arrived in Dobbs Ferry, Della Mae oriented her to her new responsibilities before assuming her own new position as principal at St. Joseph School in Spring Valley. The school was just twenty minutes away, so Theresa and Della Mae continued their ever-deepening friendship.

Sister Constance Golden, a psychology major and full-time teacher at Mercy College, was appointed the new provincial. While Theresa's job was primarily to serve as Golden's secretary, she had also been appointed councilor. As such, she joined the assistant provincial, Sister Judith Hennig, and two other councilors in making decisions that affected the province. She found the initial weeks in her new position "quite calm," but soon the mother general, Regina Cunningham, and the general council came to visit.

They met with all the New York sisters in an effort to resolve concerns about the reduction of the council from seven positions to six, and the lack of representation from northern New York. Regina was concerned that the New York Province had never properly used a council, because their councilors had additional jobs. The mother general and her council were opposed to that. From their perspective, being a provincial councilor was a full-time responsibility. Yet in the New York Province, councilor duties were light, and the appointees felt there was not enough work for them to do. They met as a council for just one morning every three weeks, "It made sense for most of them to have another job." Theresa remembers. When Della Mae had been provincial secretary, she had asked to teach part time because she was bored in the position. But since Theresa had dual responsibilities as both councilor and secretary, she did not request additional work.

A significant issue seems to have been that there was no appointed councilor from northern New York State, in the Ogdensburg diocese, where a number of the sisters worked. Apparently names from that area had not been submitted to the mother general for possible leadership positions, and there was considerable dissatisfaction. After that meeting, however, no new councilor was named.

The provincial council had important responsibilities. One was advising the provincial superior about the appointment of each sister to her specific ministerial assignment. Theresa describes the process:

> The provincial superior had a huge pad with room for all the names and slots. For example, St. Simon Stock School had so many slots and the provincial would put in the names of the people she thought would be a good fit there. Then she presented that to the council. We had to approve it. Sister Judith was the assistant, and she'd say, "No, I don't think that's good. I don't think that would work well for her. I think she'd be better over here." That's what we did. We'd go back and forth until we completed all the assignments ... Then we had to write a letter to every sister who received an assignment. It was placed on her seat in chapel on August fifteenth.

The appointments required a keen knowledge of each sister's strengths, gifts, and weaknesses. Although Theresa was the youngest person on the council, she was an excellent judge of people. In addition, her wide-ranging network of friends and acquaintances afforded her significant insight about the gifts (and foibles) of sisters of the

New York Province. She remembers one time when she advised against a school principal being given a dual appointment as superior of a local house:

> "Sister Anna" was a very good principal, but she was lacking in empathy. I happened to mention that at the council meeting because they were talking about appointing her superior. In some institutions, convents, schools, or hospitals, the administrator and the superior were the same person. In others, they divided those responsibilities.
>
> It was my judgment that she was a good administrator, but not the best to relate to sisters in the convent, so I recommended someone else. Now it so happened that Anna's very close friend was also on the council. She became annoyed and said, "How would you know that? You haven't lived with her." She was really upset with me. But the council did not appoint Sister Anna as superior, because they agreed with me.

Over the next four years, Theresa lived at the Dobbs Ferry motherhouse with the provincial and some members of the council. Even though the group lived and worked together, Theresa did not find it particularly stressful, because everyone was "on the go a lot," visiting various local houses of sisters in the province. What the gregarious Theresa did mind was that the leaders had separate living quarters and ate separately from the rest of the sisters. They lived in a small house connected by a breezeway to the main building. Although she joined the larger community in the chapel for morning and afternoon prayers, meditation, and morning Mass, she took her meals in a separate dining room with food sent separately from the kitchen. Theresa enjoyed the occasional "very nice parties" for the whole group planned by the motherhouse administrator, but says that although she was with the whole community every day, "We didn't have a great deal of time to do much talking unless they had a party."

The intervals of daily prayer remained a source of strength. For Theresa they never became a rote exercise: "I always found any time I was at prayer to be very, very helpful... It was a strong thing in my life, and I got joy from it. I always felt I was connecting with God. So it was always good."

At this time, Theresa was not bothered by the non-inclusive language of office prayers or at Mass. "I wasn't conscious at all of sexism and feminism and language. That was not a part of me. After 1969, I remember going to meetings with [Loretto Sister] Mary Luke

Tobin where we talked about women's role in the church, and then I became more aware."

In addition to her work responsibilities, Theresa found time to take evening classes at New York University, continuing her pursuit of a master's degree in public administration. She made the three-hour round trip to Manhattan by bus once a week, returning at 11:00 PM, only to rise very early for morning prayers and Mass.

As a member of the council, Theresa had the responsibility of visiting local houses in the New York Province:

> I probably had four or five houses in the city. And then, I had two or three houses upstate...I would always call ahead and make arrangements to be there for supper. After praying together, we would go to the community room and have a very nice discussion. It was good to hear what they had to say. Did they have any concerns? Every sister had to come and talk to me before I left.

Theresa was careful to stay overnight, so that there would be plenty of time to meet with each sister individually. Sometimes people came just to say hello and tell her everything was fine. Other times a sister "had big problems" with the local superior, with the job to which she had been assigned, or with the local community. Theresa would take these concerns back to the provincial council and the sister might be moved the following year if her discomfort continued, although sisters often became more settled as they adjusted to a new situation. Sometimes the conversation turned on changes resulting from Vatican II—many of which affected community life and were unfolding rapidly during Theresa's term as councilor. Of these conversations, Theresa says: "Basically I was quite supportive of what they were thinking and talking about. There were some that disagreed with where we were going. But we were at least able to talk it out." She remembers,

> I never found myself defensive when I was with them, which was always a wonderful gift for me to have later on, when I became administrator general. By then, after I had spoken my words to the pope, some people were highly critical of me. When I met with them, some were very honest, openly telling me what they thought of what I had said. They didn't like it. They didn't agree with it. I said, "I welcome any of these comments, because it's helpful for me for me to know about them and to understand your position."

Vatican II and the Renewal of Religious Life

During Theresa's final year at Port Jervis and her succeeding years serving first as councilor and then as provincial in the New York Province, momentous changes swept religious life in general and the Sisters of Mercy in particular. When Vatican II asked religious communities to examine their "manner of governing"[1] and "adjust their way of life to modern needs,"[2] the leadership of most active ministerial congregations in the United States began to consult their members about their common life together. Indeed, *Perfectae Caritatis* (the Decree on the Adaptation and Renewal of Religious Life) had specifically stipulated, "An effective renewal and adaptation demands the cooperation of all the members of the institute."[3] Religious superiors were asked to "take counsel in an appropriate way and hear the members of the order in those things which concern the future well-being of the whole institute."[4] The sisters were further enjoined to "let constitutions, directories, custom books, books of prayers and ceremonies and such like be suitably re-edited and, obsolete laws being suppressed, be adapted to the decrees of this sacred synod."[5]

Given that the decrees of the Second Vatican Council made sweeping changes in virtually every aspect of Catholic life, requesting religious communities to adapt their way of life to be congruent with the decrees was a tall order indeed. Fortunately, the sisters were up to it. The Vatican II renewal led active women religious to move out of a monastic lifestyle and into a ministerial lifestyle. Theologian and Immaculate Heart of Mary Sister Sandra Schneiders summarizes it best: "Ministry has moved from its peripheral position as a 'secondary end' of Religious Life, a controlled and restricted 'overflow' of the monastic 'primary end,' to the very center of the self-understanding and commitment of women Religious."[6]

The following brief summary of the highlights of the council provides context for the significant transformation that subsequently occurred in the lives of Theresa Kane and the Sisters of Mercy. This context is key to understanding the dynamic challenges Theresa and the Sisters of Mercy—as well as sisters from other congregations—would offer to unjust structures in the church and in society in coming years.

Because of his age, most observers had expected Pope John XXIII to be a transitional figure rather than a reforming pope. But on January 25, 1959, only three months after his election, "good Pope John" surprised everyone by announcing he would convene an ecumenical council. Generally acknowledged as the "most important religious event of the twentieth century," the Second Vatican Council saw roughly 2,200 of the world's bishops meet in four sessions between October 1962 and December 1965.[7] The bishops engaged in sweeping discussions about an extraordinarily broad range of issues. In addition to Mass in the vernacular, these issues included

> the use of the organ in church services; the place of Thomas Aquinas in the curriculum of seminaries; the legitimacy of stocking nuclear weapons; the blessing of water used for baptisms; the role of the laity in the church's ministries; the relationship of bishops to the pope; the purposes of marriage; priests' salaries; the role of conscience in moral decision-making; the proper clothing (or habit) for nuns; the church's relationship to the arts; marriage among deacons; translations of the Bible; the boundaries of dioceses; the legitimacy (or illegitimacy) of worshiping with non-Catholics; and so on, almost it might seem into infinity.[8]

By the close of Vatican II in December 1965, the bishops had hammered out a total of sixteen documents—four constitutions, nine decrees and three declarations—that created a sea change in how Catholics would understand themselves and their church. These writings addressed everything from contemporary biblical interpretation and the primacy of conscience to ecumenism and the church's relationship to non-Christian religions.[9]

After the death of Pope John XXIII in June 1963, the newly elected Pope Paul VI continued and (eventually) began to implement conciliar decisions. But first, he decided to withhold four items from the council's agenda, deeming them too sensitive or "potentially explosive" to be addressed by the assembled bishops.[10] These issues were birth control, clerical celibacy, reform of the curia, and a mechanism for implementing regular meetings of a worldwide synod of bishops after the conclusion of the council. Nevertheless, historian John W. O'Malley suggests, "these four issues, supposedly not *of* the council, were nonetheless issues *at* the council, and thus are important for understanding what happened."[11] By way of explanation, O'Malley identifies "at least" three "issues under the issues" that are key to understanding not only Vatican II but tensions in the church today:

> (1) The circumstances under which change in the church is appropriate and the arguments with which it can be justified; (2) the relationship in the church of center to periphery, or, put more concretely, how authority is properly distributed between the papacy, including the Congregations (departments

or bureaus) of the Vatican Curia, and the rest of the church; and (3) the style or model according to which that authority should be exercised.[12]

There were, in addition, three key words or concepts used to describe council deliberations at the time: "*aggiornamento* (Italian for updating or modernizing), development (an unfolding, in context—sometimes the equivalent of progress or evolution), and *ressourcement* (French for return to the sources)."[13] An important underlying assumption held by the majority of conciliar bishops was that "Catholic tradition is richer, broader, and more malleable than the way in which it had often, especially since the nineteenth century, been interpreted."[14] As will be seen, the final version of *Perfectae Caritatis* incorporates all three council concepts.

Before turning to the subject of women at the council in general and the effects of *Perfectae Caritatis* in particular, it may be helpful to reprise O'Malley's analysis of the "style" of the council, which sent its own powerful message about the exercise of authority. After an extensive analysis of the vocabulary used in Vatican II documents, O'Malley finds that "they express an overall orientation and a coherence in values and outlook that markedly contrast with those of previous councils and, indeed, with most official ecclesiastical documents up to that point."[15] For example, O'Malley's analysis finds a movement "from laws to ideals, from definition to mystery, from threats to persuasion, from coercion to conscience, from monologue to dialogue, from ruling to serving, . . . from passive acceptance to active engagement."[16] Further, while "not denying the validity of the contrasting value," the style of teaching at Vatican II,

> was the medium that conveyed the message. It did not, therefore, "define" the teaching but taught it on almost every page through the form and vocabulary it adopted. In so doing it issued an implicit call for a change in style—a style less autocratic and more collaborative, a style willing to seek out and listen to different viewpoints . . . a style eager to find common ground . . . a style less unilateral in decision-making.[17]

Of all the groups in the Catholic Church, perhaps none had internalized monarchical governance, unilateral decision-making, and a military notion of obedience more than communities of women religious. Small wonder, then, that the implicit teaching of the council on how to exercise authority yielded such dramatic changes in the decision-making structures of the Sisters of Mercy and of most US communities of women religious. While it is beyond the scope of this book to unpack each of the momentous changes wrought by the council, O'Malley's analysis provides a helpful framework for understanding why women religious—who are generally acknowledged as having internalized council decrees to a greater extent than any other segment in the church—would sometimes find themselves on a collision course with Vatican bureaucrats. In the end, the implementation of Vatican II reverted to the curia, whose churchmen were often uncomfortable with the council's vision of how authority ideally operates. It is ironic that many ensuing conflicts with US communities of women religious are a consequence of the very reforms the Vatican asked them to initiate.

WOMEN AT VATICAN II AND *PERFECTAE CARITATIS*

After the First Vatican Council, the 1917 Code of Canon Law prohibited laity from participating in council deliberations (Canon 223). Consequently, no women were invited to attend the first two sessions of the Second Vatican Council, although laymen were admitted to the second session as auditors. Finally, after Archbishop Leon Joseph Suenens of Malines and Melkite Archbishop George Hakim of Galilee called for female auditors, Pope Paul VI invited fifteen women (seven laywomen and eight religious) to audit the third session, and eight additional women to audit the fourth session (see Appendix B).[18]

Archbishop Suenens's timely 1962 book, *The Nun in the World,* was widely regarded by sisters as a guidebook to renewal. Because of his great respect for women religious, Suenens strongly critiqued the council's exclusion of women: "Women too should be invited as auditors: unless I am mistaken they make up half of the human race."[19]

While laymen were invited to address the council six times,[20] women were repeatedly denied permission to speak despite two petitions to the pope.[21] The presence of women apparently made a number of council fathers uncomfortable. In fact, the pope's decision to invite female auditors was deemed controversial enough that he deliberately leaked it ahead of time, which "gave the opposed, the reticent and the fearful a few weeks to brace themselves psychologically for the actual appearance of the women in council."[22] Such concerns were not unfounded. During the second session, a Swiss guard had physically prevented Eva Fleischner—the only female Catholic journalist in attendance—from receiving communion at an ecumenical Mass.[23]

Three women from the United States were invited to audit the final two sessions: Loretto Sister Mary Luke Tobin, who was the newly elected president of the US Conference of Major Superiors of Women (CMSW); Sister Claudia Feddish, superior general of the Sisters of St. Basil the Great, a Scranton, Pennsylvania, community of sisters from the Ukrainian Byzantine rite; and Catherine McCarthy, president of the National Council of Catholic Women. Tobin summarizes her experience of the reactions of council fathers to having women present:

> There was none of the "pedestal" mentality. I would say there was something else—either we were ignored or trivialized. Some bishops thought it was a good idea that we were there. There were three categories: (1) A minority of "good guys" really appreciated our being there (Archbishop Thomas D. Roberts, S.J., and some of our own bishops) and displayed a respectful sense of support. (2) The majority acted indifferently. Some appeared scared and shied away from even meeting us. (3) Then some clearly disapproved of our being there and avoided us totally.[24]

Pope Paul's public announcement suggested that the female auditors would "assist at several solemn rites and at some of the general congregations... during which questions will be discussed that might particularly interest the life of women."[25] Once the women arrived however, they "could not imagine what might not be 'of interest to women,'" and decided to attend everything. Despite the discomfort and disapproval of some churchmen, no one curtailed their attendance.[26]

It is a sad fact of history that although women's communities constituted 80 percent of the world's vowed religious in 1962, they were refused permission to participate in the formulation of *Perfectae Caritatis*, the council decree that would most affect their lives.[27] While Fr. Bernard Häring successfully maneuvered to have women auditors serve on the sub-commission drafting *Gaudium et Spes* (Church in the Modern World), he could not persuade conservative Cardinal Ildebrando Antoniutti to allow their input to *Perfectae Caritatis*. Häring recounts: "Efforts were made to get religious women invited for the commission on religious. Refusal!! A historical remark of Cardinal Antoniutti: 'You may try again at the fourth Vatican Council.'"[28] At the time, Antoniutti was prefect for the Congregation for Religious and president of the commission on *Perfectae Caritatis*.

Häring then lobbied Bishop Emile Guano, who headed the sub-commission drafting *Gaudium et Spes*: "I think we should get [women auditors] into our commission if they have no place even in the commission for the religious, although they are approximately 80 percent of the religious."[29] Subsequently Pilar Bellosillo (Spain), Rosemary Goldie (Australia), Sister of Charity Suzanne Guillemin (France), Loretto Sister Mary Luke Tobin (U.S.A.), Marie-Louise Monnet (France), and Marie (Rie) Vendrik (Netherlands expert/*perita*) "made excellent contributions in preparing the text and in understanding a little bit better the world today," Häring said.[30]

In fact, the women were instrumental in the final formulation of sections 29 and 32 in *Gaudium et Spes*.[31] In section 29 we find these words: "With respect to the fundamental rights of the person, every type of discrimination, whether social or cultural, whether based on sex, race, color, social condition, language, or religion, is to be overcome and eradicated as contrary to God's intent." Likewise, section 32 reads: "Hence there is in Christ and in the church no inequality on the basis of race or nationality, social condition, or sex, because 'there is neither Jew nor Greek; there is neither slave nor free[person]; there is neither male and female. For you are all one in Christ Jesus' (Gal. 3:28)."

Marie-Louise Monnet and Pilar Bellosillo also made significant contributions in the drafting of *Apostolicam Acuositatem* (On the Laity), which specifically references the contributions of women to the mission of the church: "Since in our days women take an ever more active part in the whole life of society, it is of great importance that there should be an increasingly wider participation also in the various fields of the apostolate of the church" (section 9).[32]

No review of the women of Vatican II is complete without chronicling the prophetic activities of Loretto Sister Mary Luke Tobin. Tobin was already bound for Rome when she received shipboard calls from reporters seeking reaction to the news that the pope had invited her to be a council auditor. Elected president of CMSW just months earlier, she recalls that the sisters had "suggested I go to Rome, to listen, find out all I could about what was happening about religious life, and bring it back. I never expected to go and stay, although there was talk about women being invited."[33]

Tobin exercised important leadership among the women auditors. Carmel McEnroy explains, "All the auditors I met singled her [Tobin] out as being friendly, outspoken and a prime mover for change, when many of the other sisters there were still timid and retiring in accord with their training for the cloister."[34] Theresa recalls that the Sisters of Mercy in the New York Province "were eating and drinking Vatican Council II," especially after Sister Mary Luke Tobin arrived in Rome.

> She wrote back in one of her reports that they had attended all these committee meetings with the men . . . and at those meetings, one or two European bishops brought up the fact

that we should be looking at the ordination of women. Now, that was the first time I had ever heard it...In some strange way, it must have been in my soul all those years, because all of a sudden I said, "My God, yes, of course, I can be a priest" ...That was my very first introduction...to the fact that I could be a priest.[35]

Rosemary Goldie recalled Tobin's advocacy for changing religious habits: "[She] smuggled into St. Peter's, by some trick or another, an attractive young nun to model an experimental costume before a cardinal, from whom she wished to obtain hierarchical approval."[36] Tobin also had more than her share of run-ins with Cardinal Antoniutti, the prefect who blocked women religious from contributing to *Perfectae Caritatis*:

> Every time I think of his name, I can see him instructing me what to do. I could see his eyelids flutter, but he wouldn't look at me. He gave me instructions while never looking me straight in the eye...I had to have some battles royal with him about the religious habit...I think I still have a photograph I took to him of how the sister was going to look. There she was in her little dark suit and white shirt. He took his pen and pulled her sleeve down to her wrist—and her skirt all the way down to the floor. Then the veil had to be pulled out so that the hair didn't show...
>
> Antoniutti wanted us to remain totally immersed in black serge. What defeated that was...a document that came out in 1966 decreeing that every religious community hold a special chapter initiating experimentation...We were to do away with everything we wished for even if it went against Canon Law, provided that it didn't interfere with the nature and purpose of the institute. We held on to that statement for dear life.[37]

To his credit, Antoniutti accepted (albeit hesitantly) a proposal submitted by several women religious auditors to establish the International Union of Superiors General (UISG).[38] It was conceived as "a funnel through which the Holy See could speak to religious and religious to the Holy See."[39] Guillemin saw the UISG as "creating new opportunities for responding to responsible tasks in religious life and the involvement of women religious in ecclesiastical organizations at the Roman level."[40]

After the council ended, the newly constituted UISG decided to elect a governing board. With the help of a US sociologist, Notre

Dame Sister Marie Augusta Neal, Tobin had given a presentation on government prior to the election. It disturbed some clerics who were present. That same afternoon Tobin was elected to the UISG governing board. The next morning the chair of the Commission for Religious, Paulo Philippe, OP, led a somewhat negative discussion about Tobin's presentation and tried to block her election by announcing another election that would include two other sisters from the United States. But Tobin won again:

> I was glad to be elected because I said what needed to be said. Most of the voters knew I would do that. I saw communication as a big problem, especially in dealing with bishops. I suggested earlier that a liaison committee of religious superiors and bishops be established as a kind of working, talking group that could discuss common problems. I saw UISG as serving this need and going even a step further to the international level.[41]

The creation of the UISG would prove prophetic. In 2016, Pope Francis accepted an unprecedented UISG proposal and established a new commission on the female diaconate. The issue had been on the Vatican's bureaucratic back burner for more than a decade, but because the UISG had immediate access to Pope Francis (as their founders had envisioned), they were able to bypass the red tape.

In November 1964, council fathers engaged in a "basically positive" discussion of the draft on religious life, which, "while insisting that religious institutes remain faithful to their 'purpose, particular spirit, and healthy traditions,' called for adaptation to modern conditions, an *aggiornamento*."[42] But the phrase in the draft that most signified changes to come was an injunction that that adaptation was to be done through "the cooperation of all the members of the institute." In other words, leaders of religious institutes had to involve all of their members in renewal. It was not to be done unilaterally by canonical superiors.[43] Yet many bishops were not yet satisfied, as was evident in the preliminary vote that revealed substantial opposition, with 822 bishops opposed and 1,155 in favor.[44]

Even though women religious had been denied permission to give direct input to the subcommission that created *Perfectae Caritatis*, they successfully found a way to get their concerns before the whole body of bishops. The president of the Italian Sisters Union, Charity Sister Constantina Baldinucci, asked Pope Paul VI to present the sisters' issues directly to the council, and he agreed to do so. Baldinucci then gathered the "desires, problems, and expectations" of conciliar women religious from represented countries and prepared a formal document for the pope. After his presentation to the entire body of bishops, she was gratified to hear bishops saying they left the council "much more aware of the problems and concerns of women religious."[45] The final version would be substantially revised, now with special emphasis on *ressourcement*—the need for religious institutes to return to the original spirit of their founders—as well as *aggiornamento*.[46] On October 28, 1965, Vatican II bishops overwhelmingly approved the final draft of *Perfectae Caritatis* by a vote of 2,321 to 4.[47]

Vatican II Renewal and the Sisters of Mercy

In late summer 1965 and in May of 1966 the Sisters of Mercy held their Seventh General Chapter and began discussing adaptations requested by their own sisters and affirmed by Vatican II. Although the council did not close until December 1965, many communities of women religious—such as the Sisters of Loretto and the Sisters of Mercy—had begun addressing anticipated changes during their regularly scheduled chapters at which they were canonically required to elect leaders and attend to other matters. The renewal chapters were often held in several sessions over several years in order to provide continuity of delegates and, hence, discussions.

To address the Vatican II adaptations asked of them, the Sisters of Mercy adopted the inductive methodology modeled by Pope John in preparing for the council. Mother Regina Cunningham designed the pre-chapter work "according to the schema worked out for the Second Vatican Council."[48] Four preparatory phases saw six committees appointed and 178 proposals solicited about new ways to select chapter delegates as well as "changes in formation, apostolic work and community living." As a result, the Seventh General Chapter would come to be described as "the best planned, best prepared chapter of those convened previously." Each general chapter delegate was assigned to one of the new committees: Religious Government; Formation; Apostolate; Community Life; Temporalities [Finance]; and Liturgy, Art, Music and Habit.[49]

In 1965, Theresa attended the Seventh General Chapter of the Sisters of Mercy of the Union, although she was just twenty-nine and a chapter delegate was supposed to be at least thirty. Since she had been appointed superior of the Port Jervis community, she attended in that capacity. She was one of just thirty-five delegates selected from the nine provinces, although Mother Regina was at pains to emphasize that a "tremendous effort had been made to engage the entire membership in chapter preparations." This is borne out by the large number of proposals submitted from across the Union with nearly half (82) addressing religious government and another 32 addressing community life.[50]

At the general chapter, delegates approved a process to begin revising the Union's constitutions, customs, and guides; approved a new modified habit; allowed temporarily professed sisters to have an active voice in elections; and instructed that each sister would "be free to choose the place of her meditation." In light of the ever-increasing enrollment of baby boomers in Catholic schools, the chapter also faced up to financial realities, recognizing that the provinces could no longer afford to pay for adding lay teachers to their own sponsored schools while releasing Sisters of Mercy to teach in diocesan schools. Each province was charged "to inform the bishops that no additional members will be assigned as teachers in elementary schools starting with the school year 1966-7. The community is unable to sustain the grave financial burden of lay teachers' salaries [in our own sponsored institutions]."[51]

The Seventh General Chapter launched a series of chapter meetings that, over the next twelve years, would completely transform Theresa's life and that of the Mercy sisters. As an elected chapter delegate, or in her capacity as provincial administrator, Theresa would participate in shaping decisions that brought her community into the modern world. Chapter proceedings addressed every aspect of Mercy life, from how authority would function, to how the sisters prayed, to what they would wear. Such decisions resulted in increased self-determination in the context of community life. Adult women whose lives and ministries had heretofore been shaped largely by others found greater opportunities for growth and maturation. In the process, the Mercy Union itself—however painfully at times—came to a renewed vision of itself and of what God was asking in the modern era. Theresa saw significant early changes in governance, communication, and lifestyle during her 1966–70 term as a New York provincial councilor:

> The whole union was changing. The mother general and her council would meet regularly with all the provincials...The provincials were called together to meet with them about three times a year. And it was good, because they would come back to the province, tell us what was going on in other provinces, and whatever decisions were made, they shared with us.

One of the first decisions to trickle down was an increase in leisure time. Leadership put an end to the 24/7 work week. It also relaxed the rules about when the (now modified) habit was to be worn.

> We brought up having one free day a week...We also built in that every convent had a free night where a sister didn't have to observe evening prayers and official supper. You could have supper in the convent dining room rather than the big dining room at the hospital. Things like that. And then, they made the change that, while you were in the house, you could wear casual dress—usually a duster, I guess. We weren't wearing slacks at all then...So we thought these were big changes. And of course they were at that time.

In 1968, provincial chapters were held to prepare for the June 26–August 3, 1969, Special General Chapter, which had been mandated by Rome:

> A special general chapter was not in Mother M. Regina Cunningham's plans as the Institute had concluded the Seventh General Chapter in 1966. However, in 1967, Rome mandated that all religious congregations hold special chapters before October 11, 1969. These chapters were to serve as a bridge between the past and the future, the bridge "being the 're-newal and adaptation' of our religious life to meet the needs of today."[52]

Each of the nine provincial chapters processed and finalized proposals from the membership and elected delegates to the Special General Chapter. For the first time, these local chapters were open to observers, "and in most instances, all sisters were free to speak: the workings of the community were open to all. This type of exchange had not been part of the experience of most of the membership."[53] Proposals were then forwarded to the Mercy generalate, where seven commissions involving a total of sixty-nine sisters pooled and processed them in preparing the Special General Chapter agenda. In this way, Mother Regina began to implement the Vatican II request to involve all of the sisters in renewal.

Initially four delegates to the 1969 chapter were to be selected from each province—the superior and three elected delegates with three alternates. Theresa's New York province asked that the alternates also be permitted to attend as passive observers. Fearing that seventy participants would be unwieldy, Mother Regina Cunningham denied their request.[54] But her decision was met with generalized disagreement. When delegate elections were held, each province elected six sisters—three delegates and three alternates—and an additional group of three alternates, as it was widely anticipated that once the chapter was in session, it would vote to expand representation.[55] And so it happened. In a secret ballot, chapter delegates voted forty-two to one to increase the official delegation from forty-three members to seventy by bringing the three substitute delegates from each province into full membership in the Special General Chapter. Further, the second set of alternates was permitted to attend as observers with the right to speak but not submit amendments or vote. So began decentralization of decision-making in the Sisters of Mercy of the Union.

Theresa served on the finance committee of the New York provincial chapter and was elected by the provincial council to attend the Special General Chapter. At the age of thirty-three, she would be the youngest delegate to attend, having met the requirement of being professed for ten years. She recalls the 1969 chapter as the one "when our whole community radically changed." Two of the biggest changes involved the habit and what she identifies as

> basically a decision of subsidiarity. Each sister would make the decisions that pertained to her own life, such as where she went on vacation, when she went on vacation. We each submitted a personal budget...So it really had to do with the changes in your personal life: changes in habit, being much more responsible for your prayer life.
>
> We also made decisions about ministry. Sisters would not be changed without dialogue and as much as possible, we had mutual decision-making. No one was against being moved for ministry, but it was no longer a foregone conclusion. No more would someone receive a letter on August fifteenth sending her from Dobbs Ferry up to Watertown without having had any previous communication about this.

While a modified habit had been approved in 1966, the Special General Chapter brought even greater flexibility for personal decision-making, leaving it up to each sister to decide when and where to wear it. Theresa found the proposal about the habit "very strategic":

> We never did away with the habit. We just left it to the sister to decide when and if she wore it. This was ingenious, because when we went to Rome, they said, "You did away with

the habit." But we said, "No we didn't. It is right here in our documents that it is our official garb." But because we left it up to individual sisters, we could not be accused of officially abandoning religious garb.

Indeed, Mary Regina Werntz's historical account of the habit discussion notes that chapter delegates moved from discussing several versions of the modified 1966 habit "to the question of wearing a habit at all—while some stated that a habit is a sign of religious consecration, others maintained that in a pluralistic society this may not be the case."[56] Theresa is quoted at the time as saying, "The rationale [for wearing a habit] to me seems like a defense mechanism, and I don't think it needs defense. Those sisters who want to wear a habit don't need a rationale."[57]

In the end, the decision revolved around the right of each sister to exercise personal responsibility. After a secret ballot, an amended proposal passed: "That each Sister—guided by her apostolic commitment and enlightened by community discussion—assume the responsibility of determining when she shall wear the habit."[58] This decision allowed each Sister of Mercy to gradually assume responsibility for her own apparel. Within a ten-year period (1965–75), a majority of sisters had moved from the traditional floor-length habit to a modified habit with a veil, to a modified habit without a veil, until by 1974 most—including the administrator general and council—were wearing ordinary simple clothing adorned with the official Mercy cross.[59] Theresa remembers meeting with her family for the first time without a habit:

> We all went to blue skirts and white blouses or something like that. They were pretty "habity" looking. My family said, "Oh, you look so good. Now I know you, and I can see your legs. Now you look like the old Margaret we knew." So they were fine, except that my mother felt she'd like to see us in the habit for formal ceremonies. So, when my aunt died, she said to my sister and me, "Do you think you might wear the habit when your aunt is buried, on the day of her funeral?" Nancy looked at me. I looked at her, and I said, "Mom, I don't think we will. I hope you won't mind." Her response was, "Oh, I just thought it'd be nice." That was the end of it.

In her early years as provincial of the New York Province (1971–72), Theresa initially decided to wear the modified habit for official functions, but she gradually changed her mind:

I wore the habit, as provincial, when we had official ceremonies. For profession, and for entrance, and for sisters having their jubilees. I wore it...as provincial when I went to a
final vow ceremony in 1972 with three young women who
were making final vows. None of them were wearing habits.
And I said, "Why am I doing this? I don't need to be wearing
a habit. They don't have a habit on." So I stopped wearing
the habit even for official functions.

While the evolving garb of women religious would attract a lot of
(sometimes sensationalized) attention from Catholic laity and others,
it was far from the only issue on the minds of Mercy chapter delegates in 1969. Other discussions revolved around prayer, ecumenism,
the frequency of Eucharist, and suggestions that members of the community "should try to make ourselves effective in politics wherever
we can."[60] Five discussion groups were formed to consider "basic
world issues affecting community and religious life."

Theresa reported that the sisters in one group discussed the pater-
nalistic attitude of the church hierarchy toward women. The sisters
felt compelled "to change this image of women and to not be satisfied
with a token acknowledgment but work for real acceptance. The con-
cept of the emergent woman has much impact on the future training
of our young Sisters; we must develop a positive attitude in dealing
with men."[61]

At one point, Sister Mary Aquin O'Neill (Baltimore) suggested
what the community should say to the world in light of the many
changes being introduced: "We want to remain religious women, but
these are the adaptations we see as very necessary if we are to continue to respond to the charism of Mother McAuley and the needs of
our time."[62] As the chapter drew to a close, delegates asked that the
proceedings be distributed to each sister. They were compiled into a
booklet entitled *Mercy Covenant* and would serve as the Union's interim constitutions into the next decade.

PROVINCIAL OF THE NEW YORK PROVINCE

At the 1968 New York provincial chapter, the sisters decided to experiment with a new governance model, as they had been encouraged
to do by Vatican II. A representative twenty-five-member sisters' senate and nine-member board were elected by the community at large.
The board would first select the provincial and then begin to function
as the provincial council had.

In 1970 Theresa was elected provincial in New York after the Special General Chapter approved experimental governance structures in various provinces. She was "very surprised" by her election, since she had already accepted a position as administrator of St. Michael's Home, a child-care agency in Staten Island. The previous provincial had retired six months early owing to health issues, and Theresa had encouraged the acting provincial to run for the office of provincial, but she had refused. The nine sisters elected to the province board came from diverse backgrounds and constituencies. Board members asked Theresa herself to run for provincial because she already had experience serving on the council. Two others also left their names in for consideration. Theresa recalls: "One was a very, very conservative person who said, 'I will be willing to do it if you all would want me to do it.' Well, nobody wanted her to do it." The other sister was "highly intelligent, extremely radical, with some radical proposals, but she also had vision...so the older people on the board were a little bit afraid of her."

Theresa was elected on the first ballot by an overwhelming majority. She recalls that the new group was dubbed "the schizoid board" since it included: former provincials; those who "wanted little or no renewal"; those who wanted renewal yesterday; and one member who was "highly critical of administration and governance" in general. The new structure seems to have been somewhat doomed from the start. The sisters' senate was "very active and somewhat volatile" and wanted a report on everything the province board did. Theresa did not mind providing a more detailed report, but not everyone on the province board agreed with her. As she recalls, the one-page summaries of their board meetings "said almost nothing...and so the tension got worse and worse and worse."

In April, 1971 the superior general—Regina Cunningham—visited Dobbs Ferry in response to complaints she had received. In her opinion, "the New York Province was in a state of crisis because it seemed as if many sisters were rejecting the role of authority in their lives."[63] Her subsequent address to the sisters was "perceived as negative in tone."[64] Theresa responded to Mother Regina soon thereafter, expressing her distress over the superior general's apparently one-sided view of the province: "Personally, I do not believe the weaknesses in the community outweigh the strengths we have nor the progress we have made," Theresa wrote. "Many of our sisters are sincerely interested in the community...They are struggling with the problems and tensions of our contemporary society and the place of a religious community within it, and, finally, they represent a positive force in the community and in the Church."[65]

After a year of experimentation, members of the New York Province realized their new government model was not functioning as had been hoped. "It didn't work," recalls Theresa. "It was too divisive—the sisters' senate and the province board were more at odds than anything." Still, as provincial, she worked hard to de-escalate the tensions between the province board and the senate: "I always believed in the province board. I believed in the senate—I was very faithful to all of these structures we had."

In the end, the province came up with a new structure that incorporated representative elements of the original structure. A twenty-one-member provincial assembly was elected by the whole community, which numbered about 350 sisters at the time. This assembly then elected from among themselves the provincial and four other sisters to form a five-member executive team. In 1971, Theresa was re-elected provincial of the New York Province for a term of three years. In 1974, she and one other sister on the original team were re-elected for a second three-year term.

Theresa found the new model to be "much, much better. It turned the community around. Sisters willingly entrusted leadership to a very young group of sisters. We were extremely young...And I used to be amazed at that because we were an older community."[66] Even though the New York leadership was young, they navigated the next three years with considerable aplomb. With the exception of Theresa, who, as provincial, served full time, team members chose to retain their full-time ministerial positions, meeting one weekend a month to discuss and make decisions about province business. Theresa recalls:

> The five of us set aside, faithfully, one full weekend every month. We would start Friday night and work most of Saturday. Then we went to Mass together. We went out to dinner Saturday night, and if we had to, came back on Sunday morning. They all had important positions—one was principal for a big school in the inner city. The other was principal of our largest high school in the Bronx. The third was the treasurer at the college. The fourth worked full time in a parish, and myself.

Theresa had the authority to select her own staff, and in her first term, with the full support of the provincial council, she made the innovative decision to hire non-sisters as treasurer and secretary. But Mother Regina Cunningham was not happy about this. She worried that it was counter to canon law and represented a "secularization of religious life." Theresa, however, pointed out that "the province board

was totally in support of it. This was interesting because we had former provincials who were much more conservative about many
things, and yet they had no problem with that at all. It made sense to
them. They were businesswomen." The new government structure
greatly improved interaction between sisters in various parts of the
New York Province. Theresa explains:

> It was very good for New York because we had New York
> City, and we had the Adirondacks, the upstate area. And for
> many years, only the young sisters were sent upstate. So there
> wasn't really good interaction between the sisters upstate and
> those in New York City. When we had our assemblies, we
> now traveled upstate to Watertown or Plattsburgh. The sis-
> ters from the northern part of the state then felt comfortable
> coming to those meetings, because they would go for a day,
> go home, and come back the next day. And it really brought
> us much closer together and created good solidarity.

An Unexpected Visit to Rome

In the fall of 1970—early in her first year as provincial—Theresa received a telephone call from Mother Regina Cunningham asking her
to join a delegation to Rome. In preparation for the Eighth General
Chapter (to be held in midsummer 1971), the general council had
decided that a trip to the Vatican was needed to discuss governance
and other matters with the Sacred Congregation for Religious
(SCRIS). The council chose sisters who represented a diversity of
perspectives and had attended the 1969 chapter. Theresa, Sister M.
Jeanne Salois (Detroit), and Sister M. Evangeline McSloy (Chicago),
would make the journey with Mother Regina in February 1971. The
purpose, as Theresa recalls, "was basically dialogue and conversation, and an attempt to have [SCRIS] understand the rationale for
the changes we had made and were recommending—because those
changes were supposed to be approved by Rome...especially the
habit change."

In her description of the delegation, Evangeline supplies a charm-
ing cameo of the young Theresa:

> What a diverse group we were: Mother Regina, weary from
> her years of governance; Theresa Kane, young, energetic,
> bright, sensitive; Jeanne Salois, intelligent, rather conservative;
> and me. I was full of "formation views"...I had been traveling

around the country for the Sister Formation Conference and was bound to hear and see many approaches to the topic.[67]

The Mercy sisters met with two members of SCRIS: Father Edward Heston, CSC, an American, and Father Elio Gambari, an Italian. According to Evangeline, Father Heston "seemed more Roman than American, ... somewhat rigid, desirous of implementing norms." She describes Father Gambari, on the other hand, as "freer, attentive, listening, quite aware of issues." Evangeline related that Gambari "even addressed Father Heston right in our presence: 'Father *we* can only attempt to assist, to further the Spirit's work. It is not ours to control or to dictate the Spirit's movements!'"[68]

This was Theresa's first introduction to Rome. She wore a suit to Vatican meetings, not a habit, and, as she recalls, Evangeline also wore a suit. She remembers that Mother Regina seemed "very nervous." As superior general, Regina and the general council were accountable to the Mercy membership for implementing the directions of the 1969 chapter, as well as for communicating those directions to Vatican authorities. Aside from being anxious, Regina was not in the best of health. To make matters even more difficult, she was not particularly in favor of the changes decided upon by the 1969 chapter. Yet, Theresa gratefully recalls: "I always appreciated the fact that she had great integrity, which helped me a great deal. She would say, 'This is not my personal wish, but I need to be faithful to the chapter... She was very strong about that."[69] During the various meetings with SCRIS, Theresa remembers Regina as "not having a great deal to say," instead allowing the other three to explain changes in the habit, family visitation, formation, and living situations:

> And, in fact, a couple of times [Regina] did say, "Now, monsignors, I want to tell you that the chapter made these decisions. While I know I'm the superior general, they are not personally my decisions. I don't think I would have gone in that direction, but I want to make sure you know that I support the direction." She was very good at communicating her support despite her own reservations. But she didn't add a great deal because she didn't believe in them [the directions].

Theresa learned much from watching how Regina handled Vatican officials. Soon enough she would find herself negotiating with Vatican bureaucrats over the prophetic decisions made at the visionary 1977 chapter that also elected her administrator general.[70] In February 1971, however, SCRIS officials were unsympathetic to changes in dress and lifestyle, even though they acknowledged that Vatican II documents had provided an opportunity to experiment. "They wanted us to go through some of these changes, and we may have gone beyond what was their original intent," remembers Theresa. "They did not want us to be as rigidly enclosed or to be as cloistered as formerly or to have regulations that kept us from being with our families. They had no problems with those changes." They did, however, have a problem with sisters living in apartments. Theresa recalls an energetic exchange she had with one of the SCRIS priests (probably Father Heston):

> I remember the conversation with one of the priests. He said, "Sisters live in an apartment?"
>
> "Yes," I answered. "We don't have too many living in apartments, but we have approved it."
>
> "Well, they don't have a chapel in the apartment," said the priest.
>
> I said, "Actually, some apartments do. And they're not all apartments. Some of them are local houses or convents that we've rented. You know, Monsignor, many of the priests we know in America, they live in rectories but there's no chapel in the rectory. So, we felt that we really didn't need a chapel in the house for the sisters either, because many of them live right next to the church."
>
> He didn't have a response to that, of course. He probably thought I was pretty bold. "Oh," I added, "Monsignor, I understand that many of you over here live in apartments."
>
> "Well, yes, but that's absolutely necessary. We have to," he said.
>
> So I said, "Well it's necessary for some of our sisters to do the same thing." And I tried to be rational with him, thinking: If you're doing it, buddy, why can't we?

The meeting with SCRIS was meant to keep Vatican authorities apprised of developments as the sisters implemented the wide-ranging changes asked of them by Vatican II. To Theresa's knowledge, no one in Mercy leadership ever received any communication from SCRIS that sisters should not wear ordinary clothing or live in apartments.

An Experience of Spirit

While in Rome, Theresa often left the hotel early to walk the four blocks to St. Peter's Basilica. She enjoyed wandering around inside "to pray and meditate and take in all the sights." She recalls an un-usual prayer experience that she would ponder in the days and years to come:

> One day, I went downstairs to the crypt. And I was all alone. I remember going over and kneeling before the tomb of John XXIII, and just praying and saying a prayer for the world and everybody in it and praying about our meetings with SCRIS.
>
> And I just . . . It wasn't at all a vision, it was just really . . . It is hard to describe.
>
> All I can tell you is that there I was, praying, and it was a voice, but I didn't hear anything, but it was a message. And the message was: "You are going to have an encounter with the pope. And you will be a founder of a new community." Almost—"You are going to be a Mother Founder of a new community or a woman founder of a new community."
>
> The first part of that message, which was basically very clear when I was kneeling there that morning—that I was to have an encounter with the pope—I always felt did take place.

Theresa puzzled over what had happened: "I couldn't put it to-gether. This 'encounter with the pope'—what would that mean? But I couldn't anticipate anything at all . . ." She also found the experience "a little unsettling, but I rationalized that . . . it was something that just happened. Maybe there was nothing to it . . . But then of course, when I greeted the pope in 1979, I remembered I had gotten that mes-sage." She was comforted by the views of her spiritual director, Mercy Sister Mary Ann Dillon (Dallas, PA): "I think you had a mysti-cal experience and you just have to really live in faith and see what comes." Theresa found Mary Ann's advice "very helpful in the sense of not dwelling on it, on not getting nervous or anxious about it. And I never really did. I felt very peaceful about it."

Theresa's view at the time was that the "message" was from God, not John XXIII. She had no sense of John's presence during the inter-lude. "I just appreciated him more I guess. I always did appreciate him, because I felt he was a very gentle, humble leader. And certainly, for an elderly man, he had great vision for the church."

While the first part of Theresa's "message"—that she would have an encounter with the pope—seems to have been fulfilled, she pon-ders the second part even today: "And I often think that I didn't found a new community by any means, but I certainly think that we have reformed and refounded our communities. We certainly had a whole refounding in terms of the sisters from Latin America. And I was one of the leaders of that."

Life as Provincial

Throughout her years as provincial (1970–77), Theresa and her team spent a significant amount of time helping sisters negotiate the internal changes that had resulted from the community's implementation of Vatican II. As Theresa recalls, "In the New York Province, we had consensus for change, but we also had a core of people who were really very much against it. They were very traditional, very conservative, thought we were going entirely too far... They were convinced that our adaptations and changes had not been intended by the Vatican Council and they were quite open with their objections." Some were especially opposed to the increased flexibility of prayer, clothing, and lifestyle choices. Diversity in prayer styles allowed sisters greater freedom in matters of the spirit. Theresa elaborates:

> One could decide when to go on retreat and where. This was when we started shared prayer or a group could gather for shared prayer. The sisters were encouraged to have different types of prayer. You could go outside and meditate in the morning, or you could gather in an area and have shared prayer for a half hour every day. That exercise could take the place of meditation. People really were attracted to that. We would meet in the morning at the Dobbs Ferry motherhouse, in a small parlor for a half hour... Daily Mass was considered central to our life. A sister would be strongly encouraged to attend, but it wasn't required.

To help people manage change, Theresa encouraged discussion and dialogue: "People got into discussions, and the conversation was allowed to unfold. You didn't try to get in the way, or say, 'Oh no. This is why we do it this way.'" She never felt the need to explain why things were done a certain way, but likewise, "I never hesitated to tell them my understanding of why something was being changed, because we had been very rigid. Most of the sisters agreed with the changes because they had lived under so much rigidity for so long."

Another unsettling reality facing most US communities was an increasing exodus of sisters. In just ten years, the Sisters of Mercy of the Union saw a 31 percent decline in membership. There were 7,278 sisters in 1966 compared to 5,012 in 1976. Some of the decline was natural attrition due to deaths. The rapidity of the decline, however, indicated that something else was happening. Not only were more sisters leaving but fewer were entering. In 1966, sisters in formation made up 17.4 percent of the total membership in the Sisters of Mercy of the Union. In 1976 that percentage had dropped to just 2.2 percent. Fewer and fewer women were entering religious life. Theresa's New York Province experienced a 40 percent decline in the same time frame, with 488 sisters in 1966 compared to 291 in 1976.[71] From Theresa's perspective, the rate of departures increased in 1968 because many sisters were falling in love:

> For the most part, those younger [sisters] had met somebody in college or met somebody in their ministries. "Mary Smith," who to this day is a very good friend of mine, came and talked with me at length and told me she was in love with a priest in her parish. So, she said, "Would you mind if he comes with me the next time?" . . . I said, "No. I'd be happy." They both came and took me out to supper. We sat and chatted for a couple of hours.[72]

Theresa is not of the opinion that sisters left because they felt change was not happening fast enough—at least in the Sisters of Mercy. She remembers some "highly educated" and "absolutely wonderful" sisters at the college who simply concluded that religious life "wasn't relevant anymore." Reflecting on what made sisters decide to leave, she ponders: "I think maybe they ended up not really being attuned to religious life anymore. Without making a judgment, I'm not sure they really deepened their prayer life to help them through some of this. I don't mean for that to sound harsh, but somehow, they withdrew from religious life." As provincial—perhaps to encourage a deepened prayer life—Theresa was adamant that each sister budget for an annual retreat: "Now, I couldn't ensure that they made the retreat, but they knew they had the money for their retreat."

Different provincials had different ways of dealing with sisters who departed. Theresa remembers a painful time during her tenure as provincial secretary and councilor, when "a number of her colleagues" chose to leave:

> They would either send a letter or they would call me: "Could you get me an appointment with the provincial?" "Yes. Is everything all right?" "No. I'm leaving." I would say, "Oh my God," you know? And I would have a conversation with them, and then refer them to the provincial.

The provincial at the time had a reputation for being somewhat severe with sisters who were leaving, so Theresa made a point to be around when the sister arrived for her appointment. The provincial gave each departing sister a very small amount of money and invariably asked her to return her silver profession ring. Some departing women wanted to keep the ring as a memento, so they would tell her they had lost it. "They didn't lose their rings at all," recalls Theresa. "The provincial just wanted that ring off their finger." Theresa laments:

> I felt terrible about it. It was so dehumanizing to treat someone that way, [someone] who had worked hard and had a good heart. They didn't get the respect and the thanks that were due them. For years, sisters said to me, "Oh, you were always so good to the former members." And a couple of them say, "You were better to former members than to the ones who stayed."

When Theresa herself became provincial, she dealt with departures quite differently:

> I usually counseled each one of them. "Are you sure you want to do this? We do provide for exclaustration,[73] for you to take time and consider... Is there anything we can do, as a community, that would in any way change your decision? Would you rethink it?"
>
> When it was clear that they wished to leave I would say, "When is it best for you? When is it convenient for you to return home?" One said, "God. I never thought anyone would ask me when it was convenient for me to go. I thought you were going to put me out immediately."
>
> I always gave them $500. And they were most grateful to get some money, because not every family was in a position to help them. Several asked if they could pay for their cars. I would allow that. Sometimes, I would not take any money because it was an old car. I'd say, "Use it until it's gone, and then get another one for yourself." For some, that would not be for a long time.

Theresa and the provincial team had many other responsibilities —including overseeing the financial stability of the New York Province, accepting new candidates, and approving sisters for final vows. One controversial financial decision about Mercy College occurred when Theresa was councilor and served on the college board of trustees. Originally, the Sisters of Mercy had been the sponsoring agent for the college. In 1969, in her capacity as a trustee, Theresa voted to have the school become independent of the Sisters of Mercy. This would make it eligible for funding from the state of New York, which would allow it to grow from a junior college affiliated with Fordham to a full-fledged four-year institution in its own right. Although she wasn't provincial when the decision was made, Theresa had to "live with the effects of it" in ensuing years. Some sisters were upset that the college would now be secular, "and to them it was somewhat disloyal to the Catholic Church," Theresa recalls. Yet the advantages were apparent:

> None of the sisters had to leave the college. They all received a full salary instead of a stipend. They received all of the benefits of any faculty member, including pension and health benefits...That was 1969...To this day, people still think of it as a Catholic college because we never changed the name ...Sisters of Mercy have always been on the faculty and there were tenured faculty members for forty years who were either former Sisters of Mercy or very influenced by them.

Another financial achievement was a highly successful fundraising effort to pay off the mortgage on the Mount Mercy motherhouse in Dobbs Ferry. The provincial team wanted to get the property ready to sell, since a large complex was no longer needed to house a diminishing number of sisters. Many sisters were now choosing to live in less institutional settings. Theresa relishes the memory:

> It was clear to me that down the line we had to sell Mount Mercy, so it was better to have it free and clear of mortgage. I worked very hard on that. We had an excellent fundraising committee. The sister I appointed to be director of fundraising really worked zealously. We raised enough money to pay off the mortgage and had a mortgage burning party. And we invited the sisters and some of their guests, and Cardinal Terence Cooke and Archbishop John Maguire, because they had been around when we had built it. We love to remember that evening.

In 1975, the provincial team began negotiations to sell the Mount Mercy property, but the deal fell through, and the property was not sold until 1995 when it was purchased by Mercy College.

When recalling her seven years as a provincial, Theresa finds one decision painful even to this day. Provincial leaders were responsible for approving sisters for temporary and final vows. During her first term—when the "schizoid" provincial board and the sisters' senate were at odds with one another—some of the younger sisters were "very outspoken" when they addressed the senate. "Karen Jones" was one of them. Theresa describes her:

> ...an absolutely beautiful woman. She always wore a big hat, and she was fairly quiet. But when it came time to speak, she would get up and speak well and quite critically of what was going on. She was very bright and very respectful, in my judgment. She was highly creative. She wrote poetry. I always said she walked to a different drummer.

"Betty Smith" was another outspoken younger sister. Both Betty and Karen were due to renew their vows, but Betty chose to leave instead. She told Theresa: "You know, I'm not going to stay...I don't think we'll get approved anyway...I'm sure they'll put us out." Although Theresa objected—"No. They won't do that, Betty. We won't put you out," Betty left.

Karen, on the other hand wanted to make vows. But in a secret ballot, the province board narrowly rejected her request for vows, with five against and four in favor. Theresa painfully recalls: "So I had to tell her, even though I had voted for her to make vows. And I always told her, right from day one, 'I really want you to stay.' But she was voted out." This turn of events created a crisis of conscience for the young provincial:

> Now, that became a matter of conscience for me...I often look back on it and see that, as provincial, I really had the authority to override a council decision. But somehow I couldn't.
>
> It wasn't that I wasn't courageous enough. I don't think I appreciated or had understood my authority to that degree yet.

Had she overruled the province board, Theresa firmly believes that, in conscience, she would have had to resign herself:

> My conscience decision was, I really should have said no to the council. But after that, I would have definitely had to resign, because I could not implement their decision. A majority had

voted against Karen . . . I couldn't personally have gone back as provincial if I had overridden their vote, even if they had decided they would take me back.

Theresa—a neophyte superior—had to address this wrenching dilemma at a time when her community was struggling to move away from rigid hierarchical leadership to more participative governance. In hindsight, it was a no-win situation. Nevertheless, the experience taught Theresa some valuable lessons about herself—and her conscience—that would serve her and the Sisters of Mercy well in the future. She never got over her sadness, however, even though Karen quickly forgave her. Theresa says:

I feel terrible, to this day. It is still sad for me. And she knows it. We have been very good friends for years, and years, and years. She always says, "Theresa, you've carried that too long. Forget it. I've had a wonderful life. I'm very happy." She's a social worker. She worked for many years with children and orphans.

The Growth and Development of the Mercy Sisterhood after Vatican II

While Theresa was learning (and struggling) as provincial leader of the New York Province, the Sisters of Mercy of the Union across the country were struggling to discover just who they were in the wake of Vatican II. The momentous decisions of the 1969 Special General Chapter had resulted in ever-deepening questions about what it meant to be a Sister of Mercy in the modern era.

Far-reaching decisions made at the Eighth and Ninth General Chapters chronicle the evolution of the Sisters of Mercy of the Union. They also provide both introduction and context for Theresa's energetic—and sometimes tumultuous—tenure as administrator general (1977–1984). In her capacity as provincial, Theresa both attended and contributed to these seminal gatherings. Held each summer between 1971 and 1975 the decisions and discussions of the Eighth and Ninth General Chapter sessions addressed a multitude of issues. Among these were collegial governance processes; an exploration of relatedness between the sisters, the provinces, the church, and world communities; and a search for balance between corporate ministries and creative new ministerial responses to unmet needs. All the while, increasing numbers of

Sisters of Mercy attended chapter sessions as observers and delegates, which resulted in greater ownership for the decisions made there.

The Eighth General Chapter met in three summer sessions between 1971 and 1973. Sister Concilia Moran was elected the new administrator general. A forty-year-old nurse, Concilia was the youngest general superior ever elected. Over the next six years, she would shepherd the community through a healthy—and painful—search for identity. The search would contribute to the visionary decisions made in 1977 at the Tenth General Chapter.

The 1973 session of the Eighth General Chapter foreshadowed later directions relating to women in the church. The chapter directed the generalate "to take steps to influence a change in church attitudes and structures regarding women in ministry." Likewise, newly elected general councilor Sister Doris Gottemoeller was asked "to approach her work in terms of ministry of women." Another significant decision with long-range consequences directed "that all schools staffed by Sisters of Mercy demonstrate a genuine commitment to education to justice."[74]

In 1975, the Ninth General Chapter approved a request to restore the diaconate for women in the Roman Catholic Church: "A cover letter would be sent to the United States bishops and other related groups or individuals, urging them to do all in their power to have the proposal addressed at the 1974 Synod of Bishops."[75] These and other deliberations helped shape the prophetic directions of the Tenth General Chapter that in 1977 would elect Theresa Kane as administrator general. Theresa and the administrative council would be responsible for faithfully implementing those directions. This would prove more costly than anyone could have imagined.

CHAPTER SIX

To Speak the Truth in Love

As Theresa Kane prepared to attend the first session of the 1977 chapter at the Mercy generalate in Washington, DC, she had no inkling that she would soon be elected administrator general or that the chapter's far-reaching directives would lead to significant "suffering for justice's sake" on her part and on the part of the Mercy congregation. She could not have known that her efforts to implement chapter directives would put her on a collision course with Vatican officials seeking to remove her from office because of her fidelity to her sisters' prophetic decisions.

EMERGING DIRECTIONS IN THE SISTERS OF MERCY

Over the course of the previous ten years, the Sisters of Mercy had introduced new governance structures that greatly expanded opportunities for all sisters to participate in (and therefore own) communal decisions affecting them. Significant time and energy had been spent searching for a renewed communal identity and mission in light of the Second Vatican Council's call to respond to "the signs of the times" and Catherine McAuley's founding charism. Mercy identity no longer depended upon a common style of dress, a common daily schedule, or any given work responsibility. Instead, the sisters were encouraged "to recognize ministry as a religious presence in the church and in the world and not a 'contractual agreement' that only partially occupies her time, energy and sense of responsibility to others."[1] Further, the administrative report from Mercy leaders identified a "growing sense of responsibility within many sisters for the entire Institute."[2] No longer would elected leaders be the only ones feeling responsible for communal well-being. Now everyone had a role to play in enhancing the life and mission of the Mercy community.

So what *did* the Sisters of Mercy of the Union believe themselves called to do and to be in this modern era? At the first session of the Tenth General Chapter held during Holy Week, April 2–9, 1977, the sisters' patient search for common meaning and purpose seems to have come to fruition. Chapter delegates voted "nearly unanimously" for a "deeper degree of inter-province solidarity" in order to promote Gospel justice in the world, in the church, and within their own structures:

> That this Tenth General Chapter commit the Sisters of Mercy of the Union to a deeper degree of inter-province solidarity in order to witness corporately our continuing conversion to the Gospel message and to direct our human and material resources to the promotion of justice within the world community, the Church community, and our own community.[3]

Just four months later, the president of the Leadership Conference of Women Religious (LCWR), Benedictine Sister Joan Chittister, would deliver a powerful address echoing what had just transpired among the Sisters of Mercy of the Union:

> The old vision says that the vow enables us to show what we are against...the new vision of religious life says that the purpose of vows is to be for something, to be for the poor, to be for love and justice...The old vision of religious life says that the purpose of religious life is to transcend the world, to withdraw, to be private, to be quiet. The new vision says that the purpose of a religious is to transform the world, like the Christ before it.[4]

After the vote on the new direction statement, Sister Mary Theresa Glynn (Dallas) told delegates that the Mercy community "would never go home again, they had taken a new direction and were already four days on the way."[5]

Our Relationship within the Church

A position paper developed by the Detroit Province, *Our Relationship within the Church*, presented the "most controversial"—and probably the most prophetic—material on which the chapter would act. An introductory paragraph cited Vatican II teaching and statements from US bishops that "the People of God believe they are led by the Spirit" in discerning "genuine signs of the...purpose of God,"[6] and that efforts to renew the church require "bold creative action" to both preserve "ancient truths" and "embody them in communities capable of transforming the world."[7]

An important area of concern had to do with "complex questions about the nature of authority in the Church." One difficulty named was that "authority and power were perceived as being solely in the hands of the hierarchy. This put the Sisters of Mercy...in the role of transmitters, not shapers of Church teaching."[8] Consequently, the sisters "seldom if ever" corporately questioned church teaching or took responsibility for "assisting in the church's search for truth."[9] The position paper specifically cited areas in the moral realm in which the Mercy sisters had "a responsibility to participate in the evolution of Church teaching."[10]

What gave rise to this provocative position were experiences within Mercy health ministries in which "the practice of good medicine and Church regulations had come into conflict."[11] For example, the board of trustees at Chicago's Mercy Hospital had passed a resolution saying "it was a bad practice of medicine to close a woman after a caesarian before performing a tubal ligation if it were necessary. The woman—and [the hospital doctors] were at risk if they had to open her up again to perform this procedure."[12] The Chicago provincial, Sister Catherine C. Gallagher, was also concerned about teen pregnancies: "We couldn't give teen mothers [information on contraceptives] but had to send them to another hospital."[13] In 1974, Detroit provincial Sister Emily George had expressed a similar concern, asking how a general community hospital could serve patients in a pluralistic society "where other persons of good will want our services but do not agree with our ethical position?"[14]

These realities weighed heavily on chapter delegates who, in the final analysis, were responsible for sixty-seven Mercy hospitals throughout the United States. The sister-delegates' desire to be morally accountable cannot be underestimated. "As Sisters of Mercy we can neither escape the anguish of experiencing the above concerns nor the responsibility of addressing them," the statement read. Three courses of action were named.

1. An important aspect of our current ministries can be to support the Church in its development of new teachings or new emphases within traditional teachings, in response to evolving moral contexts in the Church and in society.

2. In some areas we have a special responsibility to help change Church teaching and practice where that teaching and prac-

tice have become obsolete, inhibitive of Christian life, or injurious to individuals, the Church or society.

3. In extreme circumstances the community, and/or individuals within the community, may find it a matter of conscience not only to work actively for change in a specific Church teaching, but at the same time to dissent from the teaching.[15]

While the goal was to "explore every avenue of dialogue" with church officials, the proposal also recognized that—as a matter of conscience—responsible dissent could at times be necessary: "Corporate public dissent in the form of official statements and/or institutional policies which depart from such Church teaching may be justified when continued implementation of Church teaching and policy proves seriously harmful to persons."[16]

The proposal named "minimal criteria" for corporate dissent. After an extended discussion, the proposal *Our Relationship within the Church* passed by an overwhelming majority (see Appendix C).[17] The new Administrative Team would immediately establish the "Church/Institute Committee" to address this and other ecclesial issues in greater depth. The Sisters of Mercy (and Theresa) would pay a steep price for the sisters' courageous effort to be true to their convictions.

"Statement of Concern"
about Vatican Ban on Women's Ordination

Several chapter proposals were significantly influenced by *Inter Insigniores*, a recent Vatican declaration reaffirming the ban on women in the ministerial priesthood. Issued just six months before the April chapter by Cardinal Franjo Seper, the prefect of the Congregation for the Doctrine of the Faith (CDF), the Vatican's declaration quickly elicited widespread consternation on the part of Catholic theologians, biblical scholars, priests, historians, and women.

Just three months before the declaration's October 1976 promulgation, another Vatican department—the Pontifical Biblical Commission —had published the results of its own meeting at which biblical scholars had voted unanimously that the New Testament does not settle the question one way or the other about whether women can be ordained priests. Furthermore, a substantial majority (12–5) had voted that "Christ's plan would not be transgressed by permitting the ordination of women."[18] The findings of the Vatican's own biblical scholars were directly at odds with the *Inter Insigniores* contention that "the Church, in fidelity to the example of the Lord, does not consider herself authorized to admit women to priestly ordination."[19]

In response to the CDF declaration, the Sisters of Mercy deliberated over a "statement of concern" submitted by Sisters Arlene Violet and M. Aquin O'Neill saying the Vatican had failed to "directly involve women, reconcile divergences in the paper's conclusions with those of the Pontifical Biblical Commission, and consult with the Vatican Secretariat for Unity before its promulgation."[20] But for Sister Mary Ann Dillon, the central difficulty with *Inter Insigniores* was the argument that there must be a "natural resemblance" between Christ and the priest, because, "if the role of Christ were not taken by a man ... it would be difficult to see in the minister the image of Christ for Christ himself was and remains a man."[21] This CDF argument led many Catholics to wonder why the church is baptizing women if they cannot image Christ. Following up on Mary Ann's concern, Sister Margaret Farley shed significant light on the underlying history and theology of the CDF argument:

> The argument is that women can never resemble Christ because they don't look like Christ. The text is from Aquinas but only half is given. The other half is left out: women do not [have a] natural resemblance to Christ not because they don't look like men—it is because women are naturally inferior as human beings ... The Church is claiming that the tradition has been the natural resemblance to Christ when in fact the tradition has been that women are inferior to men.[22]

Sister Mary Aquin O'Neill found it "curious" that while the document affirms that both men and women have roles in the church, "the men get to tell women what their role is ..." Further, she pointed out, in St. Paul the gifts of the Spirit were never associated with a particular sex: "Even if you talk about ordination as being ordained to be responsible for the Church ... that was never connected with sex. Where did that happen?"[23]

Sisters who spoke in support of the statement of concern emphasized that the CDF declaration had failed to deal adequately with "the meaning of tradition, the relation of sacramental ministry to major forms of ministry in the Church, the nature of the charism of authoritative teaching in the Church, the values of equality and mutuality affirmed in principle by the document and the suitability of persons as persons to represent Jesus Christ."[24] When the votes were counted, the Mercy "statement of concern" passed nearly unanimously, with sixty-six delegates voting in favor, one opposed, and one abstention.

Chapter delegates then asked Mercy leadership to urge sisters throughout the congregation to study and analyze the issue. The chapter body also authorized the administrator general and provincials to share the community's position with the secular and religious press and the National Conference of Catholic Bishops, and to join other groups in urging the 1980 World Synod of Bishops to "reconsider the conclusions of the declaration."[25] Clearly, Theresa was on solid ground when two years later she respectfully asked Pope John Paul II to consider opening all the ministries of the church to women.

A "Dark Horse" is Elected Administrator General

In the months leading up to the 1977 chapter, Theresa had no intention of running for administrator general. After much soul-searching, she had decided to run for a third term as New York provincial. After having received many nominations from sisters in the province, she felt a "very high affirmation to stay in for another term." On the other hand, she had received just "twenty-five to thirty" nominations to serve the entire community as either "administrator general or councilor or both." She decided not to run, in part because she did not believe the number of sisters supporting her candidacy warranted it. But when Detroit provincial Sister Emily George—who was on the search committee[26]—called to ask Theresa what she planned to do, Theresa learned that she had received the most nominations of anyone. For the first time, sisters throughout the congregation could nominate candidates for administrator general and the council, but since most sisters knew only the sisters from their own province, nominations were widely dispersed.

Theresa met with her spiritual director, Fr. Joseph O'Keefe, to discuss "what I was thinking and feeling about the nominations to go to the generalate." O'Keefe advised her, "Well, if you were to be administrator general, I would consider it. If you were going to be on the council, I think they would need you more here to serve in New York as provincial." Since this confirmed what Theresa herself felt, she journeyed to the 1977 chapter with a peaceful heart. When the search committee submitted its final list of nominees for administrator general, Theresa Kane's name was not on it.

The chapter gathering was held at the Mercy generalate during Holy Week. Over the first two days Theresa remembers being "in conversation with any number of sisters. We would stop for a coffee break and people would come over and say, 'Theresa, I wish you'd leave your name in.'" When she replied, "Thank you very much. I really did think seriously about it," many sisters asked her "to rethink it."

On Tuesday afternoon, after the day's work was completed, she took a shuttle to New York to visit Sister Frederick Freese, one of her provincial councilors, who was seriously ill with metastatic cancer. She recalls that upon returning to Washington early Wednesday morning, "I had thirty to forty individual sisters either speaking to me or leaving notes under my door." That night after reviewing the list of chapter delegates, she found that nearly half of the group had asked her to reconsider. She decided to consult with the New York delegation. "I have enough people asking me that I think in fairness I should put my name in," she told them. "I don't expect to be elected, but I'll put my name in."

And so Theresa agreed to be nominated from the floor, especially after Sister Susanne Breckel suggested it would be good, "to have a diversity of views represented by the candidates."[27] The New York sisters "were very supportive," and the next day Sister Marie John Kelly— who was on the New York provincial team with Theresa—reluctantly nominated her as a candidate for administrator general. "I hated doing it," Kelly would say later. "I knew you were going to get elected."

Theresa called her closest friend, Sister Della Mae Quinn, and her blood sister Nancy (Sister Anne) to let them know she had been nominated. "And the next thing I knew, I got a call back from Della Mae. 'We're flying down, so get us two rooms.'" Both Nancy and Della Mae wanted to "make sure I'd be all right," Theresa reflected later. "But I would have been fine if I wasn't elected. I would have been glad to go home and back to my own life."

The next day, the five nominees spent time responding to questions from the delegates, a process that Theresa enjoyed because "there was no such thing as sifting out questions. We had no control over who asked what. Sometimes these processes are too scripted, and you don't get to the core of the issue."

As she walked off stage, one sister told her: "Theresa, you were great. You are not getting elected, but you were great." Theresa chalks this sister's opinion up to two controversial statements she had made. Asked for her insights about the generalate building and how she would hold on to it "because of its tradition and its meaning to the sisters," she responded, "as graciously as I could" that "if I were in any way being considered for service here I would really start to think about selling the generalate building tomorrow." Responding to audible gasps in the room, she explained:

We came here in 1929 when this was a farm, and it was all acreage...And now we are living in the middle of one of the wealthiest pieces of real estate in the county. For those reasons, I don't think we want to stay here. It is not practical. There are twenty-five sisters living here and the facility was built for two hundred. The cost is overwhelming. Why would we want to hold onto it?

As New York provincial, Theresa had for years attended meetings with the other provincials and generalate leadership. A utilization study of the generalate building suggested that no matter how the building was used, it would never be cost effective. "It was always going to be a loss and we were pouring money into it," Theresa remembers. Although Theresa's viewpoint was the logical one, Sister Doris Gottemoeller—who deeply respected Theresa's business acumen —observes that at the time there was "an awful lot of emotion invested in that building—it was emblematic of the Union."[28]

Theresa's other point had to do with the women's movement. She recalls one sister asking her, "Theresa, do you consider yourself a feminist?" Theresa's initial reply made everyone laugh: "Let me say to you what Jesus used to say to his friends: 'Who do you say I am?'" She recalls that most delegates "knew I was very active in the Women's Movement. I had attended the original Women's Ordination Conference in Detroit. And I was getting to be more vocal as provincial." She remembers responding with utmost seriousness: "Yes. I absolutely consider myself a feminist. I would like to say to this audience that I'm a radical feminist. However, I don't think I'm radical enough to say that."

Today she reflects, "But I really wanted deep down to be a radical feminist, you see. Many sisters didn't even know what I was talking about." At the time Theresa thought she needed to be more radical because feminism had not yet become "a part of her being." She wanted to be more articulate about it—and indeed, she became so two years later when she greeted the pope. For her, radical feminism would come to mean

being able to speak out publicly and to proclaim that feminism is truly a God-given gift to us. The gift of gender equality is, to me, just a basic core thing that is part of the sacred beliefs. Equality often is looked at as being political or social or civic, but I consider the whole question of equality to be religious, because if we are not equal to each other, then one or the other is idolatrous. That was an insight I came to as administrator general for the Sisters of Mercy, that truly we do have forms and expressions of idolatry in our Church.

The election for administrator general was held on Holy Thursday. After the second ballot it became apparent that the top two candidates were Theresa and Sister Doris Gottemoeller from the Cincinnati Province. Doris had served as councilor for eight years with the previous administrator general, Sister Concilia Moran. "For me, Doris was a shoo-in," recalls Theresa. "I had no question about it."

But after three ballots the tally remained inconclusive, with Theresa and Doris receiving the highest number of votes among the remaining candidates. Following Mercy election procedures, only Theresa and Doris were on the fourth ballot. A simple majority would decide who the next administrator general would be. Since this was a chapter that elected the major superior, Cardinal William Baum was in attendance to observe and confirm the election. He had been instructed to read the name of the person with the most votes (the winner) second. When Theresa heard him announce her name first and then Doris's she told Sister Miriam Joseph (St. Louis) who was sitting next to her, "Oh my God. I'm so glad Doris got it." But Miriam replied, "She didn't get it. You got it. Get up there!" The cardinal had reversed the expected order.

A surprised Theresa walked to the stage to say a few words: "I thanked all of them and said I was grateful for the trust they put in me. I would certainly do my very best and my prayer was this 'to do justice, to love with tenderness, and to walk humbly with my God'" (Micah 6:8). There was just one vote difference between the two finalists, making it "a real intense chapter of elections" in Theresa's opinion.

Theresa suspects she was selected because of her unvarnished position on the sale of the generalate. By the chapter's end the delegates would approve a proposal asking the new Administrative Team to initiate a comprehensive study of the disposition of generalate land and buildings.

Another factor in Theresa's selection was her reputation for being innovative and progressive during her term as New York provincial. Sister Helen Marie Burns recalls that during Theresa's tenure the New York Province was not afraid of experimentation even though it brought criticism from the outside. The province moved quickly to an assembly style of governance, including "shared decision making" and "a team approach to leadership," compared with other provinces.[29] Theresa "understood what needed to be done in terms of the church and the world and religious life ... early on she trusted the movements of the Spirit in a variety of settings."[30] At the same time, Burns suggests that Theresa's fidelity to what some might consider more traditional prayer and liturgical practices helped to sustain her faith at a time of rapid change.[31]

Considering the far-seeing proposals passed by chapter delegates, it is apparent that this chapter was all about change. "I think there was a really strong feeling in 1977 that we needed to move," remembers Theresa. While the delegates deeply admired previous administrative leaders, Sisters Concilia Moran and Doris Gottemoeller, a majority chose to move beyond the status quo and elect a "dark horse"—Theresa Kane—as their new leader. Doris's administrative gifts were not lost, however, because the next day she was quickly elected assistant administrator on the first ballot.[32] Three others elected to the new Administrative Team were Sister Mary Ann Dillon from Scranton, Sister Juliane Carey from St. Louis, and Sister Betty Barrett from Chicago.

On Holy Thursday evening, Theresa washed the feet of twelve sisters in a previously planned chapter ritual acknowledging her new role as a servant-leader. She remembers feeling both peaceful and humbled by the ritual: "I just felt open to whatever God wanted for me at that point. I had not planned it. I hadn't set it up, and I just ended up thinking that this was God's plan for me." But her good friend and housemate Sister Della Mae—anticipating Theresa's move to Washington—had mixed feelings. Theresa remembers her saying, "I had a feeling you were going to be elected, and I was hoping you wouldn't, but that was really selfish."

When Theresa's predecessor, Sister Concilia, met with her after the chapter ended, she told her, "My very first request of you is to bring Della Mae with you."

A surprised Theresa responded, "Really, why? Della Mae already has a job at St. Michael's home in Staten Island."

"I've been here seven years now," Concilia replied. "It doesn't work if you don't have a secretary that you really can trust completely, and someone who is your support and companion. So I think she should come."

At first Theresa was perplexed, feeling it "was like nepotism to bring your very best friend with you." But she paid attention to Concilia's advice, and after Della Mae's brother persuaded her to let him tend to their aging parents, she accompanied Theresa to Washington.

When Theresa visited her family on Easter Sunday, she found a dozen roses awaiting her. Her parents and siblings wanted to hear all about the election. A relative had called Theresa's oldest sister Mary with the exciting news: "She got elected general!" But Mary asked,

"What does that mean? I thought she had the highest position she could get as provincial."

"It was all brand new to them," Theresa recalls.

Theresa's former provincial, Sister Regina Haughney, called on Easter Monday to say, "Theresa, I can't tell you how happy I feel about what happened. I never thought I'd live to see the day when a Sister of Mercy from New York would be elected administrator general. We are the smallest of the nine provinces, and somehow or other they didn't seem to like the New Yorkers."

LIFE AS ADMINISTRATOR GENERAL

Theresa was scheduled to begin her new position on July first. In May, she and Della Mae packed a few belongings and visited the generalate ahead of time to select and begin to arrange their new rooms. On June 30, the duo loaded up the car again and drove from Dobbs Ferry to Washington, planning to arrive around 5:00 PM. Although they had made the trip many times, they somehow got lost and didn't arrive until 9:30 PM when—as in all good convents—the doors were already locked.

"So we were ringing the doorbell, and a sister from Rhode Island opened the door. 'Oh, my God!' she said. 'We thought something happened to you. We have been waiting all evening for you to come.'"

"I was the last one there," Theresa ruefully recalls. "They always laughed about that."

In a July 7 letter to the Mercy Institute, Theresa greeted "each sister personally and reverently as one in your midst who desires to serve," before thanking everyone on behalf of herself and the rest of the Administrative Team for their prayers and congratulatory messages. In her typically hospitable style, she wrote, "I ask each Sister within our institute to consider our generalate as another home where she will be welcome at any time."[33]

An advantage of having an administrative team model of governance is that leadership is shared. Consequently, important decisions have the benefit of diverse perspectives. In addition, no one sister bears the entire burden of responsibility. Theresa was always very grateful for this mode of governance: "I felt like I was one among equals. I was there. I was asked to do this, but it was just another ministry among ministries. I never felt as if I had more responsibility —or authority—than anyone else."

The new team started on July 2 and together mapped out how they wished to be present to the provinces and to the sisters in Latin America. Since Doris had served as assistant administrator, she was a great help in the transition. The team gave priority in their planning to the generalate feasibility study and the Church/Institute Committee as commissioned by the chapter. "We worked on these tirelessly in July, August, and September," recalls Theresa, "and then we divided up responsibilities." Theresa's primary responsibilities were to serve as liaison with the generalate feasibility committee, the Social Action Conference of Mercy committee, and as the managing director of the Mercy National Office in Potomac where the generalate offices were located.[34] In light of pending decisions regarding the potential sale of the land and buildings, the generalate would soon be renamed the Sisters of Mercy National Office. Theresa was also the main liaison with the nine provincial leaders serving the provinces of Baltimore, Chicago, Cincinnati, Detroit, New York, Omaha, Providence, Scranton, and St. Louis. After her election to the presidency of the Leadership Conference of Women Religious in August 1978, she spent a significant amount of time helping the national organization address common challenges and concerns of US religious orders.

Doris was liaison to Church/Institute and Government Committees, and liaison to the Mercy communications office at the Mercy National Office. Betty Barrett was liaison to the Finance Committee, the Feasibility Committee, the Mercy Action Foundation (which distributed small ministry grants), and the Mercy Higher Education Colloquium. Mary Ann Dillon connected with the Formation and Ministry Committees and with the Mercy archives office. Juliane Carey was liaison to the Health Affairs and Sponsorship Committees, Chapter Steering Committee, and the committee charged with revising the Mercy constitutions.[35]

Working in Mercy administrative leadership entailed many meetings and much networking with provincial leaders who were immediately responsible for a myriad of Mercy-sponsored ministries, as well as financial oversight in each of the nine provinces. Most decisions that affected sisters' day-to day-lives and ministries were made at the provincial level. Formation of new members was ultimately the responsibility of the Administrative Team, but much of that responsibility was delegated to provincial leaders who implemented formation programs and made recommendations for vows. The Mercy Administrative Team reserved authority to approve those women accepted for final vows.

An important function of the national office was to track and coordinate issues common to all of the provinces. During Theresa's first term, the Administrative Team initiated the General Administrative Conference, a twice-a-year meeting with provincial leaders to broaden consultation and decision-making. As Theresa recalls, another team member—she thinks Betty Barrettt—had come up with this "great, great idea." In general, Theresa remembers being very happy in her work. "I felt I was of service, but I also felt like every day I received much more than I ever gave."

The new Administrative Team lost no time in beginning to implement the 1977 chapter directives. Within the first fourteen months of their term, a company was hired to conduct a feasibility study evaluating the use of generalate land and buildings, the Church/Institute Committee was established as advisory to the Administrative Team, and members of the team travelled to Rome to share the 1977 chapter directives with officials at SCRIS and the CDF.[36]

Communicating Chapter Directives to US Bishops and to Rome

As directed by chapter delegates, before she left office, Sister Concilia Moran had written to bishops in dioceses where the Sisters of Mercy served to share information about chapter deliberations and especially their concerns about *Inter Insigniores*, the recent Vatican declaration on women's ordination. Her letter echoed the issues raised at the chapter, specifically, "the failure of the Congregation for the Doctrine of the Faith to (a) involve women more directly in the process of formulating *Inter Insigniores*; (b) to explain the divergence of its conclusions from those of the Pontifical Biblical Commission; and (c) to consult with the Vatican Secretariat for Unity before promulgating the document."[37]

The letter was also sent to officials at SCRIS—Cardinal Eduardo Pironio, prefect, and Archbishop Paul Augustin Mayer, secretary. Within two months of taking office in July 1978, Theresa, Doris Gottemoeller, and Julianne Carey journeyed to Rome to present the directives and concerns of the Tenth General Chapter to SCRIS. When they actually met with SCRIS officials, they were taken aback by the "nonchalance" shown by officials at that dicastery. Neither Archbishop Mayer nor his staff had even read the Mercy *Our Relationship within the Church* statement, which had been sent in advance.[38] A second meeting several days later was proposed by a SCRIS official so that he could read the document. Unfortunately, "the second appointment gave no evidence of better preparation, and the Sisters left Rome convinced that the nature and implications of the statement had not been understood. No expression of surprise, appreciation or caution was offered by SCRIS—nor has been to date."[39]

The sister-leaders also decided to seek a meeting with officials at the CDF. Through the good offices of Terence Cardinal Cooke, whom Theresa knew well, a meeting was arranged with Archbishop Jerome Hamer, OP, then secretary (and therefore second in command after Cardinal Seper) at the CDF. As Theresa recalls, Archbishop Hamer was "cordial" and indicated he was "most willing to discuss the work of the congregation and/or the declaration on ordination."[40]

After the trio presented what had been discussed at the chapter and the resolution on women's ordination, Hamer first expressed admiration for the role of religious women in the United States and then asked whether a woman's giftedness "must necessarily express itself in ordination." In his opinion, *Inter Insigniores* "contains no theological argument based on sex"; rather, he said the arguments are based on revelation, tradition, and the nature of the magisterium.[41] He felt the Mercy sisters were misinformed about the lack of women's participation in preparing *Inter Insigniores* and told them that "five or six women from several continents were consulted."[42] Still, it is notable that the World Union of Catholic Women's Organizations (WUCWO) had publicly criticized the Vatican's lack of consultation on *Inter Insigniores*, writing that "despite the affirmation that a large number of women were consulted in the preparatory stage to the writing and publication of the declaration, the WUCWO was not consulted [although it] represents 127 organizations which are present in 60 countries of the six continents (some 36 million women)."[43]

Hamer went on to say that the CDF had made "a very thorough study" of world reactions, and the negative reaction was "chiefly from women religious," and "almost entirely confined to the United States and Canada, with a lesser amount from Belgium."

At this point Theresa remembers responding: "Well, with all due respect, my experience of being in other countries is that very few women know how to read, so they wouldn't have been able to read your document." She remembers thinking to herself, "I mean, if you're carrying water for six hours a day, you don't have time to read a document from the Vatican."

Hamer expressed his conviction that "it was absolutely unrealistic to expect the 1980 Synod of Bishops to reexamine the declaration on ordination as such, but that the question of the role of women in the church would be a very appropriate agenda item."[44] As Theresa recalls, the archbishop reminded them that "we were, as leaders of the institute, to please make sure the sisters knew what the thinking of the church was and to follow it." She remembers reflecting that her sisters knew very well what the "thinking of the church" was, but "they just didn't agree with it."

Selling the Generalate

As directed by the 1977 chapter, over the next two years the Feasibility Committee gathered information about the value of generalate properties and conducted a survey to assess the wishes of the sisters. Survey responses were evenly divided, with forty percent of the sisters wishing to sell the property, forty-one percent desiring to retain ownership, and sixteen percent undecided.[45]

In June 1979 Theresa's opening address to the second session of the Tenth General Chapter emphasized the church's call to justice: "In light of the issues before us, inspired by our mission to serve all those in need...let the call of justice hear our corporate response and let us believe, act, and live fully realizing that 'action on behalf of justice and participation in the transformation of the world is a constitutive dimension'[46] of the preaching of the Gospel."[47] By an overwhelming majority, sister-delegates approved the sale of the generalate building and grounds.

The Administrative Team was instructed to invest the proceeds and use the interest to fund new Mercy ministries—particularly for the homeless—and for now-lowered expenses at the new national offices.[48] It was a bittersweet moment for the sisters who had long seen the Potomac generalate as a symbol of the unity within the nine provinces of the Mercy Institute. At the closing liturgy, Theresa's heartfelt reflection encouraged her sisters: "The decision we reached presents us with another approach...a call to simplicity...a call to insecurity and a call to be a pilgrim people...[It] should be an occasion for joy...It is a symbol of a new beginning."[49]

In the late summer of 1980, the generalate buildings and seventy acres of land were sold to the US Postal Service for 6.8 million dollars.[50] With the interest generated from the sale, the McAuley Institute was created in 1982 to support the development of low-income housing throughout the United States. Within seven years the McAuley Institute would provide technical and financial assistance to more than six hundred projects or groups, and its revolving loan fund would be supporting "more than $11.5 million worth of low-income housing developments."[51] Theresa's bold suggestion to sell the generalate—which she believes is why she was elected—had borne rich fruit indeed.[52]

SERVING IN THE PRESIDENCY OF LCWR

In August 1978 Theresa was elected president of the Leadership Conference of Women Religious (LCWR), an ecclesiastically recognized umbrella organization representing more than 130,000 American sisters at that time. She would serve in this position for three years, first as president-elect, then as president, and finally as immediate past president.

LCWR membership is composed of the superiors and councilors of US religious orders of women. Founded in 1956, the organization meets annually to discuss common concerns and to collaborate in "carrying out their service of leadership to further the mission of the Gospel."[53] Since the leadership of most religious orders changes on a regular basis, a much-valued service provided by LCWR over the years has been to orient new sister-leaders to their civil, canonical, and Gospel-justice responsibilities.

In the wake of Vatican II, the 1971 bylaws of LCWR "shifted focus from matters concerning 'superiors and their subjects' to the 'development of creative and responsive leadership.'"[54] LCWR expanded its vision to include all of humanity:

> In contrast to their founding sisters, the women who framed these bylaws perceived themselves to be actors whose stage was the whole world. As designated leaders of their communities in a church whose mission excluded no human concern, they considered themselves responsible for bringing their collective power to bear on the needs of contemporary humanity ...not simply in filling those needs but in shaping church and society. They did not see this end as inappropriate to their identity...On the contrary, the very Gospel in which their identity was rooted required action of them.[55]

When Theresa was elected to the LCWR presidential triad, the organization was already a hub of information sharing, mutual inspiration, and collaboration to help "shape church and society." Sisters joined the civil rights movement, engaged in advocacy for women's rights, and worked to incorporate minorities into the formerly white male enclaves of colleges and universities. They took to heart Catholic social teaching from the Vatican II constitution *The Church in the Modern World*, the 1971 Synod of Bishops' letter "Justice in the World," and Pope Paul VI's ringing challenge to religious in *Evangelica Testificatio*: "How then will the cry of the poor find an echo in your lives?"[56]

It didn't take sisters long to recognize the systemic injustices affecting women in the church. The 1972 national LCWR assembly developed the theme "Women in the Church" and canon lawyer Clara Henning shocked many as she delineated inequalities in church law that affected the female members of Christ's body.

Two years later the Ecclesial Role of Women Committee (EROWC) was formed and over several years produced consciousness-raising materials for use by sister-leaders and their communities. The *Focus on Women* kit contained booklets designed for group reflection on topics such as sex-role stereotyping, symbol and myth as vehicles of sexism, women and God, and the economic status of women.[57] LCWR officers and board members began to wrestle with questions surrounding the contemporary women's movement: "Words like 'sexism,' 'the women's issue,' and 'women's movement' came into the LCWR lexicon. And because they had firsthand experience of the power structures of the church, especially at levels transcending a single diocese, [the sister-leaders] early intuited the linkages between power and gender."[58]

From 1972 through 1979, Theresa recalls, "the theme of the annual assembly was women in the church. We never changed it." In 1976, the national assembly overwhelmingly "endorsed as a top priority 'to set in motion a process to articulate a contemporary theology of religious life consonant with the call to penetrate the world with the Gospel message.'"[59]

In the ensuing four years, a Contemporary Theology Task Force gathered data from sisters about their "perceptions and understandings" of contemporary religious life. Compilation and analysis of the input found that sisters: (1) increasingly framed the meaning of their lives in terms of the church's evangelizing mission, (2) had an evident appreciation of "a prophetic element in their calling," and (3) strongly espoused "an incarnational spirituality, which locates God's action in history."[60]

After being elected New York provincial in 1970, Theresa herself would participate in the unfolding LCWR vision. She had been very active in New York's Archdiocesan Committee on Women Religious (ACWR), a subset of LCWR Region II, which encompassed the entirety of New York State. In 1972 she was elected to the Region II executive committee and later became its chairperson. She initiated the practice of rotating the twice-yearly meetings around the state to include Syracuse, Buffalo, and Long Island rather than just the Dobbs Ferry Mercy motherhouse or the Sparkill Dominican motherhouse.

In 1977 after having been elected administrator general and moving to Potomac, Maryland, Theresa was asked to be Region IV chairperson. Washington LCWR members knew Theresa well because of her leadership in New York. By virtue of serving as Region IV chair, Theresa automatically served on the LCWR national board.

At the August 1978 annual assembly, sister-leaders from all over the United States elected Theresa president-elect of LCWR. Prior to her election, she had been invited to write a reflective piece on leadership. Published in the May 1978 LCWR newsletter, it reprised what she had learned from her eighteen years of leadership serving as a hospital administrator, provincial councilor, provincial administrator, and administrator general:

> Today's leader is a guide . . . one who encourages community members to realize and actualize their full potential in the service of their God and God's people . . . There are certain essential qualities that a leader must possess—the most important is a sense of joy in an atmosphere of hope and deep confidence in God and in humankind. We fail our members if we do not have a sense of our own dignity as a human person . . . a sense of humor coupled with a deep sense of God working in and through us. To my mind, a weakness that can appear in religious leaders is a failure to realize that the work is truly God's and we are the instruments.[61]

The August 1978 assembly was a first, since it was held jointly with the Conference of Major Superiors of Men (CMSM), the umbrella organization for male religious orders in the United States. The conference theme focused on "the systemic connection between American economic patterns and global poverty."[62] In the conference report that year, Blessed Virgin Mary Sister Joan Keleher Doyle, LCWR president, summarized LCWR's five-year effort to dismantle sexism, an effort Theresa would vigorously continue during her own tenure and beyond.

> Since 1973, the Conference has carried out extensive programs related to transforming the perceptions of and about women. We have promoted the recognition of sexism as destructive of both women and men. If we choose to continue work on this goal, from the position of our increased consciousness, we need to determine what options will most effectively insure images, structures, and ways of relating consonant with God's reign.[63]

Upon her election Theresa joined LCWR president St. Joseph Sister Mary Dooley and immediate past president Joan Doyle. Theresa describes both women as "very welcoming" and "crackerjacks" in their positions. Along with the executive secretary Divine Providence Sister Lora Ann Quiñonez, the three women in the presidency constituted LCWR's executive committee.

The LCWR executive team also networks with other umbrella organizations, such as the International Union of Superiors General (UISG), the Conference of Major Superiors of Men, Diocesan Vicars for Religious, and the National Conference of Catholic Bishops (NCCB).[64] The executive leadership works closely with the national board to plan for the annual assembly and appoints a planning committee for this major event.

Theresa describes one of the planning sessions: "After the assembly was over we stayed on for another four or five days and worked together to review the gathering just finished, look at the evaluations, identify suggestions that we thought should be implemented, and build those into the next year's program." The executive committee also provided oversight and input for various LCWR projects such as the Ecclesial Role of Women Committee and the Contemporary Theology Project mentioned above, as well as a joint project with the US bishops' liaison: *Patterns of Authority and Obedience*, discussed below.

In November 1978, three months after she was elected, Theresa, Lora Ann, Joan, and Mary journeyed to Rome for LCWR's longstanding annual meeting with Vatican officials at SCRIS. The perennial hope for these meetings was to maintain good communications with Vatican offices on behalf of American sisters who, after Vatican II seem to have perpetually perplexed—and at times dismayed—various prelates in the United States and in Rome.

In 1977, Bishop John McGann, a member of the National Conference of Catholic Bishops (NCCB) Committee for Liaison with LCWR, asked bishops to suggest topics for dialogue with a corresponding LCWR Liaison Committee. Several bishops suggested that "obedience and authority in religious congregations" could be a helpful topic. The resulting seminal study, *Patterns of Authority and Obedience*, provides excellent insight into tensions that arose between religious congregations of women and the institutional church owing to starkly differing governance models. Researched and written by LCWR executive secretary Lora Ann Quiñonez, it was published in May 1978 by members of the NCCB/ LCWR Liaison committees.[65]

The study was intended "as a starting point for dialogue between the NCCB and LCWR Liaison committees." Among other findings, it discovered "a fundamental shift from pyramidal, hierarchical to circular, horizontal models of government" in US congregations of sisters. These new structures were "increasingly designed to insure a high degree of ongoing participation by members in major corporate decisions" and "a rejection of dependence, submission, subjection, dominance of one over others... [A] peer relation has tended to replace former parent-child modalities."

With regard to the institutional church, the study found that "developments in authority/obedience patterns have led to a concern for the legitimate autonomy of the religious institute vis-à-vis both the local ordinary and the Roman Curia." Further, while recognizing that religious "are called to be part of an interdependent church," the study reported that "they are increasingly willing to insist on that flexibility and autonomy consonant with fidelity to their tradition."[66]

Religious congregations' more collaborative governance models differ markedly from the hierarchical authoritarian models of the institutional church. Consequently, the study named numerous tensions that existed within the religious communities themselves and between religious communities and the institutional church. Within communities, tensions were seen as (among other things) the "normal accompaniments of change and growth alongside the perennial dilemma of balancing personal freedom with responsibility...and the corporate mission." As for the institutional church, the report suggested, "At the root of these tensions is a serious lack of communication and consequently mutual misunderstanding and a high level of defensiveness vis-à-vis each other."

Along with conflicts between authoritarian and participative modes of governance, some bishops seemed to have a "deep suspicion of emerging collaborative structures," seeing them as "a direct challenge to their own ways of operating." Also, women's roles were at issue. "A number of bishops appear[ed] unwilling to accept women in changed ministerial and decision-making roles," and "challenge[d] the increased self-direction and autonomy of religious congregations."[67]

Theresa—along with all other LCWR leaders for decades to come —journeyed annually to meet with Vatican officials in an effort to initiate mutual communication that would diminish tensions and defensiveness. During the 1978 LCWR meeting with Franciscan Father Basil Mary Heiser, undersecretary at SCRIS, the sisters reported on their annual assembly and, as a courtesy, shared current programming and new directions. Theresa remembers being impressed with the way LCWR president Mary Dooley handled the meeting: "The 1978 meeting was basically a good conversation. Mary Dooley was always astute and strategic in what she said to them. She was highly educated, very cordial, and gracious. And SCRIS officials had great respect for her."

In addition to annual meetings with SCRIS, the LCWR presidential triad regularly attended annual November meetings of the NCCB as observers. During the years Theresa attended, she recalls that the bishops were actively working on and "very good about" the peace issue. They were also concerned about health care for the poor "but just in general—they weren't addressing birth control or any contro-versial issues," as in recent disagreements about family planning pro-visions in the Affordable Care Act. US bishops had also taken to heart the 1971 World Synod of Bishops document "Justice in the World."[68] At the time of the 1978 meeting, Archbishop John Quinn of San Francisco was president of the NCCB, Bishop James Malone of Youngstown was vice-president, and Bishop Joseph Bernardin was the general secretary.

The bishops were also following up on their bicentennial Call to Action consultation with clergy, religious, and laity held in Detroit in 1976. Plans for that gathering had begun when US bishops returned from the 1971 Synod on Justice in the World determined to bring its mandate to US dioceses. A widespread consultation process involving more than 800,000 Catholics culminated in the Detroit conference, which saw more than 100 bishops in attendance, in addition to 1,340 voting delegates and 1,500 observers. Two Sisters of Mercy, Margaret Farley (Detroit) and Norita Cooney (Omaha), served on writing com-mittees at the conference.[69] Here is an overview of the event written by a lay organization that sought to implement conference outcomes:

> At the end of three momentous days of discussion and debate, the assembly declared the church must stand up to the chronic racism, sexism, militarism, and poverty in modern society. And to do so in a credible way the church must reevaluate its positions on issues like celibacy for priests, the male-only clergy, homosexuality, birth control, and the involvement of every level of the church in important decisions. The Detroit conference recommended that each diocese take the recom-mendations home and act upon them.[70]

Unfortunately, because of the internal church-justice issues that surfaced at the conference, bishop leaders soon began to distance themselves from the movement. At the 1978 NCCB meeting, Theresa recalls, "Some of the bishops wanted the Call to Action consultation to continue and be sponsored by the bishops. But others felt it was now up to the laity to keep it moving."

And the laity did indeed "keep it moving," but not without sub-stantial opposition. In October 1978, the lay-led Call To Action (CTA) movement began in Chicago under the leadership of Dan and Sheila Daley. It quickly spread to other dioceses around the country. Because laity stood by the Detroit conference's calls for internal church reforms, CTA speakers and local chapters would, in coming decades, be banned from meeting or speaking on church property in some dioceses, and even—in one extreme case—be excommunicated from the church. Tensions escalated, especially after John Paul II issued *Ordinatio Sacerdotalis* in 1995, which sought to make the non-ordination of women "definitive" church teaching and forbade further discussion of the issue.

Theresa would herself be banned from speaking on church property in some locales. She was once threatened with excommunication by the ultra-conservative Bishop Fabian Bruskewitz of Lincoln, Nebraska, when a CTA group invited her to speak in that diocese. Bruskewitz had summarily excommunicated all members of Lincoln's CTA chapter.[71] Event planners skillfully sidestepped the issue by moving Theresa's speaking venue to the nearby Omaha diocese.

As Theresa assumed the mantle of LCWR president at the close of the 1979 annual assembly in San Antonio, Texas, 650 sister-leaders commissioned their new officers by praying: "Lead the Conference in such a spirit that we may discover ever more liberating ways to change the face of the earth." During the ceremony, Theresa shared a thoughtful reflection about the nature of prophecy and power in light of the 1971 Synod of Bishops document "Justice in the World": "A primary responsibility of leadership is to effect social change—to bring about a transformation within ourselves and within the world," she said. But if change is to happen, sister-leaders must understand and not be afraid to use their own God-given power on behalf of justice within both church and society:

> Especially we must continue to dialogue very honestly with the hierarchy of the church...No ministry can continue to exclude women who have within them the power given to them by their Creator...we can speak the truth in love about power—about our understandings of power, authority, and obedience—we can call for and work actively to promote a transformation in our church in effecting a Christian approach to power, authority, and leadership.[72]

After a thoughtful analysis of the need for prophecy and solidarity, she shared her conviction that there had been a significant change in the self-understanding of LCWR sisters: "We who are gathered together in San Antonio in 1979—we who as women gathered in another city in 1956 and called ourselves obedient *daughters* of the church—will move into the final part of this twentieth century as obedient *leaders* of our church—leaders who recognize, affirm and reverence the power that is ours."[73]

The Sisters of Mercy were proud that one of their own had been elected to the LCWR presidency. On the eve of her installation, forty-three Sisters of Mercy from California to Maine gathered at a reception in Theresa's honor. She was the second Union Mercy Sister to have been so honored. In 1959 Mother Maurice Tobin (Detroit) had also served as LCWR president. After her own installation, Theresa introduced the other members of the Mercy Administrative Team to the assembly saying: "When you take me, you take us all... I'm grateful both to the team and to my community for their commitment to LCWR and all that it means."[74] Just over a month later, Theresa Kane acted upon the power she had preached about in San Antonio and courageously asked the pope to open all the ministries in the church to women.

Awards, Father's Death, and More Media

During her 1979–80 term as LCWR president, Theresa and other LCWR executive leaders gave considerable energy to addressing the aftermath of her heartfelt appeal to Pope John Paul II at the Shrine of the Immaculate Conception in Washington. Her action elicited repercussions in the US church and in Rome.[75]

Over the next year, Theresa received numerous awards for shining a light on female inequality in the Catholic Church. In the early winter of 1980, she was named American Woman of the Year by the Saint Joan's International Alliance. Founded in 1911, the organization in 1963 became the first organization to call for the ordination of women to the priesthood.[76] Alongside luminaries such as Bella Abzug, Gloria Steinem, Rosa Parks, and Sonia Johnson, Theresa received a citation in January 1980 as a "Woman of Courage" from the Washington, DC, Women's Caucus for Art and the Coalition of Women's Art Organizations.[77]

In May 1980 *U.S. Catholic*, a monthly magazine published by the Claretian Fathers, presented her with its prestigious *U.S. Catholic* award "for furthering the cause of women in the Church." At the presentation ceremonies held in Chicago, editor and Claretian Father Mark Brummel told Theresa:

> You have revived a traditional and perhaps painful meaning of the word loyalty. Speaking difficult words in public and suffering the resulting wounds, has helped heal the wounds of those who suffered and continue to suffer in private... You focused worldwide attention on the crucial question of the rights of women, never letting that question be separated from the fundamental context of justice.[78]

In that same month, Siena Heights College in Adrian, Michigan, presented Theresa with its highest honor, the Siena Medal, during commencement exercises at the Dominican college. In a letter informing Theresa of the award, Dominican Sister Nadine Foley—who had been a coordinator of the first Women's Ordination Conference—wrote: "In this year when we celebrate the 600th anniversary of the death of Catherine of Siena, we saw the clear parallel between your courageous words to Pope John Paul II last October and Catherine's addressing Pope Gregory XI at Avignon in the 14th century." The unanimous board vote "is something of an achievement," Foley continued, noting that the two previous years the medal had been given to Piet Schoonenberg, SJ (the renowned Dutch theologian) and Dorothy Day.[79] The public proclamation said in part,

> We acclaim you, Sister Theresa Kane RSM. In times when the global village has become a reality, the geographical location of the seats of power and influence are often secondary to the psychological and sociological attitudes of those who occupy these privileged positions...Your moment of truth on October 7, 1979...continues to echo in the minds and hearts of many as...a claim upon the rights of women to stand as equals in the world's courts of influence.[80]

In the midst of this whirlwind year, two somber events impacted Theresa's life. In June 1979 Theresa's beloved father Phil became ill. Not long after celebrating fifty years of marriage to Mamie, his heart began to fail, affecting his memory. He was confused by the frequent replays of Theresa's papal greeting on October 7. Despite his grandson Tommy's patient explanations, he could not understand why "Margaret" was on television.

Phil died peacefully at home in December 1979. "We had a very beautiful funeral," Theresa recalls. In this close-knit Irish community, she still relishes the story about an altar boy who had told his mother: "Some important person must have died, because that church was filled. And there were bishops there." A good friend of the Mercy community, Archbishop John Maguire, and one other bishop from New York were in attendance.

In April 1980, Theresa attended the funeral of Mercy Sister Margaret Ann Pahl, who had been strangled and stabbed to death on Holy Saturday in the chapel at Mercy Hospital in Toledo, Ohio. On behalf of the entire Mercy Institute Theresa sought to console Sister Margaret Ann's grieving family, friends, and especially the Mercy sisters from the Cincinnati Province. She cited the scripture quotation that Sister Margaret Ann Pahl had used in her Easter card: "I ascend unto my Father and your Father; and to my God, and your God."[81] It would be two decades before a witness came forward and the priest chaplain who murdered her was brought to justice.[82]

Publicity surrounding Theresa's many awards soon led to another influx of press visitors to the Mercy National Office in Potomac, Maryland. In the early spring, Andre Truyman of Dutch Catholic Radio arrived to interview her for a documentary about American Catholic sisters. The *Washington Post*'s Marjorie Hyer wrote a lengthy feature story preserving for us a description of Theresa's office at the time: "An enormous banner with the legend 'My God I Trust You,' dominates the room," while a triptych of the Madonna and Child and a reproduction of Andrew Wyeth's painting, "Christina's World," adorns other walls. A stereo was tuned to "one of the good music stations" and on the bookshelves "books like *Roots* share space with more traditional Catholic works."[83]

Theresa told Hyer that she remained hopeful about a personal audience with the pope even though the US nuncio, Archbishop Jean Jadot, had told her that while the pope supported dialogue with US sisters, he preferred that it occur "through the proper channels" via SCRIS. But LCWR would persist, Theresa told Hyer, because, "It is important that [the Polish Pope] have an understanding of religious life, not just in one culture. The US experience of renewal in religious life is different from that in other countries."[84]

Commenting on an "exodus of American nuns from the church," Theresa admitted, "If they have experienced that kind of pain, I shouldn't say it [leaving the church] couldn't happen to me." But she doubted it ever would: "The life of faith is very, very real to me—life with God...and that can be done in the Roman Catholic Church, though the Catholic Church is not God."[85]

Paul Wilkes, on assignment from the magazine section of the *New York Times*, stayed at the generalate for three weeks to interview Theresa for a wide-ranging piece that would be published the following November. When asked if she would seek ordination herself, Wilkes describes Theresa's tentative reply: "The strong-willed, determined administrator general of the Sisters of Mercy of the Union looks down at her hands. 'I . . . I,' she hesitates, the contemplation of the priestly office bringing out a shyness and an awe she did not display before a Pope. 'I think I do want to be ordained,' she says tentatively. Then, looking up more firmly, 'I'd sure like to give it a try.'"[86]

Theresa (right) meets in 1976 with members of the General Advisory Council on which she sat by virtue of her service as provincial in New York. She would be elected administrator general the following year.

Theresa (right) with her lifelong friend Sister Della Mae Quinn in 1980.

The 1981 Administrative Team (from left): Rosemary Ronk, Betty Barrett, Theresa Kane, Emily George, and Mary Ellen Quinn.

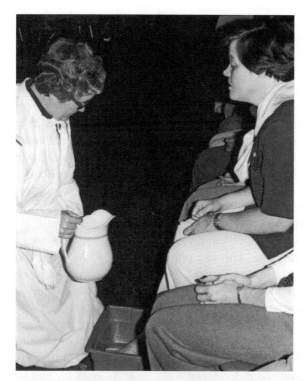

Theresa washes her sisters' feet dueing the Holy Thursday ritual after her election as administrator general in 1977.

Screen shot of the video recording of Theresa shaking hands with Pope John Paul II after greeting him on October 7, 1979.

RE-ELECTION TO ADMINISTRATOR GENERAL:
ELEVENTH GENERAL CHAPTER

After the Shrine greeting, Theresa and the rest of the Mercy Administrative Team felt it wise for her to meet personally with as many sisters as possible: "If sisters had any questions or concerns or criticism or reservations about what I had said to the pope, I wanted them to come and talk to me about it." In subsequent months, she would visit all nine provinces, giving special attention to arranging meetings with the order's senior sisters in nursing homes and retirement communities. Other sisters in any given area were also invited to come if they wished. From Theresa's perspective the meetings "went very, very well" although some sisters were quite "cautious" and asked why she could not have broached the issue with the pope privately. Others felt the "women's issue" was not suitable for the Mercy community because in these sisters' minds, feminism was always related to abortion. One sister even asked, "Well, what does sex have to do with religious life?"

Theresa remembers remaining "very calm," and "never defensive" in her interactions. She hoped to educate the older sisters about sexism, noting that "it was all new to them." It helped to remind them that the founding mission of Catherine McAuley was "to serve women, and to be present to and with women and girls." She described LCWR's fruitless efforts to meet privately with the pope before his US visit, but also candidly acknowledged, "I think I probably still would have said what I did even if we had met the pope separately, because while I was greeting him on behalf of women religious, this issue affects all women, not only sisters." Even though some sisters remained unconvinced, her efforts to reach out proved effective. Sister Laetice Williams, a delegate from the Omaha Province to the 1980 General Chapter, told that body, "When we were informed on Theresa's statement at the Shrine, the attitude changed tremendously."[87]

Before the Mercy sisters gathered to elect new leadership at the Eleventh General Chapter (March 27–29, 1980), the nominating committee published biographical information about twelve candidates from eight provinces in *Union Scope*, the newsletter of the Sisters of Mercy of the Union. Each individual was asked to share her perception of the priorities and challenges for the Sisters of Mercy in the 1980s as well as her own gifts for leadership.

A diversity of perspectives was in evidence.[88] A few more traditional candidates prioritized "putting our own house in order" by following the exhortations of Pope John Paul II about vows, religious garb, and obedience. Two candidates focused on enhancing the status

quo by prioritizing current corporate ministries and a "renewed commitment of [congregational] leadership" to individual sisters in their
ministries and to the corporate ministries. The remaining candidates
strongly prioritized justice issues, new ministries "to alleviate human
misery," and systemic change in both church and society. This last
group (Theresa among them) specifically named ongoing conversation and dialogue with the institutional church about full inclusion of
women.

As the March 1980 chapter unfolded, no one who had espoused a
more traditional mindset would be elected to leadership. Yet chapter
delegates raised many questions about the exercise of leadership:
"When does the Administrative Team speak for the Sisters of Mercy,
when for itself? Are the forums used for public statements appropriate?
Can involvement in justice issues be anything but controversial...?"[89]
The Church/Institute Committee's report detailing its work on the
issue of tubal ligation in Mercy-sponsored institutions, support for
civil rights for LGBT persons, criteria for public dissent from church
teaching, and support for women in ministry sparked significant dialogue, as did Theresa's greeting to the pope.

On Saturday, May 29, the Eleventh General Chapter "found its
center," as delegates gave two hours to "deep yet peaceful discussion"
about issues on which they did not agree. *Union Scope* would later
characterize the sisters' dialogue with the headline: "We must 'speak
the truth in love...,'" perhaps taking the phrase from Theresa's
LCWR presidential installation address.

In a wide-ranging discussion, delegates aired their perceptions,
their fears, and their dreams. Sister Ann Nelson from Providence
found a need to "distinguish between a prophet and a leader...When
I see the Administrative Team signed a statement, I feel you've committed me without asking me." Sister Emily George of Detroit responded, "Whatever generalate-level leaders do is going to bring
displeasure to some in the institute. If we go with your position, Ann,
it means generalate leadership could say virtually nothing." Ann
replied that while she did "not want to confine the Administrative
Team," she was also "a little anxious that we're not bringing our sisters with us."

Sister Pat Wolf of the New York Province was more concerned
with "what happens when leadership doesn't speak. Silence says vol-
umes. I would hope we would speak eloquently against the [military
draft]...We follow the Lord. We may not be popular if we speak the
truth of the Gospel."

There was considerable back and forth about the canonical (church
law) risks entailed by dissent within the institutional church. "I think

dissent in loyalty is always a service...If the Church/Institute Commit-tee really furthers our understanding of the human person, then the challenge to this body is to develop a process to disseminate the truth—even if unpopular," said Sister Christopher O'Rourke of Providence.

After two hours, Sister Roch Rocklage of St. Louis stood up and told the outgoing 1977–80 Administrative Team: "I think the Lord has given you the gift of prophecy, and I want to acknowledge you as a team for what you have done." Her words electrified the delegates, who rose as one and with prolonged applause, thanked Theresa, Doris Gottemoeller, Betty Barrett, and Juliane Carey for their three years of leadership on the Administrative Team.[90] As the morning drew to a close, chairperson Sister Cecilia Meighan (Dallas) praised the chapter delegates: "You are to be commended for your listening presence. The expressions on your faces, the profound silence that surrounded the discussion said much." On the same day delegates suspended usual de-liberations to attend a memorial Mass for Archbishop (and now Saint) Oscar Romero, who had been assassinated four days earlier. One won-ders to what extent this beloved advocate for the poor had inspired the day's discussion about prophecy and leadership.

The next day, Theresa was overwhelmingly re-elected to a four-year term as administrator general, receiving 56 of 68 votes on the first ballot.[91] In accepting her re-election she spoke about her own un-derstanding of religious leadership:

> We talked about leadership and prophecy and whether they are compatible. It is my conviction that prophecy is indeed an essential part of leadership...I will commit to these four years a spirit of compassion, but a spirit that is critical; a spirit of strength and gentleness; a spirit of reverence and rad-icality. I will continue to speak, to speak the truth as I see it, as I believe it in my heart.[92]

Omaha provincial administrator, Sister Norita Cooney—who had been a delegate at both the 1977 and 1980 chapters—would later tell her sisters: "One factor that strongly influenced the nomination and selection of Theresa as leader of the community was the belief on the part of chapter delegates that she was the person who could best implement the Statement of Direction developed by the Chapter body."[93] St. Joseph Sister Margaret Culbert, the associate vicar for re-ligious in the Washington archdiocese, told chapter delegates, "When I see a group as large as yours affirming Theresa's leadership and tak-ing stands on social issues, I find it very good for the image of women ...and very positive for the future."[94] Msgr. John L. Bailey, who was present as the official representative of the Archdiocese of Washington, characterized the election as "an overwhelming vote of confidence in your leadership."[95]

The election of remaining members of the new Administrative Team revealed the delegates' strong affirmation for continuing the priorities of the 1977 chapter. Using successive ballots for each position, "each team member was elected by an absolute majority on the first or second ballot."[96] Sister Emily George from Detroit was elected assistant administrator general. Sisters Mary Ellen Quinn (Omaha), Betty Barrett (Chicago) and Rosemary Ronk (Omaha) were also elected to the Administrative Team.

In her *Union Scope* write-up prior to the election, returning team member Sister Betty Barrett—who had lived in a poor neighborhood in Chicago for many years—commented: "The challenge of the 80's will be one of justice, not only to stand with the poor but to act for the transformation of the world...Mercy's option for the poor will then be obvious...Mercy will be justice." Betty, the only holdover from the previous team, would continue as liaison to the Finance Committee and oversee decisions about the distribution of funds realized from the sale of the generalate.

Newly elected assistant administrator general Sister Emily George was the current provincial administrator in Detroit. Previously she had served as president of Mercy College in Detroit. The author of three books, Emily had prioritized the alleviation of human misery, continuing a dialogic exchange with the hierarchy and fostering a "high level of unity among Congregations of Mercy," in her *Union Scope* write-up. Emily was liaison to the prophetic Church/Institute Committee (on which she already served), the communications department, and the Core Constitutions Committee with the Mercy Federation.

Before her election, Sister Mary Ellen Quinn had served as provincial administrator of the Omaha Province. She was also the national president of the Federation of the Sisters of Mercy and had served as the academic dean and vice-president of the College of St. Mary. She prioritized "proclaiming truth in and to our world, in and to our church, in and to our congregation," saying, "We must lovingly refuse to retreat from the challenges of newness and the challenges of the decade." Mary Ellen would be the liaison with Vocation/Formation entities, the Government Committee, the Prison Ministry Committee, and the Stewardship Advisory Committee charged with allocation of funds from the sale of the generalate to groups advocating for the poor.

Sister Rosemary Ronk was nominated from the floor on Saturday. Before being elected she had served as administrator of the

Mercy Fontenelle Center, a multiservice intercommunity center for the aging and for adult religious education. Previously she had been engaged in social work administration and had experience ministering to clients of all ages.[97] Rosemary was liaison to an array of Mercy groups working for systemic change and providing direct service to women, the poor, and the homeless.

Early in her second term, Theresa, with the affirmation of the rest of the Administrative Team, changed her title from administrator general to president of the Sisters of Mercy of the Union. She felt the change was appropriate in light of the sale of the generalate and the move to new offices in Silver Spring, Maryland. Over the next four years, Theresa and the new Administrative Team, would lead the Mercy community though perilous challenges to their newfound identity. Some challenges came from within, while others came from the institutional church.

Prior to her re-election, Theresa herself had submitted an insightful list of challenges and priorities to *Union Scope*. She believed that in the 1980s the Sisters of Mercy were being called to continue struggling with the call for justice in church and society and the search for ways to be in solidarity with the poor. She noted that sisters are challenged to learn from one another about "what the call to justice and solidarity means" and "to reverence, appreciate and desire diversity" in the community and in the church. At the same time, she pointed to the need to integrate spirituality and justice in the ongoing development of apostolic religious life after Vatican II.[98] Theresa then provided a rather remarkable listing of her own gifts for leadership.

> I am excited and eager to be identified with women who have a similar vision. I have a deep sense of renewed identity as a woman religious. I have a great sense of confidence in myself, in my community, and in God. I do not experience fear or apprehension about the future, yet I also approach it realistically, recognizing both the strengths and weaknesses in myself and in others. I enjoy life immensely and a spirit of peace and joy are gifts from God to me.[99]

Those who worked with Theresa during these years would readily affirm the gifts she recognized in herself. Very few sisters, however—whether through shyness or false humility—would willingly acknowledge their own gifts publicly as she had. Such was (and is) Theresa's straightforward simplicity, which leads her always to answer a question truthfully as she sees the truth, regardless of conventional ideas about propriety. She would need every one of her considerable gifts—both of nature and of grace—to meet the challenges ahead.

To Speak the Truth in Love

Five months later, at the August 1980 annual assembly of LCWR in Philadelphia, 640 sister-leaders from 361 US congregations strongly affirmed their outgoing president, Theresa Kane, with a standing ovation upon completion of her presidency. After finishing her one-year term, Theresa became past president in her third year as part of the governance triad.

The conference theme was "Once Upon a Conviction." Theresa's address "To Speak the Truth in Love"[100] was undoubtedly influenced by the Mercy General Chapter that had re-elected her the previous March and her hard-won experience as LCWR president in the past year. The title of Theresa's address is from the Letter to the Ephesians chapter 4, which exhorts the Christian community to maintain unity while respecting the diversity of gifts within Christ's body: "Some would be apostles, some prophets, some pastors and teachers...[but all gifts] equip the saints for the work of ministry...Speaking the truth in love, we must grow up in every way into Christ."

After exhorting her LCWR sisters to create a "dialogic atmosphere" over the weekend, Theresa decried the fact that over the past year some members of the hierarchy had told her, "There are issues in the church that are not open to dialogue." But such a statement, she said firmly, "causes paralysis and fear and needs to be challenged whenever it is heard."[101] She delineated four aspects of "speaking the truth in love": (1) to oneself, (2) to one another, (3) to the institutional church, and (4) to society.

For women, speaking truth to oneself involves listening "to the stirrings which are welling within them." Referencing feminist theology and spirituality, the outgoing LCWR president said, "For all too long women have followed laws and directions which have been truly 'man-made.'" To fulfill a "serious responsibility to articulate a feminist theology of religious life," sisters must be in contact with "their own feelings, experiences and reflections." One result will be a "revolutionary approach to God," no longer imaged only in male metaphor: "Such a distorted image of God must be challenged if a feminist spirituality of God is to develop among both women and men."

For Theresa, "speaking truth to each other" was already well under way in light of the revolutionary conversations religious communities had conducted among themselves both before and after

Vatican II. These had led to a profound renewal of religious dress, governance, lifestyles, and ministries. In her words to LCWR she called for "an ongoing dialogic posture" with the Vatican wherein "the SCRIS structure would reflect a new relationship of maturity, mutuality, and equality with the religious communities."

The 1971 Synod of Bishops teaching "Justice in the World" is the source of "our responsibility and obligation to speak the truth in love to our Church." That synod taught that "anyone who ventures to speak to people about justice must first be just in their eyes,"[102] therefore the institutional church "must recognize and acknowledge the serious social injustice which by its very system is imposed upon women."

Further, she sees the exclusion of women as "a root evil and a social sin" not only in the church but also in society. Therefore, women must "confront and eradicate the systemic evils of sexism, clericalism and paternalism" in both church and society. But in addressing systemic evils, Theresa cautioned, "it is essential to distinguish persons from systems." The challenge is to "retain a compassionate stance toward the persons who may be involved either consciously or unconsciously in perpetuating the sinfulness."

Theresa's outgoing address skillfully identified the systemic oppression of women in church and society and called on Catholic sisters to compassionately, but firmly, confront systemic injustice wherever it exists. She had herself experienced the costs of confrontation. Not only had she been vilified as "Judas Iscariot" and had her greeting distorted as a "harangue" that "defied the Pope," but her office had received so many vicious telephone calls that the sisters had to change the number. Protesters arrived and stayed for hours at a time in front of the generalate. Once a male caller threatened to "come over there with my shotgun... if I see her that's the end of her."

Theresa admits to being "scared to death," and police began regular surveillance of the generalate for the next several months. Fortunately, in 1978 Theresa and Della Mae moved to a nearby rented apartment where both felt relatively safe from unwanted visitors. While Theresa's Shrine greeting had brought more praise than blame, it nevertheless attracted a great deal of negative attention. In the aftermath of papal truth-telling she had ample opportunity to exercise the compassion to which she aspired. As difficult as these challenges were, Theresa's practice of speaking truth with love would be even more severely tested in the days to come.

CHAPTER SEVEN

The Perils of Prophetic Leadership

As Theresa began her second stint as administrator general, her term as president of LCWR was ending. When she delivered her outgoing presidential address, "To Speak the Truth in Love," she had already experienced both the challenges and the consequences of speaking truth. Aside from dealing with angry protesters, she had been dealing with angry prelates. As administrator general, Theresa was the team member required by church law to address all issues involving the church hierarchy—and the hierarchy was not happy with certain issues involving the Sisters of Mercy. Foremost among these was the sisters' study of tubal ligation in Mercy hospitals.

A Pastoral Approach to Elective Tubal Ligation

The Church/Institute Committee established at the 1977 Tenth General Chapter was meant to help implement that body's seminal *Our Relationship within the Church* statement. The committee functioned as "a research arm and sounding board" to advise Theresa and the rest of the Mercy Administrative Team on matters affecting the community's relationship to the institutional church. The committee was composed of sisters who had doctorates in theology (Margaret Farley and Doris Gottemoeller) as well as sisters with advanced degrees and significant experience and skill in education, health care, and administration (Sisters Concilia Moran and Emily George). Sisters outside the Mercy Institute, such as Immaculate Heart of Mary Sister Margaret Brennan and Pittsburgh Mercy Sister Betty Carroll, offered their specialized experience and expertise.

During Theresa's two terms in office the Church/Institute Committee researched and wrote background papers on numerous subjects, providing the Mercy Administrative Team with comprehensive theological, sociological, and canonical information as they sought to implement the 1977 chapter's far-seeing directives. The following list of subjects and activities by year provides a window into the visionary nature of the committee's explorations:

1. "Tubal Ligation in Hospitals Sponsored by the Sisters of Mercy of the Union" (January 1980): a study of the pastoral implications of the NCCB ethical directives on sterilization of women

2. "Women in Conversation" (1983): discussion guides and focused gatherings with Catholic women's organizations addressing women's issues

3. "Elective Office for Religious" (January 1983): a statement responding to a SCRIS inquiry and the political candidacy of a Sister of Mercy of the Union (presented at the April 1983 session of the Eleventh General Chapter)

4. "Canonical Regulation of Women's Religious Communities: Its Past and Its Future" (March 1983): presented to the Eleventh General Chapter which also authorized the Mercy Administrative Team and committee to edit, develop, and distribute the paper as background information surrounding considerations regarding the canonical status of the Sisters of Mercy of the Union.[1]

When the Church/Institute Committee began its work, Sisters of Mercy were delivering health services in fifty-seven dioceses in thirty-one states, with more than twenty-eight thousand beds in acute, long-term, and psychiatric facilities. The Sisters of Mercy Health Corporation sponsored by the Detroit Province was the "largest non-profit multi-hospital system in the United States with facilities in Michigan, Iowa and Indiana."[2] In 1980, the Mercy Health Conference (MHC) was formed to better share across the institute "expertise and abilities" in health care. For the sisters, "an integral part of Mercy leadership is to "act as advocate for people whom the [health] system puts at a disadvantage."[3]

At its first meeting, the committee carefully considered each of the topics the 1977 chapter had suggested for research. A number of considerations influenced their recommendation to the Administrative Team that the first priority should be a study of tubal ligations in Mercy hospitals. For one thing, the sisters had considerable experience with ministries involving this issue in health care, social services, and education. Because of their many hospitals, the sisters had ample op-

portunity to observe the pastoral difficulties involved with implementing the 1971 US bishops' church policy, which had forbidden tubal ligation if the main reason for the procedure was to prevent pregnancy.[4]

The bishops' directives had a long and unsettled history. After a
1973 survey of American dioceses revealed widely diverse practices in
Catholic hospitals,[5] the US bishops referred the issue to Rome. In
1975 Rome replied, forbidding direct sterilization even in light of severe health risks, including death, to the mother. In January 1978 the
administrative board of the United States Catholic Conference published a commentary to "assist the local ordinaries [bishops] and
Catholic health care personnel in the formulation of a corporate position regarding the performance of sterilization procedures."[6] The
bishops' commentary reiterated principles in the Vatican document in
which contraceptive sterilization is always wrong, a grave evil, and
may not be used to prevent physical or mental illness resulting from
pregnancy. Moral theologian Richard A. McCormick, SJ, summarized
the difficulty with this hardline position:

> But where does that leave Catholic hospitals? In a genuine
> dilemma. On the one hand, the official teaching continues to
> state that sterilization for contraceptive purposes is *always*
> (inherently) wrong. On the other, this formulation is not ac-
> cepted by a large segment of the theological community, and
> a significant number of the episcopal community.[7]

McCormick cited a passage by moral theologian Bernard Häring
as one with which many—if not most—Catholic theologians agreed:

> Whenever the direct preoccupation is responsible care for the
> health of persons or for saving a marriage (which also affects
> the total health of all persons involved), sterilization can then
> receive its justification from valid medical reasons. If, therefore,
> a competent physician can determine, in full agreement with
> this patient, that in this particular situation a new pregnancy
> must be excluded now and forever because it would be thor-
> oughly irresponsible, and if from a medical point of view steril-
> ization is the best possible solution, it cannot be against the
> principle of medical ethics, nor is it against the "natural law"
> (*recta ratio*).[8]

McCormick further noted that in 1973, G. Emmett Carter—then
bishop of London, Ontario—had concluded that sufficient theological
support existed to allow direct sterilization under specific conditions.[9]

Further, "quite a few" US bishops had told McCormick privately that they had reached the same conclusion as Carter.[10] A contemporaneous study by two Princeton researchers, Charles F. Westoff and Elise F. Jones, found that 76.4 percent of Catholics they surveyed were using some form of contraceptive compared to 79.9 percent of non-Catholics.[11] Further, 9.8 percent of Catholic women had chosen tubal ligation compared with 13.9 percent of non-Catholic women.

McCormick was careful to say, however, that permitting necessary sterilization "is not a rejection of the Church's substantial concern" about the procedure: "There is the fact that in a technologically oriented and comfort-conditioned culture many will seek sterilization where it is objectively unjustified." Further, the danger of abuse is not insubstantial. Flouting Federal regulations, over eleven thousand Medicaid patients were sterilized in Maryland, Virginia, and the District of Columbia, between 1975 and 1980.[12] "Reasons such as these," McCormick concluded, "lead me to believe that a Catholic hospital is justified in limiting its toleration to serious medical indications. It is only the absolutism of the present moral teaching and subsequent policy that is cause for concern."[13]

It is unsurprising then, that Church/Institute Committee members saw tubal ligation as "an appropriate starting point" for raising issues and engaging church leadership in developing church teaching on a topic of considerable importance to women and families. From the committee's perspective, tubal ligation was a pastoral issue insofar as it was "a medical problem, an ethical issue, and a women's question."[14]

In February 1978, the Administrative Team and provincial administrators approved the topic for research. The wider Mercy community was regularly informed of the committee's activities through Union Scope. The Mercy administration "attempted to handle communications sensitively and prudently... [but] there was no attempt to withhold knowledge of the study from the community."[15] As will be seen, this transparency, while laudable, had its drawbacks.

In early 1978 the Mercy tubal ligation study began by "reviewing the teachings of the institutional church and interpretations offered by a broad spectrum of moral theologians."[16] Simultaneously, a practical study of Union Mercy[17] hospitals was launched to "give factual information of how the official teachings of the church were implemented within a pastoral framework, thus combining knowledge of theory with practice."

The outcomes were highly informative.[18] The study found that the ethical directives of US bishops were interpreted differently in different dioceses. The directives were implemented "through various committees and decision-making processes dealing with medical-moral issues both with the dioceses and within the hospitals themselves."[19] At the time, the sixty-seven hospitals in the Union Mercy system were located in forty dioceses in twenty-four states.[20] Of the sixty-seven hospitals, sixty-five agreed to participate in the tubal ligation study. In these facilities, 202 persons were interviewed, including 70 administrators, 46 medical doctors (heads of departments), 40 nurses (usually the supervisor of surgery or obstetrics-gynecology), 31 persons in pastoral care, and 15 others (theological consultants, laboratory technicians, and medical records personnel).

When the data was analyzed, the study found that forty hospitals did not perform tubal ligations while twenty-five hospitals did. Of these twenty-five, just five performed more than twenty procedures per year. Of the forty hospitals that did not perform tubal ligations, twelve had no ob/gyn services. Thus, nearly half (47 percent) of all Union Mercy hospitals with ob/gyn facilities provided limited access to tubal ligation when pathological medical conditions or other serious obstetrical indications warranted. Pathological medical conditions included such things as severe hypertension, heart disease, kidney disease, diabetes, and thrombophlebitis, which often led to life-threatening blood clots. Obstetrical indications listed included severe recurrent hypertensive disorders of pregnancy, repeat caesarian sections with risk of uterine rupture, severe Rh sensitization of the mother, and various chromosomal or genetic diseases with significant risk of major fetal anomalies. Specific case situations put a human face on these medical conditions:

Mrs. A—28 years old with four children; suffers from thrombophlebitis, which has been complicated by a pulmonary embolism.

Mrs. B—39 years old with eight living children; has had two spontaneous miscarriages; suffers from rheumatic heart disease with mitral stenosis. Further pregnancies would accelerate her medical condition.

Mrs. F—42 years old, with three children; suffered for many years with severe bronchiectasis [permanent inflammation of bronchial tubes] with increasing difficulty each succeeding pregnancy; continual progression of pulmonary illness.[21]

The twenty-five hospitals that were performing medically indicated tubal ligations were doing so with either tacit or explicit approval from their local bishops. A survey of Catholic hospitals published on February 15, 1979, in the *American Journal of Obstetrics and Gynecology* found that 20 percent (66 of 336 responding) permitted medical sterilizations. This issue affected Catholic hospitals in dioceses across the United States.[22]

In March 1979, after a painstaking review of church teaching, developments in moral theology, and the clinical realities unfolding in Mercy hospitals, the Church/Institute Committee submitted a first draft of the study and recommendations to the Mercy Administrative Team for discussion purposes. In addition to reviewing positions from prominent theologians, the committee was at pains to note the importance of conscience in moral decision-making. Those who argue that a Catholic hospital is bound to reflect in its policies the moral teaching of the institutional church about tubal ligation "fail to acknowledge that the principle of freedom of conscience is also part of the moral teaching of the institutional Church and as such deserves to be reflected in the policies and practices of Catholic institutions."[23]

After a joint conference with some committee members and members of the Administrative Team, the tubal ligation study was completed. It was sent to the administration "with the recommendation that since the data suggested that grave circumstances warranted tubal ligation as an appropriate medical and pastoral procedure, Mercy hospitals should provide this service." The Church/Institute Committee further requested that the Mercy administration recommend this as a policy to Union hospitals.[24] Since the study revealed that "great disparity of interpretation—and consequently application—regarding tubal ligation existed across the many dioceses where Mercy hospitals [indeed all Catholic hospitals] served," the administration felt it necessary to adopt its own position before further communicating with provincial and hospital administrators.

"After seriously weighing the pros and cons," the Administrative Team wrote a tentative position statement in May of 1979. The hope was to promote dialogue within the church, thereby catalyzing a "review of official teaching on tubal ligation where the inconsistencies of interpretation and the suffering of persons could be documented."[25] Church policy could then be re-examined with a view to changing it. After further consultation and critique, the Administrative Team finalized its position in September 1979 (see Appendix D).

Since the foundational principle of a Mercy hospital is "a reverence for the sacredness and dignity of human life," the statement emphasized that "its policies should include the promotion of holistic health care and exclude whatever may cause harm to persons." It concluded:

We believe that tubal ligation, in certain circumstances is an appropriate procedure and a necessary component of holistic health care and that failure to provide this service in these circumstances may cause harm to persons. In these cases, a Mercy hospital should provide this procedure. Since our investigation shows that Church teaching in this area is not uniformly interpreted or applied and that tubal ligation is not an available option in all Mercy hospitals, we desire to draw concerned persons into dialogue about the necessity of doctrinal development of the issue and appropriate modification of hospital policies.[26]

Theresa and all involved were now ready to promote dialogue more broadly. They were "well aware that the adopted position did not reflect the church's official teaching" but also "serene that this had been done not for purposes of being at odds with the institutional church but rather to promote and advance dialogue on a critical pastoral issue"—one that affected women in particular.[27]

In the fall of 1979, the Mercy Administrative Team shared the revised study and team position with provincial administrators, one of whom encouraged sharing it with the hospital administrators who had participated in the original research. The group planned to then share it with the sisters-at-large and with US bishops.

Unfortunately, this plan was derailed when information about the confidential internal study and position statement was leaked to conservative Catholics outside the Mercy community. In October 1979, Cleveland Bishop James Hickey—then chair of the NCCB Committee on Doctrine—wrote to Theresa and requested the study results. Hickey later acknowledged that someone within the church had brought the tubal ligation study to the attention of his office. Theresa wrote back saying she could not release the study because it had yet to be shared within the Mercy community. She assertively asked for a copy of any studies the NCCB was conducting.

There were none. In November 1979, a professor from Dunwoodie seminary in New York, Father William B. Smith, published an article in the *National Catholic Register* comparing Sister Theresa Kane unfavorably to Mother Teresa of Calcutta, who had just won the Nobel Prize. He accused Theresa of seeking a "personal platform of concerned protest" in her papal greeting and likened her action to "grandstanding from the pinnacle...of a very high mountain which, of course, was an offer the Lord Himself could and did certainly refuse."[28] He criticized the confidential first draft of the Mercy position paper, which had included a sentence calling for "change in hospital policies and church teaching" rather than the final statement's request for "doctrinal development" in the matter of tubal ligation. In any case, the tubal ligation study was no longer confidential.

Theresa believes a Mercy sister who was a hospital administrator in the New York Province forwarded materials to Father Smith. Other Mercy leaders report that a hospital administrator (and Mercy sister) in the Cincinnati Province had admitted to qualms of conscience and reported the proceedings to episcopal authorities.[29] It could easily have been both of them, and perhaps several others. A vocal minority of Mercy sisters did not agree with their community's directions. Over the course of Theresa's term, a few sisters anonymously sent to church authorities media articles about her, including internal communications to all sisters, with disparaging comments written in the margins.[30]

In January 1980, Theresa met with the executive secretary of the NCCB, Bishop Tom Kelly, who told her that the tubal ligation study had been sent to the Congregation of the Doctrine of the Faith (CDF). The CDF instructed the apostolic delegate (the soon-to-be-transferred Archbishop Jean Jadot) to investigate further. Insofar as hospitals were involved, Jadot punted the CDF request to the NCCB to investigate. For the next three years, Theresa, Emily George, Mary Ellen Quinn, Rosemary Ronk, and Betty Barrett, along with Margaret Farley and selected provincial administrators such as Helen Marie Burns and Roch Rocklage, would engage in excruciating, hair-splitting meetings with US bishops and the Vatican, valiantly searching for a space for conscience—and a conscientious policy—on behalf of women and families. Their persistent and courageous efforts were doomed to fail.

In February 1980 the tubal ligation study was discussed by the Mercy General Administrative Conference, a wider consultative body that included the nine provincial administrators and the Mercy Administrative Team. While concerned about the study's implications for their congregation, the General Administrative Conference endorsed the administration's position of seeking dialogue within the church and the Mercy community—even in light of looming difficulties. It also asked the administration to be in conversation with the Mercy Health Conference, which represented health professionals from each province. In May of that year the Mercy Health Conference would also endorse the administration's position, which was to seek dialogue on tubal ligation.

Since the tubal ligation study had been addressed as part of the administration's accountability report to the Eleventh General Chapter, and the 1977 statement *Our Relationship within the Church* had been "strongly reaffirmed," the new Administrative Team had "a mandate to continue the directions set by the 1977 chapter."[31] It is evident that Theresa and the team received substantial support from the Mercy community for continuing the dialogue about medical sterilization with church officials despite episcopal resistance.

That resistance became apparent on April 29, 1980, when Theresa, Emily, and members of the Church/Institute Committee met in Chicago with a "select delegation of bishops" during the spring NCCB meeting. The bishops "clearly indicated that the issue of tubal ligation was closed and discouraged further work on it."[32] At the May executive session the NCCB reaffirmed its position on sterilization. This was later endorsed "overwhelmingly by a written vote of all the bishops," and was covered by the media.

Nevertheless, some bishops quietly allowed pastoral latitude in actual practice. Such seems to have been the case with the twenty-five Mercy hospitals (and at least forty-one additional Catholic hospitals) in which permission was given for a pastoral interpretation of church policy.

BUT NEVERTHELESS, THEY PERSISTED

In June 1980 Doris Gottemoeller confidentially updated the Mercy Health Conference about the discouraging April 29 meeting with representatives of the NCCB. In July 1980 the new Administrative Team reviewed developments related to the tubal ligation study and, after more consultation, further nuanced what would become their final position statement. The preamble of the earlier statement had extended the "principle of totality"[33] to include psychological, spiritual, and relational aspects of a person. Since the US bishops' directives had followed Pope Paul VI's explicit rejection of the use of the principle of totality in direct sterilization in *Humanae Vitae*, the revised October 1980 Mercy statement did not directly mention it. The word "harm" was deleted and "unjust injury" put in its place. The significant section of the amended version now read:

> We believe that tubal ligation, in certain circumstances, is an appropriate procedure and a necessary component of wholistic health care and that failure to provide this service in these circumstances may cause unjust injury to persons.
>
> Since our investigation shows that Church teaching in this area is not uniformly interpreted or applied and that tubal ligation is not an available option in all Mercy hospitals, we desire to draw concerned persons into dialogue about

the necessity of doctrinal development of the issue and appropriate modification of hospital policies.[34]

In August, Theresa gave her outgoing "To Speak the Truth in Love" LCWR address that decried episcopal refusal to dialogue and began her one-year term as past president of that organization.

At its fall meeting the Mercy General Administrative Conference affirmed the final tubal ligation position statement. It also discussed the administration's proposal to provide seminars educating Catholic women about pastoral and medical considerations in relationship to tubal ligations. Some provincials expressed concern about the possible effects these seminars might have on relationships with bishops in their respective dioceses.

The November issue of *Union Scope* updated the community at large about the outcomes of the tubal ligation study, the Church/ Institute Committee's recommendations and noted the Administrative Team's desire to continue dialogue with church hierarchy. It also said explicitly that the committee's conclusions, as well as the statement of the Mercy leadership on this issue, "place the Administrative Team in tension with the stance of the institutional church on this serious concern to women."[35]

In November 1980 a confidential letter was sent to all Mercy hospital administrators who had participated in the tubal ligation research to inform them of study outcomes, conclusions, and the stance of the Administrative Team. Co-signed by Emily George for the Church/ Institute Committee and Theresa for the Administrative Team, the communication did not contain specific proposals for hospital policy but emphasized the team's "intent of dialogue" which had already begun with the NCCB and various Mercy entities. The letter also stated that the committee "plans to offer within the year a seminar for the exploration of the theological, pastoral, medical, and institutional implications of providing or not providing for tubal ligations in our hospitals."[36]

An "anonymous source" sent the confidential November 12 letter to the president of the NCCB, Archbishop John Roach, who wrote to Theresa expressing his dismay and asked for the immediate withdrawal of the letter. Roach also sent his own letter to US bishops with Union Mercy hospitals in their dioceses and mistakenly implied that the Administrative Team had recommended that tubal ligations be performed in Mercy hospitals. In fact, the team had made no policy recommendation, which in any case would have been highly inappropriate, since each hospital had its own board of trustees and was accountable to the local ordinary. Theresa and Emily had simply informed involved hospital administrators of the status of the tubal ligation study and their intent to dialogue about it further with appropriate parties. But from the perspective of US church leaders, no dialogue was possible in light of recent statements from the Vatican and US bishops.

Roach asked the bishops to investigate whether or not tubal ligations were being performed in their dioceses, indicating that the April 29 meeting had been held "at the request of the Holy See." The involvement of the Vatican in the issue had never been shared with Theresa and the other sister-leaders. It sheds light on the urgency of Roach's action. He requested an immediate meeting with Theresa. On December 16, Theresa and Emily George met with Archbishop Roach; Bishop James Malone of Youngstown, who was NCCB vice-president; and NCCB general secretary Bishop Tom Kelly, who recorded the minutes.[37]

Theresa said that the sisters did not wish to be alienated from the church but saw the issue as one of serious pastoral concern. Roach observed that the issue was deeply "flavored" by the "woman's question." At one point, the archbishop said he did not have a problem with using the Church/Institute Committee's report as a basis for dialogue, but he saw the Administrative Team's endorsement as being at variance with Rome. Theresa asked if there was any possibility that Rome at a future date would address the matter of tubal ligation. Archbishop Roach replied that any issue that is genuinely pastoral is an appropriate agenda item for Rome, but Bishop Malone said this did not mean that the US bishops' conference would pursue this particular issue. After a sometimes heated and ambiguous discussion, the bishops agreed to set up a national committee to examine the issue. In closing, Bishop Kelly carefully noted that "the bishops established an environment at once cordial and non-paternal," although he said the meeting notes would be sent to Rome "because Rome was very interested in the matter."[38]

Mercy administrative leaders created a proposal to establish an interdisciplinary national committee. Archbishop Roach, however, preferred a smaller committee composed of selected bishops and Mercy leadership, including provincial administrators who had oversight of Mercy hospitals. From the beginning Archbishop Roach was clear that the meetings "should focus on ways to bring about acceptance of the traditional position of the Church...We could not enter into such a discussion unless it is clear to all participants that the Church's explicit teaching is not subject to change and that it is to be observed by Catholic hospitals."[39]

In January 1981, Bishop Kelly called Theresa to request a list of all Mercy hospitals that were performing tubal ligations. After reflection, it was the unanimous judgment of the Administrative Team that "this information was received in a confidential manner and should not be shared with anyone."[40] In March the Administrative Team appointed provincial administrators Helen Marie Burns (Detroit), Norita Cooney (Omaha), and Roch Rocklage (St. Louis) to join Theresa, Emily George, and Mary Ellen Quinn in serving on the new national committee. All of the provincial administrators had hospitals within their jurisdictions. It was also decided to postpone the proposed educational seminars for Catholic women. From March until the summer, the Administrative Team waited to hear how the bishops proposed to dialogue and which bishops would be on the national committee.

Rome Threatens to Oust Theresa from Leadership

In early 1981, news was circulating among the Washington-based Leadership Conference of Women Religious and the Conference of Major Superiors of Men that the Vatican meant to take action, even going so far as to remove Theresa from office, because the Mercy leadership continued to pursue dialogue about the tubal ligation study.[41] Bishop Tom Kelly—presumably in his role as NCCB executive secretary—had called the provincial administrator in St. Louis, Sister Roch Rocklage, to inquire if she would accept the role of president of the Sisters of Mercy of the Union if Theresa were to be removed from office. "Absolutely not," Roch had replied before immediately calling Theresa to apprise her of Kelly's request.[42]

In her capacity as past president of LCWR, Theresa journeyed to Rome in March with LCWR president Clare Fitzgerald to attend the international conference of Vicars for Religious. While there, she was able to arrange for a personal meeting with Cardinal Eduardo Pironio to discuss heightening tensions over the tubal ligation study.

The night before the meeting she was apprehensive and had difficulty sleeping. She remembers praying her favorite prayer, the *Magnificat*, and had what she calls a "very spiritual experience,"

> as if God was somehow overshadowing me—there is that part in the Gospels that says Mary was overshadowed by the Holy Spirit. I had a sense of...a cloud going over me and somehow a message came: "I am with you and I will be with you tomorrow." I felt very keenly that night that the Holy Spirit was in a sense being with me.

Theresa grew peaceful, slept soundly, and was "very comfortable going in the next day" to the meeting. As she waited alone in the antechamber of Cardinal Pironio's office, she overheard him conversing with two American bishops. The door was slightly ajar, and the walls at SCRIS were quite thin. Theresa easily identified the voice of NCCB executive secretary Bishop Thomas Kelly, but did not recognize the other American. She heard Pironio asking the prelates, "What is happening with the Theresa Kane case?"

Kelly's reply was clear: "Well, we're working on it now. We're talking about working toward some resolution on it."

A profoundly shocked Theresa remembers thinking "Oh my God. Here I am hoping to defuse this situation and they're talking about putting me out."

When she was ushered in, Theresa first told Pironio of her concerns about heightened tensions over the Mercy experience with tubal ligations and church policy. Then, with remarkable presence of mind, she confronted him with what she had overheard and asked for an explanation. "I'm very sorry that that happened. That is not supposed to happen," Theresa recalls a distressed Pironio saying. "Those doors are supposed to be closed tight."

"He wasn't sorry he said it," Theresa dryly recalls. "He was just sorry he was discovered." The cardinal then told Theresa that SCRIS had "serious concerns about her and the [tubal ligation] study," even mentioning that "the Pope had spoken to him twice about it and about 'Sister Mary Theresa's behavior.'"[43]

While in Rome Theresa herself had heard rumors—primarily from students at the North American College—that the Vatican was concerned about the study, her papal greeting, and her public advocacy of women's ordination. Yet until she took the initiative, no SCRIS official had asked to speak with her, even though her presence in Rome was known at the time—so much so that a young cassock-wearing cleric stopped her on the street and asked, "Are you Theresa Kane?" After Theresa responded that she was, he asked what she was doing in Rome. "I'm attending a meeting," Theresa told him. The cleric rudely replied: "You don't belong here. We don't want you here." Unruffled by his hostility, Theresa said simply, "Well I'm sorry about that, but I'm here and I'm attending a meeting" and then continued on her way.

On her return to the United States, with the encouragement of St. Louis provincial, Sister Roch Rocklage, Theresa quickly organized an emergency meeting of the General Administrative Conference to be held in Chicago on April 6. At this meeting Theresa shared her experience in Rome as well as the other recent threats from the hierarchical church. The Administrative Team sought advice from the Mercy provincials, and together they began to shape strategies to meet the severe threat to Mercy integrity.

After processing reactions and possible implications of recent events, the General Administrative Conference identified strategies for two possible scenarios: (1) continued dialogue with the American bishops, or (2) direct intervention by Rome. If Rome permitted the Mercy dialogue with US bishops to continue, the General Administrative Conference supported the present direction of the Administrative Team, that is, maintaining the statement on tubal ligation and encouraging dialogue with the planned national committee. If Rome intervened directly to remove Theresa, the General Administrative Conference would reconvene immediately.

In the meantime, the Conference directed the Administrative Team to seek consultation on how canon law affected their situation and to prepare a media release for provincials to use in case of precipitous action by Rome. Each provincial administrator would also share information with her team and begin to strategize appropriate ways of communicating in each province, none of which was to be in writing.[44] Over the next several months the Administrative Team consulted with national and international theologians and canonists on both the tubal ligation issue and the threat to remove Theresa from office. Mercy leadership found this assistance "invaluable" and "came to know that US bishops would not act contrary to any decisions from Rome and would not support the community in any conflict with the Holy See."[45]

A week after the emergency meeting with provincial leaders Theresa made her annual retreat at the Dominican Retreat House in Elkins Park, Pennsylvania, from April 13 to 18, 1981. It was directed by Dominican Father Luke Tancrell. Notes from her diary provide a window into her heart at this sensitive and painful time. On the first day she writes:

> O God, my life—my future is in your hands—you have control of my life. You are so present to me; truly you overshadow me—you surround and envelop me. Your awesome presence is pervading my very being. Please, God—give me strength, joy, courage and love for all persons. Be with me during these days, stay close to me, God—I need you so much.[46]

On Wednesday, April 15, Fr. Tancrell spoke about "The Meaning and Possibility of Forgiveness." In her journal Theresa emphasized "As long as you did it to one of these, *the least of my creatures*, you did it to me—God." She then wrote:

> I need to develop an attitude of heart which reverences and respects any pastor as a person while not failing in my re-

sponsibility to call those in authority to better serve their
people—pastors are servants to and for the people—the hearts
and voices of the people must be seen as God's voice and
heart if the people are sincere and of good will.[47]

MORE DIALOGUE ABOUT TUBAL LIGATION

Church officials did not precipitously remove Theresa from office,
choosing instead to continue the conversation. Over the summer, Archbishop Roach notified the Administrative Team that the NCCB had
named five bishops to the national committee to discuss their own tubal
ligation directives and the Mercy study. Bishop James Malone (co-chair
with Sr. Theresa), Bishop Raphael M. Fliss (Superior, Wisconsin), Bishop
William H. Keeler (Harrisburg), Bishop James D. Niedergeses (Nash-
ville), and Bishop William B. Friend (Alexandria-Shreveport) would represent the NCCB along with staff consultants the Rev. John Connery, SJ,
(moral theologian) and Msgr. Richard Malone (secretary).

The dialogue group had two meetings, one on September 14,
1981, and another on December 15, 1981. Bishop Friend was absent
for both meetings. Representing the Sisters of Mercy were Theresa,
Emily George, and Mary Ellen Quinn from the Administrative Team;
and Sisters Helen Marie Burns, Norita Cooney, and Rock Rocklage,
who were provincial administrators. Two moral theologians served as
their consultants, Rev. Richard McCormick, SJ, and Mercy Sister Margaret Farley. The latter was a key member of the Church/ Institute
Committee.

At the outset of the first meeting, Bishop Malone pointed out
that, while time would be allotted to hearing about problems involved in applying the directive banning tubal ligations, the dialogue
"should not be an attempt to change the teaching." He reminded the
committee of this numerous times at this meeting and subsequently.
The discussion began with an attempt to help the bishops understand
how authority operated within the Sisters of Mercy of the Union, including the critical role of the *Our Relationship within the Church*
statement from the 1977 chapter as the underlying authorization for
both the tubal ligation study and the present dialogue. Some bishops
appeared to have thought the Church/Institute Committee was solely
responsible for the tubal ligation study.

During this first meeting an attempt was made to help the bishops understand the serious dilemma faced by Mercy hospital personnel. Sister Roch Rocklage told the group that tubal ligations
were being treated by some local bishops "with as much weight as

abortions." This resulted in "refusing care to high-risk women and in performing hysterectomies in place of sterilization." For her, the central question was: "How are we to be faithful to the directives and still practice good medicine?" Malone replied that the intent of the NCCB was that medical moral committees affirm the directives in dealing with critical cases and still practice good medicine. But Sister Roch noted the inherent contradiction she experienced with bishops in the St. Louis Province: "If the [bishops'] directives forbid sterilization, then how can a medical-moral committee permit the procedure?" Sister Helen Marie Burns pointed to similar confusion among hospital personnel in the Detroit Province because interpretation of the tubal ligation directive "differed from diocese to diocese."

From Father Richard McCormick's perspective, the problem was that the bishops' tubal ligation directive "did not have the support of a growing number of theologians." But Bishop Malone said that the bishops' Committee on Doctrine had explicitly reaffirmed their tubal ligation directive and even presented it to the pope.[48] While the September meeting yielded meager progress, the six Sisters of Mercy in attendance "found the tone, the listening stance, and the pastoral concerns expressed by all present to be a hope-filled sign."[49] Acknowledging the "tension evident at the outset," the sisters were hopeful. A second meeting had been scheduled and continuing the effort seemed "worthy of energy and commitment in spite of struggle and tension."[50]

On December 12, 1981, in the midst of difficulties with the institutional church, Theresa wrote a reflection, "A Conversation with God," which was published in the Mercy newsletter, *Union Scope*. Reflecting on the completion of the 150th jubilee year of the foundation of the Sisters of Mercy, Theresa wrote that what she had learned "was the urgency of women to assume their gifted place in the church and in society. As we approach the twenty-first century, it is clear to me that the poor, that women, and that peace will have very serious claims on us."[51] After visiting thousands of refugees on Thanksgiving in La Virtud, Honduras, she reflects, "The homeless, prisoners, homosexual persons, prostitutes—all those wounded by contemporary society, these will call us to risk our lives and our reputations, even perhaps, our canonical standing, which for many of us would be more painful than life itself..."[52] Perhaps reflecting on recent covert attempts to remove her from leadership, she prayed,

> I ask especially my God, for courage for myself and for others
> to be willing to confront and critique unjust structures and
> systems, be they political, social, religious or ecclesiastical
> ...and I hope that we will receive the grace to realize that we

must address internal "disarmament" issues in our church, especially the issues of violence expressed in sexism, domination, and the abuse of power. As a church we will not be a credible force for the 21st century if we do not appropriate the human rights agenda in our own structures.[53]

The next meeting of the dialogue committee was held on December 15 at the Mercy Center in Silver Spring, Maryland.[54] This time, the dialogue was both more substantive and more pointed. Bishop Malone reiterated that the meeting had not been convened to "mediate a position of dissent," and he restated his concern about the sisters' "conviction that they had special responsibility to change church practice." Sister Helen Marie Burns countered by saying that while the bishops had stated their purpose, "the sisters have not resonated with it." Sister Margaret Farley observed that the "nub of the problem" was that the bishops and the Sisters of Mercy had "fundamentally different experiences of moral obligation" regarding sterilization. Further, she said, Roman Catholic tradition—particularly its natural law tradition—views doctrine as resting on reality and "not simply on pronouncements of authority." Perhaps the most dramatic moment arose when discussion turned to the actual medical situation of a woman with a severe heart condition. Margaret Farley vividly recalls the conversation:

> Here is a woman who has ten children. She is going to die if she has another pregnancy. Bishop Malone—after we had talked a bit about it—said, "Well, of course she would be able to have a tubal ligation." And then [Fr.] Connery said: "Sorry, Bishop Malone. She could not have had that no matter what, even if she would die."[55]

Farley grimly concludes: "And that's about where we are to this day." Sister Norita Cooney summed up the discussion:

> We have the "Directives" and the bishops' affirmation of them. We also have a number of Catholic hospitals which could be considered as not in compliance with them. Moreover, we have a number of bishops who tolerate non-compliance, and some who do not. The Sisters of Mercy have done a study on tubal ligation that raised questions for the bishops.[56]

But judging from the media surrounding the dialogue both at the time and later, the instincts of Catholic conservatives, including Pope John Paul II, seem to have been to attack the messengers—the Sisters of Mercy—who felt conscience-bound to name substantial problems in implementing hierarchical teaching. Conservative Catholic publications —*The Wanderer* and the *National Catholic Register*—carried articles between the September and December meetings denouncing the Sisters of Mercy for their "challenge" to the magisterium.[57] In responding to the media, the Administrative Team simply acknowledged that an internal study had been conducted and refused to engage in public debate about it. The sisters never wavered in their resolve to dialogue with the hierarchy face to face rather than through the media. In retrospect, in reflecting on her sessions with the bishops, Helen Marie Burns observes,

> We were trying to explain and arrive at a new point of under-
> standing on the part of those representing the official church.
> They were trying to arrive at a point of convincing the Sisters
> of Mercy of their point of view... The best you can do in
> those circumstances is create delay, so that the health systems
> can have some time to adjust, because there is no likelihood if
> you are women in the church of winning, if winning means
> your perspective would be heard.[58]

At the time, the sisters had not yet lost hope. Especially since Bishop Malone had said Rome was not insisting that the US bishops close off the dialogue. For the next meeting, Emily suggested that the committee review the tubal ligation study, but Msgr. Malone quickly countered that he thought the bishops' directives were to be the focus. It was agreed that the respective theologian consultants would prepare one-page summaries about both topics for the next meeting. Future meetings were set for March 9, 1982, and June 25, 1982.

As participants evaluated the second meeting, Bishops Malone and Niedergeses both seemed positive about moving forward and Rev. Mc-Cormick said participants had "moved to the substantive issue." Rev. Connery and Msgr. Malone were less enthused.[59] As events unfolded, it seems likely that the latter two shared their disquiet with officials in Rome.

Rome Plays Hardball

In January 1982, the Administrative Team shared the unfolding tubal ligation impasse with twenty-five major superiors of women who were responsible for hospitals, had "unique experiences" dealing with the Vatican, or who were in specialized leadership roles in LCWR.

The outcome of their dialogue with church hierarchy would affect everyone. An in-person meeting was planned for late April. But on March 2, 1982, Archbishop Roach informed Theresa that "after consultation with church authorities in the United States," the Vatican had concluded that the dialogue had "not met with success" in convincing the sisters to accept the US bishops' directives and was therefore discontinued.

At a later meeting Bishop Malone told the Administrative Team what had changed. When he went to Rome, Archbishop Roach did not intend to stop the dialogue with the Sisters of Mercy. But the matter was taken out of his hands. Vatican officials summarily informed him and NCCB general secretary Fr. Daniel Hoye that the dialogue had come to a "definitive conclusion."[60] It appears the Vatican's "consultation with authorities" was with NCCB staff members Fr. Connery and/or Msgr. Malone rather than with the US prelates who were actually responsible for conducting the dialogue with the Sisters of Mercy. Archbishop Roach evidently felt he had no option but to accede.

Now the Vatican began a lengthy coercive process to "verify" the Mercy team's obedience to a church teaching which they had no part in shaping, and which their study had found to be detrimental to the women and families they served. The decree from SCRIS officials said that "the Holy Father, who has followed all these events" was appointing a new "verification committee." Bishop Malone was appointed chairperson. The other two members were Bishop William Keeler of Harrisburg, who would later become the cardinal archbishop of Baltimore, one of the most influential sees in the United States, and Bishop Paul Waldschmidt, CSC, of Portland, Oregon. The pope instructed the committee "to conduct an authoritative inquiry to verify whether the Sisters of the Administrative Team . . . individually and together accept the teaching of the Magisterium on tubal ligation." Further, the decree required the sisters to "withdraw their November 12, 1980, circular letter with its accompanying recommendations on the same subject."[61]

The Vatican communication echoed Archbishop Roach's earlier letter to US bishops with Mercy hospitals in their dioceses that mistakenly suggested that the Mercy Administrative Team had mandated a change in hospital policy with regard to tubal ligation and that Mercy hospitals had begun to implement it. But the Administrative Team could not dictate hospital policy, even had it wanted to. Each hospital in the Mercy system had its own board of trustees that was responsible for hospital policy, and in any case, the local bishop was responsible for interpreting the tubal ligation directives. In its confidential internal communication, the Mercy leadership had simply reported on discrepancies in various bishops' interpretation of the tubal ligation directives, stated their own theologically informed perspectives, and communicated their intent to pursue dialogue with the appropriate parties. Further, the SCRIS communication wrongly said the Mercy position had received "considerable attention in the news media" although the three media articles in question were blatant distortions that had reached only a small number of ultra-conservative Catholics.

Theresa and Emily George would painstakingly point out these errors in subsequent meetings with the "Verification Committee," which, as they later discovered, harbored similar misunderstandings. The bishops had never reviewed the Mercys' painstaking tubal ligation study in depth, and the planned dialogue about it with the sisters had been circumvented by the Vatican's precipitous intervention.[62]

Over the next two years Theresa and the Sisters of Mercy consulted with some of the most highly regarded canonists, episcopal leaders, and theologians in the United States and around the world. But first Emily sent a copy of the SCRIS letter to the Mercy provincials and the theologian consultants who had helped with the original dialogue. She closed with these spirited words, "How we respond will be determined by the wisdom that comes from our shared faith and vision. Let us then keep faith and courage."[63]

At the April 14 first meeting with the Verification Committee, Bishop Malone instructed the Administrative Team that they were required to respond to two questions: "(1) Do you accept the teaching of the church on tubal ligation? (2) Will you withdraw your circular letter of November 12, 1980, with its unacceptable recommendations on tubal ligation?" The Mercy leadership was to write its response directly to Pope John Paul II. Any member who dissented was to put her sentiments in writing and sign her name. The sisters were required to respond within "a week to ten days." Theresa told the committee that it would not be possible to respond within that time frame, and after somewhat heated negotiations it was agreed that the committee would reconvene on May 11, 1982.[64]

In preparation for the April 14 meeting and before responding to the two questions, the Administrative Team consulted with provincials, a prominent canon lawyer, a progressive US archbishop, and three moral theologians. For Theresa and the other Mercy leaders, conscience was sacred, but so was their responsibility for the well-being of the Sisters of Mercy of the Union. Far-reaching consultation might help them draft a statement that would satisfy the Vatican while preserving the integrity of their community—and their consciences. "Rome is clamping down on everything," advised one progressive archbishop who told them not to expect a change in the Vatican's attitudes. He also said he would hate to see an "out and out battle."[65] Richard McCormick wrote a letter to Bishop Malone, whom he knew personally, expressing his grave concern about the SCRIS letter:

> What bothers, indeed scandalizes, me about the letter is the process. Our dialogue had only begun...we never got to the substantive concerns...The problem of tubal ligation is not going to go away. As a professional theologian I am prepared to say that the vast majority of reputable theologians throughout the world will not support the "intrinsic evil" theses of the Holy See. Furthermore, from my conversations with bishops I know that their heart is not with the absoluteness of that tenet, notwithstanding their official vote on the matter.[66]

Noting "six or seven recent incidents," McCormick also decried "a developing pattern of repression in dealing with dissent in the Church." The Administrative Team also met with Joseph A. Fuchs, SJ, a moral theologian, who, as a member of Pope Paul VI's commission on birth control, had been widely expected to oppose changing church teaching. After listening to married couples, however, Fuchs changed his mind and went on to draft the majority report that recommended a change in church teaching on artificial contraception.

> Listening to the testimony of married couples who testified to the commission, Fuchs grew in his understanding of the complexity of moral decisions about the responsible regulation of births and the right exercise of parenthood. Whereas earlier he believed that the way to apply church teachings was simply to obey them, now he realized that genuine application required adults to relate church teaching conscientiously to their personal responsibilities. From these couples, Fuchs learned the competency of a mature moral conscience.[67]

In advising the Sisters of Mercy, Fuchs emphasized that the SCRIS letter was disciplinary insofar as Rome was demanding a response in harmony with official church teaching. The Administrative Team should recognize that, for now, it could go no further with the tubal ligation issue. He suggested that they should stress the pastoral reasons the sisters had begun the study and answer only the questions posed, that is, is, they should acknowledge that the Administrative Team understood the authority of the pope and bishops as understood by the church. He cautioned them to avoid anything that asked whether or not they agreed or disagreed with church teaching.[68]

In a telephone conversation with Sister Emily George, the congregation's canon lawyer offered the opinion that "Rome will not give in on the issue, and wisdom would dictate that they answer yes to both questions." Saying "yes" to the church's teaching does not specify which church, he said, before reminding Emily, "You are the church too."[69] After further consultation with trusted theological advisors, the Church/Institute Committee, and the General Administrative Conference, the Mercy Administrative Team presented their unanimous response to Pope John Paul II at the May 11 meeting of the Verification Committee. The pertinent section reads:

> After serious, prayer, reflection, and consultation, we are moved by our love for the Church to respond to the questions posed:
>
> 1. We receive the teaching of the Church on tubal ligation with respectful fidelity in accord with *Lumen Gentium* 25 (*obsequium religiosum*).[70] We have personal disagreements as do others in the Church, including pastors and reputable theologians, with the formulation of the magisterium's teaching on sterilization. However, in light of present circumstances, we will not take an official public position contrary to this formulation.
>
> 2. We withdraw our letter of November 12, 1980, and will notify the recipients of the letter of such withdrawal.[71]

In light of the unresolved pastoral issues surrounding tubal ligation, the reply concluded with a statement of support for "continued study and consultation within the Church on this issue."

Comments recorded by Bishop Keeler of the May 11 Verification Committee meeting reflect an almost palpable sense of relief on the part of bishops around the table.[72] Bishop Keeler was impressed by the document's "theological sensitivity" and said, "I see the Holy Spirit in the writing." Bishop Malone felt the response reflected the Administrative Team's "love for the church as an existential reality," citing the their "respectful fidelity" to church teaching with reference to "current circumstances." Bishop Waldschmidt said the statement was good, clear, objective, and honest. He also noted that the issue of tubal ligation "is not a finished one," and went so far as to say that "all people in the church faced the same problems with Rome as the Sisters of Mercy." Theresa reflected that this event had been a faith-filled journey, one of "not knowing the consequences."

The meeting adjourned, and Bishop Malone sent the Mercy state-ment to Pope John Paul II through the apostolic delegate. On May 17 Theresa sent the required letter to Mercy hospital administrators withdrawing her letter of November 30, 1980. She summarized events causing the withdrawal and cited the substance of the team's May 11 response to the pope about tubal ligations.[73]

Richard McCormick provides a succinct summary of the ecclesial, moral, and theological dimensions of the Mercy attempt to "thread the needle" in meeting the demands of church hierarchy and of conscience. It is worth quoting in full here:

> The Administrative Team was aware of the fact that the *obse-quium religiosum* asserted by Vatican II does not exclude the possibility of dissent. They were also aware of the fact that, according to traditional theology, all the Church could de-mand of them in response to the teaching on tubal ligation was *obsequium religiosum*. Therefore, the Administrative Team correctly concluded that they had an airtight response.[74]

On May 9 while in Rome for a meeting, the politically astute Theresa paid a courtesy visit to Archbishop Jean Jadot, who was now pro-prefect at the Secretariat for Non-Christians. She shared the Ad-ministrative Team's response with the former US nuncio. Jadot told her the decree had probably come from the Congregation for the Doctrine of the Faith. He expressed surprise at the short seven- to ten-day timeline, saying it suggested the pope's hand in the matter: "When he wants something, he wants it immediately, although he is erratic himself."[75] He told her that while he appreciateed the US church, he had learned that it is not understood in Rome. Two days later, Theresa received his handwritten note of thanks:

> Thank you for sharing the response. I find it good—with your quotation of *Lumen Gentium* 25 and your honest decla-ration about your personal thoughts. Pastoral care and fi-delity to the Gospel values have to go together. It is not always easy... for a time. But the Holy Spirit will guide us to the whole Truth. I pray for you. + Jean Jadot[76]

While in Rome Theresa also sent a personal message to SCRIS prefect Cardinal Pironio making herself available to meet regarding the administration's statement about the tubal ligation issue. While there was no official response, she learned through informal consultation that the statement "was good and would probably be accepted."[77]

In mid-June, she received a call from the US nuncio, Archbishop Pio Laghi, indicating that the Administrative Team's response had been accepted. Several days later he met with Theresa and Emily to personally convey Rome's response. He specifically named SCRIS, the CDF, and the pope himself as having reviewed the Mercy statement, the latter "at a June 5 audience and June 7 luncheon,"[78] and assured Theresa and Emily that a written response would arrive soon. He also asked Theresa to send a copy of the withdrawal letter she had sent to hospital administrators.[79] The positive outcome was a great relief to Theresa and the rest of the Administrative Team. In a communication to provincial administrators she shared the team's sentiments:

> Even as we reflected upon Archbishop Laghi's call yesterday, we were pleased that we have not been unduly anxious about the response... We realize that the collaboration with you, the consultation with others, and finally the unity we experienced in arriving at a response that was faithful to the search to date brought a profound sense of peace... We spoke among ourselves of the support, concern, and solidarity we experienced with you amidst our struggles and tensions to faithfully exercise our responsibilities to our sisters, our church—thank you.[80]

Given all the affirmation she had received, Theresa felt she could announce Rome's acceptance of the administration's response in her annual Mercy Day communication to the sisters. She took the opportunity to thank them for their "continued thoughtfulness" shown by many notes, and remembrances, "including monetary gifts" which the team decided to give to Father Daniel Berrigan, SJ, "to further his peace efforts." Her closing request hints at one source of her strength as she tried to faithfully implement her community's prophetic directions:

> I beg your prayers for me... The conviction grows in me daily that God is in control of our lives and of the future of the world and that each of us is an instrument of God... The address by Sandra Schneiders, IHM, at the recent LCWR assembly made me reflect on how lack of faith results in feelings of insecurity. Such a consideration has helped clarify for me the areas in which I need a more enlivened faith so that God can take command... In this year commemorating the

fourth centenary of the glorification of Teresa of Avila may we grow more profoundly into women of contemplative action.[81]

In the days ahead, Theresa would need every bit of faith that she could muster.

INTO THE CRUCIBLE

The Mercy Day letter had no sooner been published than Theresa received a letter from SCRIS informing her that the pope had not accepted the sisters' response because of its "incomplete" interpretation of *Obsequium religiosum*.[82] Although it was dated August 30, Theresa did not receive it until late September. It also instructed the Administrative Team to await a follow-up explanation. In the meantime, Sister Emily George sought help from Father Charles Curran and others about how to interpret this discouraging turn of events.

Curran told Emily that Malone had recently inquired about his interpretation of *obsequium religiosum*. Surmising that Malone had made his request in light of the SCRIS communication, Curran responded and used the opportunity to ask the Youngstown prelate what the bishops intended to do about "the women's issue in the church." Malone said he did not see any hope of advancing the issue with the current pope.

Emily and Theresa subsequently met with NCCB leadership Archbishop John Robert Roach, Bishop Malone, and Monsignor Daniel Hoye seeking an explanation for Rome's abrupt turnaround. Both Roach and Malone expressed disappointment and embarrassment at the debacle. In light of the pleasure the Verification Committee had taken in the sisters' response, Malone had pressed for a speedy positive resolution. Roach was "mystified" by Archbishop Laghi's June conversation with Theresa and Emily naming SCRIS, CDF, and the pope himself as accepting their statement. Theresa and Emily quickly deduced that the NCCB knew no more than they did about Rome's recent reaction.[83]

While US Catholic leaders were mystified at the time, it is important to note that in November 1981, Joseph Ratzinger (who would become Pope Benedict XVI) was appointed cardinal-prefect of the Congregation for the Doctrine of the Faith. Archbishop Jadot had told Theresa that he believed Ratzinger at the CDF "will allow less room for dissent."[84] After the November 1982 meeting of the NCCB

Theresa called Monsignor Daniel Hoye, general secretary of the NCCB, who told her that Archbishop Roach and Bishop Malone had met with Archbishop Laghi and that the nuncio confirmed that both the pope and Archbishop Mayer from SCRIS had originally expressed pleasure at the Mercy response. He now speculated that "issues arose" when it was (again?) reviewed by the CDF, even though at their June 24 meeting he had told Theresa and Emily that he understood that the CDF had accepted the statement. As an aside, Hoye shared informally that NCCB officers and Vatican officials were "quite surprised at the positive response sent by the Sisters of Mercy." It was his sense that if the sisters had refused to comply "Rome would have acted quickly to take further action."[85]

In early December Theresa received the second letter promised by SCRIS. Dated November 21, 1982, it said the Administrative Team's interpretation of *obsequium religiosum* was incomplete. The Vatican insisted that the religious submission of mind and will (*obsequium religiosum*) "calls for the Catholic not only not to take a public position contrary to the teaching of the Church but also to direct his or her efforts, by an act of the will, to a more profound personal study of the question which would ideally lead to a deeper understanding and eventually an intellectual acceptance of the teaching in question."[86] The SCRIS letter directed the administration to send another letter to the hospitals "clearly prohibiting the performing of tubal ligations in all hospitals owned and/or operated by the Sisters of Mercy of the Union." They were further instructed to give Bishop Malone a draft of the letter for transmittal to the Vatican and that it was not to be mailed until after the Vatican had approved it.

In late January 1983, Theresa and Emily met yet again with Bishops Malone and Keeler seeking informal clarification. Malone noted that there was now a "new actor" at CDF (Cardinal Ratzinger) and surmised that the "present circumstances" and "continued study" phrases in the original Administrative Team response were seen as "evidence of dissent rather than an attempt to accept magisterial teaching." Both churchmen emphasized that "the US bishops were in complete accord with magisterial teaching" and "no bishop could be interpreted as being in dissent, regardless of his (the bishop's) application of the directives in his diocese... The NCCB was unanimous in its support of the Holy See."[87] Evidently, although US bishops permitted tubal ligations in at least sixty-one Catholic hospitals (twenty-five of which were Mercy institutions), only the Sisters of Mercy bore any responsibility once Rome became involved.

While the bishops were willing to assist and "helpful with suggestions of how to formulate a response," it became plain they were still unclear about "the nature of the November 1980 letter to hospital administrators and why the Sisters of Mercy were initially involved in a tubal ligation study." Both Keeler and Malone expressed surprise that the November letter had not told hospitals not to perform tubal ligations. Their surprise indicated that the bishops still had not understood the nuances of Mercy tubal ligation study. It was an effort to initiate dialogue, not policy. This led the Administrative Team to request an informal meeting with SCRIS officials in Rome for purposes of "mutual clarification." The team also requested that Bishop Malone and a member of the CDF be included in the informal meeting. But SCRIS declined to meet, saying it did not want to interfere in the work of the Verification Committee and the Sisters of Mercy.[88]

In the interim the Mercy leaders had begun another round of consultations with theologians, canon lawyers, and high-ranking clerics. They also began another round of soul searching for ways to preserve their integrity despite the increasingly grim outlook.

Theologians, indeed most Catholics, did not view tubal ligations as "intrinsically evil," particularly when failure to make this option available risks serious injury to mother and child. On December 21, 1982, the Mercy Administrative Team consulted with three moral theologians: Father Charles Curran, Father Richard McCormick, SJ, and their own Sister Margaret Farley. In 1968, after Pope Paul VI issued *Humane Vitae* condemning artificial contraception for spouses, Curran had helped draft a statement concluding that Catholics could responsibly use birth control if it were for the good of the marriage. He was a spokesperson and leader among the more than six hundred theologians who publicly signed the statement. Curran had been a consultant to the Sisters of Mercy all along, but kept a low profile because he himself was under investigation by the CDF for his dissent on birth control.[89]

In the course of the pre-Christmas meeting both McCormick and Curran emphasized that the Administrative Team "should not underestimate the enormous importance of the issue, especially for US women religious. That the tubal ligation issue involves women and church authority in a pastoral and disciplinary context makes the matter worth the struggle."[90] The deepening controversy throws into sharp relief the importance of Theresa's papal request to "open all the ministries of the church to women." Including women at the decision-making table could bring a bit of common sense to a teaching that apparently deemed Catholic hospital identity so fragile that it rested upon female fallopian tubes.

In an effort to be open to the Vatican's request that they re-evaluate their position, the team invited the NCCB ethical consultant, John Connery, SJ, to review official Catholic teaching on tubal ligation. Yet, "while this conference proved helpful in understanding the official teaching, it did not persuade the team to accept tubal ligation as inherently evil."[91] In February 1983, Theresa and Emily consulted with the Dominican theologian Edward Schillebeeckx, who viewed the issue as "totally political," since "there is no theological difficulty on the morality of tubal ligation." He gave the opinion that the church "is in an anti-modernistic mood" and that "prophetism cannot be the normal strategy." He also spoke about "the women's question as eventually changing the church—but how long do we have to wait?"[92]

In May, Theresa, Mary Ellen Quinn, and Rosemary Ronk attended a meeting of the International Union of Superiors General (UISG) in Rome. On May 9 the three consulted with Redemptorist Father Bernard Häring. Widely regarded as the foremost moral theologian of the twentieth century, Häring was also one of the most influential experts at the Second Vatican Council.[93] He affirmed for the sisters that the prevalent position among theologians was that tubal ligation is seen as "therapeutic for the good of the whole," as opposed to the good of the organ only. He advised the Administrative Team to "strongly question the charge against us that we have been involved in organized publicity" and demand clarification. With regard to the request that the sisters come to an agreement of intellect and will, he said, "no one can force the intellect." He emphasized that SCRIS "is making a request which is contrary to the teaching and tradition of the church. Tubal ligations, in some instances, have been and are allowed. To forbid all tubal ligations would be a contradiction." Häring's final advice was "to be honest, to continue to ask questions in order to keep the situation open, to be wise, prudent, courageous, and above all, not to allow ourselves to be bitter." The meeting concluded "with Father Häring extending his blessing and his promise of prayers."[94]

As Theresa and her sisters were being blessed by Bernard Häring in Rome, a devastating crisis was unfolding for the Sisters of Mercy in the Detroit Province. On May 9, Pope John Paul II forced a highly respected and beloved member, Sister Agnes Mary Mansour, to leave the community because of her political ministry as director of the Michigan Department of Social Services.

POLITICAL MINISTRY

As a result of the 1977 chapter's vigorous commitment to systemic change on behalf of the poor, especially poor women and children, several Sisters of Mercy sought political office as one way to live the Mercy charism. Sister Elizabeth Morancy was elected to the state legislature of Rhode Island, District #14, in 1978 and re-elected in 1980. She was praised by civic groups, even receiving a commendation from the local bishop for her commitment to the marginalized.

In May 1982, Sister Arlene Violet announced her candidacy for attorney general in Rhode Island. Also in May, Sister Agnes Mary Mansour began consultations with Detroit's provincial Administrative Team about running for state representative in Michigan's District 17. After carefully considering canon law (Canon 139.2), the 1978 SCRIS document *Religious Life and Human Promotion*, the experience of women religious already serving in elected office, and the charism of the Sisters of Mercy, the Detroit provincial team shared their opinion that Agnes Mary was free to seek public office. The province team and Agnes Mary both agreed that she would confer with Archbishop Edmund Szoka, who, "while not offering his approval, did not oppose her candidacy."[95]

In July 1982, while awaiting the Vatican's response to the Administrative Team's statement about tubal ligation in Mercy hospitals, and after rumored attempts to have her removed from office, Theresa received a letter from SCRIS inquiring about her position on Arlene Violet's candidacy for political office.[96] At the time both canon law and the SCRIS document *Religious Life and Human Promotion* permitted religious to serve in political office in special situations, if approved by the appropriate ecclesiastical authorities. Several other Catholic sisters around the country were also serving in political office.[97] However, somewhat ominously, in 1980 Pope John Paul II had ordered Father Robert Drinan, SJ, to resign from his fifth term as US congressman from Cambridge, Massachusetts. The pope had listened to conservative Republicans, including William F. Buckley Jr., Patrick Buchanan, and William Bennett who were rankled by Drinan's Democratic voting record.[98] Drinan's political ministry "had been sanctioned by the previous pope, Paul VI, as well as by the US episcopate, the cardinal of Boston, his own Jesuit superiors, and emphatically by the voters in his district."[99] Were there similar political motives behind the new SCRIS request to Theresa? Subsequent events suggest that Pope John Paul II was once again involving himself in the inner workings of Mercy governance.

Theresa acknowledged the SCRIS letter about Sister Arlene Violet within two weeks of receiving it, saying she was in a process of reflection and consultation and would communicate at a later date. On behalf of the Mercy Administrative Team, she quickly consulted with selected canonists and theologians, seeking advice, "toward the development of a well-reasoned statement, an apologia, if you will, for the inclusion of political ministry among the works appropriate to contemporary women religious."[100] She simultaneously wrote to provincial leaders and the Church/Institute Committee seeking their wisdom in relation to the letter from SCRIS.

In August 1982, Agnes Mary was defeated in the Michigan primary. In the November election in Rhode Island, Liz Morancy was elected to a third term in the state legislature, but Arlene Violet was narrowly defeated in her run for attorney general of that state.[101] In December 1982, the Church/Institute Committee completed a position paper on elective office for religious. It would be sent to the Administrative Team for their input and approval before being considered at the April 15–18, 1983, second session of the Eleventh General Chapter.

Meanwhile, Agnes Mary and the Detroit Province became entangled in a painful ecclesiastical controversy that received widespread media attention and had far-reaching ramifications. It began when the Democratic governor-elect, James Blanchard, asked Agnes Mary to consider heading Michigan's largest state agency, the Department of Social Services (D.S.S.).

Agnes Mary had significant administrative experience, having served as president of Mercy College in Detroit for more than ten years. She was an acknowledged leader among the Detroit Mercys, having been elected as a chapter delegate to the momentous 1977 chapter and again to the 1980 chapter. She was also close friends with Sister Emily George, on the Mercy Administrative Team, and Sister Margaret Farley, a leading light on the Church/Institute Committee. Sister Helen Marie Burns—who was the Detroit provincial administrator at the time—describes Agnes Mary as "a very good and loyal and consistent religious woman... She was a leader among many of the younger people, a mentor who had a leadership style that was charismatic... She understood how to bring people into a project."[102]

In her capacity as president of Mercy College, Agnes Mary had worked with James Blanchard on several issues and found herself moving in political circles. After the governor-elect asked her about assuming the directorship of social services, she immediately consulted with congregational leadership. Helen Marie recalls:

> It was clear to both of us that, if it was going to be a political appointment, the Department of Social Services was most in keeping with the tradition of Mercy... She could do some systemic work on behalf of persons who were poor, especially women and children, because those are the persons most on welfare... She was not asking for permission. That was not her style, but she was clearly exploring the consonance of the choice—not mine personally, but mine as the president of the

congregation—and we both felt it was clearly a piece that we thought was very consonant [with the Mercy charism].[103]

On December 29, 1982, Governor Blanchard appointed Agnes Mary to head the Department of Social Services. In a lengthy telephone meeting prior to the announcement, Archbishop Szoka had initially approved her appointment. In Agnes Mary's account of this conversation, he "told her to make clear her stand on abortion, to say, relative to the Medicaid payments for abortion, that she was upholding the law and not to comment further on the matter of Medicaid."[104] She did so. On December 31, Szoka was also quoted by the *Detroit Free Press* as approving the appointment:

> A lot is being made about the fact that the D.S.S. (uses Medicaid funds) to pay for abortions. It's creating a problem where there is none... As a sister, Sister Mansour must be in accord with the church. But in her job she has to follow the laws of the state, even if she doesn't agree with them... The fact that her appointment encompasses so many of the areas women religious have traditionally worked in—the poor, foster children, welfare—could give a powerful witness to the Christian dimension of the D.S.S.[105]

But weeks later, Archbishop Szoka reversed himself, saying that he had explained "the absolute necessity for her to take a clear stand against Medicaid payments for abortion" or "she would not have his support."[106] What caused his reversal?

Soon after the announcement of Agnes Mary's appointment, various local and national pro-life groups began a relentless drumbeat opposing the appointment and Archbishop Szoka's involvement. On February 11, 1983, a vicious ad in the *Wall Street Journal* accused Agnes Mary and the archbishop of being "baby killers." Postcards with the same theme deluged the archbishop's office.[107] Negative articles appeared in conservative Catholic publications. No one had anticipated these attacks. Previously the D.S.S. position had twice been held by Catholic laymen without opposition.

In February 1983, Theresa wrote in defense of Agnes Mary to those who had contacted her office with concerns about the appointment. She described Agnes Mary as "a zealous, professional, apostolic woman," who has not only "stated unequivocally her opposition to abortion but who has also publicly supported the Hatch Amendment so that citizens rather than the courts can deal with the abortion issue through their elected legislature." For her own part, Theresa said, "It is my personal conviction that the social sin of abortion can only be effectively addressed and resolved when the inherent dignity and equality of women as human beings and as citizens are recognized and proclaimed with church and societal structures." She encouraged each correspondent "to continue your struggle to humanize the social, religious and civil structures that have brought about the serious interrelated evils of our time including abortion, war, capital punishment, and euthanasia."[108]

On February 14, Archbishop Szoka met with Agnes Mary and told her that if she did not publicly oppose Medicaid payments for abortion, he would withdraw his approval of her appointment. On February 23, the archbishop issued a public statement opposing Agnes Mary's appointment and requested that the Sisters of Mercy ask her to resign from consideration for Governor Blanchard's cabinet. The provincial leadership learned of Szoka's intent just ninety minutes before his press conference but was able to issue a brief press statement affirming that Agnes Mary was a sister in good standing and that the provincial team was "taking the Archbishop's statement under advisement."[109] Helen Marie Burns well remembers the conversation she had with Agnes Mary at the time:

> I felt it my duty to ask Agnes Mary whether she could withdraw or not because it did not seem to me that I should make that decision one way or the other... And she told me clearly that she did not see in good faith and in good conscience that she could [withdraw] because the archbishop had given permission. She had given her word to the governor. She was already in the midst of taking over the office... So, the conversation I had was not to ask her to withdraw, but to say this is an option and you need to look at it. [110]

In succeeding weeks, the provincial team began a series of consultations with moral theologians, canon lawyers, members of the Sisters of Mercy, Agnes Mary, major superiors of other congregations, Theresa, Archbishop Szoka, and other bishops. The archbishop, who had been educated by the Sisters of Mercy and was considered a friend, showed little openness to moving toward mutual resolution despite significant input from moral theologians and others.[111]

On March 5, the provincial team issued a remarkable public statement detailing its position on this complex issue. It is worth quoting here in detail:

> We have carefully weighed all the considerations and conclude there is not sufficient clarity at this time for us to judge

that [Agnes Mary's] resignation would be for the greater good. Sister Agnes Mary has consistently stated her personal opposition to abortion and has indicated the need to change attitudes which encourage the choice of abortion.

As Director of Social Services we believe she is in a position which the Catholic Church defines as "material" rather than direct cooperation with the evil of abortion; that is, her intention (that abortion is evil) is consistent with Church teaching, and her position does not cause abortions to be performed: Medicaid funding of abortions would continue and individuals would choose to have abortions even if Sister Agnes Mary were to resign.

We believe that her work...is within the tradition of the religious community to serve the poor and the sick; we believe her directorship is an appropriate match for her gifts of administration and we believe—most importantly—that she is acting according to a well-formed conscience. Even in a community of believing people, conflicts about how best to maintain values can occur...We hope to be in continued discussion with authorities of the Archdiocese to bring this matter to resolution.[112]

On March 9, the Michigan Senate confirmed Agnes Mary's appointment as director of the Department of Social Services. The next day Archbishop Szoka presented a report to the apostolic nuncio, Archbishop Pio Laghi, expressing his sense that Agnes Mary's refusal to resign was "genuinely scandalous."[113] This report was immediately sent to SCRIS, and on March 23 Theresa received a letter from Archbishop Laghi telling her that SCRIS "hereby instructs you...to require Sister Agnes Mary Mansour to submit her resignation as the Director of the Department of Social Services."[114] Even though the SCRIS letter said "a careful and deliberate study of all factors" had been conducted, no one within the Sisters of Mercy had been asked to present any report to the Vatican. From the Detroit provincial team's point of view, "the matter had been taken out of our hands," insofar as the Vatican had now communicated with Theresa as the president.[115] Nevertheless, provincial leaders sought to "discover avenues of resolution" with local church authorities.[116]

All parties were instructed to keep ongoing deliberations confidential. Over the next two weeks Theresa met with Agnes Mary and Helen Marie to explore their recommendations and she consulted with the Mercy Administrative Team. On April 11 Helen Marie Burns sent a report of the situation to the bishops of Michigan acknowledging Archbishop Szoka's legitimate pastoral authority, noting their efforts to "avoid media confrontations," and sharing their hope of finding resolution at a local level.[117] Helen Marie recalls that none of the Michigan bishops responded formally, although two did respond via telephone. They said they saw no way of helping, given the hierarchical nature of the episcopacy. Archbishop Szoka, as metropolitan bishop, was at the top of the ecclesiastical ladder in Michigan. At the same time the Detroit provincial team was in regular communication with sisters in the Detroit province. Despite some initial hesitation about possible leakage to the press, Helen Marie Burn recalls,

> We came down on trusting two things about the congregation. One, they understood justice and two, they understood community. We asked them to hold confidential what we were saying, to pray with us, and to understand that this was about our ability as a congregation to continue the works of mercy...To a person they took that seriously...We had no leakage to the press.

In the meantime, Theresa was searching diligently for a way to resolve the issue with the Vatican. She sought the services of a canon lawyer who warned her, "The Vatican is really pushing hard—they want her [Agnes Mary] out. And if she is not out, they're going to put you out."

Despite these ominous developments, Theresa suggested an innovative solution to the Mercy team: "I think what we should do is approve a leave of absence for Agnes Mary. While she is in that job with the governor, she is on a leave from the community. And then when it is over, she can be fully incorporated again."

On April 11, the team granted Agnes Mary a simple leave of absence effective April 20, 1982. It allowed her to honor her conscience commitment to the people of Michigan while simultaneously establishing "the necessary distance from public identification of the [Mercy] community" in light of the controversy.[118] On the same day Theresa sent two letters to Archbishop Laghi. One said Agnes Mary had been granted a leave of absence. The other asked for a formal reconsideration by SCRIS and listed six reasons why their demand that Theresa order Agnes Mary to resign should be reevaluated. In a telephone conversation later that day, Archbishop Laghi told Theresa the material would be sent to Rome and "asked that the leave of absence not be revealed publicly and that all other matters be confidential."[119]

Theresa would later reflect that the team's initiative in granting Agnes Mary a leave of absence had "apparently sent them (SCRIS and/or the CDF) through the roof." The canon lawyer told her the Vatican accused her of "delaying tactics." Whereupon Theresa recalls telling him, "Of course I would delay. There was nothing immediate about it ... and we wanted to do it the best way we knew how."

On April 16, Cardinal Edward Pironio at SCRIS appointed Anthony Bevilacqua—an auxiliary bishop from Brooklyn, NY—to serve as the "ad hoc delegate" of the Vatican. Bevilacqua was instructed to require Sister Agnes Mary Mansour "by virtue of her vow of obedience," to resign as the Director of the Department of Social Services in the State of Michigan.[120]

In late April, Agnes Mary received a telephone call from a priest in the Archdiocese of Detroit informing her that he would be delivering a personal letter within forty-eight hours. Agnes Mary contacted Theresa, who called Archbishop Laghi. Laghi told her that SCRIS had appointed Bishop Bevilacqua to convey to Agnes Mary a decision from the Vatican about her situation.[121] Helen Marie Burns later recalls being aware that Bevilacqua was coming at some point, and "it was pretty clear that it was going to be an ultimatum." Even so, she and her Detroit leadership team strongly felt that

> it was our right canonically to protect our patrimony ... our tradition of service within the church. And if we could not find a space for negotiating, we had to at least stand [in our truth] ... There was no winning here, if winning meant Agnes Mary would continue in the position. The only way that we would avoid serious loss was if she resigned. And we knew that was not possible for her and we were not going to ask her to do that.[122]

Theresa was scheduled to leave for a meeting of the International Union of Superiors General in Rome very soon. But first she recalls checking in with the nuncio: "Archbishop Laghi, I am scheduled to go to the UISG meeting in May, but I do not want to leave if there's going to be any activity at all involving Sister Agnes Mary. So I want you to assure me that nothing will happen while I'm in Rome." She remembers Archbishop Laghi telling her, "Oh, no, Sister, no. There won't be anything going on while you're in Rome. You go ahead and go to Rome."

Although Theresa was aware that the meeting between Bishop Bevilacqua and Agnes Mary had been scheduled for May 9, it was her understanding that it would be "the beginning point of the final phase of this matter."[123] She went ahead with plans to attend the May 3–7 meeting in Rome. After her arrival there on May 1, she requested a meeting with Cardinal Pironio about the Mansour case, but received no response.

The May 9 meeting was much more than a "beginning point." When Bevilacqua arrived, he issued a written "mandate from the Holy Father" that Agnes Mary "by virtue of her vow of obedience," was to immediately resign her position as director of the Department of Social Services in the State of Michigan." Refusal to comply would result in immediate initiation of a canonical process "of imposed secularization" and dismissal from the Sisters of Mercy.[124] Bevilacqua was accompanied by two canon lawyers, Monsignor Joseph Galante of Philadelphia and Immaculate Heart of Mary Sister Sharon Holland.[125] Agnes Mary had been instructed to "feel free" to have two sisters from her province accompany her, and Sisters Helen Marie Burns and Emily George—with whom she had entered community nearly thirty years earlier—did so.

After considerable "discussion, argumentation, reflection and prayer," Agnes Mary felt the least damaging response was for her to request dispensation from her vows. An indult of secularization was issued immediately.[126] The speed with which these momentous life decisions transpired (within four hours) led canon law professor Father James Coriden to conclude that Agnes Mary had been denied due process and was treated unfairly by hierarchical clerics in the church she had served for nearly thirty years. Among other things, Coriden noted the failure to inform Agnes Mary in advance "of the radical nature of the options," the lack of competent legal counsel to inform her of her rights, "elements of suddenness and secrecy," and the "lack of candor about the nature of the confrontation."[127] He writes:

> The confrontation by a bishop-delegate of the Holy See, acting at the direction of His Holiness, Pope John Paul II, accompanied by two canon lawyers is an extraordinary intervention of the highest authority in our church. It is not only unusual and therefore unpredictable, it is overwhelming and therefore intimidating to the individual. It cuts across the normal lines of authority... Such agency is intended to insure compliance, but the result is also to limit the freedom of the person subject to it.[128]

Coriden's observation is borne out in the first sentence of Agnes Mary's press statement issued on May 11: "The evening of May 9, I requested with deep regret, sorrow, and limited freedom, a dispensation from my perpetual vows as a Sister of Mercy." The statement continues: "In order not to act in defiance of the mandate of the Holy Father, and at the same time to honor my freedom of conscience and my continuing commitment to the people of Michigan, especially the poor who are served by the Department of Social Services, I requested and was granted what for me was the least of three undesirable alternatives."[129]

The Vatican's decision to override decisions made by Agnes Mary's religious superiors (Theresa and Helen Marie) was unprecedented. Helen Marie recalls saying at the time, "What hurt me most deeply in all of it is that no one asked me as her major superior [about] the quality of her religious life. That did not seem important, and to me it was essential. You were asking her to give up what she had held and treasured and lived faithfully."

Although no one had expected the May 9 meeting to lead to immediate "secularization," neither Agnes Mary nor Helen Marie had any illusions about the probable outcome of their disagreement with the hierarchy. As Helen Marie remembers, "Agnes Mary was not caught by surprise. She had understood the possibility of [being forced to leave], and in good conscience had done what she could to prevent it."[130] Pursuing the process to the end was Agnes Mary's way of preserving her own integrity in a situation over which she had little control. For Helen Marie, her own and Theresa's integrity were central to their refusal to demand Agnes Mary's resignation from a position that had so much potential to advance the Mercy charism: "We refused to do it. We lost her, but we did not ask her to leave. That was our integrity."[131]

After Emily George telephoned Rome to relay the May 9 events to Mercy leadership, a dismayed Theresa immediately consulted with the former US nuncio, Archbishop Jean Jadot. Jadot "expressed surprise and dismay" at the action taken against Agnes Mary. He advised the sisters to get a canon lawyer based in Rome and encouraged their suggestion of pursuing a canonical appeal. He also warned that "if the case is appealed, [the Mercy sisters] should be ready to be scrutinized closely."[132] On May 18 Theresa sent a formal canonical recourse to SCRIS regarding the decision on Agnes Mary Mansour. On May 20 she sent a letter to inform the Mercy congregation at large of what had transpired. She noted, "Agnes Mary has responded to the events graciously and with great sensitivity and it is Agnes Mary's ardent desire to resume canonical relationship with the community as soon as it is possible to do so." In closing she wrote:

In the coming months and years, we will reflect, read, and speak of this extraordinary series of events. It has been painful and difficult, but it has brought us to a new moment. It is in such a spirit that we embrace the feast of Pentecost—the birth of a community known as church. On Pentecost 1983, we find ourselves a community of believers—acting in sincerity but also in conflict—a community ever in search of truth. May the magnificent prayer woven throughout these days' Scriptures be our guide: "Be slow to anger, slow to judge and slower to condemn."[133]

The leadership of the Pittsburgh Sisters of Mercy—who were not at the time aligned with the Sisters of Mercy of the Union—sent a clarifying letter to their own membership that said in part:

> The central issue in the case of Sister Agnes Mary is *not* abortion funding. The tax dollars paid by every Catholic in the United States—including Archbishop Szoka—help to finance federally funded abortion programs. To stop that and redirect public values to a truly pro-life stance, Catholics must become active in the very kind of public policy-making role which Sister Agnes Mary presently is... The central issue is whether the bishop or hierarchical authority can *autonomously* determine what apostolic ministry is proper to us as sisters of Mercy. Catherine McAuley wrestled with that in her day.[134]

Media coverage of the Vatican's unprecedented intervention led to widespread protest among activist sisters and other Catholics. The National Assembly of Religious women (NAWR) and the National Coalition of American Nuns (NCAN) issued a press release expressing "shock and anger" at the unjust treatment of Agnes Mary, who was "placed in a position of forced dispensation..." The groups called for Catholics to gather in "silent prayer and protest" on Pentecost Sunday, May 22, "as a visible witness to the arrogant abuse of power in a male-dominated church."[135] Pentecost prayer vigils were held in Chicago, Detroit, Washington, DC, and other cities.

On May 14, Mercy Administrative Team member Sister Emily George met with board members of the Catholic social justice lobby NETWORK to apprise them of events surrounding the Vatican action. NETWORK subsequently issued its own public statement supporting "Sr. Agnes Mary Mansour in her difficult conscience decision," and affirming its solidarity with the Sisters of Mercy. In a media statement, board chair Loretto Sister Mary Luke Tobin said that because NETWORK "takes seriously the need to transform political and economic structures as part of the Christian calling... we support all members of the church, religious and lay, who assume public office in order to stand with the poor in their struggle."[136]

The three areas NETWORK addressed in depth were "Catholic conscience and public policy, due process and authority in the church, and political ministry and Christian vocation."[137] NETWORK further called on its members to write letters of support to Agnes Mary as well as to Mercy leaders Theresa Kane and Helen Marie Burns. The organization suggested that members write letters of protest to their own bishop, to Bishops Szoka and Bevilacqua, and to national as well as their own local Catholic media. Women religious were encouraged to contact their leaders, asking them to request the Leadership Conference of Women Religious (LCWR) to respond, "since all US women religious are implicated."[138] The executive committee of LCWR issued a statement expressing solidarity with the Mercy leadership, finding it "incomprehensible" that a faithful woman religious should "find herself acting under duress to request dispensation from her vows." LCWR called for just processes for the exercise of authority, since "processes which are violent...are unworthy of a church called to be a sign of peace and reconciliation."[139]

Theresa visited Agnes Mary every time she was in Detroit. To this day, her eyes fill with tears as she recalls her inability to reverse the dismissal. But it was not for lack of trying. The canonical appeal to SCRIS eventually went to the Apostolic Signatura (essentially the "Supreme Court" in the Catholic Church). On July 11, 1983, Theresa received the Signatura's response informing her that since Agnes Mary's removal was at the "express command of the Holy Father," it was unable to consider the appeal insofar as the pope is the highest legal authority in the church.[140]

In ensuing months Mercy Sisters Arlene Violet and Elizabeth Morancy were also forced to choose between remaining in the Sisters of Mercy or abandoning their political ministry in service of those made poor. Theresa supported them by vigorously pursuing canonical exemptions. Morancy had been serving in the Rhode Island legislature for many years, and it was hoped that an exception would be made in her case. But all canonical recourse for both women was denied.

Few were aware that Pope John Paul II had changed the initial draft of the 1983 Code of Canon Law (still the current law of the church) from one that permitted political ministry for religious to one that forbade it. From Morancy's perspective, political and cultural issues had influenced the Polish pope's action: "I think no one will deny that one of the most political persons in the world would be our current Pope. But out of the East European experience and culture, his vision is government as the enemy."[141]

When the new code was promulgated in late November 1983, it contained provisions for reinstating a sister who wished to return to her religious institute after being dispensed from her vows. In an unusually autocratic action, Pope John Paul II specifically instructed that these provisions would not apply to "Miss Agnes Mary Mansour." On November 26, 1983, Theresa received a letter to this effect from Archbishop Laghi:

> As you know the new Code of Canon Law goes into effect on Sunday, November 27, 1983. I have received word from the Holy See that the Holy Father, as Supreme Moderator of each religious (cf. canon 590, par. 2), has made his mind clear on the application of certain provisions of the newly revised Code with regard to Miss Agnes Mary Mansour. In her case, the provision of canon 690, which permits a supreme moderator to readmit to an institute a member who had lawfully departed, does not apply. This is so in reference to Miss Mansour's re-admission to any other Religious Institute.[142]

Later Theresa would seek a private audience with the pope to plead for—among other things—a reversal of his decision. But the pope refused to meet with her. Helen Marie Burns observes that Theresa took the Mercy community's loss of Agnes Mary very personally. "It was for her—as it was for all of us—very painful. But for her it was a defeat that was very deep. And those of us who were close to Agnes Marie never faulted her for her efforts. She did everything she could."[143]

While the Sisters of Mercy lost Agnes Mary as a canonical member, they refused to lose her as a sister: "We always thought of her as our sister and she thought of herself as our sister," says Helen Marie. "And, that's the bond you don't destroy by an act of a dismissal that is not chosen in the fullest sense of that word."[144] Agnes Mary was immediately accepted as an associate member and remained a beloved and respected part of the Mercy sisterhood. She accomplished much during her four years serving as director of Social Services in Michigan. Under her meticulous leadership, the error rate in awarding Medicaid funds, food stamps and Aid to Families with Dependent children dropped to its lowest levels. She started programs to address teenage pregnancy, aid teenage mothers, and help victims of domestic violence. Her department achieved the highest national record of tracking down deadbeat parents to collect child support.[145]

Helen Marie recalls that Agnes Mary was particularly proud of two initiatives. She was able to "broaden the conversation around abortion" by bringing "the question of family planning and alternatives to abortion into the conversation in every welfare office." She also "brought educational components into the welfare requirements in ways that were helpful to bringing people off the welfare rolls."[146] Such were the activities Pope John Paul II did not understand as appropriate expressions of the Mercy charism within an admittedly imperfect political system. Agnes Mary's gifted leadership inspired an insightful response to her situation written by theologian Monika Hellwig:

> Redemption is restoration of all things in Christ...To participate in the restoration is necessarily to participate in ambivalent situations, in structures that are not morally and spiritually perfect...If there are structures of sin then there are also structures of grace; those structures that move toward the overcoming of cultural, racial, and political barriers ...that challenge and overcome oppression and greed, that redress the balance of power and resources in favor of the poor and excluded. To participate in such structures is to cooperate with grace.[147]

After suffering recurrent breast cancer in 2003, Agnes Mary was cared for at the Sisters of Mercy McAuley Center and buried in their cemetery after her death in 2004 at the age of seventy-three. An inspiring legacy of this beloved Sister of Mercy is that she not only cooperated with grace but created structures of grace on behalf of Michigan's poor.

At Agnes Mary's wake, Helen Marie Burns said: "She was always a Sister of Mercy and always a witness to our hope to stand before the world on the side of those persons who are poor, sick, and ignorant."[148] Margaret Farley's homily at her dear friend's funeral perhaps best describes the gift of Agnes Mary's life, and the shining witness of Theresa, Helen Marie, and the Sisters of Mercy:

> Every great love is no doubt a crucified love, and she did love God and her neighbor greatly. She responded to what was "done unto" her with integrity and even with visible humility. She remained faithful to her call no matter what forces tried to pluck it out of her heart. There was in her no bitterness and no loss of who she was. "I shall always be a Sister of Mercy in my heart," she said to reporters in those most painful years. Yet she came to know tears which even God did not wipe away.[149]

CHAPTER EIGHT

A Rock and a Hard Place

In light of the complex challenges facing the Mercy community, Theresa and the Administrative Team announced a special interim session of the Eleventh General Chapter to be held April 14–18, 1983, in St. Louis, Missouri.

As chapter delegates gathered, they were keenly aware of the alarming pressures being placed on the congregation by the hierarchical church. Prospects for a satisfactory resolution of the Sister Agnes Mary Mansour case looked ominous, especially since SCRIS was now pressing Theresa about "the appropriateness of political involvement for religious."[1] The hardline Vatican position that the Sisters of Mercy must adopt a dangerously rigid policy prohibiting all tubal ligations left Theresa and her sisters in a quandary. How could they follow their consciences without endangering the organizational integrity of the Sisters of Mercy? And then there were the well-founded rumors that Rome wanted to remove Theresa as major superior.

In light of these developments, the Church/Institute Committee—as part of its research mandate—initiated a study of the canonical regulation of religious communities. A draft copy was sent to each delegate beforehand. Each delegate also received a chronology of the unfolding tubal ligation impasse and a background paper on elective office.[2] At the opening of the April gathering, some Mercy sisters worried that the delegates would decide to "dissolve our canonical relation with the Church."[3] Others wondered if dissolution would not actually allow for greater freedom in living the Mercy charism. Still others questioned if Theresa and the team had gone too far.

April 1983—Chapter Deliberations and Debacles

The March issue of the Mercy publication, *Union Scope*, contained the first ever "State of the Union" report as a way of engaging—insofar as possible—the entire membership in the issues to be considered at the chapter.[4] The newsletter included a wide-ranging interview with the Mercy Administrative Team as well as a report from the General Administrative Conference.

Among other things, both the Administrative Team interview and the General Administrative Conference report addressed the importance of dialogue with the hierarchical church. The report noted that the General Administrative Conference had "repeatedly dealt with the 1977 General Chapter statement about our responsibility to assist in the church's search for truth." Furthermore, there had been "consistent consensus" to "continue in dialogue with the hierarchical church about socio-ethical questions that deeply affect the people of the church, particularly women." The GAC report said it had "confirmed the Mercy Administrative Team in its interaction with the National Conference of Catholic Bishops (NCCB) and the Holy See in regard to the tubal ligation issue."[5]

As was her customary procedure, Theresa had fully involved all levels of Mercy governance in the ongoing discernment of how best to manage increasing tensions with US bishops and with Rome. In the Administrative Team interview, Sister Betty Barrett said that in light of Vatican II's "full recognition of the dignity of the individual," the community had evaluated itself and "changed in terms of that principle." Yet even though subsidiarity and collegiality were named as values by the institutional church,

> it has not done that critique of its own structures. What seems to be inevitable . . . is that a collision takes place in terms of the ministry. If an individual, whose dignity and right to make a decision relative to her own life is now recognized, sees political ministry as her place, a collision between the two systems, the hierarchical and the collegial is unavoidable.[6]

Sister Emily George reflected that the key to the Mercy 1977 statement *Our Relationship within the Church* involved taking "an active role in helping to shape the church as a community. And that stance of active agent is part of the difficulty. The 'male cleric' portion of the church often does not see us as collaborators. They have always ministered *to* us."[7] In her own interview Theresa said: "I feel if we are serious, we must be involved in a lifelong commitment to dialogue within the church, to a love of the church that makes us willing to critique it in order to reform and transform it. And we, too, have to model that we're willing to be challenged and to be evaluated."[8]

As the chapter unfolded, the sister-delegates quickly realized that there was not nearly enough time to address the weighty matters facing them: "Too much information and clarification were still needed on the many serious issues: the tubal ligation study, canonical regulation study, elective office for sisters, and Mercy Futures [a multi-year Mercy Federation process of deciding whether to join all US-based Mercy communities into one entity]."[9] On the final day, delegates decided to convene yet another session of the Eleventh General Chapter on Labor Day, in September 1983. Accounts of the April session suggest that the sisters were overwhelmed but undaunted. One report relates, "A heaviness lay on the group as they struggled with opposing feelings. There was disappointment at accomplishing very little that was concrete and measurable, yet there was relief that they had not yielded to pressures of time by acting hastily on vital concerns."[10]

Because of the seriousness of the tubal ligation impasse, adjustments were made to the agenda "to give the Chapter body the opportunity for questions, clarification, discussion and dialogue." A panel composed of Administrative Team members and Sister Margaret Farley (who was also a chapter delegate) presented different aspects of the dilemma.[11] The delegates soon realized that the tubal ligation debacle "bore a direct connection with the 1977 chapter statement *Our Relationship within the Church*. "What has followed might be perceived," said one delegate, "as a logical outcome of that statement. We gave them [the Administrative Team] the authority and they have acted within it."[12] As a result, the 1977 statement was placed on the agenda for further consideration in September.

Theresa sought consultation from the chapter body in formulating a reply to the SCRIS request asking for her personal position in light of Mercy Sister Arlene Violet's candidacy for political office. No other religious communities had worked through a position on sisters serving in political office. The Church/Institute Committee presented a background paper on relevant church law and the discussion centered on what to do if the religious superior gave approval for elective office but the bishop did not. The three Mercy sisters already in political ministry—Arlene Violet, Liz Morancy, and Agnes Mary Mansour—were chapter delegates and provided input. While it was evident "that the delegates have no objection to the appropriateness of public office as a contemporary ministry in the church for religious," time constraints did not permit discussion of a formal statement.[13]

The presentation on canonical regulation addressed directly the "fears and questions" circulating among the Mercy membership.[14] The Church/Institute Committee's two-year canonical study must have reassured some when it concluded "that there are strong reasons for this community to maintain canonical status."[15] Margaret Farley further highlighted four key issues for the chapter body: "(1) the centralization of church authority, (2) the role and function of law in the church community, (3) the importance of cloister in canonical regulations throughout history and (4) the different application of canon law to men's and women's religious orders."[16]

The canonical study suggested further steps for a deeper understanding of canon law, including "interpreting law in a Christian sense as empowering rather than restraining, as protecting persons rather than regulating them; allowing for 'zones of freedom' within the application of the law; and including those affected by the law in its administration." In light of the above, the Church/Institute Committee framed three suggestions other than dissolution, "to stimulate conversation" among the delegates:

1. That women religious strengthen collaborative efforts in relation to the institutional church.

2. That the Sacred Congregation for Religious and Secular Institutes (SCRIS) restructure to "more adequately embody the principles of subsidiarity and collegiality."

3. That new structures be shaped "for canonical acceptance of revised constitutions and for ongoing mutual accountability between church and communities."[17]

After lengthy discussion and several suggested revisions, a substantial majority of small groups recommended that a revised draft of the canonical regulation paper would be made available as an appropriate educational tool for the Sisters of Mercy, the Leadership Conference of Women Religious, Conference of Major Superiors of Men, and other groups. A panel presentation centered on the pros and cons of pursuing the three suggested conversation items. Sr. Frances Lynch of Providence (among others) expressed concerns about the precarious timing and observed: "To discuss publicly points two and three at this time would probably be prophetic but also suicidal."[18] Time limitations did not allow for further attention, so the canonical regulation issue was referred to the September session for "major consideration."

Would Theresa Consider Resigning?

Aside from processing (and anguishing over) official chapter business, politicking was happening behind the scenes. Theresa recalls that a group of more traditional sisters from St. Louis attended the April chapter as observers. After a friend pointed out that some of them were surreptitiously audiotaping her remarks, Theresa remembers telling her, "I don't have a problem with it. What I am saying is public." In light of the well-founded rumors that the Vatican was trying to remove Theresa from office, some delegates thought it would be better if she resigned on her own.

Sister Concilia Moran, Theresa's predecessor, learned what some delegates were considering and met with her: "A proposal asking if you would be willing to resign may be put on the floor. I don't think it will go through, but I just want you to be aware of it." Theresa thanked Concilia and said,

> It would be their power and their decision to approach and ask me to resign ... but it doesn't necessarily mean that I would say yes ... I might say "No, I don't want to resign." So then they would have to raise the next question, which is "Should we put Theresa out, rather than the bishop putting her out?'"

Concilia conveyed Theresa's response to concerned parties. The idea was dropped, Theresa believes, "because they didn't want to get into the predicament where they'd have to vote to have me removed." As a provincial administrator, Helen Marie Burns also attended this chapter. She remembers, "There was a clear rumor about Theresa's possible removal [by Rome]. And there was *angst* within the congregation, even among the leaders, about her leadership going forward ... But in any kind of official discussion, the congregational leaders came down in favor of Theresa remaining." Throughout this disconcerting time Theresa felt "simple and calm" about what she faced and reflects,

> I did not want to take power from other people. I think because we are in authority, sometimes we think we have power over others. I have never felt like that, that I had power over anyone else. But neither do I think other people have power over me. Each one of us is called to ... be an agent of one's own destiny. I am called to be very responsible for my life, knowing that God is truly the one—together with me—who is designing a past, present, and future.

In a letter published in the April/May 1983 *Union Scope*, Theresa invited each Sister of Mercy to join in spirit with chapter delegates and observers, expressing hope that the fruits of this difficult chapter would in the end "strengthen us and all those to whom we are dedicated." She shared her perception,

> that although we went away from the session in a spirit of incompleteness and even powerlessness, we did not withdraw as a "house divided." What was so evident throughout the entire four days was... an acknowledgement of the rich diversity among us—diversity which at times involved tension, differences, and suffering. For me the second session was a sacred moment. Both reverence and suffering were present; sacredness or holiness is not possible without suffering, even death. The Chapter session was a moment of crisis; crisis is an opportunity for death and for birth. Both were present.[19]

Theresa asked her sisters to offer Catherine McAuley's *Suscipe* "for courage and direction" in coming months as they approached the September session of the Eleventh General Chapter. This favorite prayer of Theresa's (indeed of every Sister of Mercy) was especially apt for this anxious time in Mercy history:

> *My God, I am yours for time and eternity. Teach me to cast myself entirely into the arms of your loving Providence with a lively, unlimited confidence in your compassionate, tender pity.*
> *Grant, O most merciful Redeemer, that whatever you ordain or permit may be acceptable to me. Take from my heart all painful anxiety; let nothing sadden me but sin, nothing delight me but the hope of coming to the possession of You my God and my all, in your everlasting kingdom.*

THE QUINN COMMISSION

In late June 1983 Pope John Paul II released a letter to US bishops announcing his appointment of Archbishop John R. Quinn of San Francisco to head a special commission of three bishops ostensibly to "facilitate the pastoral work of their brother Bishops in helping the religious of your country... to live their ecclesial vocation to the full." The letter was dated April 3 but not released until late June. The pope encouraged what would become known as the "Quinn Commission" to work together with SCRIS, which was in the process of developing guidelines.

In May 1983, the SCRIS guidelines "Essential Elements" of religious life was published.[20] The *New York Times* religion editor, Kenneth

Briggs, describes it as "the most aggressive effort yet to restrain what the Vatican saw as renegade renewal."[21] "Essential Elements" paid scant attention to the deeply valued renewal experience of US sisters. It recommended a return to a monastic lifestyle that involved a religious habit, set hours for prayer, and common life. As we have seen, this was something long sought by the Vatican, but not by most US sisters. Initially, Theresa and other US women's communities viewed the "Quinn Commission" with alarm. Theresa suspected that the Mercy tubal ligation study was one underlying factor that impelled the pope to try to rein in US religious orders. Although concerns about the decline in religious vocations was touted as the main premise for the Quinn study, many feared at the time that this was simply "a pretext to undermine the gains that many nuns cherished."[22]

Happily, Archbishop Quinn patiently transformed what could have been a disastrous conflict with US sisters into an opportunity for greater mutual understanding. On November 16, in what was described as a "stirring 45-minute speech" to the National Conference of Catholic Bishops, Quinn "stressed that what they [the bishops] were being called to was first and foremost a 'special pastoral service' to Religious, the 'most essential element of which was dialogue.'"[23] In coming months, he urged bishops to "go beyond the old dichotomy of control-autonomy and instead invoke a mutual partnership."[24]

Three years later Archbishop Quinn's report to the Vatican included "a ringing appeal for improved treatment of women both in society and the church, noting that many Catholic women chafed at being excluded from 'policy and decision-making roles in the church.'"[25] Linking this exclusion to the decline in vocations to the sisterhood, he said, "In light of this [lack of] potential, candidates find other modes of service and hesitate to enter religious life."[26]

In 1989 Pope John Paul II relented and wrote a three-thousand-word letter to US bishops praising the "largely positive assessment of religious orders" reached under Quinn's diplomatic leadership. He affirmed the status of LCWR and CMSM as the two "leading conferences representing men's and women's religious orders."[27]

At the outset of the commission's work, this diplomatic outcome was far from assured. It testifies to the uncommon pastoral skill of Archbishop Quinn, arguably one of the finest US churchmen of the twentieth century.[28] Archbishop Thomas Kelly, who was also on the Quinn commission, optimistically (and prematurely) said at the time, "I think we've turned a corner in relationships between Rome and women religious."[29] Remarking on the sad reality of "traditional clerics," who in 2009 launched yet another meritless investigation of US sisters, Briggs later observed, "Had greater openness and insight followed Archbishop Quinn's careful study, the path forward might have been harmonious and mutually enhancing. Though that wasn't to be, the archbishop's gifts of perception, compassion and spirit brought signs of hope in that brief moment."[30]

Theresa frequently wrote Archbishop Quinn about her concerns, especially seeking his advice and support about approaching the pope.[31] In fact, both Theresa and the papal nuncio, Archbishop Pio Laghi, asked him for guidance about the difficult issues that Theresa worked hard to resolve. To Theresa, Quinn offered wisdom about navigating through—and negotiating with—Roman hierarchical culture. He also confidentially wrote the nuncio in support of a personal meeting between Theresa and the pope to discuss the Mansour case.[32] He provided insight, moreover, about the culture of women religious and advised Archbishop Laghi against further censuring Theresa as she prepared to leave office.[33]

In June 1984, just weeks before leaving office, Theresa had a "pleasant, enjoyable visit" with Archbishop Quinn, who hosted a luncheon at his San Francisco home with her and Sister Margaret Cafferty, then-president of LCWR. In her letter of thanks, Theresa expressed a desire to reciprocate when Quinn visited "out East," extending "a promise of prayers and best wishes as you continue your dedicated, zealous service."[34]

LATIN AMERICA PROVIDES PERSPECTIVE

As difficult as tensions with the church hierarchy were, they paled in comparison with the struggles of the poor—and those of sisters who ministered to them—in Latin America. That their suffering profoundly impacted many sisters in the United States was due in no small part to the brutal murders of four American churchwomen in El Salvador on December 2, 1980. Maryknoll Sisters Ita Ford and Maura Clarke, lay missioner Jean Donovan, and Ursuline Sister Dorothy Kazel were raped by Salvadoran soldiers before being summarily shot and buried in a shallow grave.

The sisters' martyrdom was deeply felt by the Sisters of Mercy. Dorothy had written to Theresa one week before she was killed. She had read a *National Catholic Reporter* account of Theresa's "To Speak the Truth in Love" presentation to LCWR:

> I was especially impressed with what you had to say about the "middle-class nature" of U.S. nuns' work—and how important it is to serve the poor and oppressed. I believe that wholeheartedly—that is why I am here in El Salvador... Actually, my real reason for writing to you was to share a "resurrection"

experience. A very good friend of mine, a Maryknoll sister—Carla Piette—was drowned while crossing a river after taking a political prisoner home. I think her beliefs, her life, her whole being go along with what you are saying. Do continue to be spirit-filled and challenging.[35]

An excerpt of Dorothy's letter was reprinted in *Union Scope*, prompting that publication to declare that "the Sisters of Mercy feel a spiritual closeness to Ursuline Sister Dorothy, to Maryknoll Sisters Maura Clarke and Ita Ford, to lay volunteer Jean Donovan and to all of those who have lost their lives in El Salvador." The article went on to say that "the brutal murders of the women serve as a grim reminder that violent death is an ordinary daily happening in El Salvador" and repeated an appeal from Maryknoll asking the US government to stop intervening in that country.

The following December 2, 1981, Theresa and other members of the Administrative Team gathered on the steps of the US Capitol as part of a national day of remembrance for the four churchwomen. Because the Salvadoran government was complicit in the murder both of the four women and of Salvador's beloved archbishop (and later saint) Oscar Romero, the group called for an end to US aid to the corrupt oligarchy that controlled the country. Nine months before the churchwomen were murdered, Romero had been gunned down while saying Mass in a small hospital chapel in San Salvador.

The next year, in December 1982, Mercy Administrative Team members Sisters Betty Barrett, Rosemary Ronk, and ten other women were arrested for civil disobedience as they prayed in memory of the Salvadoran martyrs in the capitol rotunda. Observing that women and men religious serving in Central America have access to information that "is not the information that the State Department is getting," Sister Betty firmly explained, "We stand in the halls of Congress until they listen to us."[36] After leaving leadership, Betty would herself minister among the poor of Latin America.

Because the Sisters of Mercy had indigenous and US sisters in various Latin American settings, they stayed in close touch with socioeconomic and political developments there. In October 1978, Theresa and the Administrative Team surveyed the sisters working in Latin America to see how members in the United States and Latin America could mutually benefit and support one another. Their individual responses identified a need for "realistic links with other [Sisters of Mercy] in Central and South America and the Caribbean," and suggested gathering together "to share apostolic experiences, discuss mutual concerns, and seek mutual support and collaboration."[37]

The first planning meeting was held in Guyana in 1979 with sixteen Union Sisters of Mercy from six countries and the United States in attendance. This group organized the first Latin American Caribbean Conference (LA/CC) in Jamaica in 1980. It invited all Sisters of Mercy ministering in the region, including those belonging to other Mercy congregations outside the Union. Subsequent gatherings occurred annually. The LA/CC would become "an on-going process of theological-pastoral reflection on the Latin American/Caribbean realities... [and] a means of bonding [Sisters of Mercy] cross-culturally, interpreting their charism, and making them responsible to one another and to their people."[38]

While in leadership, Theresa herself made several trips to the region. In 1981, as a board member of the Washington Office on Latin America (WOLA), she joined an international team invited by the Honduran government to monitor the first presidential election to be held in almost twenty years. She was the only female independent observer. Noting that Honduras is the second-poorest country in Latin America, she criticized US policy: "How strange it seems... that our government generously offers economic aid while U.S. business corporations rape the country of its economic resources with a minimum of capital return for the exports, notably coffee and bananas, that we receive from Honduras."[39]

In October 1982, Theresa visited Belize—formerly known as British Honduras—which a year earlier had become independent. The Mercy community in that country celebrated a history-making profession of the first Honduran Sister of Mercy to make vows in Latin America rather than in the United States.

Theresa also revisited Honduras on this trip. She found that, in comparison to her visit a year earlier, the political and economic situation was now critical. Tensions were high, and there was an increased military presence in the larger cities.[40] One suspects that as difficult as it was to manage rising tensions with the institutional church over tubal ligations in Mercy hospitals, Theresa's—indeed the Mercy community's—closeness to those devastated by poverty and violence brought a certain perspective.

A SPIRITED ATTEMPT TO ADDRESS THE VATICAN MANDATE

On May 27, 1983, Theresa wrote to Bishop James Malone in his capacity as the chairperson of the Verification Committee regarding the Vatican's tubal ligation mandate. She included a preliminary draft letter to hospital administrators and carefully clarified, "We interpret the November 21, 1982 SCRIS communication to require one letter."[41] Before offering a list of June dates on which to meet, Theresa reprised recent events:

> A deliberate re-evaluation through additional consultation with theologians, including Rev. John Connery, S.J., and a thorough and extensive consultation with our General Chapter delegates occurred between January and May, 1983. In addition, we made several personal attempts to offer and receive clarification of the entire issue with you, the Committee of Verification and SCRIS in the past few months.[42]

On June 13, 1983, Theresa and the Administrative Team had a substantive meeting with Verification Committee members Bishops James Malone, William Keeler, and Paul Waldschmidt.[43] Aside from reviewing the draft letter, the Administrative Team addressed areas of significant tension having to do with the process.

From the viewpoint of the Sisters of Mercy, neither the US bishops nor SCRIS had ever actually reviewed the tubal ligation study itself. Despite repeated requests, the Administrative Team was not given an opportunity to explain or clarify the document. Sister Emily George asked how it could have been that the Verification Committee had been so pleased with the Mercy sisters' May 11, 1982, letter to Pope John Paul II, only to have Vatican offices reject it. Malone acknowledged that the Verification Committee was "acting as a conduit" and "agent of transmittal," for the Vatican.

Betty Barrett, called attention to exaggerations (not to say distortions) in the November 21, 1982, SCRIS response regarding "organized public dissent" involving "significant publicity." She asked the bishops "to transmit to the Holy See clarification of these issues," but Malone suggested that the Administrative Team should do this instead. When Theresa observed that "the study indicated that tubal ligations were performed with the knowledge and permission of the local ordinaries," Malone responded, "The error on the part of the bishops should not be explained away." He suggested that the bishops would "have to reckon with the congregation to which they are responsible." Theresa said she had refused the NCCB's request for a list of the hospitals performing tubal ligations "in order to protect the local ordinaries." While bishops are accountable to the Congregation for Bishops, only the Sisters of Mercy knew which bishops had adopted a pastoral approach in allowing tubal ligations in pathological situations. Therefore, it was unlikely that any US bishop would be able to help Roman authorities understand why he had taken the pastoral position he had.

In essence, the Mercy community was being held accountable for permissions that had been given by the local bishops.

Theresa expressed dismay that "the message to and from Rome was that the Sisters of Mercy were not cooperative," and she was "further disappointed in not having the opportunity to meet with either the Congregation for Religious or the Verification Committee to offer and to receive clarifications on the tubal ligation study." The three bishops made a few suggestions about the Administrative Team's draft letter to SCRIS and carefully stipulated that their role was evaluative only: "... to judge how clearly the draft meets the instructions of the Congregation for Religious."

On July 6, 1983, Theresa sent Bishop Malone a cover letter to Cardinal Pironio with the required "draft of a letter to be sent to the chief executive officers of our hospitals." The final letter would not be sent until SCRIS approved the text. It read:

> Dear Chief Executive Officer:
>
> On November 21, 1983, the Sacred Congregation for Religious and Secular Institutes (SCRIS) requested that we write stating our reevaluation of tubal ligation and clearly prohibiting the performance of tubal ligations in Mercy hospitals owned and/or operated by the Sisters of Mercy of the Union.
>
> As requested by SCRIS to reevaluate, we, the Mercy Administrative Team, have spent additional time in study and consultation on tubal ligation. In obedience to the magisterium we will take no public position on this matter contrary to church teaching. As you face pastoral problems regarding tubal ligation, we ask that you continue to work in close collaboration with your local ordinary in implementing church teaching.[44]

Theresa's letter to Cardinal Pironio included her heartfelt—albeit veiled—hope that the "pastoral situation" of women with serious medical issues in need of tubal ligations will be brought to visibility in the church community: "My ardent hope and prayer is that the church as community is more visible among us because of the pastoral situation which has engaged us during these recent times."[45]

SEPTEMBER SESSION OF THE ELEVENTH GENERAL CHAPTER

The third session of the Eleventh General Chapter was held September 1–6 in Cincinnati, Ohio. Theresa's opening presentation set the context for the gathering by addressing what she described as "three moments" which had occurred since the April session had recessed: (1) the tubal ligation issue; (2) the papal letter and the "Essential Elements" document on religious life (aka the "Quinn Commission"); (3) Sister Agnes Mary Mansour and the Mansour case.[46]

After updating chapter delegates about meetings with the Verification Committee and the draft letter to hospital CEOs now awaiting SCRIS approval, Theresa voiced her belief that "the five of us experienced and continue to experience great dis-ease about the final response as it does not advance the serious pastoral issue facing Catholic women."[47] She shared what she had told Bishop Malone: "What we are engaged in is carrying out the letter of the law and not the spirit of the law—we all know that the letter of the law kills the spirit," and she concluded, "I do hope that some of our spirit has not died through this difficult experience."[48]

Of the second moment, she first observed that the "Essential Elements" document and the new Code of Canon Law "clearly institutionalize one form of religious life and situate ministry directly within the hierarchy." Theresa then reflected, "Our renewal efforts have produced a new form of religious life which is striving to be neither hierarchical nor institutional."[49] Further, she commented that while the pope had validated one vision of religious life, "It is simply that—one vision." Theresa predicted that in the coming decade, "Women who find themselves with other visions of religious life will be called to bring spirit, form, and flesh to the newer visions in order that such forms can be woven into the fabric of the church's life."[50]

As for "the third moment"—Agnes Mary Mansour—Theresa told her sister-delegates, "For me this moment has been a cause of suffering; I and many others grieve deeply about it. Sister Agnes Mary Mansour is our sister—theologically, spiritually, and psychologically." She told of the efforts to appeal Agnes Mary's case to Rome, and informed delegates that the Detroit Province had chosen to leave her place at chapter vacant as "a symbolic gesture from the Detroit community." For Theresa, the "predominant theme" in this third painful moment is "the overwhelming sense of violence which occurred. The violence experienced by Agnes Mary as a person and the violence towards the religious community was evident in the secretive, harsh, militaristic manner in which the canonical process was executed."

Relating the "moments" to chapter decisions facing them, Theresa identified "the challenge of conscience formation and the primacy of conscience in the life of a religious person—that is a person bound to God by belief in the Divine."[51] Theresa voiced her "ardent hope and prayer" that this chapter and others in the future would address issues surrounding the primacy of conscience. She concluded with a resounding—and prophetic—ecclesial vision that could be considered the *leitmotif* of her leadership:

> If Church as a community of persons is to be a witness to the dignity of the individual, the primacy of person over structures and institutions, the belief that a person is the primary agent of her/his own destiny, then such a community of believers must raise the issue of conscience development with its accompanying challenges to church structures; to canonical regulations and the role of governance as servants to the community; in the papacy, the hierarchy, the religious life and other forms of legitimate authority. Authority seen as service and not domination will bring Church as community to a labor of love.[52]

A great deal of chapter time was given to explaining and clarifying events surrounding the Agnes Mary Mansour case. Agnes Mary's provincial, Helen Marie Burns, pointed out that she did not know if a canonical process had been followed because "it was very difficult to get any information as to what the canonical process was. Now, looking back, we have a sense of it . . . it wasn't known at the time."[53]

After "extended deliberation" a proposal addressing the unjust processes surrounding Agnes Mary's removal passed with 54 affirmative votes, 12 opposing, and 1 abstention. Among the issues named were lack of due process and bypassing the legitimate authority of the Mercy community. Serious concern was expressed over a Vatican action that manifested "what seem to us to be profound discrepancies between our understanding of the nature and role of religious congregations in the Church and the understanding which was operative in this enforcement of the law." The statement concluded by calling for the development of processes which reflect greater mutuality within the community of believers.[54]

In discussing the 1977 statement on *Our Relationship within the Church,* delegates desired "a more positive thrust rather than focusing attention solely on the idea of corporate public dissent." Because the delegates were hesitant to either affirm or rescind the original statement as a definitive document, a new proposal called for a "recognition of the '77 statement as a substantive beginning of an articulation of our relationship within the church" and asked for "a task force to further that articulation." Appointed by the Mercy Administrative Team, the task force would be responsible for (1) designing and implementing a theological reflection process with the membership about their experience as an apostolic religious congregation in the church,

(2) articulating the understandings which will result from the process, (3) and drawing out implications for service within the church. The proposal passed unanimously.[55]

Chapter delegates revisited the Canonical Regulation Study and chose to take no direct action. Instead, they felt that the study "stands as a committee-produced background paper which has assisted the chapter's ongoing reflection on the question of canonical regulation and related matters."[56] Further—perhaps to allay concerns about losing canonical recognition—the delegates took care to say there was no "implied endorsement" of the paper "except insofar as the Chapter accepts it as responsible research which can profitably be shared by others."[57]

With regard to the tubal ligation study, chapter delegates tabled a proposal to "recognize and support" the Administrative Team because they were unable to reach consensus on the wording. In light of recent developments with the Vatican and the expanded discussion of the 1977 *Our Relationship within the Church* statement, "no further action was thought to be called for."[58]

After considerable discussion, the chapter passed a proposal that the Administrative Team authorize a task force to "undertake a study of political ministry as an appropriate expression of the charism of the Sisters of Mercy" and recommended that it "include some experience-based research" and engage "the perspectives of both the United States and the Latin American/Caribbean regions."[59]

The chapter body also spent time considering "Mercy Futures," an ongoing process exploring unified governance for all Sisters of Mercy who were members of the Federation of the Sisters of Mercy of the Americas. A proposal to continue the work of the Mercy Futures Task Force in considering a new governing structure and several models of decision-making passed unanimously.[60]

"Let us go as women anointed . . ."

As this emotionally wrenching yet highly productive chapter session drew to a close, Theresa reflected on the meaning of that moment in Mercy history and in church history. For her, the fruit of the Eleventh General Chapter was "a clear vision of the twofold nature of church —that is: the pursuit of truth, and service to and with the poor and oppressed."[61]

Noting that one vision of the 1977 statement *Our Relationship within the Church* was the pursuit of truth in the context of problematic church structures and teachings that "project an image of possessing truth," Theresa suggested that conflict was "inevitable." Yet if the Sisters of Mercy were serious about pursuing truth, she said, then they were also called to "confront and address conflict within both church and societal structures." Perhaps reflecting on her own experience, she stated that "the pursuit of truth produces criticism, suffering and at times rejection." She prayed that the community's conviction about truth "will indeed encourage us to embrace the risks, the doubts, the vulnerability inherent in the pursuit of truth."

She challenged her sisters to "recognize and remove" from their spirit any fear of opening their "hearts, minds, and lives to be in solidarity with the poor and oppressed." Alluding to recent struggles, she added: "Only when one experiences powerlessness, insecurity, and fear can one truly be capable of identifying with the poor. It is my hope and prayer that the experience of powerlessness felt by ourselves so often this week will move us to a deeper level of compassion, nonviolence, and charity toward all people." Theresa suggested that the "profound attention [of Jesus] to the poor and outcast was precisely because he suffered deeply himself."

"We too have suffered," she said, and she predicted that "more suffering will be asked of us." Theresa's prayer was that the sisters' faith and love for God and one another "will serve as a glorious moment amidst the powerlessness and pain."[62] She formally concluded the Eleventh General Chapter with a powerful prayer,

> As we go forth from this session let us go as women anointed —as women being sent by the Spirit, as Jesus was, to proclaim joyfully the gospel message... The spirit of God is upon you—God has anointed you—She has sent you to bring glad tidings to the poor—to proclaim freedom to those in bondage —recovery of sight to the blind and release to prisoners—to announce this year as a year of favor from your God... May God bless you and keep you. May God let her face shine upon you and be gracious to you. May God look upon you kindly, and grant you peace.[63]

THE VATICAN MAKES NEW RESTRICTIVE DEMANDS

On the day the chapter ended, Theresa received a telephone call from Bishop Malone informing her that he had received a response from Cardinal Pironio and that SCRIS required new and more restrictive language in the tubal ligation letter to hospital administrators. Malone's follow-up letter on September 7 contained instructions that the second and third sentences of the letter were to contain this exact wording:

In obedience to the *Magisterium* we will continue to study
and reflect on Church teaching with a view to accepting it.
We, therefore, direct that the performance of tubal ligations
be prohibited in all hospitals owned and/or operated by the
Sisters of Mercy of the Union.[64]

SCRIS further asked that Theresa and Administrative Team members accept the revision "within a reasonable but short period of time."
Ominously, the letter also said: "If you or any other member of the
Mercy Administrative Team, do not accept the requirement of the Congregation, that dissent by individual members of the Mercy Administrative Team (MAT) is to be specified in writing and with signatures."[65]

Since Theresa was about to embark on a much-needed two-week
vacation, Malone agreed to a late September date for the Administrative Team's reply. Malone's letter further clarified that the SCRIS
command was a "formal precept" from the Congregation, "meaning
that you either accept the revision or not, and that no further compromises or word changes in the draft letter will be entertained by the
Congregation on the matter."[66]

While Theresa was away, the assistant administrator general, Sister Emily George, again reached out to canon lawyers, moral theologians, and other churchmen to apprise them of the latest development
and seek their counsel. On behalf of the Administrative Team, she
also asked the nine Mercy provincials for their opinions on how to respond. Father James Provost, who was the executive secretary of the
Canon Law Society of America at the time, replied that a formal precept had "serious binding force" and the penalties for disobeying
could include removal from office or even censure such as interdict
and excommunication. In his opinion the sisters had no option but to
comply. That said, he suggested that additional steps could be taken
"to place the required statement in a proper ecclesial context, or to
refer its interpretation to the principles approved by the American
bishops in their ethical guidelines for hospitals."[67] Also, the statement
did not preclude in-service sessions for hospital boards and other personnel on the interpretation and application of the precept.[68]

Father Frank Morrissey, the canon lawyer for the Sisters of Mercy,
wrote: "In a feeling of helplessness, I can only suggest that the best
thing to do would be to send out the letter and let the matter rest in
peace for a while."[69] Father Sean O'Riordan, CSSR, who was teaching
at the Collegio Sant' Alfonso in Rome, wrote to Theresa advising acceptance of the wording and suggested publicizing that it had come
from SCRIS: "The gun had been put to your head and what else could
you do but act as you were ordered—making it clear, though, that you

were carrying out an order."[70] O'Riordan had consulted even "quite conservative" theologians in Rome who favored tubal ligations in very serious circumstances. But, they told him, "authorities here were simply not interested in pursuing a theological dialogue ... They were stating a hard line, imposing it as far as they could and not listening to any other views on the matter."[71]

In a telephone conversation with Sister Emily George, moral theologian Rev. Joseph Fuchs, who was also in Rome, said that while he could not give advice, for him personally it would be against his conscience to accept the statement. He added that he had attempted to reach Cardinal Ratzinger to discuss the issue because in his view "SCRIS is going beyond its jurisdiction."[72]

While Father Charles Curran suggested trying to continue to borrow time,[73] Father Bryan Hehir did not agree. In a telephone conversation with Emily, he said it would be "totally unwise" to press the issue further, especially in light of John Paul's recent statements against contraception. To do so would be to invite severe consequences: "Morally, when one has done all one can to move an issue intellectually, and only force [coercion] results, prudence dictates that the consequences enter into the decision."[74]

Provincial Leaders Respond

Without exception, the leadership of the nine Mercy provinces either advised accepting the SCRIS revision or expressed support for whatever the Administrative Team would decide. Letters from the provincials reveal sensitivity and compassion for the position between a "rock and a hard place" from which the Administrative Team must now discern. In a sentiment echoed by others, leaders in the Omaha Province advised, "The immediate result of non-compliance would probably be the removal of the Administrative Team from office and possibly dispensation from vows. It is not worth this sacrifice ... We feel that compliance with the request can also be done with integrity. We have lost the battle but not the war."

In a closing paragraph, Omaha's provincial, Sr. Norita Cooney, wrote: "Theresa, everyone on our Team wants the Administrative Team to know that we feel ultimately that the decision is yours. You have to do what you feel, in your best judgment, needs to be done at this time. Know that we will support you in whatever decision you make."[75]

Several provinces consulted with the chief executive officers of their hospitals and were of the opinion that the SCRIS-mandated revision would not change current practice. One wrote: "The practice [of

allowing medically indicated tubal ligation] will not change if the letter is sent and not sending the letter will not encourage other hospitals to allow tubal ligations."[76] Provincial leaders in Chicago observed
that the notion of Mercy corporate dissent was unresolved and "remained a question" at the recently concluded chapters and among the
membership.

Perhaps the most heart-wrenching response was the personal letter to Theresa from the New York provincial, Sister Marie John Kelly,
who had first placed Theresa's name in nomination for administrator
general. She lamented,

> We have never been allowed to tell our story. We have never
> been heard. No one is listening—within the church structure
> at least—and that is a grave violation to our personal in-
> tegrity and right as faithful and faith-filled women of the
> church. I do believe God is listening and God will effect the
> change someday—somehow.[77]

After stipulating that "... in no way do I want you or the Team to
go against your consciences," Marie John says she doesn't see how losing Theresa or any member of the Administrative Team "will achieve
any good ... We need your leadership, your gifts. Your resignation—or
worse due to non-compliance with the letter—would cause great confusion and a possible split in the community and beyond." In closing
she wrote, "Theresa, you are greatly loved and respected. The integrity
of the team is recognized—you all have rendered, with great suffering,
marvelous leadership and service to our community and the church. I
pray that the Spirit of God will continue to guide you and give you
courage and strength."[78]

In early October, Theresa asked Peter Shannon—who was both a
canon lawyer and a civil attorney—for an opinion about the civil law
implications of publishing the SCRIS statement without referencing the
Catholic bishops' 1980 directives on tubal ligation. Bishop Malone's
September 7 letter said that SCRIS had stipulated there were to be "no
further compromises or word changes" in the draft letter to Mercy hospitals. But Shannon saw potential civil law repercussions if the Mercy
Administrative Team sent a directive absolutely prohibiting all tubal ligations. He explained, "Such a directive might be proffered as a defense
by a physician in a Mercy hospital, where a specific pathology warranted excision of the fallopian tubes (a so called 'indirect sterilization')
and where the physician negligently failed to diagnose the pathology or
perform the surgery to the detriment of the patient."[79] So-called "indi-

rect sterilizations," are permitted in the NCCB 1980 directives. Shannon telephoned Bishop Malone to make him aware of these legal concerns. NCCB attorneys and Shannon then consulted with one another. The issue was unresolved when the Administrative Team members began meeting to consider their final decision.

Decision—Between a Rock and a Hard Place

Before arriving at a decision, the five members of the Mercy Administrative team sought to discover what each was pondering individually. Theresa recalls that one team member was leaning toward noncompliance with the SCRIS mandate, saying, "I think we should go ahead, do what we think is best for the church [and refuse to comply], even if it is against what [the hierarchy] believes right now." Theresa and another team member agreed with her. A fourth team member was "a little bit on the fence," while the fifth felt it was best to comply, especially in light of the potentially severe consequences.

After considerable prayer and discussion, the Mercy Administrative Team unanimously agreed to comply with SCRIS demands. As Theresa remembers it, "We didn't think we had a really strong unanimous conviction, so we went the safer way."

As they were sharing their views, the team received word that Bishop Malone and the Verification Committee had agreed to include a phrase referencing the US Bishops' 1980 directives in the final draft. For Mary Ellen Quinn, "That ninth-hour intervention—word of which was received during the actual prayer service when team members were sharing their decisions about the directive—was a great relief. In reality, now, the directive indicates no change from what had been operative."[80]

Three months later, each member of the Administrative Team wrote a reflection about her experience of wrestling with conscience and consequences regarding the tubal ligation decision. The reflections were made available to community members who wished to receive them. The following excerpts are both poignant and enlightening:

> Through these last few months, I have kept a quotation from Thoreau on my desk. "When then should one defy authority? When the law requires you to be an agent of injustice to another." My question then was this: Does the prohibition of tubal ligations in our hospitals make me an agent of injustice? Our research and pastoral experience said "yes." However, unlike Thoreau I am not totally free to act as an individual

...Our prayer service on the Capitol Rotunda on December 2, 1982 was a witness against the inaction of our government on behalf of the slain Central American missionaries... I consider my decision not to say 'no" as another non-action. I must live with it. Pray for me. —*Sister Betty Barrett* [81]

As best I could ascertain, the MAT [Mercy Administrative Team] could not maintain its original focus, the pastoral care of women, if engaged in open confrontation with the hierarchy ...I had to see if I could intellectually accept the statement the Vatican was asking us to convey to the hospitals. I discovered that I could—though very difficult. The statement was carefully crafted. It did not say we accepted magisterial teaching on tubal ligation; rather we would open ourselves toward acceptance by study and reflection. —*Sister Emily George* [82]

Perhaps our collaborative exploration would have developed a nuancing of the tubal ligation teaching in the United States similar to the nuanced directives in Canada and Germany. We will not know, however, because no substantive discussion of the issue was permitted... When we came to the final decision to send the directive as written by SCRIS I agreed because there was no alternative for reasonable people...I have experienced a loss of innocence about the Vatican that is so profound I am sure my efforts of church renewal will soar to new heights of creativity! —*Sister Rosemary Ronk* [83]

Had I not been in a leadership position in our congregation, I do not believe I could have complied with the directive. My personal convictions are such that compliance would not have been an option...My original anger and frustration have given way to a rather profound sadness and deep pain at what I have seen in the church I dearly love...I have learned that ours is a church whose stewards are truly human with both strengths and frailties... We are not the real victims; for them we must continue our efforts, our ministry...I am struck by a statement of Edward Schillebeeckx in his book on ministry: "... Even in suffering, ministers are those who bring joy." Let us know that the cross and joy are also paradoxical but they are our life. —*Sister Mary Ellen Quinn* [84]

Throughout the experience I found myself reflecting on the virtue of chastity in its richest meaning. Chastity is a call not only to purity of body but very specially to a purity of soul, mind, and spirit. I was moved to probe my own motivation ...I had to acknowledge the fear I was experiencing and to ascertain if my decision was being made primarily out of fear, recognizing that it was not possible to eliminate fear completely. Although the ultimate decision was personally very difficult, I found the purgation and purification within my heart and spirit a sacred experience. —*Sister Theresa Kane*[85]

On October 26, 1983 Theresa sent the SCRIS-mandated letter to Mercy hospital CEO's:

Dear Chief Executive Officer:
    The Sacred Congregation for Religious and Secular Institutes has directed us, the Mercy Administrative Team, to write you stating our reevaluation of tubal ligation and clearly prohibiting the performance of tubal ligations in Mercy hospitals owned and/or operated by the Sisters of Mercy of the Union.
    We have spent additional time in study and consultation on tubal ligation. In obedience to the magisterium we will study and reflect on Church teaching with a view to accepting it. We therefore direct that the performance of tubal ligations be prohibited in all hospitals owned and/or operated by the Sisters of Mercy of the Union. This directive is to be interpreted in light of the National Conference of Catholic Bishops' statement of July 3, 1980, titled *NCCB Statement on Tubal Ligation*.[86]

As requested, Theresa also sent a copy of the final letter to Bishop Malone. In closing she told him, "Your kindness and pastoral concern through this experience has been deeply appreciated, thank you." Although Theresa and the Administrative Team had had many difficult exchanges with Bishop Malone, she was appreciative of the pastoral skill and finesse with which the Youngstown prelate had tried to fulfill his responsibilities. By the time the tubal ligation debacle concluded, it was apparent that the rigidity surrounding hierarchical teaching emanated more from the Vatican than from US bishops. The bishops were also caught between a rock and a hard place.
    On October 27, 1983, Theresa wrote to the Mercy community at large to inform them of the Mercy Administrative Team's unanimous decision. She noted that "...some within both our religious and larger church community will be pleased with our response. Others will experience distress," and she promised to make available

the Administrative Team reflections, urging her community to "freely discuss our decision" in respectful dialogue.

"For me," she wrote, "the decision was influenced by a trust which bonds you and me—a profound sense of obedience to the women who chose me to serve as Presider until June 1985." In the letter's touching—if tongue in cheek—closing paragraph, Theresa referred to the five-hundredth anniversary of Martin Luther and then said, "May we come to understand how diligently we as a religious community and as part of a church community need to recommit ourselves to a relentless pursuit of truth. Even when we fail in truth, may we never let die its holy pursuit!"[87]

Catholic media publicized the resolution of the tubal ligation conflict in considerable depth, usually with headlines indicating that the Sisters of Mercy had acted because of pressure from Rome.[88] In succeeding months progressive Catholics occasionally asked moral theologian Rev. Charles Curran about why he was able to dissent over contraception while (in their view) the leaders of the Sisters of Mercy had "backed down." Curran explained:

> You know the primary concern for them had to be the good of their order. I was a lone ranger. I was speaking only for myself. Nobody else was going to be involved in that decision or the consequences of it but myself. They obviously were not speaking just for themselves. They were speaking for the whole Mercy order. And I am sure that was a factor that weighed very heavily on them... Whereas frankly I did not have to worry about that.[89]

Final Months as President of the Sisters of Mercy of the Union

On the second weekend of November 1983, Theresa found herself extraordinarily busy. She was committed to multiple dialogic events, including Mercy leadership with bishops, women claiming their identity as "Woman-Church," and a workshop sponsored by Catholic bishops on the topic of women in the church.

On November 11, she welcomed a group of ten bishop-ordinaries to a Chicago meeting with the Mercy General Administrative Conference. The invited bishops led dioceses where Mercy provincial and administrative centers were located. The meeting was a wise effort to normalize relationships with US ordinaries in light of negative impressions created by past NCCB communications and conservative

Catholic media. Designed to be an opportunity to dialogue about "the experience of the Sisters of Mercy as a national group since 1978," the presentations and discussion centered on the 1977 Statement *Our Relationship within the Church*, the tubal ligation study, and political ministry.

Participants felt there was a "sense of respectful listening" on the part of both bishops and Mercy leadership, while also admitting to "difficult moments" in which "hard things were said." Theresa found that the gathering "gave the bishops a view of the provincial administrator 'as part of the larger whole' and of the province as 'related to and interrelated to the larger Union.'" For Betty Barrett, "The agenda, was a beautiful example of...a group of women with leadership shared among them."[90]

At a November 12–13 workshop Theresa represented the Women's Ordination Conference in a dialogue with more than a hundred US bishops and at least ten national organizations on the topic of women in the church. Held in Washington, DC, the workshop had sponsorship from a subcommittee of the National Conference of Catholic Bishops. This is noteworthy because, at a September 1983 *ad limina* visit, Pope John Paul II had urged a small group of US bishops to withdraw support "from individuals or groups who in the name of progress, justice or compassion, or for any other alleged reason, promote the ordination of women to the priesthood."[91]

The Washington gathering included prominent women scholars, such as Sister of St. Agnes Dianne Bergant of the Catholic Theological Union, who spoke on "Women in the Bible"; Professor Francine Cardman of Weston School of Theology, who spoke on "Historical and Theological Reflections on the Origins of Ministry"; and Elisabeth Schüssler Fiorenza of the University of Notre Dame, who spoke on "Patriarchal Structures and Christian Community."[92] Theresa thought the bishops were "receptive," observing that the topic of patriarchy "seemed to generate the most curiosity and interest" among them.[93]

On the evening of November 11, Theresa was among over twelve hundred women from all over the United States, Canada, England, and Latin America who attended a two-day conference titled "From Generation to Generation: Woman Church Speaks" held in in Chicago. Because of her involvement with the NCCB workshop on women, she was able to attend only the Friday evening sessions. She found the atmosphere "electrifying," describing it as "a spirit of a new Pentecost" because "so many other Catholic women wanted to be together to speak of their experiences of God and of church." They were women who were "eager and ready to move ahead, not in isolation but together as women who have a vision."[94]

Theresa's "Pastoral on Women"

In January 1984, as a New Year's message to the Sisters of Mercy of the Union, Theresa wrote a special "Pastoral on Women."[95] It is her creative manifesto about women's equality in church and society. The letter would lead to yet another concerted effort by Vatican officials to sanction her. It also attracted an unusually virulent response from at least one member of her own community. Theresa began her "epistle" with an inclusive version of passages from Genesis and Wisdom:

> Then God said: Let us make woman in our image, after our likeness... God created woman in her image; in the divine image she created her. (Genesis 1:26–27)

> For God formed woman to be imperishable; in the image of her own nature she made her. (Wisdom 2:23)

She then summarized Elisabeth Schüssler Fiorenza's book *In Memory of Her*, explaining that in the early church "women and men were joined in a discipleship as equals" and that "with the gradual formation of a patriarchal church, women were eliminated from church leadership." She reviewed statistics about the status of women in the 1980s, cited here in part: (1) two thirds of the eight hundred million illiterate people in the world are women, and women own less than 1 percent of the land; (2) one of every three women in the United States is raped in her lifetime, with just one rape in sixty leading to conviction; (3) one of every four female children is sexually abused during childhood, and 80 percent of women who work outside the home report being sexually harassed on the job.[96] Sadly, these statistics are not significantly improved today.[97]

Sexism, wrote Theresa, "is not just the issue of economic exploitation. Its life-destroying power perpetuates violence against women, a violence that is often overlooked or condoned by the churches." The grim statistics call for both "profound meditation" and "dignified assertive action" by women. She added that the fact that "women have been considered inferior and evil throughout church history is a painful recognition." If the church is called to alleviate and eradicate poverty, she believes, "it must be committed in attitude, structure and behavior in acknowledging and proclaiming the inherent dignity of all women." Further, the proclamation must occur in the context of "promoting human rights, a nuclear-free world and protection of the helpless."

What most offended Vatican officials was the paragraph in which Theresa denounced the structural exclusion of women from Catholic decision-making:

A serious obstacle to women serving in all ministries within the church is the structural prohibition of ordination. To proclaim that women as persons are capable of receiving all sacraments but one is a form of idolatry. Ordination for women is key in renewal of church structures as it symbolizes exclusion, and in practical terms prohibits women from functioning as fully participating members in decision-making roles. The continuance of this structural barrier is a social sin and must be regarded in the same way as slavery, once considered natural and divinely ordered.[98]

She argued that women have "a serious responsibility to strengthen their conviction that before God they are equal and to live out of such a conviction." It is "not a question of women 'forcing' their way into all ministries within the church," Theresa wrote, but of recognizing that "women by their very nature and baptism 'belong' within all ministries of our church."

After sharing her views, Theresa invited other Sisters of Mercy to develop their own. She concluded her pastoral letter with these words: "We are women made in God's image and likeness. As such we truly have a 'place' and 'belong' in every level of human effort, whether in church or in society, where God is to be imaged for the continued redemption of the word."[99]

Theresa's New Year's letter triggered a visceral response from one threatened sister who anonymously returned it to her with over forty annotations written in the margins. A sampling follows: "You are not a daughter of Catherine McAuley but a daughter of Satan. We Sisters of Mercy are ashamed of you. Get out of our order and take your followers with you." The sister dismissed global statistics about the status of women as "all materialistic" and urged Theresa to "get at the source [of the problem] and instruct [women] to be modest in their dress and start fighting pornography." She warned Theresa about "rebelliousness," saying, "You women ought to get off your high horses and learn what true humility means." Finding Theresa "utterly cheap and despicable," she instructed her to "see a psychiatrist to help you and your followers overcome your horrible, diabolic and hate-filled obsessions... The devil is pleased with you!" This disturbed sister even sent a copy of her annotated letter to Archbishop Quinn, informing him that

Sister Theresa Kane and her followers continue in their willful disobedience to the Holy Father who directed us to return to the wearing of the Habit and living in convents, not in apartments. This point-by-point rebuttal was intended for Sister Theresa's eyes only. However, as the Bishops Commission is studying Religious Life, they ought to know the inside story as well.[100]

Eight months later, Archbishop Quinn would write to the papal nuncio expressing "serious misgivings" about the desire of the Congregation for the Doctrine of the Faith to censure Theresa over her pastoral letter. Rome had apparently been sent a copy of Theresa's pastoral letter too.

While the censure never materialized, this sad saga illuminates the challenges progressive Catholics often faced at a time when Rome frequently responded to (and therefore empowered) ultra-conservative persons or groups who were having difficulty accepting the changes brought by Vatican II. In any case, it seems evident that Vatican offices were increasingly concerned about any discussion of women's ordination.

In Theresa's mind, framing her communication as a pastoral letter was one way to make sure her sisters would actually read it. Communications from the generalate were easily overlooked: "It was an administrative judgment that I made. I wanted a final letter to go out to the sisters that would be both personal and a creative approach . . . If I wrote this as an epistle to the sisters, it would get their attention." Her "epistle" seems to have attracted more attention than she or anyone else had bargained for.

On Coming to Maturity in a Patriarchal Church

Although this was an extremely stressful time, Theresa remembers never feeling alone or isolated in her exercise of leadership. "I always felt so supported . . . I had a very strong team that worked very closely together, so I never felt I was alone in any of it. Not at all." Yet because of the many institutional pressures they were dealing with, Theresa and the Team did begin consulting with a mental health professional. A Sister of Mercy—who was also a clinical psychologist—met with them together and individually. She then made recommendations about who could benefit from further counseling. Theresa was one of them.

Over a period of two years Theresa journeyed every other month from Washington, DC, to Albany, New York, to meet with a male psychologist. "He told me this is like going through a divorce," she remembers. The psychologist suggested that her relationship with the institutional church was changing "from being a child in the church to being a woman in the church with your own authority." Remembering the experience today, Theresa reflects:

> I think it purified my relationship with the hierarchy and with authority and maybe particularly with men who were in ecclesial authority. We grew up in a setting where, even though theoretically we all knew we were equal...at the same time we still had that inhibition towards authority and towards men who were bishops. And I think that I, in a sense, moved out of that, where I became free of those constraints, and I felt strong and equal to them.

It is interesting that Theresa chose the word purification to describe her changed relationship. She explains,

> [Purity] is a word that means a great deal to me in terms of my spiritual life. You know we talk about sin and about offending God, and for me it is like the interior spirit is trying to have a purification...It is like my inner spirit with God. The term we used to use was to be chaste. I want myself to be as pure as I can be...so [if there is] anything that is not of God, I want to have it cleared from my consciousness, from my spirit, from my life.

For Theresa, subordination is not of God, and cleansing her "interior spirit" of an unconscious tendency to defer to male authority solely because of its maleness was both purifying and liberating. This "purification" may be one source of her remarkable ability to persevere in the face of so many obstacles, both within and without.

POPE JOHN PAUL WILL NOT MEET

In January 1984, Theresa wrote a personal letter to the pope asking for a private audience before concluding her service as president of the Sisters of Mercy of the Union on June 30, 1984. Two months later she received a reply from Cardinal Edward Martinez at the Vatican

Secretariat of State, inquiring "what expectations you may have regarding the nature of such a meeting."[101]

On Holy Thursday, Theresa wrote directly to the pope detailing her requests to (1) clarify some "perceptual distortions" regarding the quality of spiritual renewal in the Sisters of Mercy; (2) respond to concerns the pope may have had about public attention over the tubal ligation study and political ministry, including the Mansour and Violet cases; (3) tell him personally of the "many expressions of prayer and support," and "renewed fidelity to the mission of the church" that had come directly from delegates to the Mercy's Twelfth General Chapter; (4) offer a perspective and indicate cooperation with Archbishop Quinn's commission; (5) include present and future members of the Mercy Administrative Team, in the dialogue—specifically, Sisters Emily George, Helen Amos, and Helen Marie Burns.[102]

On August 3, after she had already left office, Theresa received a letter from the papal nuncio, Archbishop Laghi, informing her that although "careful consideration" had been given to the matters raised, these concerns "could be referred for examination" to SCRIS, and "it has been deemed inopportune" to grant her a private audience with the pope.[103] Altogether, between 1980 and 1984 Theresa made five formal requests to meet with Pope John Paul: three on behalf of LCWR and two as president of the Sisters of Mercy of the Union. All were refused.[104]

It is notable, therefore, that in 1998—nearly twenty years after Theresa's greeting at the Shrine—the pope inquired after her at a luncheon with officials from the US Conference of Catholic Bishops (USCCB). Cleveland Bishop Anthony M. Pilla—who was president of the USCCB at the time—invited Sister of Mercy Sharon Euart to accompany him to their annual meeting with Vatican officials. A canon lawyer, Sharon was the associate general secretary of the USCCB at the time. This was the first time the associate general secretary had been invited to attend,[105] and it was unusual for a female canon lawyer to be present at Vatican meetings.[106] Vice-president Joseph A. Fiorenza, bishop of Galveston-Houston, and General Secretary Father Dennis M. Schnurr also went to Rome as part of the delegation.[107]

As their meetings concluded, the four were invited to join Pope John Paul II in his residence to enjoy a noon meal with the pontiff. After Bishop Pilla introduced Sharon as the associate general secretary and a Sister of Mercy, the pope paused, looked at her, and asked "Sister of Mercy?"

"Yes, your holiness" replied Sharon.

"Do you know Sister Theresa Kane?" he inquired.

Sharon affirmed that she did indeed know Theresa.

The pope then asked, "What is she doing now?"

Sharon replied that Theresa was an associate professor at Mercy College in Dobbs Ferry, New York.

"Then there was this long pause again," Sharon remembers, bfore the pope asked her, "Will you please give her my greetings?" Sharon immediately agreed.

As the group was taking its leave, the pope put his hand on Sharon's shoulder and reminded her, "Please do not forget to give my greetings to Sister Theresa."

Stunned, Sharon returned home and immediately called Theresa to relay the pope's message: "She was speechless... It was very powerful, because this was 1998. This was twenty years later and he still remembered her and knew she was a Sister of Mercy."

Theresa herself was puzzled and uncertain about how to interpret the pope's outreach:

I wasn't sure if it was highly political or if somehow over those twenty years he had come to some new insights himself ...It is possible that he had better feelings toward me for at least being able to stand up and speak to him about the women in the church... He would not ever have been supportive of Agnes Mary... Certainly, on the issue of women in the church one hoped he was more educated by now. He had many women's [church reform] groups going over to the Vatican to relay their concerns.[108]

Indeed, beginning in 1988, Pope John Paul wrote several official documents about the dignity of women. But he adamantly refused to consider opening ordination to women, even to the point of creating canonical sanctions for Catholics who continued discussing it.[109] Some Catholics were (and are) of the opinion that rather than upholding women's dignity, the pope sought to silence them.

As word got around about the pope's personal greeting, some of Theresa's acquaintances urged her to write him again and request a meeting. She adamantly refused: "I have written to that man five times already. Twice for the Sisters of Mercy and three times for LCWR. It was no, no, no...I am not writing to him anymore. If I have anything to say to him, I'll do it when I meet him in heaven."

Election of New Leadership:
Twelfth General Chapter, March 23–27, 1984

In her last chapter address as president, Theresa shared a vision of a future in which "the Roman Catholic community is being called to a transfiguration both in attitudes and in structures . . . We cannot continue to denounce political, economic, and social structures without simultaneously analyzing and critiquing church structures."

She spoke again of her "deep anguish and suffering" over the loss of Agnes Mary Mansour and Arlene Violet, both of whom had been forced to choose between religious life and their call to political ministry. Theresa painfully acknowledged that she experienced "an overwhelming sense of powerlessness about this ecclesiastical conflict. I was impotent to act as an instrument to mediate, resolve, or transform the conflict that has radically altered the course of two woman's lives—women who are suffering because of the conflict." She entreated the delegates to "be women of vision" invoking the same biblical text at the end of her term as at its beginning: "This is what Yahweh, God, asks of us—that we act justly—love tenderly—and walk humbly with our God, with one another, and with all peoples of the earth (Micah 6:8)."[110]

Election of the new Mercy Administrative Team was a priority at this chapter. To a person, the nominees emphasized a need to be in ongoing dialogue with the institutional church. As the election process unfolded, each new sister-leader was elected on the first ballot. Unprecedented in the history of Mercy elections, the vote testified to an unusual degree of consensus about what was needed in their future leaders. Sister Helen Amos was elected president/administrator. Sister Helen Marie Burns was elected vice-president, and Sisters Camilla Verret, Gretchen Elliott, and Patricia Wolf were elected Administrative Team members.

Among other priorities, Helen—the Baltimore provincial administrator and president of the Federation of the Sisters of Mercy—cited the mandate from the April chapter to conduct a study of political ministry, and to design a theological reflection process about "our experience as an apostolic religious congregation." She suggested it was a time "to commit our leadership to the fullest possible cooperation with the American bishops' recent efforts on behalf of the struggle for peace and to true collaboration in their present efforts to articulate the role of women in our Church and our world."[111]

Helen Marie—the Detroit provincial administrator and a past president of the Mercy Federation—identified specific movements in the congregation. These included a growing awareness of Mercy internationality; Mercy reorganization in the United States; efforts to define as well as understand the gift religious life is to the People of God; efforts to conserve and utilize resources for service; and efforts to join with "others of good will in the struggle for truth, the struggle for peace, the struggle for justice."[112]

Priorities for Camilla Verret of Omaha were the need to model "real dialogue" with the institutional church and "calling together key forums for ethical reflection and decision making."[113] Among other priorities, Gretchen Elliott from Detroit said "the next MAT [Mercy Administrative Team] must support the Eleventh General Chapter's decision to further the articulation of our relationship within the church," and support the Mercy Futures movement.[114] Patricia Wolf of the New York Province was nominated from the floor. At the time she was elected, Patricia was heavily involved in advocating for corporate responsibility as a consultant with the Intercommunity Center for Justice and Peace in New York City.[115] The newly elected Mercy Administrative Team was clearly well equipped to continue the legacy of the previous team and to shepherd the next evolution of chapter decisions and directions.

Other chapter business included "an expression of concern" for Arlene Violet and a pledge of "continuing efforts to clarify the role of religious in political ministry." A resolution to request a dispensation that would permit Sister Elizabeth Morancy to continue in public office received overwhelming support. Unfortunately, on May 9, 1984, the Vatican denied the dispensation request.[116] Sr. Elizabeth made the unhappy decision to continue her political ministry outside the Sisters of Mercy. At one point, a delegate from Latin America expressed her deep gratitude for the leadership of Theresa and the Administrative Team that had brought a new sense of empowerment and direction:

> A big thank you for the direction you have given to the Latin American Conference...I can best describe your leadership as a leadership of empowering of people, and I don't know how we could ever thank you for that. I have a sense that never before have the regions of Latin America and the Caribbean been known—I mean the issues have never before been put to the fore, as a whole, and I think that has given us a sense of our value to the Institute.[117]

Perhaps following up on Theresa's prayer at the previous chapter to "embrace the risks" of pursuing truth, the discussion around the 1977 *Our Relationship within the Church* statement identified "the church's search for truth and our part in that," as a focus.[118] In 1985 the task force would offer workshops in all nine provinces with the theme of "The Communal Search for Truth" to further reflect upon "our relationship with the church."[119]

After discussing a previously requested evaluation of the Church/ Institute Committee, the Twelfth General Chapter overwhelmingly passed a resolution affirming the committee's accountability to the Mercy Administrative Team and its mission of "providing scholarly research on questions and issues that are raised by our relationship to the institutional church."[120] Even though a small number of individual Sisters of Mercy were unsettled by—and even vehemently opposed to— some of the prophetic directions established by the 1977 chapter, the congregation's duly elected leaders continued their strong support of those directions.

As the chapter was drawing to a close, Theresa and newly elected president Helen Amos reflected together on Mary's *Magnificat*. Their words of love and inspiration reflect grace in the midst of struggle and are reprinted here in part.

Helen: Theresa, all of us who have had the privilege of spending a considerable amount of time in your company are well aware of your great devotion to this scripture passage... You have reminded us time and again to carry our experiences of every kind to our faith and subject them there to that very crucial test—Have we remembered that God's mercy is from age to age? And have we learned that God's mercy drives out fear?

Theresa: It is friendship that encourages us to be without fear... And if I have any message for the new team it is not to be afraid... I do not think we are ever without fear... it is being able to endure the fear and still know that God is with us in our fears... perhaps that's really what faith is—to be able to believe even though we are afraid.

Helen: Because both joy and fear come up in the passage they remind us... how God reverses things to bring about justice. God not only reverses our fear and allows it to come out joy... but reverses the position of the lowly and makes it a great position...

Theresa: When Mary came to Elizabeth and said that *Magnificat* she... had no idea of the tremendous change that would occur in her life... She would be a woman with [Jesus] on his journey and she would suffer with him... There will be suffering, there will be death, but I do believe that we must continue to "fear not"... and to believe that nothing is impossible with God.

LCWR Honors Theresa—And So Do Some Bishops

None were in a better position to understand what Theresa faced in dealing with labyrinthine Vatican politics than the former presidents of the Leadership Conference of Women Religious. While many of them had faced very difficult challenges, no one had been threatened with being ejected from office as Theresa had. On May 24, 1984, eight past LCWR presidents, the current president, and the president-elect gathered in Denver, Colorado, to support, honor, and congratulate Theresa as she completed her term of office.

In an introduction, Sister Mary Luke Tobin—who had represented LCWR at Vatican II—reminded the group that each of them had first been elected by her own community, and then elected again by community leaders from all over the United States. She said, "We wish to present our testimony to these sisters whom we have represented, represent now, and will represent. We testify not only to our affection for Theresa Kane, but also to our admiration for the courage which inspires hope. Only such prophetic qualities have the potential of leading us into the future."[121]

Theresa's good friend and mentor, Mercy Sister Betty Carroll, journeyed from Peru to attend. She addressed one of Theresa's favorite themes: "Third World Women, First World Women and the Church." Mary Luke presented a book of tributes written by fifteen of Theresa's LCWR colleagues. Theresa was also given an artistic rendering of a powerful quotation from her 1980 LCWR conference report. She treasures these mementos to this day. The loving accolades acclaim her as a "valiant woman of the Gospel" and praise her courage, simplicity, prayerfulness, compassion, and unwavering commitment to dialogue:[122]

There are few people who have affected either religious life or the Church as profoundly as you have... Besides being admired, Theresa, you are also loved... You have that rare and precious gift of combining great personal strength with what seems to be boundless compassion. Popes and

archbishops may quake at the sound of your name; we celebrate a great woman who represents the best of religious life.
—Margaret Cafferty, PBVM

I think what has always struck me about Theresa is her beautiful simplicity and sensitivity toward "the other." Involved in events and projects that have consistently thrust her into the public domain, she never failed to be aware of and responsive to the "little" and "unimportant" others in any gathering. For her no one was ever "little" or "unimportant" and that quality, more than any other is, I believe, a mark of greatness.
—Betty Moslander, CSJ

The human family and especially women need to experience today the power of a new form of obedience, a listening and liberating obedience. The ministry of [Theresa's] leadership invites us to release that power of choosing in harmony with our deepest truth for the sake of the world entrusted to us.
—Francis B. Rothluebber, OSF

Unlike those who may experience Theresa as a voice crying in the wilderness, we who hear her word welcome it as the message of God. We laud the strength with which she addresses unjust and dehumanizing structures in the church and society. We rejoice in her love which flows from a heart that is free. We share her dream for reconciliation, for equity, for peace.
—Barbara Lawler Thomas, SCN

I celebrate Theresa... For persisting in holding out a hand in reconciliation even though others refused to talk... For determinedly maintaining that dialogue and church should be inseparable, perhaps synonymous... For steadfast insistence that every person counts... For simplicity... For hoping, for hoping still. *—Lora Ann Quiñonez, CDP*

In addition to those named above, other former presidents at the celebration included Benedictine Sister Joan Chittister,[123] Franciscan Sister Francine Zeller, and Sister of Charity Helen Flaherty. As the festivities drew to a close, the group joined in singing a musical tribute, "We Are All Sisters of Mercy." The original composition was created by Sister of Loretto Rosa A. Liddell and captures well the meaning Theresa's prophetic leadership had at the time—not only for women religious but also for many thousands of ordinary Catholics:

Chorus   "We are All Sisters of Mercy" (x2)

First Singer: I ask you?
                    How has Theresa been a Sister of Mercy?

Second Singer: 1. Helping us hope together,
                    and share that hope with those
                    who see no reason for hope.

                 2. Being willing to be challenged,
                    open to change, ever seeking reconciliation.

First Singer: Therefore, we salute her! (chorus)

                 3. Speaking strong words,
                    words that reflect the desires of all women
                    who yearn to be free (chorus)

                 4. Telling a kind of truth
                    that kept others honest.
                    It had the kind of power
                    that empowers the powerless (chorus)

                 5. For steadfast insistence
                    that every person counts (chorus)[124]

In 2003, LCWR presented its first ever Outstanding Leadership Award to Sister Mary Luke Tobin, recognizing her unparalleled leadership during the Second Vatican Council. In 2004, it went to Sister Theresa Kane, recognizing that she "has given her life's energies, time and skills to fostering religious life, creating peace, and working for the rights of women and the rights of people who are impoverished."

In addition to LCWR, some US bishops and other religious leaders wrote to thank Theresa and the Administrative Team. Walter F. Sullivan, Bishop of Richmond, wrote to say:

Words seem inadequate to express to you my appreciation for the leadership you have given, not only to the Sisters of Mercy, but also to the religious women of our country. Your witness to the gospel has not only been an edification but also an example of prophetic call. I certainly empathized with you in some of your recent struggles with the Vatican.

Your response has not only been heroic but also reflective of the example of Jesus. There are many, including myself, who both admire you and are grateful to you for your leadership at a most critical time in the history of the church.[125]

Francis A. Quinn, the Bishop of Sacramento, wished "to add my voice to the many others who express their gratitude for your service in the Church...It must be a source of great joy and satisfaction for you to look back and know the good you have done for so many people, especially your Religious Sisters."[126]

Sister Christine Marie Rody, General Superior of the Vincentian Sisters of Charity in Bedford, Ohio, shared:

Although I have not completed a full year in administration as superior of our community, I have been fully aware of the dedication and vision of the Religious Sisters of Mercy concerning major decisions and policies which would open new vistas for women religious in our Church in America. The challenges and sacrifices involved can be viewed as richly rewarded because of the encouragement they have offered to other religious communities. Know that we of smaller congregations appreciate the generous sharing of Sisters like yourself from larger groups...May you reap God's choicest blessings for the love and concern you have shown for God's church.[127]

Father Anthony Bellagamba, IMC, the executive director of the United States Catholic Mission Association (USMCA) said:

We wish to thank you, Sr. Theresa and all the other members of your Generalate, for your support of the USMCA and for the prophetic example you all have given to the whole Church. When these past few years will be history, it will be evident to all what is clear to some of us now: that you have been real prophets and true women of the kingdom and of the Church. We thank you for that and we admire you a lot.[128]

"I CAN NO OTHER ANSWER MAKE BUT THANKS..."

In her final "Accountability Report" to the Mercy community, Theresa thanked her sisters on behalf of the entire Mercy Administrative Team for the "graced opportunity and the privilege that have been ours to serve you...The full impact of these brief years is written in our hearts, and in our lives and memories." She briefly reviewed the journey the Mercy community had taken over the previous fifteen years when "we have attempted to incorporate as lived experience the vision of Vatican II, especially its teaching about the primacy of the person," which "has had revolutionary effects upon the life and mission of Catholics and their church." She reminded sisters of their call to "continuing conversion" and of the community's prophetic 1977 chapter decision "to direct [our] human and material resources in promoting justice" within society, the church and the Mercy community itself.

In a poignant passage she wrote, "These past seven years have been years of special grace. Today they seem as but an instant. There have been many joys; there has also been suffering. I struggle to integrate both joy and sorrow and to understand God's Mercy—a Mercy which is akin to amnesty (amnesia), a Mercy that not only forgives but forgets..." She felt that she had a "deeper belief in the inherent goodness of humanity..." and that "we are gifted co-creators with God, yet limited, fearful, and fragile creatures of the earth. God knows all, this God who is Mercy, Justice and Peace."[129]

The front page of the last issue of *Union Scope* for which Theresa would ever be responsible featured her photograph alongside those of the other four members of this gifted Administrative Team: Emily George, Mary Ellen Quinn, Betty Barrett, and Rosemary Ronk. A headline from Shakespeare's *Twelfth Night* read: "I can no other answer make but thanks, and thanks, and ever thanks."

Perhaps even more telling was a photograph of the artistic rendering given her in May by the LCWR presidents who quoted her own words: "Let us courageously confront the changes needed in our church and society. Confrontation when coupled with reverence, honesty, and charity is a Christian responsibility. How essential it is to approach our future with fidelity, perseverance and non-violence."[130]

CHAPTER NINE

A Lifetime of Prophetic Service

The summer Theresa completed her term as president was filled with transitions. Her mother Mamie had become very ill and required hospitalization soon after the family celebrated her eighty-sixth birthday. Theresa was able to spend precious time with Mamie before she died during the last week of June, just as the Administrative Team was transferring leadership. The entire team—Sisters Emily George, Rosemary Ronk, Betty Barrett, and Mary Ellen Quinn, along with Theresa's good friend Della Mae, attended Mamie's wake and funeral in New York. They returned to Washington in time for a previously planned farewell celebration that, in addition to Sisters of Mercy, included a number of bishops from the NCCB Committee on Women who were in town for a meeting.

Shortly thereafter, Theresa flew to Belize for a meeting of the Mercy Latin American Conference. With Betty Barrett, Theresa was intimately involved in founding the new group and had been asked to be present at the early July gathering. She reflects, "It was almost a week after my mother died and I remember being in Belize near the ocean, thinking about her and saying to myself 'It is so strange that...she died, and here I am down in Belize. Two very different worlds...'"

In August, Theresa attended the LCWR assembly for the last time as an officeholder. As a past president, however, she was invited to attend future assemblies anytime she chose. In the years that followed she rarely missed the annual event and reveled in catching up with old friends and encouraging new sister-leaders.

That fall, Theresa entered into a sabbatical time to reflect, decompress, and heal from the pressures (and the pain) that had accompanied her high-profile leadership. Her journal from this time—the only time in her life that she regularly kept one—reveals vulnerabilities that she rarely allowed others to see. It also chronicles her slow transition into the next stages of her life's journey. She recalls that on the day she began her sabbatical she went to church and spent time reflecting on her experiences as administrator general:

> I was looking at the crucifix and remember just being struck by the fact that Jesus was stripped naked hanging on the cross. I never really felt I was in any way crucified. I never had that sense that people were picking on me...I just knew that we were trying to [respond to] the legitimate cries and calls of the sisters and trying to be very faithful about it, realizing that not everybody understood it. Not everyone agreed with it. But we still wanted to follow our consciences. It was as if I were naked—in the sense of being pure and standing before God and saying that I have done as much as I think I was called to do or should have done.

RESOLUTION OF ATTEMPTS TO CENSURE THERESA

In late August, Theresa received a call from the new president, Sister Helen Amos. Helen told her she had received a letter from Archbishop Jerome Hamer at the Congregation for the Doctrine of the Faith (CDF) instructing her to either publicly censure Theresa or take some kind of action to differentiate the new Mercy leaders from their predecessors.[1] The CDF was particularly perturbed by the pastoral letter Theresa had written the previous January.[2] They took exception to her suggestion that restricting church leadership to men constituted "a form and expression of idolatry."[3]

Helen recalls being "totally appalled" by the idea of public censure. "What the letter asked of us was so far from what we considered right and just, it was ridiculous."[4] Furthermore, she felt it would be inflammatory to the broader Mercy community if it learned what the Vatican was asking them to do.

Theresa asked Helen if she could see the CDF communication. Helen said yes and invited her input. "The letter was addressed to them, not to me," Theresa reflected. "They were the ones who in their consciences had to make a decision about how they wanted to respond." She wrote to Helen expressing her appreciation for being included and advised that "in my judgment you and your team need to pray and reflect about this and make the decision that you believe is appropriate."

On September 24 (Theresa's birthday and Mercy Day), she met in person with Helen and the Administrative Team. She remembers saying that the previous team "had done what we thought was right according to [the decisions of] the chapter..." At the same time—while she recognized that the new Mercy Administrative Team would approach things differently—she voiced her expectation that they would be faithful to chapter directions. "This is just political, highly political," she said. "They want to make sure that you don't continue the same way that we [the previous team] did." After the meeting adjourned, Helen Amos and the other Mercy leaders began pondering their response. At the time, Helen explained:

> We as a community were feeling really embattled. There was a sense that we could barely conduct our business for all the public attention we were getting. There was criticism, much of it extremely unfair, and prejudice against anything the Sisters of Mercy would do...My sense was that we had to continue what this was about at its root, the search for truth. We had accepted...responsibility for the communal search for truth and could not back off from it. But we had to try to pursue it under calmer circumstances.[5]

At the Twelfth General Chapter, discussion about the 1977 *Our Relationship within the Church* statement had moved away from focusing on specific women's issues and identified "the church's search for truth and our part in that..." as a new direction.[6] The vice-president of the congregation, Sister Helen Marie Burns, recalls that "clearly nobody was going to censure Theresa...but at the same time the chapter itself had pulled back...Legitimately Helen could have said that we're not in the same place now as we were before."[7] Helen Amos suggests that the fact that the chapter had elected her—a "known quantity"—signaled that the sister-delegates wanted a slightly different approach: "I was a person who was not going to be the fearlessly vocal proponent of the message, but neither would I be unfaithful to the message."[8] She remembers the new Mercy Administrative Team asking:

> How can we lift up the unity—by concentrating on the charism of mercy—without quashing the individuality, the diversity as it is expressed in different personal opinions and proclivities...? How can we continue to develop our self-understanding as responsible members of the church in order to contribute collaboratively in the church community...? Everybody doesn't feel the same way, [and] there are very strongly held convictions. But we need to be one in some way, and we need to be one within the church.[9]

Helen Amos recalls seeking the counsel of Archbishop John R. Quinn, who translated a Latin adage about Vatican politics for her: "You are right, but we are not wrong." From this she deduced, "He was sympathetic to the bind we were in, but also signaling to me that there are certain battles you are not going to win even if you're right."[10]

In October, the Mercy Administrative Team found a way to respond to Rome without censuring Theresa. Helen Amos wrote a private letter to the CDF essentially saying that the new team would "not be continuing with the same controversial issues," as the previous administration.[11] On October 24, she shared the letter with Theresa, who was very distressed by it and requested a follow-up meeting with the Administrative Team. This meeting was set for Tuesday, November 6.

On the Friday beforehand, Theresa flew to New York to attend her first provincial assembly meeting as a rank-and-file member, someone not in a position of leadership. She wrote in her journal at the time: "How much I experienced 'You can never go home again' feelings at the end of the meeting. I worked to incorporate myself into the meeting—perhaps too hard—It was like trying to put the 'toothpaste back in the tube!' I found it difficult."[12] On November 6 she met with the Administrative Team and shared her concerns:

I thanked them for meeting with me and said, "I realize that you're in a very delicate position here and you're trying to follow your vision and set your goals. I just want you to know I was disappointed in the response because so much of what we did was from the vision of the 1977 chapter. It was not just from me personally...

At the chapter's behest, Doris [Gottemoeller] and I went to Rome and spoke to [SCRIS and the CDF] about women's ordination. We told them that our community had endorsed it. We followed up with Church/Institute Committee recommendations about tubal ligation. We also were actively involved in political ministry with Agnes Mary. We had been asked by the chapter to do that. The chapter endorsed political ministry for the Sisters of Mercy.

From Theresa's perspective, she had done only what she was obligated to do as administrator general. Helen Amos gently said, "I'm sorry, Theresa. We prayed about it and this was the best we could do." Theresa's journal—written two days after the meeting—provides an immediate window into her sentiments at the time:

I met with the [Administrative Team] on Tuesday and shared my four concerns about the October letter to Archbishop Hamer. I was more anxious and nervous at it than I'd anticipated. They listened and responded so reverently and graciously. I expected some hostility and defensiveness but there was none. More and more I feel like a revered "elder." It is a rather new experience and I need to care for the role delicately. Meeting with team was a graced moment. Helen Burns was extraordinary.[13]

On December 12, Theresa noted in her journal: "The Vatican accepted Helen Amos's letter. I was relieved but not joyous... How very frightened I get—how very much I need to truly trust so deeply in my loving God who is especially close in times of difficulties. I pray for a great deepening of faith."[14]

An Unexpected Healing

While the Administrative Team was struggling to address a potentially incendiary demand to censure her, Theresa was enjoying a less hectic schedule that included time for daily swims at the local pool, writing in her journal, and watching Geraldine Ferraro debate as the first major party female candidate for vice-president. She also continued occasional visits to her psychologist in Albany, who anticipated that their work together would soon be completed.

In mid-October 1984, Theresa attended Sunday noon Mass at St. John the Baptist parish in Silver Spring, Maryland. The sacrament of the sick had been planned as part of the liturgy. Although Theresa had not submitted her name as a participant, she decided to "enter into the spirit of the service and receive and experience healing for myself and for our world."[15] She remembers "reflecting on my own brokenness and the areas of alienation, hostility, and fear in my life."[16] Her last session with her therapist had "unearthed some painful things about myself in my relationships with my parents,"[17] and she found herself remembering the harrowing struggles with the institutional church. Her journal recounts what happened at the Mass.

I was overwhelmed with a tremendous sense of God's presence and a profound sense of healing within myself. It was as if the difficulties and the suffering of the past years, especially the suffering of the most recent years with the ecclesiastical authorities had just been washed away. I felt an overwhelming sense of relief, peace, love and as if something heavy had been removed from me. I was very overwhelmed by the experience and I began to cry quietly but very deeply.

A young child—a girl who was accompanied by an adult—reached over and grasped my hand. She wanted to give me consolation. It was a beautiful moment and I thought immediately of the phrases in scripture referring to a child leading us—the child having insights—the love and simplicity of a child.

I prayed so earnestly to be as that young child—loving, pure, gentle, caressing, joyous, and simple. I wanted so to wash away any ugliness, any bitterness, hostility, and fear from within my very being and spirit. I prayed so that my life, my heart, and my spirit would become pure, loving, fearless, and so trusting in God and Her Providence to me.

I reached out in spirit to join hands with John Paul II, Pio Laghi, the bishops in general—and to reach out to all humankind in all parts of our earth.

I feel that I have been healed in spirit and wish to continue on a journey towards greater purification of thought, motive, words, and actions—wanting only what God wants and wanting only good for all persons—grieving at any thought of violence, hostility, suffering and harm which we do to one another.[18]

WHAT HAPPENED TO THERESA'S LEADERSHIP COLLEAGUES?

Theresa's first year out of office was marked not only by the death of her mother, but also by the deaths of two of her Mercy Administrative teammates. On August 26, her fellow Administrative Team member and friend, Sister Rosemary Ronk from Omaha, lost a yearlong battle with recurrent cancer. Before she died, Rosemary wrote this message to her friends:

I will be passing through the event of death in order to continue on with my life. I thank each of you for your gracious and loving assistance to me during this unique moment of life . . . I am as excited and as curious about what lies ahead—after death—as I have always been about the future.[19]

When Rosemary died, the annual LCWR meeting was in progress in Kansas City. Theresa comments, "You would not believe all the sisters who left that meeting to go to her funeral. They were crazy about her. She was on the committee for the assembly that year and was always actively involved in both national and regional leadership for LCWR."

While the Mercy community had time to prepare for the loss of Rosemary, shockwaves went through the ranks when Sister Emily George died instantly in a car accident on December 6, 1984. She had encountered a bad snowstorm while driving back to the University of Notre Dame from a board meeting at Mercy College in Detroit.

On December 12 Theresa recorded her feelings:

> I am in great sorrow... the overwhelming experience is a void—an empty feeling—I have such an urge to fill the hole but know that I cannot and should not—I must take within my heart and spirit this emptiness, this void. Time, friends, God's mercy and love will eventually heal it. She became such a part of my life in these past four years... She and I shared such intense experiences that we became as one in so many ways.[20]

In a homily eulogizing her lifelong friend, Sister Margaret Farley recalled that a foundational belief in Emily's life was a passage from the Song of Songs as it relates to the saving mystery of Jesus: "'Love is as strong as death.'[Song of Songs 8:6] And the Good News is just that—given in the revelation of God in Jesus Christ."[21] In searching for "a perfect biblical figure" to describe Emily, Margaret reflected,

> It would be that of a woman who could weep like Rachel, press for wisdom and justice like Deborah, strategize around incompetence and malice like Miriam, and bear a sword of sorrow like Mary, but sing with a free and peaceful heart, "My soul glorifies the Lord, and My spirit rejoices in God my Savior."[22]

In Detroit for Emily's funeral, Theresa recalls that people kept saying, "Emily's work was done." But for Theresa, "Her work was just beginning. She was so passionate about women in history. She was a great historian. I knew she was going to do great work on the history of women." About a week after Emily's funeral Theresa received an unexpected sympathy letter from the papal nuncio, Archbishop Pio Laghi. She and Emily had met with him many times in the difficult negotiations surrounding the Mercy tubal ligation study and other matters. Theresa reflected in her journal:

It was so strange to get a note from him, and yet his sentiments did console me. God somehow was using him as an instrument for me—the paradoxes of life—when Pio and I have had such conflicts and even now he has not granted my request for a personal appointment with him. This may be his only way of reaching out at this time.

How much I need to be wise—to be compassionate—to be loving, gentle and strong amidst suffering, anguish, and pain both from those with whom I share life and with those who are so present to me through death—my Mom and Dad— Emily and Rosie...[23]

The other members of the 1980–84 Mercy Administrative Team went on to ministries that typify the community's Vatican II passion to bring mercy and justice to a broken world. For many years Sister Mary Ellen Quinn served as the administrator of a very poor parish along the southwest border of New Mexico in the diocese of Las Cruces. "She absolutely loved it," remembers Theresa. Mary Ellen returned to Omaha to help care for her ailing mother and died suddenly in her sleep on December 3, 2008.

Sister Betty Barrett returned to Chicago and worked in poor neighborhoods for a time before she began a seven-year ministry in Honduras. Betty was greatly beloved by the Honduran people. Theresa recalls, "One of the Honduran sisters told me that if you visited the neighborhood people, you would find three pictures on the wall: John Kennedy, John Paul II, and Betty Barrett." When Betty celebrated her fiftieth jubilee in Honduras, her provincial called Theresa, "Betty doesn't want anything for her jubilee. Nothing at all. We came up with the idea that we would send you to her." Theresa spent two weeks experiencing firsthand Betty's great love for the Honduran people,

She always had a group of women around her. She was so pastoral. "Come in, come in, come in," she would say and then she would fix tea for them. She sat in the living room patiently an hour, an hour and a half. These were very, very busy women and they had about ten kids each, but they loved coming in and sitting talking to her.

Theresa chuckles over this story because Betty was not fluent in Spanish and often had no idea what people were actually saying. "The only thing I'm doing in Honduras is a ministry of presence," Betty would explain. "I'm here. They see me. I smile. I hug them. I bless them and that's all." For Theresa, "She was like the priest among them or the pope."

After Betty returned from Honduras, she ministered in Aurora, Illinois. She and Theresa stayed in close touch over the years. In 2001, Betty traveled to New York to be present with Della Mae when Theresa was hospitalized with a life-threatening illness. A year before Betty's death in 2011, Theresa organized a ninetieth birthday party for her, traveling from New York to Chicago to celebrate with her dear friend.

SABBATICAL LEARNINGS

In the months before leaving office, Theresa was encouraged to consider pursuing whatever she wished during her time off. Two things attracted her. One was to spend time in a missionary environment and the other was to spend time in a cloister. As a young woman she had been attracted to both lifestyles but had pursued a different path in her earlier life as a Sister of Mercy. On her sabbatical, she felt that "it would fulfill some need in me to be in the missionary area and also to be with the Carmelite sisters."

From January 11 through February 20, 1985, Theresa ministered with the Sisters of Mercy at their hospital in Guyana. She spent the month of April with the Carmelite sisters in Beacon, New York. Both experiences provided her with what some might call a desert experience—away from her usual supports—which allowed for significant reflection about what had been, and what was yet to be.

Theresa had chosen Guyana because it was English-speaking and she was already familiar with the sisters and the hospital, having visited several times. She worked with various hospital departments, helping them prepare financial statements and budgets, and lived at the Georgetown convent of the Sisters of Mercy. The work was not difficult, but it was tedious since everything had to be done manually. Theresa found herself "in awe of the staff members who do their extensive paperwork with such care and precision." While she was away, she missed Della Mae and her US friends more than she had anticipated.

In some ways the experience echoed—albeit to a lesser degree—her earliest months with the Sisters of Mercy. Her journal on January 22 notes: "Since I have come, I was so very lonesome the first few days...I am getting better, but I didn't realize it would be so hard ...the great distance and the inability to pick up a phone and talk freely and leisurely [to Della Mae] has made the separation very painful." In the same entry she reflected:

Perhaps the central lesson I am learning is something that is so obvious, but it came home to me again—that wherever I go, I bring myself. The biggest challenge before me is to know myself well...to be very honest with myself and to study my thoughts, behavior, words, and actions so I can live my life according to what God wants of and for me...It is such a challenge to become interiorly free—and to create an environment where others can be free to be who and what they are without any prejudgments or prejudices from me.[24]

In considering her experience in Guyana many years later, Theresa believes she developed "a great appreciation of what it was really like to be so economically poor. When we grew up, we were economically poor, but this was really very severe poverty...And you could see it. Just walk through the streets, and you saw it. So that was very touching to me." She also gained a deeper insight into her own racism.

It helped me to move into a setting where everybody was black...and to live among black and brown sisters. And then meeting and going among the men, who were very, very black, helped me get over maybe some racism that I had, and I didn't even realize it. I found myself a little bit afraid of black men. And I think that came from how I grew up.

On February 2, 1985, while she was in Guyana, Theresa celebrated the thirtieth anniversary of her entrance into the Sisters of Mercy. In the afternoon she recorded precious memories about the day she entered, noting, "I am so in touch with my beautiful and loving parents—I never would have imagined that on this day they would both be dead and that I would be in Guyana, South America— a long way from 415 Brook Avenue in the Bronx."[25] She also spent a good deal of time reflecting on her own fears and what her struggles with the institutional church now seemed to require.

I need to meditate on the fears I feel...to make an act of faith and trust in God when I am afraid. To know that God who has created and sustained me until now loves me and every other creature she/he has made and that we are called to be at one with each other...To not only forgive but to forget—the amnesia of God—how much I need to learn about remembrance and amnesty...

The essence of love is a forgetfulness of events which hindered or stifled the love...It is in forgetfulness that love continues to grow, create, and develop. In the remembrance of hurt, despair, [and] hostility, destruction occurs—a form of hell... How I need to meditate on and learn the essence of the justice of God—how God remembers, forgets, and in her/his time, rights the wrongs without harming or destroying those who cause or are instruments of the harm.[26]

That same evening, Theresa renewed her vows privately in the convent chapel,

> I recommit and rededicate the rest of my life to the Core and Center—God. And to be and live in a relationship of charity in heart and spirit to every human being—almost five billion of us inhabit this planet—perhaps there are others in other parts of the universe. It is to God—not institutions or structures that I rededicate my future.[27]

Immediately after this she wrote, almost as an afterthought, "I am growing more anxious at Mass with our hierarchical sexist symbols. I try not to direct my concern toward the priest. I need patience and wisdom to know how to [behave] as Mary, Jesus, and other holy persons might behave... Please O God, help me to turn to you for guidance during such times."[28] In the years ahead, Theresa would speak publicly many, many times about the need for inclusive language in worship.

On the plane ride home on February 20, Theresa listed some personal learnings from her time in Guyana. These included her love of using her talents and gifts to help others; her love of accounting, analyzing reports, and working with figures; her desire to become more relational in her task-oriented approach to work; and her "high oral needs and continued desires to eat and drink, especially after the work day is over."[29] She had enjoyed the relaxation afforded by a greater opportunity to read, and she greatly appreciated the "tremendous example and inspiration" each of the sisters serving in Guyana had been to her, especially "their goodness and care, amidst overwhelming problems and deprivations."[30]

A month later, she wrote that the experience had helped her to realize "how vast, how different, how rich and yet how poor our world is... and how much I need to become and stay attuned to peoples all over the globe." Shopping at the local supermarket at home in Dobbs Ferry, she became "overwhelmed with the excessiveness of the goods and food available," and pondered the impossibility of ordinary people in the United States "ever imagining that people are poor and starving."[31] For the rest of her life Theresa never forgot the reality of global poverty, and she spoke about it frequently in presentations to various audiences across the country and in Canada.

Theresa was looking forward to her month-long retreat at Carmel, although she was "a little afraid of it also...it may be a new moment for me." She prayed for a readiness "to enter fully and wholly into whatever God is asking of me for this moment and whatever my God you will ask of me for my future—for our future together."[32] Perhaps to prepare for her retreat, she asked Father Charles Curran to be the minister of the sacrament of reconciliation for her. A long-time friend and prophetic figure himself, Charlie well understood the spiritual pitfalls that can accompany a call to challenge the clerical system out of love for the People of God. Theresa's journal records that the two met for about an hour and that "it was such a good experience for him and for me":

> I mentioned a number of attitudes, feeling within my heart— some tendencies and motivations within me. Charlie spoke of the need to be so attuned to the merciful, loving, gentle, compassionate God—whom we call Father/Mother—and the need for continuing self-criticism. He spoke of the importance of community—church as community—church which strengthens, nurtures and cares for us and we for each other. We conversed about the need for and grace of avoiding bitterness and cynicism [which are] forms of self-destruction.

> My resolve: Monitoring my interior dispositions—my attitudes of charity—to deepen a sense of love, kindness, and gentleness towards all people. The need for a deep, attentive presence to every person and every event. To be active in my attitude of receiving the present moment...To enter into the heart, life, and concern of another—to truly be compassionate ...to empathize with others.[33]

Curran agreed to Theresa's request to meet for reconciliation three or four times a year, "at the beginning of the year, during Lent, before the summer and perhaps again in the fall." The two met until 1986 when he left Washington, DC, after being forced out of his position at the Catholic University of America. Reflecting on the meetings with Theresa, Curran comments,

> It was sort of a mutual kind of thing—it wasn't a one-way street. Obviously, we both shared the same basic positions. She had been chastised by the pope and I had been chastised by Ratzinger and the pope. I immediately recognized that she

was really a woman of great holiness and that there was much more to Theresa than simply what people saw on a television screen.[34]

In 1985 Curran dedicated his book *Directions in Fundamental Moral Theology* to the two recently deceased members of the 1980–84 Mercy Administrative Team, Sisters Rosemary Ronk and Emily George. He would maintain a warm friendship with the Sisters of Mercy and with Theresa for many years to come.

Theresa's stay at the monastery was fruitful for her. She arrived on March 27 and was warmly welcomed by the sisters who—after having lived for many years in Theresa's hometown of the Bronx—had moved to Beacon, New York, three years previously. She was delighted to have been invited to live among them, join them for prayer, and share their evening meal two nights a week. Theresa met daily with a sister-scholar who was an expert on Teresa of Avila. Otherwise she spent her days in silence. She did not find it difficult, "because during the day, I would be in the chapel praying. I did a lot of walking in the afternoon, and I did my own reading every day."

While Theresa was at the monastery, Della Mae's mother died after a long illness. Theresa left her monastic retreat to attend the services and support her friend. She returned shortly thereafter, but said, "I felt bad about it because [Della Mae] could have used me at that point."

Summarizing her experiences with the Carmelite sisters, Theresa comments, "I really had a [greater] appreciation of what I had gone through myself. I had time to review and go over my years in leadership ... It was a contemplative experience for me, for sure, and I certainly felt closer to God as a result of it." She also came away with the insight that the life of a contemplative sister "was probably not the life for me ... I left knowing that what I had done with my life seemed a better fit than going to a Carmelite monastery. I needed to be active, to be of service."

Moving Forward: 1985–1995

After her sojourns in Guyana and at the monastery, Theresa was asked by the Washington-based Center of Concern to be an observer at the United Nations Third International World Conference on Women. Held in Nairobi, Kenya, from July 15 to 26, 1985, the conference mandate was to establish concrete measures to overcome obstacles to achieving "the goals of the UN Decade for Women." There were nineteen hundred delegates from 157 member states in attendance. A parallel NGO (non-governmental organization) event attracted twelve thousand participants.[35]

Conference planners designed ten days of grassroots workshops that preceded the actual conference. Women were invited to lead these. As Theresa remembers, "You could participate in so many workshops. It was ten dollars a day. Many of the native women went to it because they could afford that." There were workshops on domestic violence, wife abuse, children, and the education of girls. Theresa found the structure itself empowering because it allowed for "self-education by the women themselves. Women came from all these little villages. They got up at four o'clock in the morning and spent hours to get there on a bus."

Adrian Dominican Sister Maria Reilly from the Center of Concern accompanied Theresa, who had made arrangements for them to stay with the Sisters of Mercy in Nairobi. Founded by Irish sisters, the Nairobi community was diverse, and it included African sisters from various (and sometimes competing) tribes, Irish sisters, and sisters from the Indian subcontinent.

Returning to the United States, Theresa began a second year of sabbatical. Since Della Mae was still working for LCWR and Theresa's future ministry had yet to emerge, they remained in their Washington, DC, apartment. Theresa decided to complete the master's degree in public administration that she had begun so many years earlier at New York University. She took the train to New York City every week, attended classes for two days, and commuted home. The Sisters of Charity graciously offered hospitality at their convent on Washington Square.

It was a relaxing schedule especially because Theresa did not find her graduate studies difficult. At this time, she humorously recalls, "I started being the domestic partner at home." Previously, Della Mae had done all of the grocery shopping and cooking to accommodate Theresa's busy schedule as president. Theresa now assumed those chores saying, "That was a reverse and it was enjoyable. I loved doing it." When Della Mae came home, dinner would be ready, and the ever-sociable Theresa would discuss the day's highlights, "I have to tell you what happened when I went to Stop & Shop." Della Mae would laugh, "I never met anybody who has an experience every time she goes out . . . you [Theresa] always have such stories when you go to the store."

The slower pace gave Theresa time to consider what she wanted to do next. As a younger sister, she had been attracted to teaching high school. Now, as her sabbatical drew to a close, she wrote to inquire about a faculty position at a Mercy high school in the Bronx and offered "to do whatever you think I can do." The high school did not have an opening. Meanwhile, the New York provincial visited Washington to ask a favor. A Sister of Mercy who administered a nursing home on Tupper Lake in the Adirondacks wanted to attract more sisters to work on her staff. The facility needed help in the finance office and in fundraising. As Theresa tells it, Della Mae "almost died." Me? Going to the Adirondacks?

City girls born and bred, neither Della Mae nor Theresa could really see themselves in this bucolic setting, but since the provincial "seemed so desperate to get sisters there," they agreed to go. Theresa later described the decision as "a complete disaster." The finance office had an outmoded system of recordkeeping and the billing was significantly in arrears. Theresa worked to get the accounts payable in order, but it was difficult because some bills were more than ten years past due. Della Mae had no real background in fundraising and did not find the position a good fit for her skills. Theresa soon realized that what the agency actually needed was someone familiar with recent Medicaid and Medicare third-party billing practices. Not only was she not up to date with these, she was not inclined to learn about them either. "I don't want to do finances for the next ten years . . . I don't think God is calling me there," she remembers saying to herself.

Over the Christmas holidays the two met with the provincial again. Theresa told her that while both had wanted to help, the Tupper Lake ministry was not working out. "We'd be better off hiring someone who's really a professional finance person, who's up to date on nursing home finances, and let that person get started. We're just delaying the inevitable," Theresa said. While she may have viewed the Tupper Lake experience as "a disaster," it did clarify for Theresa what she did not want to be doing in coming years.

In February 1987 Theresa and Della Mae left Tupper Lake and moved to a "very nice" three-bedroom apartment in Yonkers. Della Mae soon found work at Phelps Hospital in nearby Tarrytown, and later at Cabrini Hospital. The principal of Our Lady of Victory Academy in Dobbs Ferry, Sister Mary Dillane, had heard that Theresa and Della Mae were moving to the area and offered Theresa a campus ministry position at the all-girls high school. Although Theresa had no prior experience, Mary was eager to have sisters on staff and promised to work with her.

Over the next three and a half years Theresa organized numerous social justice activities and gathered groups of girls to help her plan school-wide eucharistic celebrations. On Thanksgiving mornings, she drove a contingent of girls to the Bowery to serve homeless men, returning in the early afternoon. Once she invited Father Dan Berrigan, SJ, to celebrate Mass. Mary wisely suggested that Theresa send a note advising parents that the controversial peace activist would visit the school. Several students returned with notes asking if their mothers could come to the Mass too. "So we had four or five mothers at the Mass," Theresa remembers. "They wanted to see Dan Berrigan. And the kids didn't have a clue who he was."

When Berrigan asked Theresa what Gospel reading she planned to use, she told him, "I only have one Gospel, Dan, it is the *Magnificat*. I use that for everything." After a student read the Gospel, Theresa remembers that Berrigan "gave a little homily and then went down among them with his microphone. He asked what they thought of this and that and the other thing. He was wonderful. They loved him."

The high school often had difficulty finding priests for Mass or the sacrament of reconciliation. But because of Theresa's prodigious social network, she could usually convince someone to come: "I'd call them up and say, 'Just give me an hour, that's all. An hour and a half and then you're outta here...'" During Lent, she remembers, "we would have a penance service followed by individual confessions, which they never had there before because they couldn't find a priest."

In 1990 Theresa was asked to serve on the formation team for new members in the Sisters of Mercy. She served for about seven years, three of which were as director of formation. From 1992 until 1996 she was the administrator of the Dobbs Ferry motherhouse until it was sold to Mercy College in 1995. The decision to sell the motherhouse had been made ten years earlier but the buyer financing had not materialized.[36] In hindsight, Theresa found this "providential" since the mission of Mercy College was more consonant with the vision of the Sisters of Mercy than selling to real estate developers would have been. In addition, the college was already utilizing several wings of the motherhouse for students.

Along with her colleagues, Theresa helped prepare the motherhouse for sale. She then helped to relocate some seventy retired sisters. Using funds realized from the sale of the property, Mercy leadership solicited funding from four other communities of women religious and together the women built a retirement facility for sisters from their respective orders. In 2001 Marian Woods opened in Hartsdale, New York. Theresa and Della Mae would move there in 2002, and Theresa lives there today.

While willing to administer the motherhouse for a short time, Theresa soon realized it was time to move on to a different ministry. "I gave my youth to administration. I was done," she remembers. In

1992, a professor at Mercy College asked her to teach a course on the history of women and she realized she wanted to teach at the college level. "I came to the conclusion that although I had thought all along that I wanted to teach in a high school, once I was there, I found them quite immature...Some were very interested, some were not. I would rather be in a college setting where students are there because they want to be there."

A friend at the college advised that she would need a liberal arts preparation in religion or history. Theresa had always enjoyed history and decided that, "having come out of years of experience of doing women in church and society, I would like to focus on women's history." In 1992 there were only two places that offered a graduate degree in women's history—Sarah Lawrence College in Bronxville[37] and Rutgers, the State University of New Jersey.

Sarah Lawrence was very close to home, so, in addition to her administrator's job, Theresa pursued part-time graduate studies in Bronxville for the next several years. These included courses on women in world history, gender in politics, and gender and sexuality. For her dissertation, Theresa interviewed ten women religious about their experiences twenty years before Vatican II and ten sisters who entered religious life after the Vatican Council. She found it "absolutely fascinating. The older sisters said that for thirty years no matter what house they lived in, they didn't need to even look at the daily schedule because everyone did everything at the same time."

In 1995 Theresa received a master of arts in women's history from Sarah Lawrence College, and in the late summer she attended the Fourth UN World Conference on Women in Beijing as a delegate of the Sisters of Mercy. When she returned, she gave presentations about her experiences to various groups around the country. For the 1995–96 school year she began teaching in earnest as an adjunct professor of religion at Mercy College.

A Gifted Teacher

From 1995 until this writing, Theresa has taught thousands of students at Mercy College on three of its four campuses in the greater New York City area. Consonant with the values of its sister-founders, Mercy College's mission is "to provide educational access for traditional and non-traditional students. These include students who may be demographically underrepresented in higher education, who have high financial need, and/or view themselves as first-generation college students."[38] The college values affordability. On average, its costs are 50 percent lower than those of surrounding private colleges, and it offers significant financial aid in the form of scholarships, grants, and work-study programs. Approximately 85 percent of Mercy College students receive some form of financial assistance. Diversity is highly valued, with students hailing from thirty-five countries and thirty-eight states.

Theresa usually taught at the Bronx and Dobbs Ferry campuses of Mercy College. In 2000 she became an associate professor in a new Master's in Public Administration program and began teaching graduate students. She continued teaching undergraduates with courses on the history of women, the history of world religions, sociology, and religion and psychology. For many years she taught religion in the Bronx to first generation Latino/a students hailing from the Dominican Republic, Honduras, Puerto Rico, Cuba, and the Caribbean. Many were also the first in their families to attend college. Although religion was part of the family heritage, Theresa observed, "[Religion] just wasn't part of [the students'] lives, at least not formal religion …They would say "my father is a retired Catholic. He doesn't go anymore. I made my baptism and my communion in the church but I haven't been back since." Even so, she remembers that her religion classes "were always packed" with the school maximum of thirty students. Faculty advisors often told struggling students to "sign up for Professor Kane. She teaches a good course in religion."

Theresa was fond of assigning creative, experiential projects. She asked her students to visit religious sites of any denomination, attend a service or ceremony at the site, and write a five-page paper about the experience. She provided addresses for nearby churches, synagogues, Zen temples, mosques, and even storefronts. Students could go alone or with friends and family. The idea was to have a personal experience of some religious expression of worship. In Theresa's mind, this was important because

> you can come to class and you are getting all this knowledge, …But the field trip experience makes it more real for you. The students go to the church, the synagogue, or the mosque and it's a little overwhelming and a little frightening. But they get through the experience, and then they have a better sense of religion.

At first some students "hated doing the project." But on their course evaluations at semester's end, the vast majority found it worthwhile.

Several even told Theresa, "You know I really should have been going [to church]. I'm going to start going back." She wryly clarifies: "Now that might mean once or twice a year."

Another assignment was perhaps even more meaningful. She asked that they "choose a figure of inspiration,...pick out someone that you really think is passionately alive and interview them." She explained the experience would help them know "what religion is all about—it is to put spirit and life and passion into another." Many students interviewed family members—especially parents or siblings—who had displayed great courage in dealing with an illness or disability. The stories were beautiful, but a good many were also very sad. "They actually sat down with their mother and found out she had been abused," Theresa lamented. "That came up over and over again—how much their mothers had been sexually abused or beaten in the past." When students shared their stories in class, they would weep, "and everyone in the room would be crying too." Still, she felt

> it helped them to go into another person's life. I used to say, "Now, this is very vulnerable for you because you're telling us something very personal. However, you have the solidarity in this room. We're all friends, we're peers here." I said, "You're going to feel a stronger relationship with each other after it," and they did.

At the completion of each student's story, Theresa honored the experience by gently suggesting "Let's just take a couple of moments of quiet." She found the other students "were just in awe of these young women or men who got up and told those stories. They were so moved by them." Although she had attended panels on domestic abuse in Nairobi and Beijing, Theresa was somewhat shocked at the prevalence of abuse in her students' families. "Any number of these were Hispanic women, and they ended up usually getting a divorce and then remarrying. Sometimes it was better and sometimes it was worse."

Theresa brought the same values of mutuality and empowerment to her teaching ministry that she had espoused in all of her previous ministries, a habit that endeared her to faculty and students alike. She especially enjoyed interacting with the students: "I always said to them, 'We're very different ages, but you come in here with experiences that I've never had. And I come with experiences that you never had, so it is a sense of mutuality, where we learn from each other about these experiences.'" She admired how solicitous her students were of one another.

> And they were forever texting. One would run up and say, "Joe said he's going to be a little bit late, but he'll be here as soon as he can." I think that was good. If someone in somebody's family was sick, they would ask, "How are they doing?" Even though there were strangers in the room, they were willing to talk with each other. I had them working in small groups most of the time, so they got to know each other well. Friendship was very important to them.

At this writing, Theresa no longer teaches undergraduates but continues to mentor graduate students in the Master's in Public Administration program in health leadership. In 1999 she received the Outstanding Teacher Award from students on the Bronx campus and in 2005 the faculty of Mercy College honored her with its Outstanding Teacher Award. On July 15, 2015, the college gave her its prestigious lifetime achievement award at the annual Trustees Scholarship Dinner. A brief video created at the time reprised her life, from her widely publicized address to the pope, to a time of quiet prayer in the Marian Woods chapel.[39]

Dr. Ann Grow, professor of philosophy at Mercy College, praised her: "Theresa is the valiant woman of the Old Testament, brave, humble, and strong... The spirit of the Sisters of Mercy is still alive at Mercy College because of her—and others—who love educating those that haven't had a chance." Professor Eileen McMahon saw Theresa as "an agent of change... It is this quiet, passionate, consistent service of those who need it—for the joy of it, for the joy of serving." In the video, a frail, soft-spoken Daniel Berrigan, SJ, said, "I want to congratulate [Theresa] and say thank you—you walked straight into the fire but that is the story of your faith."[40]

HEALTH CHALLENGES

In the early 1990s Theresa's sister Nancy (Sister Ann) was diagnosed with a rare form of Alzheimer's disease. Just sixty years old, she was living in a Sisters of Mercy–owned apartment in Yonkers with several other Mercy sisters at the time. When her housemates relocated to other ministries, Theresa and Della Mae moved in to be with Nancy.

Della Mae had accepted a position at nearby Lady of Victory Academy, so it was easy to drop Nancy off at the motherhouse adult day care program on her way to work. When Nancy's condition worsened, she agreed to move to the motherhouse, where more care was available. After the sale of the motherhouse in 1995, Theresa's family agreed to relocate Nancy to a facility in the Bronx—St. Patrick's Home—which was close to relatives. She would live there until her death in 2004. Watching her beloved older sister slowly deteriorate was very painful for Theresa: "She was decidedly getting worse and worse...You would have a short time in the morning when there was some kind of spontaneous life going on and then she was gone. It's a terrible disease."

From 1995 to 1996 Della Mae took a sabbatical in celebration of her golden jubilee as a Sister of Mercy. She studied theology and embarked upon a ten-day pilgrimage to Israel that she had fortuitously won. Thanks to "the tremendous amount of frequent flyer miles" Theresa had accumulated as administrator general, the two visited Hawaii, Ireland, and Rome before the year was out.

In September, as she prepared to return to work, Della Mae suffered a serious stroke that affected her speech. With therapy, her physical strength and mobility slowly returned, but she required intensive speech therapy for several years. At the beginning Della Mae could not speak at all. Two weeks after her stroke, Theresa, who had committed to give a presentation in Connecticut, asked her sister Rose, who was a good friend of Della Mae, to stay with her on the weekend. When Rose arrived, Della Mae spoke for the first time, "Hello Margaret," she said. "I'm not Margaret, I'm Rose," said Rose. "Oh," Della Mae said, "I mean hello Rose!"

Theresa relishes the story because from that day forward Della Mae always called her Margaret, whereas before the stroke she had called her Theresa. Della Mae made a very good recovery, although her speech never fully returned to normal. Theresa remembers how, in the immediate aftermath of the stroke, her sisters were so worried about her. "I was a wreck. They called me every night and I cried and cried...Barbara said to me, 'Maggie, you have to take care of yourself. You're going to have a nervous breakdown. She needs you, you can't do that.'"

Theresa was able to arrange her teaching schedule to help Della Mae with her therapies, and the two continued living in their Yonkers apartment. Della Mae eventually returned to sewing her own clothing, driving short distances to appointments, and working at the motherhouse several days a week. As her condition stabilized, Theresa remembers her sister telling her: "You know, we thought you were going to have a stroke because you were so upset." At the time Theresa asked God, "Why didn't it happen to me instead of Della Mae?" Later (perhaps relaying God's reply) she told Barbara,

> I never could have done what [Della Mae] did. She was amazing. I never saw her cry. Never saw her depressed, even though that is what usually happens when you have a stroke. [I think it was because] her mind wasn't affected. Her brain was still good. She wasn't able to talk, but she knew everything that was going on.

By early 2001 things had almost returned to normal at the Yonkers apartment. Theresa was now teaching full time as an associate professor at Mercy College, and Della Mae enjoyed her mornings at the new Mercy administrative offices in nearby Hartsdale. Theresa occasionally broached the subject of moving to Marian Woods, the community's retirement center. Della Mae was getting older and Theresa worried that her companion was wearing herself out with housekeeping, laundry, and grocery shopping. Their apartment was on the top floor, which required trekking up and down two flights of stairs. Della Mae was adamant that she did not want to move.

In the months that followed, Theresa's own severe health challenges would precipitate a change. She suffered a freak accident at the airport in the summer of 2001 as she was returning from having helped a friend in Florida. Her driver pulled away from the curb without realizing Theresa was still retrieving her bags from the back seat. She fell and injured her back, but adamantly refused to go to the hospital, insisting she was well enough to get on the plane for her flight to LaGuardia. After she explained the cause of her injury, the van service Theresa regularly used between Yonkers and LaGuardia agreed to pick her up at the airport. She notified Della Mae to watch for the van but waited to see her before explaining what had happened. An alarmed Della Mae immediately drove Theresa to the hospital. The emergency room providers were dumbfounded when they discovered that she had flown all the way from Florida with a broken back. Fortunately, while the injury was serious, no permanent neurological damage was done. Theresa had to wear a back brace for six very hot weeks during the summer, but her activities were only minimally limited.

In October Theresa contracted a severe *Clostridium difficile* (C. *diff*) infection after surgery to remove an ovarian cyst. From November 2001 through February 2002 she was in and out of the hospital with severe and unrelenting diarrhea. Fifteen months earlier she had vowed to lose weight when she turned sixty-five. Before surgery she was very proud to have reached her goal of 165 pounds. Over the next three months she lost another 50 pounds. By February 2002 she weighed an alarming 115 pounds. A specialist at Phelps Hospital in Tarrytown was finally able to help her, and she began to improve slightly.

The following month Theresa's sister Rose died after a yearlong struggle with pancreatic cancer. Following a round of chemotherapy, she had briefly improved, but in September 2001 her condition worsened. Theresa was able to visit her in Connecticut before she was hospitalized herself. Despite her weakened condition, Rose made frequent trips to see Theresa in the Tarrytown hospital. "Nobody came to see me as often as Rose she did," Theresa recalls. "Every time I turned around, she was in the hospital. Drive over, stay an hour, and go home. And she was getting weaker and weaker herself."

Theresa's oldest sister, Mary, a nurse, was later convinced that Rose's death weakened Theresa's immune system even further. The C. diff infection returned with a vengeance. There were few alternatives at the time except for surgery.[41] On April 10 Theresa underwent extensive abdominal surgery to remove part of her colon. All of Theresa's surviving sisters, Mary, Honey, and Barbara hastened to her bedside. She was so weak that the surgeon told them he was not sure she would survive, but that she had to have the surgery. He said nothing of this to Theresa, who, in any case had no intention of dying. "He didn't know me . . . he should have been talking to my primary doctor who knew me very well."

Before leaving the hospital that night, Theresa's sisters and Della Mae visited her—unsure if she would live to see the morning. Immediately after surgery Theresa had had one frightening episode of low blood pressure—which she remembers—but she soon recovered and was transferred to intensive care, where she stayed for five days. During the ensuing ten-day hospitalization, Theresa learned how to manage her ileostomy, which she had been told would be temporary. She remembers having no difficulty dealing with the medical paraphernalia: "I did extraordinarily well . . . the ostomy nurse at the hospital was great. She taught me how to do it."

A year later, the surgeon told Theresa that the ileostomy could not be reversed and would have to be permanent. Theresa accepted this difficult news with equanimity. To this day she manages her condition so unobtrusively that most people are unaware that she has this health challenge.

At the end of April, Theresa was transferred to St. Patrick's Home for three weeks of rehabilitation during which she slowly regained her strength. In the interim, she remembers that the Mercy provincial, Sister Pat Vetrano, spoke to Della Mae. "I think it might be time for both of you to come to Marian Woods because Theresa's not going to be up to doing a lot for a while," Pat said gently. Theresa's niece and two nephews spent a marathon day at the apartment packing boxes for the moving van. On July 1, Theresa and Della Mae moved into Marian Woods. Eventually they were able to arrange apartments next to one another.

Theresa marvels at Della Mae's faithfulness throughout this harrowing time: "Every single day from November 4th until May 4th she never missed a day at the hospital or at St. Patrick's home. It was six full months. She had to leave Yonkers and drive to the Bronx, which was not easy."

Despite her ordeal, Theresa was determined to continue teaching. Mercy College had found substitutes for the winter 2002 semester when she was so gravely ill. After finishing rehabilitation in mid-May, she took the summer to recuperate and was well enough to return to work in September 2002. She negotiated a reduced load of three courses for the fall semester but was well enough to resume full-time teaching in January 2003.

LIFE AT MARIAN WOODS

Over the next ten years Theresa and Della Mae enjoyed being together in the midst of work, community meetings, and Theresa's ever-present travel schedule. Women's and church renewal groups across the country frequently invited her to give retreats and/or speak about women's issues in church and society. She was obligated, moreover, to attend meetings of the many nonprofit boards on which she sat. Three mornings each week, Della Mae walked to a Mercy administrative office on the Marian Woods property to help out with community mailings. She returned for dinner at noon and then rested or watched CNN in the afternoon.

When Theresa was home, the two ate breakfast and dinner in the dining room and enjoyed a light evening supper together in the community room close to their apartments. "We had our own little community within a community," Theresa recalls. "Many times, when I was home, either she came to my room in the evening to watch TV, or I went to her room. We kept each other company like that."

Shortly after Della Mae's eightieth birthday in 2005 Theresa began to notice that her friend was slowing down a bit. About a year after her brother Jack's death in 2007 Della Mae began to experience some mild memory loss. Theresa recalls her saying, "I can't keep that straight now. I'm not sure. I don't know what's going on." Yet Della Mae managed fairly well for the next several years. Theresa remembers that "she was always attentive to dress, looks, and money matters as well as her devotion to prayer and Mass." But soon episodes of confusion became both more frequent and more noticeable.

In 2010 Theresa wished to surprise Della Mae with an eighty-fifth birthday party, but she didn't at first understand that the celebration was for her. "She had no idea what was going on," Theresa sadly recalls. Sometimes when Theresa was away, Della Mae would forget where her apartment was. The other sisters helped her find it, making sure to inform Theresa when she returned. As Della Mae diminished, she forgot how to use the telephone and the TV remote. Theresa always helped her with these.

In 2012 Della Mae fell and suffered a broken shoulder and then developed pneumonia. Her condition worsened. Theresa planned to remain at the hospital the night of November 12, but having been assured her lifelong friend was improving, she went home. Before she left, however, the two prayed Catherine McAuley's *Suscipe* prayer together, just as they had done every night during Della Mae's hospital stay.

The next morning Theresa was shocked to learn that Della Mae had died during the night. She consoled herself with the knowledge that her dearest friend had been prepared to die. When her family had visited, Della Mae had asked Theresa, "They think I'm going to die, don't they?" Theresa gently replied "It's possible that you might. How would you feel about it?" Della Mae answered, "I don't mind. I'm not afraid to die."

In her eulogy, Theresa emphasized Della Mae's "fidelity, her courage, and her absolute passion for service as a Sister of Mercy." She "never got hung up on 'community,'" Theresa said. "She thought we spent entirely too much time talking about it. What we were about was service. What you want is to be out there serving the people and taking care of them, and the community comes along automatically..." She shared how unhappy her friend had been at one point in her life when she lived in "a beautiful brand-new convent" in a wealthy suburban parish. Della Mae told Theresa, "I want to go back to the city. They don't need us up here."

Six years after Della Mae's death, Theresa reflects that her loss "gets harder as time goes on... If you said to me I would feel this bad after six years, I wouldn't have anticipated that... it is still deep, deep, deep... we were very close for forty-five years. People say, 'Oh, you were so good to her'... but nobody knows how good she was to me."

LOCAL AND NATIONAL BOARD SERVICE

In the course of her long ministerial career Theresa served on many nonprofit boards. Leadership within the congregation brought with it a number of automatic board appointments to groups founded by the Sisters of Mercy. Even after she left office, however, Theresa was much sought after by diverse nonprofit boards that admired her business acumen and passionate advocacy. In 1980 she became a founding member on the board of the Association for the Rights of Catholics in the Church (ARCC), an organization formed after the Vatican's condemnation of progressive theologian Hans Küng in 1979. Today ARCC seeks to promote and protect the rights of all Catholics within the institutional church.[42] Theresa also served on two social service organizations that minister to women and children in the Bronx. From 2000 to 2006 she was on the board of Mercy Center in Mott Haven, a community center dedicated to empowering women and families by offering adult education and workforce readiness programs, immigrant services, and services for children. From 2001 to 2011 she was on the board of the Thorpe Residence, serving three of those years as board president. The facility, sponsored by the Sparkill Dominicans and located in the South Bronx, is a transitional housing program and shelter for women and children.

Theresa has been a proud member of the Women's Ordination Conference since its founding in 1975. She served on its board from 1990 to 1996, and at this writing remains a valued advisor.

In 1995, at the age of fifteen, Erin Saiz Hanna first heard about Sister Theresa Kane at her Mercy high school in Rhode Island: "And I remember thinking 'well, that's awesome. I really hope I'm a cool rebel nun like that one day.'"[43] While she never became a nun (Hanna was introduced to her husband by a Sister of Mercy), she became a passionate Mercy associate member. In 2008, she became the executive director of the Women's Ordination Conference, serving in that capacity until 2017.

Hanna often reached out to Theresa for advice and counsel: "She was always willing to lend her prophetic voice to the movement, speaking at conferences and workshops and adding her name to important petitions."[44] Born a year after Theresa's visionary 1979 address, Hanna reflects, "When I took over at WOC thirty years later, so much had happened. Women had been silenced, women had been excommunicated... but Theresa Kane and so many of the older WOC [Women's Ordination Conference] activists that I met were so inspiring... they persisted... she persisted through all these years."[45]

After posting Theresa's address to Pope John Paul II on social media, Hanna found it continues to resonate.

> I posted [Theresa's papal greeting] on social media, saying this happened thirty years ago. People seeing it for the first time were blown away by it. Theresa was a nun with authority, and she led with her example. She gave good Catholics the ability and the permission to question for themselves the injustices within the church...It was a very pivotal public moment that resonated with a lot of people and continues to resonate today.[46]

In 2015, the Women's Ordination Worldwide Conference presented its inaugural "Theresa Kane Woman of Vision and Courage" awards to four women who, "like Theresa Kane, prophetically live out their visions of an inclusive, equal and just Roman Catholic Church." One of the awardees was Jamie Manson, a native New Yorker and *National Catholic Reporter* (NCR) books editor and columnist. Manson writes about issues of equality in the church, particularly those that affect women and LGBTQ individuals.[47] While she was deeply touched by the honor, Manson also felt "a certain weightiness to what this means...to honor what Theresa did and to continue on that path." The award brought her a heightened sense of responsibility "to stay in the fight, even when all I want to do sometimes is run away, get a nice job with even nicer security on Wall Street."[48] One of the things Manson loves about Theresa Kane is her commitment to teaching first-generation working-class undergraduates in the Bronx. "She really loves young people," Manson observes. "She wants to be actively engaged with younger adults like me and Erin [Saiz Hanna]. She has been really supportive...rather than wringing her hands about the future...she wants to know your story and just hang out with you."[49]

The Women's Ordination Worldwide Conference was held in Philadelphia, September 18–20, 2015, just days before Pope Francis would make his first pastoral visit to the United States. When the "Theresa Kane Woman of Vision and Courage Award" was announced, a packed audience rose to their feet clapping and cheering in an extended ovation as Theresa approached the podium. As she had done thirty-six years earlier, Theresa publicly addressed the pope about the need to eradicate gender inequality:

> Pope Francis, although your formal titles are: Holy Father and Supreme Pontiff, I take this sacred opportunity to greet

you as a brother, a friend, a collaborator in our service to and with God and with others...

I have come to the conviction that anything less than all women in the Catholic community having the possibility of being in all ministries or our church is not only a deficit, not only wrong; it is a scandal to our church and to our world...For the Catholic Church to be agents of God's message in our 21st century, we need to have a vision that the degradation of women worldwide, in all countries of our planet, is the primary root issue of social and religious violence, and not of God...

I urge you Pope Francis to listen to the women of our church and world who cry out in anguish as women throughout the ages have done. Only radical (at its roots) gender equality in church and in society will begin to diminish the violence, hatred and other forms of inhumanity in our world today.[50] (See Appendix E)

From 2000 to 2009 Theresa served on the board of the *National Catholic Reporter* (NCR), an independent progressive media outlet. Today, NCR's biweekly newspaper reaches over one hundred thousand subscribers and has an even larger online readership. Tom Fox—the publication's widely respected CEO/president and former editor—first met Theresa when she gave him an exclusive interview a year after her papal greeting. For Fox, the primary gift that Theresa brought to the NCR board was simply "her presence...the quality of her personality, its integrity...She anchors all activities by just being herself. Her strength is contagious and inspiring. She does not necessarily have to say much. When she talks, however, one listens carefully because her comments are full of wisdom."[51] Theresa was on the NCR board as Pope John Paul II's papacy was ending and Pope Benedict XVI's was beginning. During this time, Fox observed:

Theresa spoke her mind and was resilient in expressing her love for the church and its primary values, starting with the gospels and social teachings, while not allowing herself to become depressed by its failings. She has always been a feminist, one who includes all life in her circle. She lives beyond gender, preaching inclusiveness in all she says and does.[52]

Theresa with a group of Loyola of Chicago students at a 2002 workshop hosted by FutureChurch at the annual Call To Action Conference. She spoke eloquently even though just seven months earlier she nearly died from an abdominal infection. (Photo by author)

Theresa with Agnes Mary Mansour in 2004.

With NCR columnist Jamie Manson, who received the first ever Sister Theresa Kane Award at the Women's Ordination Worldwide Conference held in Philadelphia in 2015. (Photo by author)

Theresa and Sr. Margaret Ann Brown celebrating respectively their 60th and 70th Jubilees in April 2009 at the Marion Woods retirement community in Hartsdale, NY.

National Speaking Ministry

After receiving dozens of speaking requests following her greeting to the pope in 1979, Theresa remembers thinking, "This is probably the beginning of a journey and not just a one-time thing. I have a responsibility... [The October 7 greeting] could not be the end of it. Now that I've said it, and I believe it, and I proclaimed it, how do I continue to actualize it?"[53] In a 2014 interview with the Women's Alliance for Theology Ethics and Ritual she said her papal message had "become a vision. It has certainly become a passion and I guess in many ways it has become a focus for my life."[54]

Although some in the hierarchical church expected Theresa's influence to wane after she left the presidency of the Sisters of Mercy,[55] it did not. Over the next three decades she became a popular conference speaker and retreat leader for groups in every walk of Catholic life. She gave presentations and led retreats for sisters, priests, high school and college students, and Catholic laity. Large crowds flocked to hear her speak at national church reform events, including the annual Call To Action (CTA) conference, which attracted thousands of Catholics each year for well over two decades.[56] Other reform organizations that invited her to speak included FutureChurch, the Women's Ordination Conference, Voice of the Faithful, and the married priest organization CORPUS.

Theresa is especially beloved for her support of LGBTQ rights. New Ways Ministry cofounder Loretto Sister Jeannine Gramick describes her as a "visionary" on the issue. In the late 1970s the Mercy Administrative team endorsed a New Ways newspaper ad supporting the civil rights of LGBTQ people. Gramick recalls that, when she met with the team to discuss the issue,

> Theresa went a step further, asking about ways to support gay and lesbian priests and nuns. We weren't even talking about gay priests or lesbian nuns in 1978. A couple of years later in, 1981, we had our first major symposium for Catholic leaders, including diocesan leaders, LCWR, and CMSM. Theresa was one of the major speakers about what we should be doing as leaders on this issue.[57]

In later years Theresa twice preached at a special LGBTQ Mass the night before Manhattan's Gay Pride Parade and gave presentations at conferences sponsored by New Ways Ministry and Dignity, another Catholic advocacy organization.

Often conservative Catholics chanting and carrying signs demonstrated against her appearance. Sometimes the venue had to be changed because the local bishop would not allow her to speak at a diocesan-owned facility. Once she was scheduled to speak at Bishop Thomas Gumbleton's parish in Detroit, but the archdiocese refused permission. Gumbleton is a member of Elephants in the Living Room, a progressive organization of Catholic clergy and laity in the Detroit Archdiocese.[58] Theresa's presentation was quickly moved to Detroit Mercy College. An event that had been expected to attract about four hundred people drew eight hundred justice-minded Detroit Catholics.

Theresa never hesitated to speak frankly when she saw injustice, especially injustice in the church. In 2009 she criticized yet another Vatican investigation of US nuns. Addressing the fortieth anniversary conference of the National Coalition of American Nuns (NCAN), she said, "Regarding the present interrogation, I think the male hierarchy is truly impotent, incapable of equality, or co-responsibility in adult behavior. In the church today, we are experiencing a dictatorial mindset and spiritual violence."[59]

Teaching at Mercy College was a distinct advantage. Theresa did not have to worry about losing her job because of opposition from conservative Catholics. While deeply rooted in Mercy values and vision, the school was not subject to Catholic hierarchical authority. Theresa's teaching schedule was flexible, and the college itself was supportive.

Being at Mercy College was a great blessing to me. Whenever I gave a talk, I always sent a copy to the president and provost, because I identified myself as an associate professor at Mercy College. I wanted the college to be recognized. That meant a lot to them...I really could not have been in a better place to get that kind of understanding and support. Many were just very thrilled that I was there [at Mercy College] because they thought it was prestigious for them.

More frequently than not, Theresa was invited to speak on women's issues in a presentation she titled "Women in Church and Society: A Twenty-First-Century Vision." It was important to her to situate her comments within the demands of social justice that necessarily require "leadership from women, in all areas in the church and society." Years earlier she had been surprised by sisters who told her they were uninterested in issues pertaining to the poor and marginalized, "You know, this is social justice that you're interested in, but not all of us are interested." She pondered how Catholics had become conditioned to believe that "certain issues belong to justice, but they do not belong to God."

I began to realize that spirituality and social justice are two sides of the same coin. They are intricately related... "How do I love God, whom I don't see, but I don't love you, whom I see?"...I was very much inspired by the World Synod of Bishops where they came back and said "Social justice is a constitutive element of the Gospel."

A 2002 presentation at Call To Action exemplifies Theresa's preferred approach. She began by pointing to an increased use of US "smart bombs" in Afghanistan and the need for women to be leaders in peacemaking. Increased militarization leaves fewer resources for basic necessities such as food and clean water. This focus disproportionately impacts women and children, who make up most of the world's poor. "God is not American, Asian or African," she told the audience. "The Old Testament tells us that we are made in the image and likeness of God. [The text] is not talking only about Americans, but about everyone who is created. This is a call to all of us... we are all made in God's image." From this vantage point, Theresa moved to her signature theme.

Until women are in all ministries of the Church, we will continue forms and expressions of idolatry. We are diminished when the male can offer the Eucharist, but women are always recipients and never initiators of it. These are forms of idolatry that are still with us and therefore our community and the Eucharist are diminished because of it.

The need to find practical ways of incorporating inclusive language is another of Theresa's favorite topics. At a 2010 presentation for FutureChurch in Cleveland, Ohio, she shared a true story.

I was planning to receive ashes one Ash Wednesday when I heard the priest say "Remember, man, that you are dust and unto dust you shall return." Now I have gotten to a point where I just can't take that quietly. So I said to myself, "Well, I don't need to get ashes...I mean it's not even a holy day." So I was not going to get in line. Finally, I said to myself, "No I'm getting in line." So I went up.
    When I approached the priest, I put my hand up and said quietly, "Father when you give me ashes, please don't say man." He got flustered, but he did as I had asked. Instead he said, "Remember that you are dust..." When I got back to my seat, I heard him again say "Remember you are dust," and

then I heard him say, "Remember man, you are dust." When
it was a woman receiving ashes he didn't use the word "man."

Afterwards, I spoke to him, "I'm the woman who asked
you not to say 'man.'" And he told me, "I never thought of
such a thing before. You're right, most of those parishioners
were women, and I was calling them all 'man.'"

When the appreciative audience finished chuckling, Theresa gently
drove home her point: "There are certain things we need to do because it's good for us to do. It just may not be the orthodox thing to
do."

The death of Theresa's father was a turning point in her evolving
understanding of the mystery of God. "It is the strangest thing. I
began to see God as mother as well as father. I was uncomfortable for
a while, when we say, 'Our Father, who art in heaven.' I'd say, 'Our
Father and Mother,' but I didn't say it out loud because it wasn't yet
deep in my soul." Since her father had never been abusive or domi-
neering, Theresa found the timing of her new understanding somewhat mysterious. She began to realize she was still thinking of God as
a parent and, as she explained, "I'm at a point in my life where I
don't really need a parent. I'm grateful for my parents, but I don't
need a parent in my life. I need a companion and a friend." She
started exploring non-sexist language, moving more deeply into "new
language about God, new images of God, anything I could read about
our relationship with God and how I contemplated God. I referred to
God as 'She' as well as 'He' because I wanted to keep expanding [my
understanding of] God." Her explorations led to the insight that, "for
me, God is a divine spirit. That is the closest I can get...I can't really
image God. All I can do is try to feebly articulate how I believe God is
in my life at this point."

And how does Theresa "feebly articulate" about God in her life?
Her words echo those of many mystics who struggle to explain their
experience of human freedom and the divine creativity at work within it.

God is clearly a spirit, a spirit that is pervasive in this universe and in every part of the universe. And I do think that although I'm the author of my own destiny, God is the ultimate
author...but no one else is. God is and I am. So I'm fully responsible for my destiny and for my future. But God is also
clearly in charge—and I mean in a loving way. God is really
my mover and shaker—and the one who is directing my life
and my activity.

Theresa's national speaking ministry occurred during a time of division and opposition to new ideas in the Catholic Church. This tension led to persecution of theologians, nuns, and laypeople by conservative Catholics, by some bishops, and by some Vatican officials. At her speaking events Theresa invariably encouraged women to be "confident, courageous, and compassionate" in living their call to be made in God's image. Asked about the source of her own hope in continuing to advocate for opening all the ministries of the church to women, Theresa replied. "I find hope in contemplating God, being with the creator God in new and creative ways. I have found great comfort in discovering God as my friend, as my companion, and as my advocate."

Conclusion

There is perhaps no better way to conclude a biography about a beloved Sister of Mercy who made history than with words from another Sister of Mercy. Sister Helen Marie Burns was intimately involved in every aspect of Theresa's challenging time as president of the Sisters of Mercy of the Union. She was the Detroit provincial when Sister Agnes Mary Mansour was forced out of her community because of her embrace of political ministry on behalf of Michigan's poor.[60] She was a member of the special Mercy committee that engaged US bishops in dialogue about the need for pastoral (and safer) tubal ligation policies. Immediately following Theresa's term of office, Helen Marie was elected vice-president of the Mercy congregation. She had many opportunities to observe Theresa's leadership during an extraordinarily painful and difficult time. Her views on the meaning of Theresa's life and ministry are illuminating.

Theresa never acted without a sense of wanting to be of service to the church ... Circumstances shaped her into a voice for women, for women's rightful place in the church, and for women's empowerment. And she gladly utilized that voice.

That is why I think she was not depleted by the negativity or the pressure or the outright criticism and disrespect that she received. She understood it wasn't about her. It was about this larger reality and she was an instrument. And she didn't mind being an instrument and she would be that as well as she could be.

I would want people to remember Theresa as a very simple woman ... her sense of faith is rooted in a simple relationship with a God of love. And, I would say, a God of truth.[61]

Epilogue

The story of Theresa Kane and the Sisters of Mercy is an important chapter in the history of US women religious, indeed in the history of the People of God. The Second Vatican Council invited all the faithful to embrace a new spiritual maturity. Prior to Vatican II most Catholics had been content to have priests and bishops tell them what to do. Their job was to obey whatever rules the hierarchy set forth and then their salvation would be assured. While women religious exercised significant initiative inaugurating new education and health ministries, they were subject to a hierarchy that expected the same blind obedience from them as from the rest of the laity.

But Vatican II recognized anew the power of the Holy Spirit at work in the lives of the faithful, who, it said, were "marvelously called and wonderfully prepared so that ever more abundant fruits of the Spirit may be produced in them" (*Lumen Gentium* 34). The council taught that the prophetic mission of Christ is expressed not only through the ordained but also "through the laity whom He made His witnesses and to whom He gave understanding of the faith (*sensus fidei*) and an attractiveness in speech so that the power of the Gospel might shine forth." (*LG* 35). Vatican II further enjoined ordinary Catholics to freely make their needs and desires known to church leaders, even saying they had at times an obligation "to express their opinion on those things which concern the good of the church" (*LG* 37).

Yet, as Theresa's story—and that of the Sisters of Mercy—reveal, many, if not most, in the church's hierarchy were not ready to hear their experience of God's leading their lives of service. Catholic sisters embraced conciliar teachings more than any other group in the church. The council created a compelling theological vision of the church as the People of God. It did not create the structures that would help to make that vision a reality. Instead, council fathers hoped and expected new structures would be developed by future synods of the world's bishops.

This turns out to have been a vain hope. Reactions from Catholic conservatives—angry and upset over change in a church they thought would never change—contributed to the many theological controversies and conflicts that Catholicism experienced in the ensuing fifty years. There were few safe spaces where faithful—albeit widely differing—Catholics could talk with one another about "things which concern the good of the church." Despite a deepening worldwide priest shortage, significant polarization occurred over such issues as ordaining married as well as celibate priests and opening the diaconate and priesthood to women. In the United States, Catholic social teaching about justice and peace was eclipsed by issues related to human sexuality, such as the human rights of LGBTQ Catholics and moral decision-making in human reproduction. One's beliefs about the latter two issues became for some a litmus test for the Catholic "brand"—that is, who was a "true Catholic" and who was not.

Hierarchical politics also played a role in the failure to develop structures that encouraged expanded dialogue and participation in church decision-making. Pope John Paul II centralized power in the Vatican to a degree unprecedented in modern times. Many, if not most, non-doctrinal decisions by national bishops' conferences had to be approved by Rome. In English-speaking countries, Vatican officials overturned a new English Mass and Lectionary translation, almost twenty years in the making, even though the world's English-speaking bishops' conferences had already approved the new text by wide margins.[1] This ruling upended a long-standing precedent wherein a country's bishops had final authority over liturgical translations. Worse, the final decision on the widely criticized new Mass translation was made by a small group of Vatican clerics, rather than the international team of English-speaking experts who had been developing accessible translations over many years.[2]

Such was the hierarchical church within which Theresa and the Sisters of Mercy—and other religious orders—sought to "speak the truth in love." Thirty years after Theresa's greeting to Pope John Paul II, his successor, Pope Benedict XVI (Joseph Ratzinger), authorized dual investigations of US sisters. Ratzinger was prefect of the Congregation for the Doctrine of the Faith (CDF) when, in late 1984, it tried to censure Theresa Kane. As documented in chapters 7 and 8, this same CDF, probably at the behest of conservative staffers at the US bishops' conference, undercut US bishops in their attempts to negotiate with the Sisters of Mercy about pastoral approaches to tubal ligations in Mercy hospitals.

Past, it seems, is indeed prologue. In February 2009, the CDF, under the leadership of American Cardinal William Levada, announced a "doctrinal assessment" of the Leadership Conference of

Women Religious (LCWR, an umbrella group representing 80 percent of active US sisters).[3] Just a month earlier Cardinal Franc Rodé, the prefect of the Vatican's Congregation for Institutes of Consecrated Life and Societies of Apostolic Life, announced a wide ranging "Apostolic Visitation" of 341 female US religious orders comprising over fifty thousand sisters. Described as "probably the largest investigation in church history," the Vatican said the purpose was to "look into the quality of life of religious women in the United States."[4] Such was the twenty-first-century hierarchical church within which a new generation of sister-leaders would seek to speak truth with love.

Catholics in the United States quickly rallied to support the sisters. In the ensuing six years, widespread media coverage chronicled the sister-leaders' ongoing patient dialogue with Vatican officials as well as vigorous support for the sisters from tens of thousands of ordinary Catholics. Hundreds of prayer vigils were held in cities across the United States and over a hundred thousand people wrote or signed letters and petitions to church officials.[5]

The unprecedented nature of the investigations prompted widespread speculation.[6] Were US bishops diverting attention from their own problems resulting from their cover-up of clergy sex abuse?[7] Was the investigation "payback" for LCWR's support of the Catholic Hospital Association's decision to back the Affordable Care Act after US bishops withdrew their support, ostensibly over the scientifically untenable belief that IUDs and birth control pills are abortifacient?[8] In light of demands for extensive reports about each order's financial status, were bishops looking for ways to shore up their own coffers to help pay legal fees from clergy sex abuse?[9] No one knew the answers to those questions.

Perhaps in response to a widespread outcry from laity and many influential Catholic benefactors, Vatican officials soon realized their investigations were at best ill-advised. In August 2010, Pope Benedict appointed American Archbishop Joseph W. Tobin, a former superior general of the Redemptorists, as secretary of the Congregation for Institutes of Consecrated Life and Societies of Apostolic Life. Tobin quickly acknowledged the "harm that had been done in the early stages" of the Vatican investigation and advocated for a more dialogic process.[10] Shortly thereafter, Benedict appointed a new prefect of the congregation, Brazilian Archbishop João Braz de Aviz, who also worked to "build mutual trust" between the Vatican and religious orders.[11] The Brazilian archbishop replaced Cardinal Franc Rodé, who, because of the Cold War, had never attended Vatican II. Rodé was particularly ill-suited to understanding the changes in religious life that had emerged from the council.

In April 2012, as one of his last acts at the CDF, Cardinal Levada officially censured LCWR, accusing it of having a "radical feminist ideology,"[12] expressing political positions different from those of US bishops, and spending too much time on poverty and social justice issues rather than opposing abortion and gay marriage.[13] He issued a mandate requiring oversight of the Conference statutes, programs, and prayer practices. Braz de Aviz lamented that Cardinal Levada had never consulted him before making his decision in 2012 to censure LCWR.[14] This is a surprising omission insofar as the Congregation for Institutes of Consecrated Life and Societies of Apostolic Life is the Vatican office responsible for the world's religious orders. It should have been consulted before Levada approved such a serious and potentially destructive action. This failure of communication is one example of the runaway curia that eventually led to Pope Benedict's early resignation.[15] The CDF censure dashed any newfound hope—in light of dialogic overtures from Tobin and Braz de Aviz—for a pastoral resolution to the controversial investigations of Catholic sisters.[16]

It soon became apparent that sister-leaders were determined to defend their own moral agency and exercise their obligation "to express their opinion on those things which concern the good of the church." In her 2012 keynote address, LCWR president Sister Pat Farrell urged her sisters to be "truthful and fearless" in dealing with the doctrinal assessment. "They can crush a few flowers, but they cannot hold back the springtime," she told them, quoting from a Spanish phrase she had learned while ministering under a military dictatorship in Chile.[17]

LCWR was also being honored for its faithful service to the Gospel. In 2011 it received the Mandatum Award from the National Federation of Priests' Councils because its "service to the Gospel of Jesus Christ exemplifies the purpose and goals of the federation."[18] In 2013 the organization received the prestigious Herbert Haag Religious Freedom prize "in recognition of its extensive efforts in helping the poor, the marginalized and people in difficult circumstances and of '[its] careful reflection of the signs of the times in the spirit of the Second Vatican Council.'"[19]

Pope Benedict's resignation and the election of Pope Francis in March 2013 eventually led to a marked turnaround in the Vatican approach to US sisters. On December 14, 2014, in a live-stream presentation from the Vatican, a panel of sisters and Vatican officials, including now-Cardinal Braz de Aviz and LCWR president Sister Sharon Holland, issued a "roundly positive, even laudatory" report about the Apostolic Visitation of US sisters. The report stated that the congregation "wishes to express the profound gratitude of the Apostolic See and the Church in the United States for the dedicated and selfless service of women religious in all the essential areas of the life of the Church and society."[20] In the midst of many expressions of gratitude,[21] some concerns were identified. After acknowledging that communities already had written guidelines for their spiritual practices, the report asked sisters "to discern what measures need to be taken to further foster the sisters' intimate relationship with Christ and a healthy communal spirituality based on the Church's sacramental life and sacred Scripture."[22] Allaying earlier fears that the Vatican wanted sisters to stop their social justice advocacy, the report praised and encouraged sisters to work toward "the elimination of the structural causes of poverty" and continue their direct service to the poor.[23]

LCWR president Sister Sharon Holland found the statement "affirmative and realistic," noting that "it is not a document of blame or simplistic solutions. One can read the text and feel appreciated and trusted to carry on."[24] In closing, the report cited Pope Francis's call "to create still broader opportunities for a more incisive female presence in the church," but made no specific recommendations.

In an unexpected meeting on April 16, 2015, Pope Francis met for nearly an hour with four members of the LCWR leadership just after a joint final report officially ended the doctrinal assessment of the conference. The new CDF prefect, Cardinal Gerhard Müller, said: "At the conclusion of this process, the Congregation [CDF] is confident that LCWR has made clear its mission to support its member Institutes by fostering a vision of religious life that is centered on the Person of Jesus Christ and is rooted in the Tradition of the Church. It is this vision that makes religious women and men radical witnesses to the Gospel, and, therefore, is essential for the flourishing of religious life in the Church."[25] Eileen Burke-Sullivan, a Creighton University theologian and consultant for women's religious orders told the *New York Times* that the lengthy meeting with the pope was "about as close to an apology, I would think, as the Catholic Church is officially going to render."[26]

There are at least three historic precedents that emerged from the sisters' experience of being investigated by two Vatican offices. The first is that contemporary expressions of religious life were finally affirmed publicly, not only by the tens of thousands of ordinary Catholics who strongly supported the sisters but by the Vatican itself. Consider this excerpt from the Apostolic Visitation report:

In response to the appeal of *Perfectae Caritatis* to return to the Gospel, "the ultimate norm of religious life" and to "their

founder's spirit and special aim" (PC, 2 a & b) women religious sought to adapt their lifestyle and mission in ways that
might enable them to more effectively respond to contemporary needs. In a spirit of creative fidelity to their charisms,
they branched out in new ministries to those most on the
margins of the Church and society. Women religious in the
United States also notably pursued ongoing theological and
professional formation seeking to further their ability to serve
the Church's evangelizing mission and to prepare others to
collaborate in it as well.[27]

It is no small thing to receive official approbation from Vatican offices after many years of exclusion, criticism, and struggle—beginning
with Loretto Sister Mary Luke Tobin's fruitless efforts to have sisters
included in the Vatican II meetings that directly affected their lives,
or Theresa's under-appreciated efforts to help Vatican officials understand that sisters who chose to live in neighborhoods did so because they found it was the best way to bring the Gospel to ordinary
people.

The second historic precedent was the surprising joint statement
from LCWR leaders and the CDF. Soon after the doctrinal assessment
ended, Sister Sharon Holland—who worked at the Congregation for
Institutes of Consecrated Life and Societies of Apostolic Life for many
years before becoming LCWR president—observed, "Those who are
familiar with procedures of the Roman Curia will recognize that the
results of a CDF study of the doctrinal stances of an individual or
group normally end with a statement from the dicastery. This process
ended with a joint report."[28] The CDF is not in the habit of issuing
joint statements with anyone, let alone an organization it had roundly
criticized just a few years earlier.

The third historic precedent is the April 16, 2015, private meeting
between Pope Francis and LCWR leadership. This marks the first
time any pope ever met privately with LCWR leadership—although
LCWR leaders had tried to arrange such a meeting many times. Consider Theresa Kane's five formal requests to meet with Pope John Paul
II in the 1980s—all of which were denied.

Clearly much had changed between US women religious leaders
and Vatican officials since the time Theresa and the Sisters of Mercy
initiated dialogue about women's moral agency and equality in the
church. When Mercy leaders attempted to discuss their community's
prophetic *Our Relationship within the Church* statement, the Congregation for Religious[29] had not even read it beforehand. The document
forthrightly named the Mercy community's sense of responsibility

"for assisting in the Church's search for truth," and "to participate in the evolution of church teaching." Yet officials at the CDF opposed the sisters' exercise of moral agency and decision-making authority on behalf of the women they served and punished the sisters for seeking to dialogue about it.

While women religious leaders—indeed all of the non-ordained—are not permitted to exercise equal decision-making authority in the church today, some small progress may be in evidence. It is a positive sign that both Vatican dicasteries provided at least an appearance of mutuality at the public events announcing the conclusion of the investigations of US sisters. Both offices also acknowledged and praised the critical importance of the Gospel witness of US women religious. But perhaps the most important outcome of the Vatican investigations is that US sister-leaders were finally at the table. Their concerns—and their moral agency—were taken seriously, albeit at considerable personal cost, and notwithstanding substantial suspicion on the part of Vatican officials.

To what can we attribute the Vatican's change in attitude? The election of Pope Francis and strong public support from ordinary Catholics were undoubtedly influential. Most critical by far, however, was the early determination of sister-leaders to avoid public confrontation and to engage in persistent, painstaking dialogue with Vatican officials, however long that might take. In the final statement ending the LCWR investigation, Seattle Archbishop Peter Sartain—who was delegated by the CDF to oversee its mandate to LCWR—alluded to the efficacy of this decision:

> Our work together was undertaken in an atmosphere of love for the Church and profound respect for the critical place of religious life in the United States, and the very fact of such substantive dialogue between bishops and religious women has been mutually beneficial and a blessing from the Lord.[30]

Sartain himself made important contributions that enhanced mutual understanding. LCWR president Sister Sharon Holland praised him for breaking "the pattern of institutionalized perceptions" when he asked for resources "to help him understand how LCWR congregations had gone about the renewal called for by Vatican Council II."[31] The LCWR national offices prepared executive summaries of influential books for the archbishop and discussed them with him as he required. Archbishop Sartain also tried to understand the situation from LCWR's vantage point and "worked tirelessly to translate understanding between CDF and LCWR . . . patiently helping CDF officials and LCWR officials understand what was happening between them."[32] In the final joint statement, Holland summarized the nature of the dialogue that had taken place and an important learning.

> We are pleased at the completion of the Mandate, which in-volved long and challenging exchanges of our understandings of and perspectives on critical matters of Religious Life and its practice. Through these exchanges, conducted always in a spirit of prayer and mutual respect, we were brought to deeper understandings of one another's experiences, roles, re-sponsibilities, and hopes for the Church and the people it serves. We learned that what we hold in common is much greater than any of our differences.[33]

In 2018 LCWR leaders who had been involved in the arduous six-year investigation wrote a small book—*However Long the Night*—that includes reflections about the meaning they found within what had for them become a spiritual journey. Their insights illumine the transformative power of embracing Theresa's discipline of "speaking the truth in love," in a church and world greatly in need of both. Saint Joseph Sister Janet Mock—the executive director of LCWR dur-ing the investigation—shed light on some of the seemingly insur-mountable challenges the women initially faced,

> How does one go about developing an authentic relationship with a group of people who, in our experience, took words out of context and acted against us on that misrepresentation of truth? When there is no truth, there is no trust—and con-sequently no authentic relationship...
> The men with whom we were speaking interpreted the way we prayed together and spoke about God and the things of God as a violation of Catholic orthodoxy. We in turn had spent more than 50 years as an organization, encouraging member congregations to study and pray with the documents of Vatican II which resulted in well-developed spiritualities consistent with each congregation's charism.[34]

An important guiding principle for LCWR throughout was "to always hold the greater good of the People of God before us and refuse to demonize and defame the CDF."[35] Mock describes a patient process that eventually led to common ground: "LCWR officers at-tempted to listen carefully to the cardinals and archbishops... to truly understand their position. In the process, we began to meet these men as brothers in Christ who held a deep commitment to Jesus Christ and the Catholic Church. This was a ground of common meaning and with some, the beginning of trust."[36]

Recurrent learnings that emerged for LCWR leaders were that the Vatican mandate pointed to larger issues beyond LCWR, including the role of the laity, the nature and function of authority, and the absence of safe spaces in which to discuss one's experience of God. Sister Florence Deacon found that the Vatican investigation had much to do with the ongoing implementation of Vatican II, particularly "the ecclesial roles of women religious and of the laity, especially women; understandings of authority, faithful dissent, and obedience, and the need for spaces where honest, probing questions about faith and belief can be raised and discussed."[37] Sister Carol Zinn comments that a key issue guiding how LCWR "understood its responsible use of influence at this time" concerned the Vatican II renewal that had led to "an adult, educated laity."

> There was a deeper conversation that yearned to emerge, a broader understanding of the core issues, and a profound movement of the Spirit prompting all of us to discernment and fidelity in new and challenging ways. The CDF mandate was about an adult, educated laity, in this case, a group of women religious, whose vision of a Vatican II church had guided their renewal, framed their discernment for more than 50 years, and claimed their fidelity.[38]

The positive conclusion of the Vatican's two investigations of US sisters suggests that fidelity to the truth of one's experience of God's leading is costly but ultimately transformative both for the individual and for the church. No less important is persistence in speaking those truths in a way that neither alienates nor refuses to hear the sacred truths of another. It is just this sort of exchange that Theresa Kane espoused—indeed relished—in her exercise of leadership. Many Sisters of Mercy and LCWR leaders were influenced by her example of forthrightly putting her truth on the table and making room for others to place their truths there as well.

Theresa's vision of full ministerial equality for women in the Catholic Church is far from being realized, yet we may be closer to that long-sought ideal because of the dialogic breakthrough that was ultimately the unforeseen blessing of the Vatican's rebuke of Catholic sisters. The sisters' contemplative approach and decision-making processes made room for the Spirit of God to lead and guide them and the prelates Rome had appointed to investigate them. Full equality in the Catholic Church will not happen until the structures of Catholicism are themselves transformed to allow women and men, gay and straight, lay and ordained, to bring their own contemplative experiences of God, in Jesus Christ, to the discernment and decision-making table. Because in the end, it really is about what God wants "on earth as in heaven."

Theresa's passionate life and witness arise from her own deep experience of the mystery of God. It is here that she found strength, despite substantial persecution, to pursue a vision of equality and justice for women in the church and in society. It is here that she learned to speak the truth in love.

With Mercy College students from the Bronx, April 2017. (Photo by author)

Appendix A

WELCOME TO POPE JOHN PAUL II
By Sister M. Theresa Kane, RSM

October 7, 1979
The National Shrine of the Immaculate Conception
Washington, DC

In the name of the women religious gathered in this Shrine dedicated to Mary, I greet you, Your Holiness Pope John Paul II. It is an honor, a privilege, and an awesome responsibility to express in a few moments the sentiments of women present at this shrine dedicated to Mary the Patroness of the United States and the Mother of all humankind. It is appropriate that a woman's voice be heard in this shrine and I call upon Mary to direct what is in my heart and on my lips during these moments of greeting.

I welcome you sincerely; I extend greetings of profound respect, esteem, and affection from women religious throughout this country. With the sentiments experienced by Elizabeth when visited by Mary, our hearts too leap with joy as we welcome you—you who have been called the Pope of the people. As I welcome you today, I am mindful of the countless number of women religious who have dedicated their lives to the church in this country in the past. The lives of many valiant women who were the catalysts of growth for the United States Church continue to serve as heroines of inspiration to us as we too struggle to be women of courage and hope during these times.

Women religious in the United States entered into the renewal efforts in an obedient response to the call of Vatican II. We have experienced both joy and suffering in our efforts. As a result of such renewal women religious approach the next decade with a renewed identity and a deep sense of our responsibilities to, with, and in the Church.

Your Holiness, the women of this country have been inspired by your spirit of courage. We thank you for exemplifying such courage in speaking to us so directly about our responsibilities to the poor and oppressed throughout the world. We who live in the United States, one of the wealthiest nations of the earth, need to become ever more conscious of the suffering that is present among so many of our brothers and sisters, recognizing that systemic injustices are serious moral and social issues that need to be confronted courageously. We pledge ourselves in solidarity with you in your efforts to respond to the cry of the poor.

As I share this privileged moment with you, Your Holiness, I urge you to be mindful of the intense suffering and pain which is part of the life of so many women in these United States. I call upon you to listen with compassion and to hear the call of women who comprise half of humankind. As women we have heard the powerful messages of our Church addressing the dignity and reverence for all persons. As women we have pondered upon these words. Our contemplation leads us to state that our Church in its struggle to be faithful to its call for reverence and charity for all persons must respond by providing the possibility of women as persons being included in all the ministries of our Church. I urge you, Your Holiness, to be open and to respond to the voices coming from the women of this country who are desirous of serving in and through the church as fully participating members.

Finally, I assure you, Pope John Paul, of the prayers, support, and fidelity of the women religious in this country as you continue to challenge us to be women of holiness for the sake of the Kingdom. With these few words from the joyous, hope-filled prayer, the *Magnificat*, we call upon Mary to be your continued source of inspiration, courage, and hope: "May your whole being proclaim and magnify the Lord; may your spirit always rejoice in God your Saviour; the Lord who is mighty has done great things for you; Holy is God's Name."

Appendix B

LIST OF WOMEN AUDITORS PRESENT
AT THE SECOND VATICAN COUNCIL*

Luz-Marie Alvarez-Icaza (Mexico; 4th session, 1965)

Constantina Baldinucci, S.C. (Italy; 3rd and 4th sessions, 1964–65)

Pilar Bellosillo (Spain; 3rd and 4th sessions, 1964–65)

Jerome Maria Chimy, S.S.M.I. (Ukrainian rite, Canada; 4th session, 1965)

Gertrud Ehrle (Germany; 4th session, 1965)

Cristina Estrada, A.C.J. (Spain; 3rd and 4th sessions, 1964–65)

Claudia Feddish, O.S.B.M. (Ukrainian rite, U.S.A.; 3rd and 4th sessions, 1964–65)

Henriette Ghanem, S.S.C.C. (Coptic rite, Lebanon; 3rd and 4th sessions, 1964–65)

Rosemary Goldie (Australia; 3rd and 4th sessions, 1964–65)

Ida Grillo (Italy; 3rd and 4th sessions 1964–65)

Suzanne Guillemin, D.C. (France; 3rd and 4th sessions, 1964–65)

---

*Carmel McEnroy, *Guests in Their Own House: The Women of Vatican II* (New York: Crossroad, 1996), 297.

Marie de la Croix Khouzam, R.E.S.C. (Coptic rite, Egypt; 3rd and 4th sessions, 1964–65)

Catherine McCarthy (U.S.A.; 3rd and 4th sessions, 1964–65)

Alda Miceli (Secular Institute, Italy; 3rd and 4th sessions, 1964–65)

Marie-Louise Monnet (France; 3rd and 4th sessions, 1964–65)

Marchesa Amalia di Montezemolo (Italy; 3rd and 4th sessions, 1964–65)

Margarita Moyano Llerena (Argentina; 4th session, 1965)

Gladys Parentelli (Uruguay; 4th session 1965)

Anne-Marie Roeloffzen (Belgium; 3rd and 4th sessions, 1964–65)

Hedwig Skoda (Czechoslovakia, 4th session, 1965)

Juliana Thomas, A.D. J. (Germany; 3rd and 4th sessions, 1964–65)

Mary Luke Tobin, S.L. (U.S.A.; 3rd and 4th sessions, 1964–65)

Sabine de Valon, R.S.C.J. (France; 3rd and 4th sessions, 1964–65)

Appendix C

Tenth General Chapter
Sisters of Mercy of the Union
April 1977

Our efforts as Sisters of Mercy to ponder our relationship with the Church took spirit from Vatican II: "The people of God believe that they are led by the Spirit... Moved by that faith they try to discern in the events, the needs, and the longing which they share with other people of our time, what may be genuine signs of the... purpose of God." More recently influenced by the U.S. Bishops' Conference on Liberty and Justice for All, we are aware that "the effort to renew the Church in changing circumstances is at the heart of Christian life... Always the Christian faith, carried to... new times, required of its adherents bold, creative action to preserve the ancient truths and embody them in communities capable of transforming the world."

Since Vatican II there have been many efforts to understand the Church in richer ways. It is variously spoken of as a "community," as "institution," as "servant," etc. We intend here to focus on two of these ways of describing the reality of the Church—the Church as "community" and the Church as "institution." We understand the Church as community to be all those persons who are bonded together in the life of Jesus Christ. This is actualized in many forms within the one Church. We understand the Church as institution to be its structures, rules, and delineated roles. Both of these ways of understanding the Church are important and they are interrelated. The institutionalization of the Church is precisely for the sake of the continued existence of the Church as community and as servant in the world.

We as Sisters of Mercy experience the Church under its aspect of community in many ways: we are baptized into a worshiping community; we live in a religious community, we participate in parish community, we form communities of service. From the beginning the Sisters of Mercy have also had an important relationship with the Church as institution; we have canonical status with the Church; our vows are received by the Church; our charism of mercy is publicly recognized within the Church; we relate to parish and diocesan structures; we sponsor institutions in the name of the Church.

At this historical moment in the development of the Church there are two aspects of the institutional Church that present special concerns. The first concern relates to the way in which institutional structures facilitate and express the Church as community. Since Vatican II important changes have taken place in traditional structures, e.g., the parish. These changes have furthered the growth of Church as community. However, there is still an urgent need to discover new and creative forms of community to complement traditional Church structures.

The second area of concern relates to the complex questions about the nature of authority in the Church. In the Church's role as teacher and healer, often authority and power are perceived to be solely placed in the hierarchy and clergy. Nonetheless, the Church's tradition has always affirmed that there are many ways in which the truth and life of Jesus empower each person as a thinker and doer in his name. The contemporary challenge is to understand more clearly that the empowerment of the individual is actualized in relation to the Church as community and as institution.

As Sisters of Mercy we can neither escape the anguish of experiencing the above concerns nor the responsibility of addressing them. We experience them among ourselves and encounter them in our ministry.

The question of new models of community raises itself for us as for the Church. The question of relating to many communities simultaneously and of discerning fidelity to sometimes conflicting commitments is our question as well as that of each person in the Church. Precisely as members of a religious community we have today the special responsibility to witness to the viability of new forms of faithful, worshiping communities and actively to foster their growth. It is possible for us to take leadership in stimulating change in existing structures and in creating alternate models of community. We can do this by providing meaningful liturgical experiences within our local communities and community institutions, participating in the formation of Church communities other than the traditional parish, actively working toward adopting new models of Church structure. Our efforts to be faithful members of local communities, parish communities, ministry communities, etc. can serve to add insight to the efforts of others to live with similar demands.

The question of authority in the Church also raises itself for us in a special way. We are identified with the institutional Church as teachers and healers, yet we have often thought of ourselves as without authority and power, as only transmitters of the truth formulated by the Church hierarchy... We have, consequently, seldom if ever allowed ourselves to question corporately Church teaching or to develop policies in ministry which depart from Church discipline. Perhaps more importantly, we have also not accustomed ourselves to take responsibility for assisting in the Church's search for truth.

Now, however, we are sharing more and more in the whole Church's growing understanding of the dignity and responsibility of each person to think and to do. As a community of women, we are growing in self-understanding of our role as women, as persons, and as a Christian community. This includes an increasing urgency to form our consciences, and to recognize ourselves as moral agents in our teaching and healing. We experience, then, a call to greater relationship with and in the Church. Even when we find ourselves in disagreement/conflict with some teachings of some Church authorities, our desire to challenge is never a desire to break with the institutional Church. When we are faced with structures which do not allow fully creative collaboration and reflective disagreement with Church authorities, we experience ourselves as responsible to help generate alternative structures.

While affirming the official Church teaching, there are areas, particularly in the moral realm, in which we as a community have a responsibility to participate in the evolution of Church teachings:

1. An important aspect of our current ministries can be to support the Church in its development of new teachings or new emphases within traditional teachings, in response to evolving moral contexts in the Church and in society.

2. In some areas we have a special responsibility to help change Church teaching and practice where that teaching and practice

have become obsolete, inhibitive of Christian life, or injurious to individuals, the Church or society.

3. In extreme circumstances the community, and/or individuals within the community, may find it a matter of conscience not only to work actively for change in a specific Church teaching, but at the same time, to dissent from the teaching.

Corporate public dissent in the form of official statements and/or institutional policies which depart from such Church teaching may be justified when continued implementation of Church teaching and policies proves seriously harmful to persons. Minimal criteria for justifying corporate public dissent include:

1. Continued implementation of the teaching entails grave harm done to persons.

2. Strong theological or ethical reasons support a position in opposition to the teaching.

3. Corporate public dissent is seen to serve the overall good of the Church in this instance.

4. The public has a right to know about the dissent in order to take it into account in conscience formation.

5. Public dissent is a *last resort* after all other avenues of dialogue have been exhausted.

6. The dissent is authorized by the appropriate authority in the community.

As we work toward a more responsible posture in relation to the Church, we recognize that it is necessary to explore every avenue of dialogue. We shall do this in continuity with our tradition as Sisters of Mercy. We do it also in continuity with the authentic tradition of the Church wherein new life has always demanded ongoing reform and renewal, ongoing humble but courageous love.

Appendix D

Sisters of Mercy of the Union
September 1979

STATEMENT OF THE GENERAL ADMINISTRATIVE TEAM
RELATIVE TO
HOSPITAL POLICY ON TUBAL LIGATION

A Response to the Recommendations
of the Church/Institute Committee

As a leadership group of religious women in the Church, we believe that part of our responsibility is an ongoing attempt to understand and articulate the Gospel in the light of ever-changing circumstances.

As Sisters of Mercy, we believe that our search for understanding is situated in a pastoral context; that is, it must be oriented toward the service of the poor, sick, and uneducated. Furthermore, we desire to carry out our search in respectful dialogue with the teaching Church, and by means of strategies commensurate with our commitment to collegiality and subsidiarity.

As a community engaged in health services, we acknowledge a special responsibility to search for new understandings in the developing areas of medical and sexual ethics.

Our search is guided by...

> ... An affirmation of the sacredness and dignity of human life;

> ... An affirmation that the principle of totality is appropriately extended to include not only the physical aspects of

273

the person, but also the psychological, the spiritual, and the relational (e.g., relationships to family and to the larger community);

... An affirmation of the teaching of Vatican II relative to marriage, i.e., "Marriage is not merely for the procreation of children: its nature as an indissoluble compact between two people and the good of the children demands that the mutual love of the partners be properly shown, (and) that it should grow and mature." Also: "When it is a question of harmonizing married love with the responsible transmission of life, ... objective criteria must be used, criteria drawn from the nature of the human person and human action, criteria which respect the total meaning of mutual self-giving and human procreation in the context of true love." (*Gaudium et Spes*, #50–51)

The Institute of the Sisters of Mercy is founded "to extend the Church's ministries of teaching and healing" (*Mercy Covenant*, W-1). A Mercy hospital is an exemplification of that ecclesial mission; its foundational principle is a reverence for the sacredness and dignity of human life. Therefore, its policies should include the promotion of holistic health care and exclude whatever may cause harm to persons. We believe that tubal ligation, in certain circumstances, is an appropriate procedure and a necessary component of holistic health care and that failure to provide this service in these circumstances may cause harm to persons. In these cases a Mercy hospital should provide this procedure.

Since our investigation shows that Church teaching in this area is not uniformly interpreted or applied and that tubal ligation is not an available option in all Mercy hospitals, we desire to draw concerned persons into dialogue about the necessity of doctrinal development of the issue and appropriate modification of hospital policies.

Appendix E

Sister Theresa Kane, RSM
September 18, 2015

Pope Francis, although your formal titles are Holy Father and Supreme Pontiff, I take this sacred opportunity to greet you as a brother, a friend, a collaborator in our service to and with God and with others.

I have no doubt your many years in Argentina engaged with the many economically poor people has been a powerful source of strength and grace. Those experiences prepared you to be noted for your deep pastoral spirit, your desire for collegiality and your vision that all of us in the Catholic community are called to be holy—to be saints!

I am a Catholic woman, a woman religious, a Sister of Mercy, born and raised in the United States, New York City. Through both education and life experiences, I have come to a conviction that anything less than all women in the Catholic community having the possibility of being in all ministries of our church is not only a deficit, not only wrong; it is a scandal to our church and to our world.

For a long time I have believed the Catholic community might serve as a role model and an instrument of reform for governments and religions throughout our world that allow and even legislate that women are less than fully human; that women are objects to be exploited; that it is acceptable and even at times believed natural to violate, to beat and abuse women physically, psychologically and sexually.

For the Catholic church to be agents of God's message to our 21st century, we need to have a vision that the degradation of women worldwide, in all countries of our planet, is the primary, root issue of social and religious violence and not of God.

We as a Catholic community are called to proclaim fully and lovingly to our entire planet community that such scandalous beliefs and actions of gender inequality are forms and expressions of idolatry. When idolatry is present God is not in our midst. We need to bring a loving, caring, creative God into the center of our everyday lives by eradicating all forms of gender inequality. Only then will God as Companion, as Mother, Father, as our Divine Source of grace be present in our world.

I urge you, Pope Francis, to listen to the women of our church and world who cry out in anguish as women throughout the ages have done. Only radical (at its roots) gender equality in church and in society will begin to diminish the violence, hatred and other forms of inhumanity in our world today.

Notes

CHAPTER 1: THE ELEPHANT IN THE SANCTUARY

1. See Appendix A for full text of the October 7 address.

2. Theresa Kane, interviews with author, February, June, October 2017. Unless otherwise indicated, all quotations from Theresa Kane are from audiotaped interviews with the author that are now stored at the Mercy Heritage Center Archives, Belmont, NC.

3. Law would go on to become the cardinal archbishop of Boston and—after fleeing to Rome—became a poster child for how not to handle clergy sex abuse.

4. Declaration of the Sacred Congregation for the Doctrine of the Faith, *Inter Insigniores,"* On the Question of Admission of Women to the Ministerial Priesthood," October 15, 1976. See https://tinyurl.com/kjwzxlz.

5. Mary Regina Werntz, RSM, *Our Beloved Union: A History of the Sisters of Mercy of the Union* (Westminster, MD: Christian Classics, Inc., 1989), 344.

6. Ibid.

7. Ibid.

8. Jeremy Daigler, RSM, *Incompatible with God's Design: A History of the Women's Ordination Movement in the U.S. Roman Catholic Church* (Plymouth, UK: The Scarecrow Press, 2012), 69–70.

9. George Vecsey, "53 Nuns, After a Night of Prayer, Stand in Silent Protest to Pontiff," *New York Times,* October 8, 1979.

10. Leadership Conference of Women Religious, *The Status and Roles of Women: Another Perspective,* 22–23 (1976). Mercy Heritage Center Archives, Belmont, NC. The document also supported passage of the Equal Rights Amendment.

11. Ruth McDonough Fitzpatrick, "Women in Ministry: Response to Sister Theresa Kane and Pope John Paul II," Document #11, *Theology in the Americas,* New York, 4.

12. Three years later, Kelly would become the archbishop of Louisville.

13. Theresa Kane, interview with author, June 5, 2017.

14. Author interviews with Dominican Sister Carol Coston, August 2018; Loretto Sister Maureen Fiedler, July 2018; Ms. Dolly Pomerleau; and Loretto Sister Jeannine Gramick, April 2019.

15. At the time, Fiedler was a member of the Erie Sisters of Mercy who were not affiliated with Theresa's Sisters of Mercy of the Union. She later transferred to the Sisters of Loretto.

16. All three organizations were founded in the wake of the US bishops' 1976 Call to Action gathering in Detroit, convened by Cardinal Dearden. Hand-picked lay leaders deliberated for several days and suggested prophetic directions for the US church, in areas such as disarmament, women's equality, primacy of conscience, gay rights, justice for those made poor, and opening ordination to married men and women. When the bishops did not follow up on the conference outcomes, a number of independent Catholic non-profits were founded to carry the vision forward.

17. Carol Coston, interview with author, August 14, 2018.

18. Vecsey, "53 Nuns."

19. The flyer was developed by the Quixote Center. Mercy Heritage Center Archives, Belmont, NC.

20. Theresa Kane, interview with author, June 5, 2017.

21. LCWR past president Joan Doyle was from Dubuque, Iowa.

22. This small vignette throws light on systemic difficulties long endured by Catholic sisters. Women leaders can address the highest authorities of their church only through male mediators. The pope's 1979 visit was no exception.

23. Leadership Conference of Women Religious, 1979/1980 Conference Report 8. Mercy Heritage Center Archives, Belmont, NC.

24. The Center of Concern is a global Catholic social justice think tank founded in 1971 "to create a world where economic, political, and cultural systems promote sustainable flourishing of the global community." https://www.coc.org.

25. John Paul II, homily at Philadelphia Cathedral Mass for Priests, October 4, 1979. https://tinyurl.com/ycynqdjd.

26. George Weigel, *Witness to Hope: The Biography of Pope John Paul II* (New York: Cliff Street Books, Harper Collins, 1999), 350.

27. See Mark Winarski, "Theresa Kane Stance Wins Support, But Not in Rome," *National Catholic Reporter*, October 19, 1979; and Stephenie Overman, "Everybody Is Talking, But...," *Chicago Catholic*, October 16, 1979, National Catholic News Service.

28. Marjorie Hyer and Megan Rosenfield, "A Challenge from Nuns," *Washington Post*, October 8, 1979.

29. Ibid.

30. Peter Hebblethwaite, in his column of the same name, *National Catholic Reporter*, October 19, 1979.

31. Hyer and Rosenfeld, "A Challenge from Nuns."

32. Hebblethwaite, *National Catholic Reporter*.

33. Helen Scarry, interview with author, June 2, 2018.

34. Winarski, "Theresa Kane Stance."

35. Dolly Pomerleau, interview with author, July 18, 2018.

36. Carol Coston, interview with author, August 14, 2018.

37. Dolly Pomerleau, interview with author, July 2018.

38. Helen Amos, interview with author, January 25, 2018.

39. Margaret Farley, interview with author, June 28, 2018.

40. Doris Gottemoeller, interview with author, January 8, 2018.

41. Pope John Paul II, "Prayer at the National Shrine of the Immaculate Conception," Washington, DC, October 7, 1979. See https://tinyurl.com/y9jgvo62.

42. George Vecsey, "53 Nuns."

43. Kenneth L. Woodward with Mary Lord, "A Sister Speaks Up," *Newsweek*, October 22, 1979.

44. Hebblethwaite, *National Catholic Reporter*.

45. It is unclear to what Pope John Paul II is referring. This passage is not included in his original text (see https://tinyurl.com/ydcczbgf) but was directly quoted by Peter Hebblethwaite, who was present and reported it in *The National Catholic Reporter* on October 19, 1979. It is logical to assume that the pope added this at the last minute, perhaps in response to Theresa's greeting or to the petition from Catholic Advocates for Equality.

46. Hebblethwaite, *National Catholic Reporter*.

47. Hyer and Rosenfeld, "A Challenge from Nuns."

48. Russell Chandler, "Nun Confronts Pope, Calls for Women Priests," *Los Angeles Times*, October 8, 1979.

49. Despite pleas from other council fathers such as Cardinal Leo Joseph Suenens, Antoniutti had resolutely refused to allow women religious auditors to attend meetings of the Vatican II Commission on Religious Life. At the time, 80 percent of the world's religious were female. See Carmel McEnroy, *Guests in Their Own House: The Women of Vatican II* (New York: Crossroad Publishing, 1996), chapter 5, and Ann Carey, *Sisters in Crisis Revisited* (San Francisco: Ignatius Press, 2013), 238.

50. Hyer and Rosenfeld, "A Challenge from Nuns." The article did not supply last names or religious community identifications for sisters who were quoted.

51. Theresa Kane, interview with author, June 2017.

52. Theresa Kane, press statement, October 8, 1979. Mercy Heritage Center Archives, Belmont, NC.

53. Dolly Pomerleau, interview with author, July 2018.

54. Mother M. Sixtina, "Apology," advertisement published in the *Washington Post*, October 12, 1979.

55. Mother M. Claudia, IHM, "We Are Happy to Be Sisters...We Love Our Life," *Philadelphia Inquirer*, October 17,1979.

56. George W. Cornell, "Sister Who Challenged Pope Likened to St. Joan of Arc," *Long Beach Independent Press-Telegram*, October 13, 1979.

57. Editorial, "Sister Kane's Action Lacked Respect for Pope," *Southern Cross* (official newspaper of the dioceses of San Diego and San Bernardino), October 1979.

58. John F. Kavanaugh, SJ, "Neither Praise nor Scorn Alters Dissent Like St. Catherine's," *St. Louis Review*, October 19, 1979.

59. Editorial, "The Loyal Dissent," *St. Cloud Visitor*, October 13, 1979.

60. Editorial, "Lacking in Good Form or an Honorable Thing to Do?" *Catholic Messenger*, Davenport, Iowa, October 18, 1979.

61. "Archbishop Lauds Rights Plea," National Catholic News Service. Published in *Catholic Herald*, Sacramento, CA, November 8, 1979.

62. Frank J. Rodimer, "Sister Theresa and the Pope," *Beacon*, October 16, 1979. Rodimer was bishop of the Paterson, NJ, diocese from 1997 to 2004.

63. "Early Christian References to Priesthood Included Women, Says Scripture Scholar," Religion News Service. *Catholic Messenger*, Davenport, Iowa, October 18, 1979.

64. Richard L. Kenyon, "Pope Out of Touch with US, Nun Says. Nun Sees Peril in US Reaction to Pope," *Milwaukee Journal*, October 21, 1979.

65. "National Papers Divided on Remarks by Sister Kane," National Catholic News Service, October 14, 1979.

66. Father Henry Haacke, Kenton, KY, "Dishonored Guest," letter to the editor in *Our Sunday Visitor*, October, 1979.

67. Overman, "Everybody Is Talking, But..."

68. ¡La Monja Que Se Enfrentó a un Papa!, *El Visitante Dominical*, November 11, 1979.

69. "Aftershock from a Papal Visit," *Time*, October 22, 1979.

70. Kenneth L. Woodward with Mary Lord, "A Sister Speaks Up."

71. James Bradley Burke, "Two Different Reactions in Chicagoland," *Chicago Catholic*, October 19, 1979.

72. *Sacramento Bee*, editorial October 10, 1979.

73. Marjorie Hyer, "Mormon Bishop Excommunicates Woman Who is Supporting ERA," *Washington Post*, December 6, 1979. Linda Sillitoe, "Church Politics and Sonia Johnson: The Central Conundrum," *Sunstone 5*, no. 1 (January–February 1980). Sonia Johnson, "Patriarchal Panic: Sexual Politics in the Mormon Church," paper presented at the American Psychological Association meetings, New York City, September 1, 1979. Johnson was chair of Mormons for ERA. See https://tinyurl.com/ycfuyhkc.

74. Paul Wilkes, "Equal Rights on the Altar of God?" *New York Times Magazine*, November 30, 1980.

75. Theresa Kane, "Communication to the Members of the Leadership Conference of Women Religious," October 19, 1979, and "Communication to Every Sister of Our Mercy Institute," October 22, 1979. Mercy Heritage Center Archives, Belmont, NC.

76. Lora Ann Quiñonez, CDP, and Mary Daniel Turner, SNDdeN, *The Transformation of American Catholic Sisters* (Philadelphia: Temple University Press, 1992), 157.

77. Ibid.

78. Sister Mary Patricia Barrett, major superior of the Sisters of Charity of St. Augustine, "LCWR Leader Is Supported in her Remarks to the Pope," *Catholic Universe Bulletin*, October 19, 1979.

79. Dominican Leadership Conference, February 9, 1980. University of Notre Dame Archives, LCWR files CLCW, 2007–2175, Theresa Kane, RSM, Correspondence, 1979–80.

80. George W. Cornell, "Mercy Order Leader Seeks Clergywomen," *Sacramento Morning News*, October 14, 1979.

81. Suzanne Noffke, OP, "Beyond Pain and Anger." Unpublished LCWR analyses of Shrine letters. University of Notre Dame Archives, LCWR files CLCW, 2007–2175, Theresa Kane, RSM, Correspondence, 1979–80.

82. Unpublished introduction to LCWR analyses of Shrine letters. University of Notre Dame Archives, LCWR files CLCW, 2007–2175, Theresa Kane, RSM, Correspondence, 1979–80.

83. Mary Collins OSB, "The Pope and Every Catholic: Conflicting Expectations," April 7–9, 1981. Unpublished LCWR analyses of Shrine letters. University of Notre Dame Archives, LCWR files CLCW, 2007–2175, Theresa Kane, RSM, Correspondence, 1979–80.

84. Ibid.

85. Unpublished introduction to LCWR analyses of Shrine letters.

86. Collins, "The Pope and Every Catholic: Conflicting Expectations." All preceding quotations and references in this paragraph are from the Collins analysis.

87. Unpublished introduction to LCWR analyses of Shrine letters.

88. Theresa Kane, "Communication to the Members of the Leadership Conference of Women Religious," and "Communication to Every Sister of Our Mercy Institute."

89. Ibid.

90. After the Second Vatican Council all religious communities were asked to review their way of life and revise their constitutions accordingly.

91. Theresa Kane to Eduardo Cardinal Pironio, September 17, 1979. LCWR correspondence. Mercy Heritage Center Archives, Belmont, NC.

92. Theresa Kane to Most Reverend Augustin Mayer, OSB, October,1979. LCWR correspondence. Mercy Heritage Center Archives, Belmont, NC.

93. Theresa Kane, "Communication to the Members of the LCWR National Board," November 20, 1979. LCWR correspondence. Mercy Heritage Center Archives, Belmont, NC.

94. Lora Ann Quiñonez, Memorandum re: Reports to LCWR Members of November Meeting in Rome, December 28, 1979. In CMAS 3/31 CPC National Assembly April 1980. University of Notre Dame Archives.

95. Ibid.

96. Theresa interprets this text as inviting study and dialogue: "The controversies raised in our days over the ordination of women are for all

Christians a pressing invitation to meditate on the mystery of the Church, to study in greater detail the meaning of the episcopate and the priesthood, and to rediscover the real and pre-eminent place of the priest in the community of the baptized" (*Inter Insigniores*, 5). http://www.papalencyclicals.net/paul06/p6interi.htm.

97. Theresa Kane, interview with author, June 2017.

98. Quiñonez, Report of Meeting Between LCWR Representatives and Cardinal Pironio, Rome, Italy, November, 1979. In CMAS 3/31 Consortium National Assembly. University of Notre Dame Archives.

99. Ibid.

100. Ibid.

101. Kane, "Communication to the Members of the LCWR National Board," November 20, 1979.

102. Ibid.

CHAPTER 2: DAUGHTER OF IMMIGRANTS

1. Unless otherwise noted, all quotations from Theresa's sisters and nieces are from October 2017 interviews with the author.

2. Orchard Beach is a public beach and part of Pelham Bay Park in the Bronx.

3. Theresa Kane, interview with author, October 2017.

4. Theresa Kane, "Chronicle of highs and lows of my life—where God touched me directly and/or through others," personal journal, July 1982, written during Omaha Assembly, Estes Park, Colorado.

5. Ibid.

6. Ibid.

CHAPTER 3: CATHERINE MCAULEY AND THE SISTERS OF MERCY

1. Mary C. Sullivan, *The Path of Mercy: The Life of Catherine McAuley* (Washington, DC: The Catholic University of American Press, 2012), 20.

2. Helen Marie Burns and Sheila Carney, *Praying with Catherine McAuley* (Winona, MN: St. Mary's Press, 1996), 17.

3. Sullivan, *Path of Mercy*, 24.

4. Ibid., 60.

5. Burns and Carney, *Praying*, 19.

6. Sullivan, *Path of Mercy*, 40.

7. Ibid., 35.

8. Ibid., 34.

9. Burns and Carney, *Praying with Catherine McAuley*, 40.

10. Sullivan, *Path of Mercy*, 53.

11. Angela Bolster, "Catherine McAuley in Her Own Words" (Dublin:

Dublin Diocesan Office for Causes, 1978), 31, as cited by Burns and Carney, *Praying with Catherine McAuley*, 14.

12. Sullivan, *Path of Mercy*, 41.

13. Ibid.

14. Burns and Carney, *Praying with Catherine McAuley*, 21.

15. Ignatia Neumann, ed., Letters of Catherine McAuley, 154–55, in Burns and Carney, *Praying with Catherine McAuley*, 23.

16. Sullivan, *Path of Mercy*, 68.

17. Helen Marie Burns, RSM, email communication, July 12, 2018.

18. Burns and Carney, *Praying with Catherine McAuley*, 25.

19. Ibid., 14.

20. Mary Regina Werntz, RSM, *Our Beloved Union: A History of the Sisters of Mercy of the Union* (Westminster, MD: Christian Classics, Inc., 1989), 1.

21. Ibid., 235.

22. Ibid., 161.

23. Ibid., 164.

24. Ibid., 203.

25. Burns and Carney, *Praying with Catherine McAuley*, 91.

26. Ibid.

27. Ibid., 92.

28. Ibid.

29. Sullivan, *Path of Mercy*, 362.

30. Burns and Carney, *Praying with Catherine McAuley*, 29.

31. Ibid., 29–30.

32. Sandra Schneiders, "Discerning Ministerial Religious Life Today," *National Catholic Reporter*, October 2, 2009, (print issue); original headline, "The Past and Future of Ministerial Religious Life," https://tinyurl.com/y9b fqdl2.

33. Burns and Carney, *Praying with Catherine McAuley*, 28.

CHAPTER 4: "MY GOD I TRUST IN YOU"

1. Paul de Jaegher, SJ, *The Virtue of Trust* (New York: P. J. Kenedy and Sons, 1932), 42.

CHAPTER 5: INNOVATIVE PROVINCIAL: IMPLEMENTING VATICAN II

1. *Perfectae Caritatis* (Decree on the Adaptation and Renewal of Religious Life), 3, 4. https://tinyurl.com/7hlux.

2. Ibid., 10.

3. Ibid., 4.

4. Ibid.

5. Ibid., 3.

6. Sandra M. Schneiders, *Prophets in Their Own Country* (Maryknoll, NY: Orbis Books, 2011), 61.

7. John W. O'Malley, *What Happened at Vatican II* (Cambridge, MA: Harvard University Press, 2010), 1.

8. Ibid., 5.

9. Highest ranked, and central to the other documents are the four constitutions, which include On the Liturgy (*Sacrosanctum Concilium*), On the Church (*Lumen Gentium*), On Divine Revelation (*Dei Verbum*), and On the Church in the Modern World (*Gaudium et Spes*). The nine decrees are On the Mass Media (*Inter Mirifica*), On the Eastern Churches (*Orientalium Ecclesiarum*), On Ecumenism (*Unitatis Redintegratio*), On Bishops (*Christus Dominus*), On the Adaptation and Renewal of Religious Life (*Perfectae Caritatis*), On the Training of Priests (*Optatum Totius*), On the Apostolate of the Laity (*Apostolicam Actuositatem*), On Missionary Activity (*Ad Gentes Divinitus*), and On the Ministry and Life of Priests (*Presbyterorum Ordinis*). The three declarations are On Christian Education (*Gravissimum Educationis*), On Non-Christian Religions (*Nostra Aetate*), and On Religious Liberty (*Dignitatis Humanae*).

10. O'Malley, *What Happened at Vatican II*, 6.

11. Ibid.

12. Ibid., 8.

13. Ibid., 37.

14. Ibid.

15. Ibid., 306.

16. Ibid., 307.

17. Ibid.

18. Carmel McEnroy, *Guests in Their Own House: The Women of Vatican II* (New York: Crossroad Publishing, 1996), 35.

19. Ibid.

20. The laymen spoke about the lay apostolate, world poverty, and the mission of the laity in the modern world. See O'Malley, *What Happened at Vatican II*, 27. See also McEnroy, *Guests in Their Own House*, 157.

21. McEnroy, *Guests in Their Own House*, 157.

22. Ibid., 43–44.

23. Ibid., 99.

24. Ibid., 97. Mary Luke Tobin, interviewed by Carmel McEnroy, Nerinx, KY, April 29, 1988.

25. McEnroy, *Guests in Their Own House*, 44.

26. Ibid., 100.

27. Ibid.,126.

28. Ibid., 126, 160–61.

29. Ibid., 127.

30. Ibid.

31. Ibid., 150.

32. Ibid., 129–31, 149–50.

33. Ibid., 58. Mary Luke Tobin, interviewed by Carmel McEnroy.

34. McEnroy, *Guests in Their Own House*, 189

35. Theresa Kane, interview with author, June 2017.

36. McEnroy, *Guests in Their Own House*, 167.

37. Ibid. Mary Luke Tobin, interviewed by Carmel McEnroy.

38. The idea was first conceived by Henriette Ghanem, SSCC (Lebanon-Coptic rite) and Suzanne Guillemin, DC (France). Sabine de Valon, RSCJ (France) and her secretary general Françoise de Lambilly, RSCJ, were also instrumental in founding UISG.

39. McEnroy, *Guests in Their Own House*, 183. Letter to Carmel McEnroy from Maureen Aggeler, May 12, 1989.

40. Ibid., 283.

41. Ibid., 185, Mary Luke Tobin, interviewed by Carmel McEnroy.

42. O'Malley, *What Happened at Vatican II*, 239.

43. Ibid.

44. Ibid.

45. McEnroy, *Guests in Their Own House*, 169.

46. O'Malley, *What Happened at Vatican II*, 239.

47. Ibid.

48. Mary Regina Werntz, RSM, *Our Beloved Union: A History of the Sisters of Mercy of the Union* (Westminster, MD: Christian Classics, Inc., 1989), 240–41.

49. Ibid., 241

50. Ibid., 242, 244.

51. Ibid., 248.

52. Ibid., 255. Quoted segment by Mother Regina Cunningham to the sisters, December 29, 1967, box VIII, 1969 Special General Chapter File, Mercy Heritage Center Archives, Belmont, NC.

53. Werntz, *Our Beloved Union*, 257.

54. Ibid., 256.

55. While in session, the chapter constitutes the highest authority in a religious institute and can therefore overrule decisions made by the major superior.

56. Werntz, *Our Beloved Union*, 273.

57. Ibid.

58. Ibid. The vote was 47 in favor and 20 against.

59. Werntz, *Our Beloved Union*, review photos of 1965–71 Seventh General Council, 244 and 250; 1969 chapter, 258; Eighth General Council, 1971, 307; 1972 Eighth General Chapter, 311; and Ninth General Council, 326.

60. Werntz, *Our Beloved Union*, 264.

61. Ibid., 265.

62. Ibid., 261.

63. Ibid., 294.

64. Ibid.

65. Ibid. Werntz also cites letter from Kane to Cunningham, May 24, 1971.

66. Four members of the executive team, including Theresa, were under the age of thirty-five and the fifth member was over forty.

67. Werntz, *Our Beloved Union*, 299.

68. Ibid.

69. Under canon law, the decisions of the chapter constitute the highest authority in a religious community, and the superior is duty bound to implement them.

70. The Mercy community changed the title from "superior general" to "administrator general" when Theresa's predecessor, Sister Concilia Moran, was elected.

71. All statistics from Werntz, *Our Beloved Union*, 340.

72. Names have been changed to protect the privacy of individuals involved.

73. Canon law requires that finally professed religious be given adequate time to come to a good decision about their future. The community must support them financially during this period of time, which is called exclaustration.

74. Werntz, *Our Beloved Union*, 320.

75. Ibid., 327.

CHAPTER 6: TO SPEAK THE TRUTH IN LOVE

1. Mary Regina Werntz, RSM, *Our Beloved Union: A History of the Sisters of Mercy of the Union* (Westminster, MD: Christian Classics, Inc., 1989), 340.

2. Ibid., 378.

3. Ibid., 344. The vote was 62 yes, 4 no, 2 abstentions.

4. Joan Chittister, "Making the Future Possible," in *Spiritual Leadership for Challenging Times: Presidential Addresses from the Leadership Conference of Women Religious* (Maryknoll, NY: Orbis Books, 2014), 12–13.

5. Werntz, *Our Beloved Union*, 345.

6. *Gaudium et Spes*, 11. https://tinyurl.com/34xrhq.

7. US Bishops' Conference document "On Liberty and Justice for All," as cited in *Our Relationship within the Church*, Tenth General Chapter. April 1977. Mercy Heritage Center Archives, Belmont, NC.

8. Werntz, *Our Beloved Union*, 342.

9. Sisters of Mercy of the Union, *Our Relationship within the Church*, Tenth General Chapter, April, 1977. Mercy Heritage Center Archives, Belmont, NC.

10. Sisters of Mercy of the Union, *Our Relationship within the Church*.

11. Werntz, *Our Beloved Union*, 341.

12. Ibid., 341.

13. Ibid., 341–42.

14. Ibid., 342.

15. *Our Relationship within the Church*.

16. Ibid.

17. Werntz, *Our Beloved Union*, 343. The vote was 64 yes, 2 no, and 2 abstentions.

18. John R. Donahue, "A Tale of Two Documents," in *Women Priests*, edited by Leonard Swidler and Arlene Swidler (New York: Paulist Press, 1977), 25.

19. *Inter Insigniores*, 5. https://tinyurl.com/kjwzxlz.

20. Werntz, *Our Beloved Union*, 343.

21. Ibid. (Text footnote cites *Inter Insigniores*, 5, paragraph 3).

22. Ibid.

23. Ibid.

24. Ibid., 343–44.

25. Ibid., 344.

26. According to Sister Helen Marie Burns, this was the first and last time nominees would be reviewed by a search committee. In subsequent elections, the congregation returned to the previous method of nomination by the members-at-large. Those receiving a select number of nominations were given the option of accepting or declining to have their name placed in nomination. Those who accepted became the slate of nominees submitted to the chapter body.

27. Werntz, *Our Beloved Union*, 345.

28. Doris Gottemoeller RSM, interview with author, January 8, 2018.

29. Helen Marie Burns, interview with author, January 2018.

30. Ibid.

31. Ibid.

32. Gottemoeller would soon be asked by the Mercy Federation to spearhead the Mercy Futures Project, which laid the groundwork for the 1991 merger of seventeen autonomous congregations of Sisters of Mercy into the Institute of the Sisters of Mercy of the Americas. She would be elected the first president of the new institute.

33. Theresa Kane, "Communication to Each Sister within our Mercy Institute," July 7, 1977. Mercy Heritage Center Archives, Belmont, NC.

34. "GAT [General Administrative Team] Activities from Inside-Out," *Union Scope*, January 1979, 10. Mercy Heritage Center Archives, Belmont, NC.

35. Ibid.

36. Werntz, *Our Beloved Union*, 349.

37. Sister M. Concilia Moran, RSM, letter to church hierarchy, April 19, 1977. Mercy Heritage Center Archives, Belmont, NC.

38. Msgr. Richard Malone, Notes from December 15, 1981, meeting with NCCB officials and Mercy Administrative Team (MAT) in an attempt

to dialogue over the need for a pastoral approach to women with severe medical issues in need of elective sterilization. Mercy Heritage Center Archives, Belmont, NC.

39. Emily George, RSM, "History of the Tubal Ligation Study Since 1977," unpublished internal report written for Mercy leadership in April, 1983. Mercy Heritage Center Archives, Belmont, NC.

40. "Visit with Archbishop Jerome Hamer, OP," Meeting summary from Mercy Heritage Center Archives, Belmont, NC.

41. Ibid.

42. Ibid.

43. Carmel McEnroy, *Guests in Their Own House: The Women of Vatican II* (New York: Crossroad Publishing, 1996), 270. McEnroy notes that officials from WUCWO had themselves visited CDF officials several months earlier, in June of 1977. The WUCWO statement is found in their publication *Pro Mundi Vita* 10.

44. "Visit with Archbishop Jerome Hamer, OP."

45. "Key Findings in Sisters' Survey," *Union Scope*, March 1979, 4. Mercy Heritage Center Archives, Belmont, NC.

46. World Synod of Catholic Bishops, "Justice in the World," 6, 1971.

47. Theresa Kane, "Opening Reflections to the Delegates at the Second Session of the Tenth General Chapter, June 25, 1979. Mercy Heritage Center Archives, Belmont, NC.

48. "Chapter: Sell Potomac Land, Buildings," *Union Scope*, July 1979

49. Theresa Kane, Closing Remarks at the Eucharistic Liturgy on Thursday June 28, 1979, concluding the second session of the Tenth General Chapter of the Sisters of Mercy of the Union, Potomac, MD. Mercy Heritage Center Archives, Belmont, NC.

50. "Mercy Day Marks Closing of National Center," *Union Scope*, September-October 1980, 1. Mercy Heritage Center Archives, Belmont, NC.

51. Werntz, *Our Beloved Union*, 359.

52. In 2005 the work of the McAuley Institute drew to a close. Its loan fund was transferred to Mercy Housing, Inc., in Denver Colorado, and all viable programs were transferred to other housing endeavors. (Institute Leadership Team Accountability Report, Phase3, 1999–2005, *Walking the Path of Mercy*.)

53. See https://lcwr.org/about.

54. Lora Ann Quiñonez, CDP, and Mary Daniel Turner, SNDdeN, *The Transformation of American Catholic Sisters* (Philadelphia: Temple University Press, 1992), 21.

55. Ibid., 22.

56. Pope Paul VI, *Evangelica Testificatio*, 18, and Quiñonez and Turner, *Transformation of American Catholic Sisters*, 22.

57. Quiñonez and Turner, *Transformation of American Catholic Sisters*, 98.

58. Ibid., 99.

59. Ibid., 57.

60. Ibid., 59.

61. Theresa Kane, "Reflection on Leadership," LCWR Newsletter, May, 1978. Mercy Heritage Center Archives, Belmont, NC.

62. Quiñonez and Turner, *Transformation of American Catholic Sisters*, 81.

63. Joan Keleher Doyle, BVM, LCWR Conference Report, 1980. Mercy Heritage Center Archives, Belmont, NC.

64. In 2001 the conference—which until then had focused primarily on church affairs—combined with the United States Catholic Conference (which addressed social justice issues) into one entity now named the United States Conference of Catholic Bishops (USCCB).

65. Lora Ann Quiñonez, *Patterns in Authority and Obedience: An Overview of Authority/Obedience Developments among US Women Religious* (Washington, DC: Leadership Conference of Women Religious, May 15, 1978).

66. Unless otherwise noted, all quotations in this paragraph are from Quiñonez, *Patterns in Authority and Obedience*.

67. Quiñonez, 13. While *Patterns in Authority and Obedience* was written more than forty years ago, its findings remain relevant today. One wonders if the recent painful conflicts reflected in the 2008–2015 Vatican investigation of US women religious would have been avoided had the dialogue so deeply desired by LCWR leadership begun in earnest forty years ago.

68. World Synod of Catholic Bishops, "Justice in the World," 1971.

69. Farley served on the Personhood Committee and Cooney served on the Neighborhood Committee.

70. See: https://cta-usa.org/history/.

71. The excommunication was removed by his successor, Bishop James Conley. See https://tinyurl.com/yb4fh5gn.

72. Theresa Kane, "Reflections from the Incoming President," LCWR Assembly, San Antonio, TX, August 30, 1979. Mercy Heritage Center Archives, Belmont NC.

73. Ibid.

74. "LCWR Commissions New Officers," *Union Scope*, October 1979, 3. Mercy Heritage Center Archives, Belmont NC.

75. A detailed discussion is found in chapter 1.

76. "Woman of Year," *Catholic Telegraph*, Cincinnati, Ohio, February 1980. Also see telephone message from Ms. Bernice McNeela, president of St. Joan's International Alliance, US Section, January 21, 1980. Mercy Heritage Center Archives, Belmont, NC.

77. Elisabeth Bumiller, "Seven Profiles in Courage," *Washington Post*, January 14, 1980.

78. Father Mark Brummel, CMF, as reprinted in *Union Scope*, June 1980, 8. Mercy Heritage Center Archives, Belmont, NC.

79. Nadine Foley, OP, Letter to Theresa Kane, RSM, February 21, 1980. Mercy Heritage Center Archives, Belmont, NC.

80. Siena Medal Recipient, Theresa Kane, RSM, Commencement Program. Mercy Heritage Center Archives, Belmont, NC.

81. "Sister Dies Tragically," *Union Scope*, June 1980, 11. Mercy Heritage Center Archives, Belmont, NC.

82. John Schwartz, "Gerald Robinson, Priest Convicted of Killing Ohio Nun, Dies at 76," *New York Times*, July 4, 2014. https://tinyurl.com/ydfgc8tu.

83. Marjorie Hyer, "Nun Who Spoke Out to the Pope Has No Regrets," *Washington Post*, May 20, 1980.

84. Ibid.

85. Ibid.

86. Paul Wilkes, "Equal Rights on the Altar of God?" *New York Times Magazine*, November 30, 1980.

87. "We Must 'Speak the Truth in Love,'" *Union Scope*, April 1980, 12. Mercy Heritage Center Archives, Belmont, NC.

88. See *Union Scope*, February 1980 and March 1980. Mercy Heritage Center Archives, Belmont, NC.

89. Unless otherwise indicated, all quotations in this paragraph are from *Union Scope*, April 1980. Mercy Heritage Center Archives, Belmont, NC.6

90. In 1979 Sister Mary Ann Dillon had been elected provincial administrator of the province of Scranton and no longer served on the Administrative Team.

91. The June 1979 chapter of affairs expanded the term of the Mercy Administrative Team from three years to four.

92. "A Leader's Vision..." *Union Scope*, April 1980, 2. Mercy Heritage Center Archives, Belmont, NC.

93. Norita Cooney, RSM, "Sterilization Chronology; Sisters of Mercy of the Union April 1977–April 1983." Mercy Heritage Center Archives, Belmont, NC.

94. "Official Observers Comment," *Union Scope* April 1980, 15. Mercy Heritage Center Archives, Belmont, NC.

95. Ibid.

96. "Institute Chooses Leaders for 1980–84," *Union Scope*, April 1980, 1. Mercy Heritage Center Archives, Belmont, NC.

97. Unless otherwise noted, information and quotations in this paragraph were found in *Union Scope*, March 1980. Mercy Heritage Center Archives, Belmont, NC.

98. "GAT Nominees Speak Out on Issues," *Union Scope*, March 1980, 8. Mercy Heritage Center Archives, Belmont, NC.

99. Ibid., 8–9.

100. Theresa Kane, "To Speak the Truth in Love," Address to Leadership Conference of Women Religious Assembly, August 24, 1980. Mercy Heritage Center Archives, Belmont, NC. Reprinted in Annmarie Sanders,

IHM, ed., *Spiritual Leadership for Challenging Times: Presidential Addresses from the Leadership Conference of Women Religious* (Maryknoll, NY: Orbis Books, 2014), 16–27.

101. Unless otherwise indicated, all quotations in this paragraph are from Theresa Kane, "To Speak the Truth in Love."

102. World Synod of Catholic Bishops, "Justice in the World," 1971.

CHAPTER 7: THE PERILS OF PROPHETIC LEADERSHIP

1. "1980–84 Accountability Report: Church/Institute Committee," *Union Scope*, March 1984, 6. Mercy Heritage Center Archives, Belmont, NC.

2. "Mercy Health Services Challenge Injustices," *Union Scope*, January/February 1981, 7. Mercy Heritage Center Archives, Belmont, NC.

3. Ibid.

4. National Conference of Catholic Bishops, "Ethical and Religious Directives for Catholic Health Facilities," *Hospital Progress* (December 1971): 17–17d.

5. Anthony Kosnick, "The Present Status of the Ethical and Religious Directives for Catholic Health Facilities," *Linacre Quarterly* 40 (1973): 81–90.

6. United States Catholic Conference Administrative Board, "Commentary on Sterilization," *Hospital Progress* (January 1978): 26–27.

7. Richard A. McCormick, SJ, *The Critical Calling: Reflections on Moral Dilemmas Since Vatican II* (Washington, DC: Georgetown University Press, 1989), 279.

8. Bernard Häring, *Medical Ethics* (Notre Dame, IN: Fides, 1973), 90.

9. Policy Manual of St. Joseph's Hospital (London, Ontario), 1973, "Foreword."

10. McCormick, *The Critical Calling*, 275.

11. Charles E. Westoff and Elise F. Jones, "The Secularization of U.S. Birth Control Practices," *Family Planning Perspectives* 9, no. 5 (1977): 203–7.

12. *Washington Star*, June 22, 1980, 1.

13. McCormick, *The Critical Calling*, 279–80.

14. Emily George, "History of the Tubal Ligation Study Since 1977," unpublished internal report written for Mercy leadership in April, 1983. Mercy Heritage Center Archives, Belmont, NC.

15. Ibid.

16. Ibid.

17. Before 1991, the nine provinces Theresa served as administrator general/president referred to themselves as "Sisters of Mercy of the Union." In 1991 the Union joined with sixteen other autonomous congregations to become the Institute of the Sisters of Mercy of the Americas. See Denise

Colgan, RSM, and Doris Gottemoeller, RSM, *Union and Charity: The Story of the Sisters of Mercy of the Americas* (Silver Spring, MD: Institute of the Sisters of Mercy of the Americas, 2017), 1.

18. Unless otherwise indicated, all outcome data is found in "Working Paper: Report from the Sterilization Subcommittee," Sisters of Mercy Church/Institute Committee, October 10, 1977, 7–16. Mercy Heritage Center Archives, Belmont, NC.

19. George, "History of the Tubal Ligation Study."

20. As noted earlier, the Sisters of Mercy had "health services" in fifty-seven dioceses in thirty-one states, but not all "health services" were hospitals.

21. Working Paper: Report from the Sterilization Subcommittee, 19.

22. John M. O'Lane, MD, "Sterilization and Contraceptive Services in Catholic Hospitals," *American Journal of Obstetrics and Gynecology* 133, no. 4 (1979): 355–57.

23. Working Paper: Report from the Sterilization Subcommittee, 26.

24. George, "History of the Tubal Ligation Study."

25. Ibid., 4.

26. "Statement of the General Administrative Team Relative to Hospital Policy on Tubal Ligation: A Response to the Recommendations of the Church/Institute Committee." Mercy Heritage Center Archives, Belmont, NC.

27. George, "History of the Tubal Ligation Study," 5.

28. William B. Smith, "A Tale of Two Sisters," *National Catholic Register*, November 25, 1979.

29. Helen Marie Burns, interview with author, January 29, 2018.

30. Media folders about Sr. Theresa Kane. Mercy Heritage Center Archives, Belmont, NC. Correspondence of Archbishop John Quinn, University of Notre Dame archives.

31. George, "History of the Tubal Ligation Study," 6.

32. Ibid., 7.

33. In Catholic medical ethics, the principle of totality says that each part of the human body exists for the good of the whole organism. It is therefore ethical, for example, to remove a damaged organ if it threatens the life of the entire body. Pope Paul VI followed Pius XII's rejection of the principle in tubal ligation because the danger to the mother does not come from the fallopian tubes themselves but "only if a voluntary sexual activity brings about a pregnancy..." *Acta Apostolica Sedis* 45 (1953): 674–75.

34. Emily George, "The Tubal Ligation Study: Reflection of a Mercy Administrative Team Member," August 1984, 5. Mercy Heritage Center Archives, Belmont, NC.

35. *Union Scope*, November 1980, 3. Mercy Heritage Center Archives, Belmont, NC.

36. Theresa Kane, Emily George, Letter to hospital administrators November 12, 1980. Mercy Heritage Center Archives, Belmont, NC.

37. What follows is a partial account of meeting details taken from "Meeting of Sisters Theresa Kane, R.S.M., and Emily George, R.S.M., with Archbishop John Roach and Bishop James Malone, President and Vice-President, NCCB," December 16, 1980, United States Catholic Conference, Washington, DC. Mercy Heritage Center Archives, Belmont, NC.

38. Ibid.

39. Letter from Archbishop John Quinn to Sister Theresa Kane, February 12, 1981. Mercy Heritage Center Archives, Belmont, NC.

40. "Chronology of Events Sisters of Mercy of the Union and the National Conference of Catholic Bishops," Fall 1979–Spring 1981. Mercy Heritage Center Archives, Belmont, NC.

41. George, "The Tubal Ligation Study," 8.

42. Theresa Kane, interview with author, June 2017.

43. George, "The Tubal Ligation Study," 8.

44. Specifics about the April General Administrative Conference meeting are from General Administrative Conference Minutes: Special Meeting, Monday April 6, 1981. Mercy Heritage Center Archives, Belmont, NC.

45. George, "History of the Tubal Ligation Study."

46. Theresa Kane, "Holy Week Retreat, April 13–18, 1981," Dominican Retreat House, Elkins Park, Pennsylvania. Notes from her personal journal.

47. Ibid.

48. The preceding narrative about the September 14 meeting is taken from "Summary of Meeting of NCCB and MAT [Mercy Administrative Team] regarding Tubal Ligation Report," September 14, 1981, USCC, Washington, DC. Mercy Heritage Center Archives, Belmont, NC.

49. "Bishops and Mercy Administration in Dialogue," *Union Scope*, September 1981, 3. Mercy Heritage Center Archives, Belmont, NC.

50. Ibid.

51. Theresa Kane, "A Conversation with God," *Union Scope*, December 1981. Mercy Heritage Center Archives, Belmont, NC.

52. Ibid.

53. Ibid.

54. Narrative that follows is from "Minutes from Conference between the Sisters of Mercy and the NCCB: Second Meeting," December 15, 1981, Mercy Center Washington. Mercy Heritage Center Archives, Belmont, NC.

55. Margaret Farley, interview with author, June 28, 2018.

56. "Minutes from Conference between the Sisters of Mercy and the NCCB: Second Meeting."

57. Frank Teskey, "Sisters of Mercy Challenge Magisterium on Medical Ethics," *The Wanderer*, October 15, 1982. James Hitchcock, "Mount Carmel Mercy: Catholicism Revised," *National Catholic Register*, October 18, 1981.

58. Helen Marie Burns, interview with author, January 29, 2018.

59. "Minutes from Conference between the Sisters of Mercy and the NCCB: Second Meeting."

60. "Minutes of the Mercy Administrative Team with the Committee of Verification," Mercy Center, Washington, April 14, 1982. Mercy Heritage Center Archives, Belmont, NC.

61. *Sacra Congregazione Per I Religiosi E. Gli Institui Secolari*, Prot. N. 40137/81. Mercy Heritage Center Archives, Belmont, NC.

62. "Meeting of Sisters Theresa Kane and Emily George, RSM with Bishops James Malone and William Keeler regarding the Tubal Ligation Study," Center for Applied Research in the Apostolate, Washington, DC, January 24, 1983. Mercy Heritage Center Archives, Belmont, NC.

63. Emily George, "Memorandum to Provincials and Consultants to Bishops/MAT Meeting on Tubal Ligation," March 29, 1982. Mercy Heritage Center Archives, Belmont, NC.

64. "Minutes of the Mercy Administrative Team with the Committee of Verification."

65. Elizabeth Carroll, RSM, "Confidential Report on Telephone Conversation with Archbishop Rembert Weakland re: Tubal Ligation," April 7, 1982. Mercy Heritage Center Archives, Belmont, NC.

66. Richard A. McCormick, SJ, Letter to Most Reverend James W. Malone, March 31, 1982. Mercy Heritage Center Archives, Belmont, NC. Also cited in McCormick, *The Critical Calling*, 279–80.

67. James F. Keenan, "Champion of Conscience," *America*, April 4, 2005. https://tinyurl.com/yd3vy7jh.

68. "Matters Regarding Tubal Ligation Study," Summary of Three Meetings, Spring 1982. Mercy Heritage Center Archives, Belmont, NC.

69. Ibid. Phone consultation of Sister Emily George with Francis Morrissey, OMI, Ottawa, Canada, April 21, 1982. Mercy Heritage Center Archives, Belmont, NC.

70. Commonly interpreted by Catholic moral theologians as the "religious submission of mind and will" (McCormick, *The Critical Calling*, 283).

71. Letter from Mercy Administrative Team to Pope John Paul II responding to two questions about their stance on tubal ligation, May 11, 1982. Mercy Heritage Center Archives, Belmont, NC.

72. Notes for the Meeting of the Committee of Verification with the Mercy Administrative Team, May 11, 1982, Mercy Center Washington. (Bishop Keeler took the official minutes.) Mercy Heritage Center Archives, Belmont, NC.

73. Theresa Kane, Letter to hospital CEO Mr. Edward J. Connors, May 17, 1982. Mercy Heritage Center Archives, Belmont, NC.

74. McCormick, *The Critical Calling*, 283.

75. Matters Regarding Tubal Ligation Study: Courtesy Visit to Archbishop Jean Jadot by Sisters Theresa Kane and Emily George, Rome, Italy, May 19, 1982. Mercy Heritage Center Archives, Belmont, NC.

76. Ibid.

77. George, "History of the Tubal Ligation Study," 10.

78. "Matters Regarding Tubal Ligation: Meeting of Archbishop Pio Laghi with Sisters Theresa Kane and Emily George," Apostolic Delegate's residence, Washington, DC, June 24, 1982. Mercy Heritage Center Archives, Belmont, NC.

79. Ibid.

80. Theresa Kane, "Communication to the Provincial Administrators," June 18, 1982. Mercy Heritage Center Archives, Belmont, NC.

81. Theresa Kane, Letter to all sisters on for Mercy Day, 1982 (September 24, 1982). Mercy Heritage Center Archives, Belmont, NC.

82. Eduardo Cardinal Pironio, Prot. N. 40137/81, August 30, 1982. Mercy Heritage Center Archives, Belmont, NC.

83. Notes from "Meeting of Sisters Theresa Kane and Emily George, RSM, with Archbishop John Roach and Bishop James Malone," November 4, 1982. Mercy Heritage Center Archives, Belmont, NC.

84. "Matters Regarding Tubal Ligation Study: Courtesy Visit to Archbishop Jean Jadot by Sisters Theresa Kane and Emily George, Rome, Italy, May 19, 1982." Mercy Heritage Center Archives, Belmont, NC.

85. Telephone conversation between Sr. M. Theresa Kane, RSM, and Msgr. Daniel Hoye, NCCB. A copy was sent to the provincial administrators and other members of the Administrative Team. Mercy Heritage Center Archives, Belmont, NC.

86. Letter from Sacred Congregation of Religious and Institutes of Secular Life, to Sister Mary Theresa Kane, R.S.M., Prot. N. 40138/81, November 21, 2018. Mercy Heritage Center Archives, Belmont, NC.

87. Notes from meeting of Sisters Theresa Kane and Emily George, RSM, with Bishops James Malone and William Keeler regarding the Tubal Ligation Study, CARA, Washington, DC, January 24, 1983. Mercy Heritage Center Archives, Belmont, NC.

88. George, "History of the Tubal Ligation Study."

89. Charles Curran, "Bernard Häring: A Witness of Critical Love for the Church," *National Catholic Reporter*, November 24, 2012. https://tinyurl.com/y7rklew2.

90. "Summary Report: MAT [Mercy Administrative Team] Meeting with Consultants, Tubal Ligation Issue," Silver Spring, MD, December 21, 1982. Mercy Heritage Center Archives, Belmont, NC.

91. George, "History of the Tubal Ligation Study," 11.

92. Notes from "Meeting of Sisters Theresa Kane and Emily George RSM with Rev. Edward Schillebeeckx, O.P." Union Theological Seminary, New York, February 3, 1983. Mercy Heritage Center Archives, Belmont, NC.

93. Charles Curran, "Bernard Häring: A Moral Theologian Whose Soul Matched His Scholarship," *National Catholic Reporter*, July 17, 1998. https://tinyurl.com/ybgxughy.

94. Notes from "Consultations in Rome, May 9–14, 1983. Sisters Theresa Kane, Mary Ellen Quinn, and Rosemary Ronk.

95. Madonna Kolbenschlag, ed., *Authority, Community, and Conflict* (Kansas City, MO: Sheed and Ward, 1986), 140.

96. Ibid.

97. St. Joseph Sister Clare Dunn served as minority leader in the Arizona legislature until her untimely death in a car accident in 1981. Likewise, Dominican Sister Ardeth Platte served as city councilwoman in Saginaw, Michigan, for over ten years. See Madonna Kolbenschlag, "Sister Mansour Is Not Alone," *Commonweal*, June 17, 1983.

98. Colman McCarthy, "Father Drinan, Model of Moral Tenacity," *Washington Post*, January 30, 2007. https://tinyurl.com/25a88s.

99. Ibid.

100. Helen Marie Burns, "Case Study," in *Authority, Community and Conflict*, ed. Kolbenschlag, 4.

101. Violet would win in 1985, becoming the first woman ever elected as a state's attorney general. Marjorie Hyer, "Two Rhode Island Nuns Challenging Papal Edict," *Washington Post*, January 28, 1984. https://tinyurl.com/y9kxscac.

102. Helen Marie Burns, interview with author, January 15, 2018.

103. Ibid.

104. Burns, "Case Study," 6.

105. Ibid.

106. Ibid.

107. Ibid., 6, 7.

108. Theresa Kane, Letter to persons who wrote of concerns about Agnes Mary Mansour's appointment, February 1983. Mercy Heritage Center Archives, Belmont, NC.

109. Burns, "Case Study," 7.

110. Helen Marie Burns, interview with author, January 15, 2018.

111. Report of the Sisters of Mercy Province of Detroit Relative to the Appointment of Sister Agnes Mary Mansour, RSM, Director of the Department of Social Services in the State of Michigan, February 23–March 5. Mercy Heritage Center Archives, Belmont, NC.

112. Statement of the Provincial Administrative Team of the Sisters of Mercy, Province of Detroit, regarding Sister Agnes Mary Mansour, March 5, 1983. Mercy Heritage Center Archives, Belmont, NC.

113. Bishop Anthony J. Bevilacqua, Ad Hoc Delegate of the Holy See, "Chronology of Events in the Matter of Sister Agnes Mary Mansour," March 10, 1983. Mercy Heritage Center Archives, Belmont, NC.

114. Archbishop Pio Laghi, Letter to Sr. Theresa Kane (no. 268.83.8), March 23, 1983, in Kolbenschlag, *Authority, Community and Conflict*, 157.

115. Detroit Provincial Administrative Team, "Chronology of Events Surrounding Sister Agnes Mary Mansour's Appointment as Director of the Department of Social Services," Communication to Sisters of Mercy, Province of Detroit, May 12, 1983. Mercy Heritage Center Archives, Belmont, NC.

116. Ibid.

117. Ibid.

118. Ibid.

119. Ibid.

120. Burns, "Case Study," 10–11. Bevilacqua would later become the cardinal archbishop of Philadelphia. He died in the midst of a priest sex abuse controversy after the Philadelphia grand jury ruled that he and his predecessor, John Cardinal Krol, had systematically covered up the child sex abuse of hundreds of Philadelphia priests. See "Cardinal Anthony Bevilacqua Dies at 88," *Philadelphia Inquirer*, February 1, 2012. https://tinyurl.com/yawhlo8h.

121. Detroit Provincial Administrative Team, "Chronology of Events Surrounding Sister Agnes Mary Mansour's appointment as Director of the Department of Social Services."

122. Helen Marie Burns, interview with author, January 15, 2018.

123. Burns, "Case Study," 11.

124. Bishop Anthony J. Bevilacqua, "Formal Precept of the Holy See to Sister Agnes Mary Mansour R.S.M.," in *Authority, Community, and Conflict*, ed. Kolbenschlag, 168–73.

125. Sharon would later regretfully tell Theresa that there were issues about the Mansour case of which she was unaware at the time of this meeting. Helen Marie recalls that Sharon had been quite helpful earlier in the process. Theresa Kane, interview with author, June 2017, and Helen Marie Burns, interview with author, January 2018.

126. Burns, "Case Study," 11-12.

127. James Coriden, "Fair Process," in *Authority, Community, and Conflict*, ed. Kolbenschlag, 32–33.

128. Ibid., 33.

129. Agnes Mary Mansour, Press Statement, May 11, 1983. Mercy Heritage Center Archives, Belmont, NC.

130. Helen Marie Burns, interview with author, January 15, 2018.

131. Ibid.

132. "Consultations in Rome," May 9–14, 1983, Sisters Theresa Kane, Mary Ellen Quinn, Rosemary Ronk. Mercy Heritage Center Archives, Belmont, NC.

133. Theresa Kane, Letter to Sisters, May 20, 1983. Mercy Heritage Center Archives, Belmont, NC. The biblical text refers to James 1:19.

134. Letter from Pittsburgh Mercy leadership to their members, May 13, 1983. Notre Dame Archives, LCWR Mansour case, communications and correspondence about Mansour case, May 13, 1983–September 1983.

135. "National organizations protest Vatican decisions," media release from National Assembly of Religious Women (NARW) and National Coalition of American Nuns (NCAN). May 13, 1983. Mercy Heritage Center Archives, Belmont, NC.

136. NETWORK news release and public statement, May 18, 1983. Mercy Heritage Center Archives, Belmont, NC.

137. Ibid.

138. NETWORK action alert, May 18, 1983. Mercy Heritage Center Archives, Belmont, NC.

139. "Statement of the Executive Committee of the LCWR regarding the Mansour Case," media release, May 1983. Mercy Heritage Center Archives, Belmont, NC.

140. Letter from the *Supremum Signaturae Apostolicae Tribunal* Prot. N. 15363/83 CA to Sr. Mary Theresa Kane R.S.M., July 4, 1983, in *Authority, Community, and Conflict*, ed. Kolbenschlag, 184.

141. "Two Nuns Who Quit Order Defend Political Role," *New York Times*, May 6, 1984. Associated Press. https://tinyurl.com/y8ljxd5p.

142. Confidential letter of Archbishop Pio Laghi to Sr. Theresa Kane R.S.M. No. 923/83/2, November 26, 1983, in *Authority, Community, and Conflict*, ed. Kolbenschlag, 186.

143. Helen Marie Burns, interview with author, January 15, 2018.

144. Ibid.

145. Wikipedia, Agnes Mary Mansour, https://tinyurl.com/yd76x68j.

146. Helen Marie Burns, interview with author, January 18, 2018.

147. Monika K. Hellwig, "A Theological Perspective," in *Authority, Community, and Conflict*, ed. Kolbenschlag, 135, 137.

148. Helen Marie Burns, "Reflections for Agnes Mary's Wake Service," December 20, 2004. Personal papers.

149. Margaret Farley, "Homily Delivered at the Funeral Mass for Agnes Mary Mansour," December 21, 2004. Personal papers.

CHAPTER 8: A ROCK AND A HARD PLACE

1. "Eleventh General Chapter: 1983 Session," *Union Scope*, December 1982. Mercy Heritage Center Archives, Belmont, NC.

2. *Union Scope*, April/May 1983, 3, 5, 6. Mercy Heritage Center Archives, Belmont, NC.

3. Ibid., 7.

4. The general chapters of the Sisters of Mercy had always received an accountability report from the current Administrative Team. The "State of the Union" report, however, initiated a larger accountability to the membership-at-large. (Email communication from Sister Helen Marie Burns, January 2, 2019.)

5. "GAC [General Administrative Conference]: An Evolution for the '80s," "State of the Union Report," Sisters of Mercy of the Union, *Union Scope*, March 1993, 2. Mercy Heritage Center Archives, Belmont, NC.

6. Sister Barbara Valuckas, SSND, "A Conversation with MAT [Mercy Administrative Team]: Looking Toward the Future," *State of the Union Report*, Sisters of Mercy of the Union, *Union Scope*, March 1993, 2.

7. Ibid.

8. Ibid.

9. "General Chapter Recesses until September," *Union Scope*, April/May 1983. Mercy Heritage Center Archives, Belmont, NC.

10. Ibid.

11. Farley participated because she is a moral theologian and had been a member of the Church/Institute Committee.

12. Sr. Anne Vaccarest, "Tubal Ligation Study: Chapter Discussion Focuses on Question and Clarification," *Union Scope*, April/May 1983, 3. Mercy Heritage Center Archives, Belmont, NC.

13. Sr. Moira Kenny, "Elective Office—Recess Leaves Questions Unanswered," *Union Scope*, April/May 1983, 5. Mercy Heritage Center Archives, Belmont, NC.

14. Sr. Joy Clough, "Canonical Regulation Study Focuses Delegate Discussion," *Union Scope*, April/May 1983, 6. Mercy Heritage Center Archives, Belmont, NC.

15. "Canonical Regulation of Women's Religious Communities: Its Past and Its Future," written by Margaret Farley with input from Emily George, Church/Institute Committee, Sisters of Mercy, 1983. Unpublished papers of Margaret Farley.

16. Clough, "Canonical Regulation Study."

17. Ibid.

18. Ibid.

19. Theresa Kane, Letter to Sisters of Mercy, *Union Scope*, April/May 1983, 1.

20. One wonders why the "Essential Elements" document was made public before the more moderate papal letter, which was written before the guidelines but not made public until much later. ttps://tinyurl.com/ya6ldo3k.

21. Kenneth A. Briggs, *Double Crossed: Uncovering the Catholic Church's Betrayal of American Nuns* (New York: Doubleday, 2006), 198.

22. Ibid., 199.

23. Jerry Filteau, "Bishops Taking on 'Risks': Speaking on New Areas, Controversy," *The Voice, Catholic Archdiocese of Miami,* November 25, 1983 (Catholic News Service): 1, 4. https://tinyurl.com/y8xlcmke.

24. Ibid.

25. Kenneth Briggs, "John R. Quinn: A Spiritual Emissary," *National Catholic Reporter*, June 26, 2017. https://tinyurl.com/y9fnkaqq.

26. Ibid.

27. Peter Steinfels, "Pope Is Content with U.S. Religious Orders," *New York Times*, April 2, 1989. https://tinyurl.com/y85erykm.

28. See William Grimes, "John R. Quinn, Archbishop and Liberal Voice in Church, Dies at 88," *New York Times,* July 6, 2017, https://tinyurl.com/y7pglbql. See also Briggs, "John R. Quinn: A Spiritual Emissary."

29. Steinfels, "Pope Is Content with Religious Orders."

30. Briggs, "John R. Quinn: A Spiritual Emissary."

31. John R. Quinn, Letter to Sister M. Theresa Kane, R.S.M., January 25, 1984. Notre Dame Archives, DJRQ 1/20 Correspondence.

32. John R. Quinn, Letter to Archbishop Pio Laghi, January 19, 1984 Prot. N. 114/84/6, and Letter to Archbishop Pio Laghi, February 2, 1984. Notre Dame Archives, DJRQ 1/20 Correspondence.

33. Ibid.

34. Theresa Kane, Letter to Archbishop John Quinn, June 22, 1984. Notre Dame Archives, DJRQ 1/20 Correspondence.

35. Dorothy Kazel, "Keep the People of El Salvador before the Lord," *Union Scope,* January/February, 1981, 3.

36. "Sisters Speak Out in the US Capitol Building," *Union Scope,* December 1983, 1. Mercy Heritage Center Archives, Belmont, NC.

37. Mary Regina Werntz, RSM, *Our Beloved Union: A History of the Sisters of Mercy of the Union* (Westminster, MD: Christian Classics, Inc, 1989), 365.

38. "1980–84 Accountability Report," *Union Scope,* March 1984, 4.

39. Theresa Kane, "Sr. Theresa Kane Observes Honduran Elections," *Union Scope,* December 1981, 8. Mercy Heritage Center Archives, Belmont, NC.

40. "Sister Theresa Kane Visits Honduras, Belize," *Union Scope,* December, 1983, 3. Mercy Heritage Center Archives, Belmont, NC.

41. Rather than a rewrite of the first part of their original May 11 reply to the pope addressing adherence to the magisterium and invoking *obsequium religiosum.*

42. Theresa Kane, Letter to Bishop James V. Malone, May 27, 1983. Mercy Heritage Center Archives, Belmont, NC.

43. Unless otherwise noted all meeting quotations are from "Meeting of the Mercy Administrative Team with the Committee of Verification," June 13, 1983, International Inn, Washington, DC. Mercy Heritage Center Archives, Belmont, NC.

44. Theresa Kane, Letter and enclosures, "Draft letter to Chief Executive Officer" and "Letter to Cardinal Pironio and Archbishop Mayer" sent to Bishop James V. Malone, July 6, 1983. Mercy Heritage Center Archives, Belmont, NC.

45. Theresa Kane, enclosure "Letter to Cardinal Pironio" sent via Bishop James V. Malone, July 6, 1983. Mercy Heritage Center Archives, Belmont, NC.

46. Theresa Kane, "Opening Address to Third Session of Eleventh General Chapter, September 1, 1983," reprinted in *Union Scope,* September 1983, 1–2. Mercy Heritage Center Archives, Belmont, NC.

47. Ibid.

48. Ibid.

49. Ibid.

50. Ibid.

51. Ibid.

52. Theresa Kane, "Opening Address to Third Session of Eleventh General Chapter, September 1, 1983."

53. "Clarification and Information on the Mansour Case," *Union Scope,* September 1983, 3. Mercy Heritage Center Archives, Belmont, NC.

54. "Proposals, Statement Accepted by Eleventh General Chapter"; "Statement Re: Agnes Mary Mansour," *Union Scope,* September 1983, 4. Mercy Heritage Center Archives, Belmont, NC.

55. Proposals, Statement Accepted by Eleventh General Chapter"; *Our Relationship within the Church, Union Scope,* September 1983, 5. Mercy Heritage Center Archives, Belmont, NC.

56. "Other Chapter Action," *Union Scope,* September 1983, 5. Mercy Heritage Center Archives, Belmont, NC.

57. Ibid.

58. "Chapter Looks at Individual Proposals," *Union Scope,* September 1983, 6. Mercy Heritage Center Archives, Belmont, NC.

59. "Proposals, Statement Accepted by Eleventh General Chapter"; "Political Ministry," *Union Scope,* September 1983, 4. Mercy Heritage Center Archives, Belmont, NC.

60. "'Mercy Futures' Is Topic of Panel, Floor Discussions," *Union Scope,* September 1983, 5. Mercy Heritage Center Archives, Belmont, NC.

61. Theresa Kane, "Let Us Go as Women Anointed . . . , " *Union Scope,* September 1983, 8. Mercy Heritage Center Archives, Belmont, NC.

62. All quotations in this section from Theresa Kane, "Let Us Go as Women Anointed . . ." *Union Scope,* September 1983, 8.

63. Theresa Kane, "Let Us Go as Women Anointed . . . , " *Union Scope,* September 1983, 8.

64. Bishop James W. Malone, Letter to Sister Mary Theresa Kane R.S.M., September 7, 1983. Mercy Heritage Center Archives, Belmont, NC.

65. Ibid.

66. Ibid. According to Fr. James A. Provost, the 1983 Code of Canon Law describes a precept as "a decree by which a person or persons are directly and legitimately required to do or omit something" or be liable to a penalty. Letter to Sr. M. Theresa Kane, RSM, October 5, 1983. Mercy Heritage Center Archives, Belmont, NC.

67. James A. Provost, Letter to Sr. M. Theresa Kane, RSM, October 5, 1983. Mercy Heritage Center Archives, Belmont, NC.

68. Ibid.

69. Francis G. Morrisey, O.M.I., Letter to Sister Emily George, RSM, September 29, 1983. Mercy Heritage Center Archives, Belmont, NC.

70. Rev. Sean O'Riordan, C.SS.R., Letter to Theresa Kane, October 21, 1983. Mercy Heritage Center Archives, Belmont, NC.

71. Ibid.

72. Emily George, "Memo re: Telephone Conversation with Joseph Fuchs, S.J., re: Tubal Ligation Issue," October 10, 1983. Mercy Heritage Center Archives, Belmont, NC.

73. Emily George, summary of conversation with Father Charles Curran, September 23, 1983. Mercy Heritage Center Archives, Belmont, NC.

74. Emily George, handwritten account of two conversations with Father Bryan Hehir, September–October 1983. Mercy Heritage Center Archives, Belmont, NC.

75. Norita Cooney, RSM, Letter to Sister Mary Theresa Kane, RSM, September 16, 1983. Mercy Heritage Center Archives, Belmont, NC.

76. See letters from provincial leadership responding to tubal ligation issue, tubal ligation file. Mercy Heritage Center Archives, Belmont, NC.

77. Marie John Kelly, Letter to Theresa Kane, September 17, 1983. Mercy Heritage Center Archives, Belmont, NC.

78. Ibid.

79. Peter Shannon, Letter to Sisters of Mercy Administrative Team, c/o Sister Mary Theresa Kane, RSM. October 26, 1983. This letter summarizes a series of events regarding civil issues related to the mandated tubal ligation letter and the eventual resolution thereof. Mercy Heritage Center Archives, Belmont, NC.

80. Mary Ellen Quinn, "Reflections of Sister Mary Ellen Quinn," in "MAT [Mercy Administrative Team] Reflections on the Tubal Ligation Decision," January 1984. Mercy Heritage Center Archives, Belmont, NC.

81. Betty Barrett, RSM, "Reflections of Sister Betty Barrett," in "MAT Reflections on the Tubal Ligation Decision."

82. Emily George, RSM, "Reflections of Sister Emily George," in "MAT Reflections on the Tubal Ligation Decision."

83. Rosemary Ronk, RSM, "Reflections of Sister Rosemary Ronk," in "MAT Reflections on the Tubal Ligation Decision."

84. Mary Ellen Quinn, RSM, "Reflections of Sister Mary Ellen Quinn," in "MAT Reflections on the Tubal Ligation Decision."

85. Theresa Kane, RSM in "Reflections of Sister M. Theresa Kane," in "MAT Reflections on the Tubal Ligation Decision."

86. Theresa Kane, RSM, Letter to Chief Executive Officers of Mercy Hospitals, October 26, 1983. Mercy Heritage Center Archives, Belmont, NC.

87. Theresa Kane, RSM, Letter to Sisters of Mercy of the Union, October 27, 1983. Mercy Heritage Center Archives, Belmont, NC.

88. Robert J. McClory, "Sterilization: Forbidden by Rome, Pushed by U.S: Sisters Obey Rome, Forbid Tubal Ligations," National Catholic Reporter, November 11, 1983. "Rome Tells Mercy Sisters to Stop Tubal Ligations," National Catholic News Service, December 3, 1983.

89. Charles Curran, interview with author January 18, 2018.

90. "GAC and Bishops Meet and Dialogue in Chicago," Union Scope, November/December 1983, 3. Mercy Heritage Center Archives, Belmont, NC.

91. Pope John Paul II, "Address of Pope John Paul II to a Group of Bishops from the United States of America on Their ad limina apostolorum Visit" September 5, 1983. https://tinyurl.com/yaa5b28d.

92. "On Women: NCCB Workshop" *Union Scope*, November/December 1983, 4. Mercy Heritage Center Archives, Belmont, NC.

93. Ibid.

94. "Woman Church Speaks," *Union Scope*, November/December 1983, 4. Mercy Heritage Center Archives, Belmont, NC.

95. Unless otherwise noted, quotations below are from: Theresa Kane, RSM, "1984 New Year Message from Theresa Kane: A Pastoral on Women," January 1984. Mercy Heritage Center Archives, Belmont, NC.

96. Theresa cited statistics from Teresa Hommel's article "Sexism and Conversion," published in the May 1981 issue of the NETWORK newsletter.

97. Two thirds of the world's 774 million illiterate adults are women (https://tinyurl.com/yaomvxs8). Fewer than 20 percent of the world's landowners are women (https://tinyurl.com/o6nml5h). In the United States, one in five women and one in seventy-one men will be raped at some point in their lifetime (https://tinyurl.com/y9fbrjyp). Only five of every thousand reported rapes will lead to a conviction (https://tinyurl.com/h6jqprr). One in five girls and one in twenty boys is a victim of child sex abuse (https://tinyurl.com/y8e9crru). Eighty-one percent of women have been sexually harassed at work (https://tinyurl.com/yaj7akmv).

98. Theresa Kane, "1984 New Year Message from Theresa Kane: A Pastoral on Women," January 1984. Mercy Heritage Center Archives, Belmont, NC.

99. Ibid.

100. Unsigned cover letter to Archbishop John Quinn accompanying Theresa Kane's "1984 New Year Message from Theresa Kane: A Pastoral on Women," January 1984. Archives, University of Notre Dame, DJRQ. Sister Theresa Kane folder,

101. Edward Cardinal Martinez, Letter no. 128.198 to Sister Mary Theresa Kane, March 6, 1984. Mercy Heritage Center Archives, Belmont, NC.

102. Theresa Kane, RSM, Letter to Pope John Paul II, Holy Thursday, April 19, 1984. Mercy Heritage Center Archives, Belmont, NC.

103. Archbishop Pio Laghi, Letter to Sister Theresa M. Kane, R.S.M., no. 2987/84/8, August 3, 1984. Mercy Heritage Center Archives, Belmont, NC.

104. Theresa Kane, RSM, Letters as President of LCWR to Pope John Paul II on November 14, 1979; March 25, 1980; and June 15, 1980. Letters as President of the Sisters of Mercy of the Union, January 6, 1984, and April 19, 1984. Letter from Archbishop Pio Laghi to Sr. M. Theresa Kane, RSM, no. 2987/84/8, August 3, 1984. Mercy Heritage Center Archives, Belmont, NC.

105. As a thirty-year resident of the diocese of Cleveland, I can attest to the fact that Bishop Pilla is well known for respecting women religious and appointing women (both lay and religious) to positions of responsibility leading parishes and diocesan offices.

106. Details of the papal luncheon and its aftermath are from Sharon Euart's interview with the author in January 2018.

107. Father Schnurr would be ordained a bishop in 2001 and in 2008 installed as archbishop in the Archdiocese of Cincinnati.

108. Theresa Kane, interview with author, June 2017.

109. See *Ad Tuendam Fidem*, 1998 (https://tinyurl.com/yd5y8lay). *Ordinatio Sacerdotalis*, 1994 (https://tinyurl.com/qx7c9yz). and *Responsum ad Dubium*, 1995 (https://tinyurl.com/bq25dv7). Also *Mulieris Dignitatem*, 1988 (https://tinyurl.com/nphq2r6) and *Letter to Women*, 1995 (https://tinyurl.com/nyx6ug2).

110. Theresa Kane, "Let Us Be Women of Vision," *Union Scope*, April 1984, 2. Mercy Heritage Center Archives, Belmont, NC.

111. "Nominees for 1984–88 Union Leadership: For Administrator," *Union Scope*, January 1984, 1. Mercy Heritage Center Archives, Belmont, NC.

112. Ibid.

113. Ibid.

114. Ibid.

115. Ibid.

116. Letter from the Sacred Congregation for Religious and Secular Institutes to Sister Theresa Kane, Prot. N. 60407/84, May 9, 1984, in *Authority, Community, and Conflict*, ed. Madonna Kolbenschlag (Kansas City, MO: Sheed and Ward, 1986), 205.

117. Sue Kamler and Anne Vaccarest, "MAT/Delegates Discuss Accountability," *Union Scope*, April 1984, 4. "Mercy Heritage Center Archives, Belmont, NC.

118. "1977 Statement: A Progress Report," *Union Scope*, April 1984. Mercy Heritage Center Archives, Belmont, NC.

119. "Reflection Workshop: Searching Together for Truth," *Union Scope*, November/December 1984. Mercy Heritage Center Archives, Belmont, NC.

120. "Church/Institute Committee Is Affirmed," *Union Scope*, April 1984, 9. Mercy Heritage Center Archives, Belmont, NC.

121. Mary Luke Tobin, SL, introduction to *Tributes Honoring Theresa Kane, R.S.M.* Personal papers of Sr. Theresa Kane.

122. All quotations in this section taken from *Tributes Honoring Theresa Kane R.S.M.* Personal papers of Sr. Theresa Kane.

123. Joan Chittister's tribute is reprinted on the dedication page of this book.

124. From personal papers of Sr. Theresa Kane. Reproduced from original musical score.

125. Letter from Bishop Walter F. Sullivan, Bishop of Richmond to Sister Theresa Kane, President, Sisters of Mercy of the Union. May 30, 1984. Mercy Heritage Center Archives, Belmont, NC.

126. Letter from Bishop Francis A. Quinn to Sister M. Theresa Kane, May 7, 1984. Mercy Heritage Center Archives, Belmont, NC.

127. Letter from Sister Christine Marie Rody, VSC, to Sister Theresa Kane, RSM, May 8, 1984. Mercy Heritage Center Archives, Belmont, NC.

128. Letter from Rev. Anthony Bellagamba, IMC, to Sister M. Theresa Kane, RSM, April 16, 1984. Mercy Heritage Center Archives, Belmont, NC.

129. Theresa Kane, "Conclusion: One Vision from the Center," in "1980–84 Accountability Report," *Union Scope*, March 1984, 14. Mercy Heritage Center Archives, Belmont, NC.

130. "I can no other answer make but thanks," *Union Scope*, May/June 1984, 1. Mercy Heritage Center Archives, Belmont, NC.

CHAPTER 9: A LIFETIME OF PROPHETIC SERVICE

1. Helen Amos, interview with author, January 2018.

2. Letter of Archbishop John R. Quinn to Archbishop Pio Laghi, August 17, 1984. Archbishop John R. Quinn correspondence August 1983–January 8, 1985. University of Notre Dame Archives.

3. Unless otherwise indicated, all quotations of Theresa Kane are from interviews with the author. Each of Kane's entries from her personal journal are footnoted.

4. Helen Amos, interview with author, January 2018.

5. Mary Regina Werntz, RSM, *Our Beloved Union: A History of the Sisters of Mercy of the Union* (Westminster, MD: Christian Classics, Inc, 1989), 359. (Helen Amos, telephone interview with author, December 20, 1988).

6. "1977 Statement: A Progress Report," *Union Scope*, April 1984. Mercy Heritage Center Archives, Belmont, NC.

7. Helen Marie Burns, interview with author, January 2018.

8. Helen Amos, interview with author, January 2018.

9. Ibid.

10. Ibid.

11. Ibid., and Theresa Kane, interview with author, August 2018.

12. Theresa Kane, journal entry, November 6, 1984.

13. Theresa Kane, journal entry, November 8, 1984.

14. Theresa Kane, journal entry, December 12, 1984

15. Theresa Kane, journal entry, October 17, 1984.

16. Ibid.

17. Ibid.

18. Ibid.

19. "Rosemary Ronk, RSM—Passed from Life to New Life August 26, 1984," *Union Scope*, September 1984, 1. Mercy Heritage Center Archives, Belmont, NC.

20. Theresa Kane journal, December 12, 1984, Foundation Day.

21. Margaret Farley, "Love Is Stronger Than Death," homily delivered at the Funeral Mass for Sister Emily George, RSM, December 8, 1984. Personal papers shared with author.

22. Ibid.

23. Theresa Kane, journal entry, December 12, 1984, Foundation Day. Personal papers.

24. Theresa Kane, journal entry, January 22, 1985.

25. Theresa Kane, journal entry, February 2, 1985.

26. Ibid.

27. Ibid.

28. Ibid.

29. Theresa Kane, journal entry, February 20, 1985.

30. Ibid.

31. Theresa Kane, journal entry, March 28, 1985.

32. Ibid.

33. Ibid.

34. Rev. Charles Curran, interview with author, January 18, 2018.

35. United Nations World Conferences on Women. See https://tinyurl. com/ y769g69c.

36. See chapter 5

37. In 1972 Sarah Lawrence became the first US college to offer a graduate degree in women's history. https://tinyurl.com/y84946dl.

38. "About Mercy College," https://tinyurl.com/yb3dv9o6.

39. "Mercy College Honors Theresa Kane." https://tinyurl.com/yccyedyc.

40. Berrigan died less than a year later on April 30, 2016, at the age of ninety-four.

41. Today there are effective medical treatments for this dreaded condition. See Mayo Clinic "C. difficile infection." https://tinyurl.com/ydypmf92.

42. See https://tinyurl.com/ycnbnhlm.

43. Erin Saiz Hanna, interview with author, December 2018.

44. Ibid.

45. Ibid.

46. Ibid.

47. The others were Bishop Patricia Fresen of the Roman Catholic Women Priests movement; Regina Bannan, a former professor at Temple University and former president of the Women's Ordination Conference; and Judy Heffernan, a member of the Southeastern Pennsylvania Women's Ordination Conference.

48. Jamie Manson, interview with author, December 2018.

49. Ibid.

50. Theresa Kane, "My Message to Pope Francis in Philadelphia— September 2015." Personal papers. See Appendix E.

51. Tom Fox e-mailed response to interview questions from author January 2019.

52. Ibid.

53. "Making History, Making Change: A Conversation with Theresa Kane," podcast from Women's Alliance for Theology, Ethics and Ritual (WATER), October 28, 2014.

54. Ibid.

55. John R. Quinn, Letter to Archbishop Pio Laghi, August 17, 1984. Archbishop John R. Quinn correspondence, August 1983–January 8, 1985, University of Notre Dame Archives, DJRQ 1/20 Correspondence.

56. At this writing, Call To Action conferences continue attract hundreds of Catholics although not in the same numbers as previously.

57. Loretto Sister Jeannine Gramick, interview with author, April 15, 2019.

58. Members are willing to discuss the many "elephants" in the church's living room.

59. "Mercy Sister Theresa Kane Criticizes Church Hierarchy," *National Catholic Reporter*, September 29, 2009. https://tinyurl.com/ycex89sq. At the same conference, NCAN presented an award to Sister of Charity Sister Louise Lears, who was banned from church ministries and sacraments by St. Louis Archbishop Raymond Burke because she supported women's ordination.

60. See chapter 7. The Vatican forced Mansour to leave the Sisters of Mercy because she would not resign her position as the director of Social Services for the state of Michigan. At the time, Medicaid funds paid for abortions for poor women. Two Catholic men had served in this position previous to Mansour and were never asked to step down.

61. Helen Marie Burns, RSM, interview with author, January 2018.

Epilogue

1. Bryan Cones, "Where Did the New Mass Translations Come From?" *U.S. Catholic*, December 2011. https://tinyurl.com/y9ber4ww.

2. See "Liturgists Worry about Upcoming Implementation," *America*, February 14, 2011 (https://tinyurl.com/y7d6htfa) and "Peter Jeffery on *Liturgiam authenticam*," Pray Tell blog, July 17, 2010 (https://tinyurl.com/yb6gt6sy). To his credit, in September 2017 Pope Francis returned decision-making about vernacular translations to the local bishops. See "Pope Pushes Decentralization in Translation of Liturgical Texts," *Crux*, September 9, 2017 (https://tinyurl.com/y8tzlmal).

3. Levada was a protégé of both Joseph Cardinal Bernardin and Joseph Cardinal Ratzinger. Bernardin recommended his appointment to the Congregation for the Doctrine of the Faith, where he worked with the prefect, Cardinal Ratzinger, before being named auxiliary bishop of Los Angeles in 1982. He was named archbishop of Portland, Oregon, in 1986 before becoming archbishop of San Francisco in 1995. When Ratzinger became Pope Benedict, he immediately appointed Levada to replace him as the prefect of the CDF in May 2005.

4. Joshua J. McElwee, "Visitation Report Takes Mostly Positive Tone towards US Sisters, "*National Catholic Reporter, Global Sisters Report*, December 16, 2014. https://tinyurl.com/y7b3g8jy.

5. Christine Schenk, "For US Sisters, Ordinary Catholics Made a Way Where There Was No Way," *National Catholic Reporter*, May 21, 2013. https://tinyurl.com/ychc67zp.

6. Mary Gordon, "Francis and the Nuns: Is the New Vatican All Talk?" *Harpers Magazine*, August 2014. https://tinyurl.com/y8aowgsb.

7. Judith Best, "Reflection on the Apostolic Visitation, 2008–2017," *National Catholic Reporter, Global Sisters Report*, July 5, 2017. https://tinyurl.com/yd7nadq5.

8. Jamie Manson, "What an Abortifacient Is and What It Isn't," *National Catholic Reporter*, February 20, 2012 (https://tinyurl.com/ya2nqfh4). See also Gordon, "Francis and the Nuns."

9. Sister X, "Cross Examination: Why Is Rome Investigating US Nuns?" *US Catholic*, October 21, 2009. https://tinyurl.com/y95cj6rj.

10. Cindy Wooden, "Vatican Aims to Regain Trust of US Religious Women, Official Says," Catholic News Service, August 10, 2011. https://tinyurl.com/yysfhfm7.

11. John Thavis, "Calming the Waters: New Vatican Official Tries Different Approach," *National Catholic Reporter*, June 6, 2011. https://tinyurl.com/ybtn25vs.

12. Sadhbh Walshe, "Pope Francis Is Throwing Nuns under the Bus for Sharing His Own Beliefs," *The Guardian*, May 8, 2014. https://tinyurl.com/ycsmxcqt.

13. Andrew Stern, Catholic Nuns' Group 'Stunned' by Vatican Slap," *Washington Post*, April 20, 2012. https://tinyurl.com/ybmrjud7.

14. Joshua J. McElwee, "Vatican Religious Prefect: 'I was left out of LCWR finding,'" *National Catholic Reporter*, May 5, 2013. https://tinyurl.com/ybgecwgs.

15. Tom Heneghan, "Vatican Crisis Highlights Pope Failure to Reform Curia," Reuters, May 30, 2012. https://tinyurl.com/y8zjv28b; Desmond O'Grady, "Can Francis Cure the Curia?" *Commonweal*, August 31, 2013. https://tinyurl.com/ydbsk7vj.

16. McElwee, "Vatican Religious Prefect; 'I was left out...'"

17. Joshua J. McElwee, "LCWR President to Sisters: Be 'Fearless' on Vatican Mandate,'" *National Catholic Reporter*, August 10, 2012. https://tinyurl.com/y8h2e8oo.

18. "National Federation of Priests' Councils Honors LCWR," *Update: A Publication of the Leadership Conference of Women Religious*, June 2011. https://tinyurl.com/y93ypblr.

19. "'Rebel' Nuns Receive Religious Freedom Award," *Vatican Insider: World News*, November 19, 2012. https://tinyurl.com/y7pea9gg.

20. McElwee, "Visitation Report."

21. The word "gratitude" appears eight times in the twelve-page report.

22. McElwee, "Visitation Report."

23. Laurie Goodstein, "Vatican Report Cites Achievements and Chal-

lenges of US Nuns," *New York Times,* December 16, 2014, https://tinyurl.com/ycrmkobd.

24. McElwee, "Visitation Report."

25. "Press Release and Final Report on the Implementation of the Doctrinal Assessment of the Leadership Conference of Women Religious (LCWR) and Mandate of the Congregation of the Doctrine of the Faith (CDF)," April 16, 2015. https://tinyurl.com/y7f3guz8.

26. Laurie Goodstein, "Vatican Ends Battle with US Catholic Nuns' Group," *New York Times,* April 16, 2015. https://tinyurl.com/yclvmnwk.

27. "Apostolic Visitation Final Report," December 16, 2014. https://tinyurl.com/yd84andq.

28. Sharon Holland, "The Power of Secrecy and Perceptions," in *However Long the Night: A Spiritual Journey of The Leadership Conference of Women Religious,* ed. Annmarie Sanders (Washington, DC: Leadership Conference of Women Religious, 2018), 115.

29. Then called Sacred Congregation for Religious and Secular Institutes (SCRIS).

30. "Press Release and Final Report on the Implementation of the Doctrinal Assessment of the Leadership Conference of Women Religious (LCWR) and Mandate of the Congregation of the Doctrine of the Faith (CDF)," April 16, 2015. https://tinyurl.com/y7f3guz8.

31. Sharon Holland, "The Power of Secrecy and Perceptions," 115.

32. Ibid.

33. Ibid.

34. Janet Mock, "Common Journey Through Diverse Paths," in *However Long the Night: A Spiritual Journey of the Leadership Conference of Women Religious,* ed. Annmarie Sanders (Washington, DC: Leadership Conference of Women Religious, 2018), 57.

35. Ibid., 65.

36. Ibid., 59.

37. Florence Deacon, "Relationships Matter: Nonviolence and the Pressure to React," in *However Long the Night: A Spiritual Journey of the Leadership Conference of Women Religious,* ed. Annmarie Sanders (Washington, DC: Leadership Conference of Women Religious, 2018), 80. Deacon served in the LCWR presidency from from 2011 to 2014.

38. Carol Zinn, "Embarking on an Unknown Journey," in *However Long the Night: A Spiritual Journey of the Leadership Conference of Women Religious,* ed. Annmarie Sanders (Washington, DC: Leadership Conference of Women Religious, 2018), 99. Zinn served in the LCWR presidency from 2012 to 2015.

Bibliography

Briggs, Kenneth A. *Double Crossed: Uncovering the Catholic Church's Betrayal of American Nuns*. New York: Doubleday, 2006.

Burns, Helen Marie, and Sheila Carney. *Praying with Catherine McAuley*. Winona, MN: St. Mary's Press, 1996.

Burns, Helen Marie. "Case Study." In *Authority, Community, and Conflict*, edited by Madonna Kolbenschlag, 1–19. Kansas City, MO: Sheed and Ward, 1986.

Carey, Ann. *Sisters in Crisis Revisited*. San Francisco: Ignatius Press, 2013.

Chittister, Joan. "Making the Future Possible." In *Spiritual Leadership for Challenging Times: Presidential Addresses from the Leadership Conference of Women Religious*, 12–13. Maryknoll, NY: Orbis Books, 2014.

Coriden, James. "Fair Process." In *Authority, Community, and Conflict*, edited by Madonna Kolbenschlag, 31–33. Kansas City, MO: Sheed and Ward, 1986.

Daigler, Jeremy. *Incompatible with God's Design: A History of the Women's Ordination Movement in the U.S. Roman Catholic Church*. Plymouth, UK: The Scarecrow Press, 2012.

Deacon, Florence. "Relationships Matter: Nonviolence and the Pressure to React." In *However Long the Night: A Spiritual Journey of the Leadership Conference of Women Religious*, edited by Annmarie Sanders, 69–83. Washington, DC: Leadership Conference of Women Religious, 2018.

Donahue John R. "A Tale of Two Documents." In *Women Priests*, edited by Leonard Swidler and Arlene Swidler, 25–34. New York: Paulist Press, 1977.

Häring, Bernard. *Medical Ethics*. Notre Dame, IN: Fides, 1973.

Hellwig, Monika K. "A Theological Perspective." In *Authority, Community and Conflict*, edited by Madonna Kolbenschlag, 134–38. Kansas City, MO: Sheed and Ward, 1986.

Holland, Sharon. "The Power of Secrecy and Perceptions." In *However Long the Night: A Spiritual Journey of the Leadership Conference of Women Religious,* edited by Annmarie Sanders, 108–17. Washington, DC: Leadership Conference of Women Religious, 2018.

Kolbenschlag, Madonna, ed. *Authority, Community, and Conflict.* Kansas City, MO: Sheed and Ward, 1986.

McCormick, Richard A. *The Critical Calling: Reflections on Moral Dilemmas Since Vatican II.* Washington, DC: Georgetown University Press, 1989.

McEnroy, Carmel. *Guests in Their Own House: The Women of Vatican II.* New York: Crossroad Publishing, 1996.

Mock, Janet. "Common Journey Through Diverse Paths." In *However Long the Night: A Spiritual Journey of the Leadership Conference of Women Religious,* edited by Annmarie Sanders, 55–67. Washington, DC: Leadership Conference of Women Religious, 2018.

O'Malley, John W. *What Happened at Vatican II?* Cambridge, MA: Harvard University Press, 2010.

Quiñonez, Lora Ann and Turner, Mary Daniel. *The Transformation of American Catholic Sisters.* Philadelphia: Temple University Press, 1992.

Quiñonez, Lora Ann, *Patterns in Authority and Obedience: An Overview of Authority/Obedience Developments Among US Women Religious.* Washington, DC: Leadership Conference of Women Religious 1978.

Sanders, Annmarie, ed. *However Long the Night: A Spiritual Journey of the Leadership Conference of Women Religious.* Washington, DC: Leadership Conference of Women Religious, 2018.

Schneiders, Sandra M. *Prophets in Their Own Country.* Maryknoll, New York: Orbis Books, 2011.

Sullivan, Mary C. *The Path of Mercy: The Life of Catherine McAuley.* Washington DC: The Catholic University of American Press, 2012.

Weigel, George. *Witness to Hope: The Biography of Pope John Paul II.* New York: Cliff Street Books, Harper Collins, 1999.

Werntz, Mary Regina. *Our Beloved Union: A History of the Sisters of Mercy of the Union.* Westminster, Maryland: Christian Classics, Inc., 1989.

Zinn, Carol. "Embarking on an Unknown Journey." In *However Long the Night: A Spiritual Journey of the Leadership Conference of Women Religious,* edited by Annmarie Sanders, 94–107. Washington, DC: Leadership Conference of Women Religious, 2018.

Index

papal feedback, 210, 226
pastoral tubal ligation policies, need
   for, 254
as a post-caesarian procedure, 109
SCRIS prohibition on procedure, 161,
   163–64, 197–203
*See also Our Relationship within the
   Church*
Tupper Lake nursing home, 234

UISG. *See* International Union of Superi-
   ors General
Union Scope newsletter, 137
   "A Conversation with God" reflec-
      tion, 156
   April/May 1983 letter from Sister
      Theresa, 186–87
   challenges and priorities of the order,
      138
   Dorothy Kazel letter excerpt, 190
   Eleventh General Chapter reporting,
      134, 135
   State of the Union report, 182–83
   tubal ligation study updates, 144, 150
United Nations Third International World
   Conference on Women, 232–33
United States Catholic Conference, 143
U.S. Catholic, 129
U.S. Catholic Award, 3, 129

Valenta, Kathleen, 20–21
Vatican
   Congregation for Institutes of Conse-
      crated Life and Societies of Apos-
      tolic Life, 257, 258, 260
   on contraceptive sterilization, 143
   Inter Insigniores ban on women's or-
      dination, 2, 19, 30, 110–11,
      119–20
   John Paul II, centralizing the power
      of, 256
   Quinn report, receiving results of, 188
   removal of Sister Theresa from office,
      requesting, 32, 107
   Special General Chapter mandate,
      90–92
Vatican II, 57, 73, 79
   The Church in the Modern World
      constitution, 122
   conservative reactions to, 255–56
   dignity of all persons, calling for
      recognition of, 6, 183
   highlights of the council, 80–81
   Kane dissertation on pre/post council
      religious life, 236

Perfectae Caritatis decree, 80, 82,
   83–88, 259–60
   Sisters of Mercy of the Union, response
      to, 85–86, 88–93, 100–105, 107–8
   spirit of founders, requesting orders
      return to, 56, 88, 107, 260
   US sisters, effect of council on, 3, 13,
      80, 82–83, 262–63
   women in attendance, 83–88, 267–68
Vendrik, Sister Marie, 85
Vetrano, Sister Pat, 243
Violet, Sister Arlene
   papal feedback on case, requesting,
      210
   political ministry of, 169–70, 179,
      184, 212, 213
   "statement of concern" submission to
      Vatican, 111
Virtue of Trust (de Jaegher), 62, 68

Waldschmidt, Bishop Paul, 159, 162, 192
Wall Street Journal, 171
The Wanderer, 20, 29–30, 158
Warde, Frances, 24, 54
Washington Office on Latin America
   (WOLA), 191
Washington Post, 14, 17, 18, 20, 131
Weigel, George, 7
Werntz, M. Regina, 92
Westoff, Charles, 144
Wilkes, Paul, 22, 131
Williams, Sister Laetice, 134
Wolf, Sister Pat, 135
Women and Ministry study, 6, 27
"Women in Church and Society" (presen-
   tation), 251
Women's Caucus for Art and the Coali-
   tion of Women's Art Organiza-
   tions, 129
Women's Ordination Conference (WOC),
   5, 130, 205
   Detroit conference, 2–3, 114
   Kane as a board member, 245
   Kane as a conference speaker, 25
Women's Ordination Worldwide Confer-
   ence, 246–47
Woodward, Kenneth, 20
World Synod of Bishops, 106, 252, 255
   1980 Synod, 2, 112, 120
   "Justice in the World" document, 122,
      127, 128, 140
World Union of Catholic Women's Orga-
   nizations (WUCWO), 120

Zinn, Sister Carol, 263